The
ADOBE
KINGDOM

OTHER BOOKS BY DONALD L. LUCERO FROM SUNSTONE PRESS

A Nation of Shepherds

The Rosas Affair

The
ADOBE
KINGDOM
New Mexico 1598–1958

As experienced by the families
Lucero de Godoy y Baca

Donald L. Lucero

SUNSTONE
PRESS

SANTA FE

Sunstone books may be purchased for educational, business, or sales promotional use.
For information please write: Special Markets Department, Sunstone Press,
P.O. Box 2321, Santa Fe, New Mexico 87504-2321.

Book design ›Vicki Ahl
Body typeface › Chaparral Pro ♦ Display typeface › Charlemagne
Printed on acid free paper

Library of Congress Cataloging-in-Publication Data

Lucero, Donald L., 1935-
The adobe kingdom : New Mexico, 1598-1958, as experienced by the families Lucero
de Godoy y Baca / by Donald L. Lucero. -- [2nd ed.].
    p. cm.
Includes bibliographical references and index.
ISBN 978-0-86534-669-7 (softcover : alk. paper)
1. New Mexico--History. 2. New Mexico--Genealogy. 3. Lucero family. 4. Baca
family. I. Title.
F796.L834 2009
929'.20973--dc22
                                            2009007678

WWW.SUNSTONEPRESS.COM
SUNSTONE PRESS / POST OFFICE BOX 2321 / SANTA FE, NM 87504-2321 /USA
(505) 988-4418 / ORDERS ONLY (800) 243-5644 / FAX (505) 988-1025

This book is dedicated to my children Jennifer Lyn Lucero and Marisa Lucero Ferreira who are the legacy of the history presented here and to my parents of twelve generations who experienced it.

CONTENTS

PREFACE TO THE SECOND EDITION

This new edition corrects typographical errors, misplaced punctuation, and digressions, as well as a few minor slips that were in the first edition. I have not, however, completely determined the correct number or gender of Manuel Baca's children. We now know that Juana (*La Vieja*) was his sister rather than his daughter, and that he had two additional children: Gregorio, born c 1689 [and thus too young to bear arms in 1693], and Bernardina, born c 1690, who were omitted from the original list of settlers who returned to New Mexico. No attempt has been made to incorporate them into the study.

PREFACE TO THE FIRST EDITION

H istory is not the sole province of captains and kings. It is also the proper dominion of ordinary people. It is the story of their heroic acts as well as their more mundane occupations, from digging irrigation canals to herding sheep.

This history may break little new ground. Its focus, however, is on 12 generations of two colonial families: the Bacas and the Luceros, who are representative of the untold millions of individuals who have sought to establish new homelands. Such a focus provides the reader with a continuity and synthesis not available in other works regarding the New Mexican experience.

The Adobe Kingdom recounts the history of a people from the top down, from the bottom up, and from the outside in. Like any history, this one is colored by cultural biases. Dependent as it is on published primary and secondary sources, it also risks perpetuating the perspectives of these sources. There are, in addition, the added dangers involved in accurately recording family histories: the propensity to provide only that data which presents ones forebears in a favorable light, or worse, to withhold information which might detract from some very personal concept of "ideal."

There has been a concerted effort to present events as they actually occurred, to view as many published sources as possible to make these determinations, and to provide a historically accurate analysis of these events.

There were, however, two instances in which I departed from this approach: in my account of events surrounding the assassination of Governor Luis de Rosas, and in my description of the marriage of Miguel Antonio Lucero de Godoy. It seemed important to me to provide my reader with the emotional glue which would make the Rosas assassination and the Lucero de Godoy marriage meaningful occurrences. This need, in the

Rosas affair, resulted from my realization that had Alonso Baca or Luis Martín Serrano (I), been executed in the political intrigues which occurred 350 years ago, I would not be here.

In the case of Miguel Antonio Lucero de Godoy's marriage, I chose to highlight an event—the wedding of a 72-year-old gentleman to a woman perhaps 50 years his junior because it was the only way I could put flesh on the bones of an important figure in this family chronicle. Miguel Antonio played a pivotal role on his grandfather's lands at *Cañada de Cochiti*, at *La Soledad* north of San Juan, at the *Plaza del Río de Chama*, and finally at *San Miguel del Bado*. He appears to have lived forever in communities throughout the kingdom, and the recounting of his life provided me with a central focus for discussing the transition of settlers from north-central New Mexico out onto the eastern plains.

This work is a thoroughly researched and accurately recorded account of a people who walked and herded for 800 miles, froze in the snow, and buried their loved ones in nameless graves throughout the Spanish borderlands. In individual drive, stubborn will, and indefatigable courage, they were the match of any people, and this is their story.

—Donald L. Lucero de Godoy y Baca
Dartmouth, Massachusetts

ACKNOWLEDGEMENTS

N o one can write a family history embedded within the history of New Mexico without incurring a large debt to a number of individuals whose writings were a source of insight, inspiration, and illumination. The task of writing such a book covering ground well trodden by scholars of previous generations would not have been possible without the benefit of their work. These are listed in the bibliography, and I gratefully acknowledge their assistance.

This book started several years ago when I got a call from my brother-in-law, Carlos Gómez, who suggested that we collaborate on researching our family histories. We agreed to do our own research and to share our findings, with Carlos concentrating on the genealogy, me on the history. Through the ensuing years of painstaking research, Carlos uncovered reams of genealogical data, peeling back, as it were, layer upon layer of parentage, following line after line of ascendancy as each receded into the distant past. As Fray Angélico Chávez had completed the genealogical research for the first seven generations of New Mexico's colonists, Carlos concentrated on the period 1821-1902. He was able to reconstruct three complete generations of 14 individuals, and more fragmented bloodlines for an additional two. Through his efforts we were able to make a connection between the work of Fray Chávez and a second genealogist, Margaret Buxton. This genealogical tie, in the person of Miguel Antonio Lucero de Godoy (born in 1755), allowed us to link 10 complete generations of Luceros. I am indebted to Carlos Gómez for allowing me to fill the gaps and, therefore, construct the history of our ancestors.

In addition, my debt of gratitude to Fray Angélico Chávez, OFM, cannot be overstated. In three major books, and an inaugural address, Fray Chávez's work presented me with the possibility of writing a family history. Through the years I have filled notebook after notebook with disparate items largely gleaned from his work: Oñate's Colonists, Those

Killed at Ácoma, Those Killed or Who Lost Family Members in 1680, Those Who Escaped the Rebellion, Principals in the Rosas Affair, and my favorite, Less Than Perfect. I tried to categorize the participants of particular missionary supply caravans, the names of the *encomenderos*, signatories at El Morro and constructed genealogical charts by the score. The listings went on and on. I will probably never throw these notes away—they have become too precious—but the present work has given me an opportunity to try to make sense of them and, I hope, to use Fray Chávez's work as he intended.

My understanding and knowledge of the Spanish colonial period (1598-1821) comes from a number of different sources, most notably the works of Fray Angélico Chávez, Ramón Gutiérrez, Paul Horgan, John Kessell, France Scholes, and Marc Simmons. I have counted 140 different citations to John Kessell in my end-notes. There could as well have been 240. It was through the work of John Kessell that I truly began to understand the Spanish settler, his life and times; the preferential treatment given to the colonist born in Spain; the deep-seated Spanish belief that a man lost status by working with his hands; and the psychology of a nation of shepherds. John Kessell's, *Kiva, Cross, and Crown*, regarding the period 1540-1840, is without a doubt the one which most accurately details the tensions between the Pueblo Indians, Franciscan Friars, and Spanish authorities as they fought over the adobe kingdom.

The revisionist treatments provided Governor Manuel Armijo, Gertrudis Barceló, and Padre Antonio José Martínez are supported by the writings of Janet Lecompte, and especially E. H. Mares, Ray John de Aragón, and Thomas Steele. The new perspectives provided by the latter three, especially, require that we review the treatments provided Father Martínez in other works, and demand that we completely discount the mauling given him in Willa Cather's great American classic, *Death Comes for the Archbishop*.

For the discussion and description of the founding of Las Vegas, I am most indebted to Lynn Perrigo under whom I studied while completing my undergraduate work in history at New Mexico Highlands University. For my understanding of don Celso Baca and Santa Rosa, I am most indebted to two local historians, Davy Delgado and Andrés Hernández. Here, one senses that there is much yet to be learned regarding the Spanish and Mexican systems of land tenure, and of that turbulent period of American History, westward expansion and the settlement of the plains.

To these and to many others I am indebted: Marian Meyer Ackerman, Las Vegas, New Mexico for sharing the Baca genealogy compiled by her aunt, Guadalupe Baca y Vaughn; Darleen Baca Martínez, Carnegie Public Library, Las Vegas, New Mexico; José Eligio Baca, Sr., Chupaderos, New Mexico; James Hugo Cabeza de Vaca for his work regarding Governor Bartolomé Baca; Joan Chávez, Moise Memorial Library, Santa Rosa, New Mexico; José Antonio Esquibel for his study regarding the Esquibel family; T. G. Futch, III, President, and Ann Chaney Young, Program Director, American Studies Foundation, Hacienda de Los Luceros, New Mexico; Henry Gallegos and Roberta Quintana Gallegos, Santa Fe, New Mexico for their support and many kindnesses; Stanley M. Hordes, Ph.D., Adjunct Research Professor, Latin American Institute, University of New Mexico, Albuquerque; David Joseph, LICSW, Providence, Rhode Island, Roy Luján, Ph.D., New Mexico Highlands University, and James Sewell, M.D., Las Vegas, New Mexico, who consented to read portions of the manuscript.

Christine Gómez Lloyd for numerous genealogical material but especially for her work on the García and Gonzáles families; Tony Martínez, Los Luceros, New Mexico; Jonathan Ortega for his study regarding Juan Manuel Baca and Vacaville, California; Orlando Romero, Librarian, History Library, Palace of the Governors, Santa Fe, New Mexico; David Gonzáles and Jonathan Ortega for their study of Elfego Baca; Eufracio Salazar, Lagunita, New Mexico; J. Richard Salazar, State Archivist, Santa Fe, New Mexico; Stella Tapia, Reference Librarian, New Mexico Highlands University, Las Vegas; William Zamora for his work on the Zamora family; the staffs of three major institutions or facilities; Church of Jesus Christ of Latter-Day Saints Genealogical Library, Albuquerque, Special Collections Branch of the Albuquerque Public Library, and the State of New Mexico Records Center and Archives, Santa Fe.

Mary Ouimet Viera, New Bedford, Massachusetts, and Charlene García Simms, for their editorial assistance. Their helpful suggestions and practiced eye made this a much better manuscript both in terms of scholarship and presentation; Shirley Clayton, President of the Genealogical Society of Hispanic America for her undying faith in the project; and Eduard Terrones Simms of *El Escritorio* for helping bring the first edition to fruition.

To those of my family who may have found me distant while I became imbued with the spirit of the past, and especially, to my Aunt Aurora Lucero-White Lea, who encouraged me to look up in my search for potsherds and worked stone, and to listen for the voices in the stillness. I alone, of course, am responsible for any errors contained within. Individuals with evidence which will confirm, correct, or supplement the statements made should write to the author.

A GENEALOGY GUIDE

Relationships: The following is a 12 generational study of two nuclear and extended families, the Bacas and the Luceros de Godoy, who were among the first to colonize New Mexico. Names emboldened in the text represent possible, probable and confirmed lines of descent to the author starting with Chapter I. Proper names that are italicized represent hypothesized relationships. The genealogical determinations made result from research conducted over a number of years using hundreds of historical and genealogical sources. These sources for each entry may be found in the Genealogical Name Index.

Kinship: In a study of this nature it is important to understand the concept of "kinship," the guiding principle in nearly all aspects of colonial social organization. This was an age in which kinship, both consanguineal (by blood), and affinal (by marriage), was an important concept, a concept which may be appreciated by today's older generation, but perhaps not fully understood.

The kinship system included socially recognized genealogical ties. Relatives of different genetic relationships were placed in the same kinship system. Thus, the colonization of New Mexico was a family affair: married couples with both their married and unmarried children; joint families with two or more nuclear families linked through either the paternal or maternal line; married and unmarried adult siblings of both genders; and clans. In contrast to most nuclear families which are temporary and cease to exist with the death of the parents, the kinship groupings of this study were corporate, seemed to transcend the lives of its individual members and appeared to go on indefinitely. The interconnectedness and interrelationship of these early families will provide hours of speculation.

Dates: The dates in the body of this book follow the Gregorian calendar which was proclaimed by Pope Gregory XIII in 1582. Although there was a new official calendar, its existence and manner of construction were known to only a few. The annual calendars we now take for granted were not known during the early period of this study (1598-1846). Individuals were dependent on the church calendar for regulating the periods of their lives. Birthdays, for example, were celebrated on the saint's day for whom the individual was named, or alternately, an individual was named for the saint on whose feast day he or she was born. The dependence on the church calendar in a frontier society often resulted in people giving wrong or conflicting ages, resulting in errors of up to 10 years—or more.

Generations: A generation is defined as one step or degree in the descent of a family. This period is generally considered to be about 20 or 30 years. This study commemorates the parents of 12 generations. The number of generations, however, is quite variable. Cristóbal Baca (I) and Ana Ortiz Pacheco, for example, had five children, four of whom are followed in this study. The descent of Cristóbal (I)/Ana through their son, Alonso, involves both 11 and 12 degrees of descent, 12 steps are identified through Antonio, 15 through María and 12 through Isabel. These differences result from the length of a generation in these four lines.

Examples that demonstrate this anomaly can be seen in Charts I, VI and IX. In the main line of descent through Alonso there are six known birth dates, or birth parameters, for individuals born between 1570 and 1808. The number of years between generations in this line range from a low of 22 to a high of 58 for an average of 33.7 years. Descent through María presents an entirely different picture. Fully eight of the first nine descendants were women who culturally tended to marry much younger than men. By using the three known birth dates for individuals born during the same time period (1570/1806 for Alonso, 1570/1808 for María), I determined that the average number of years between generations was only 21.7 years. The reader will note that these averages coincide rather closely with the upper and lower limits of a generation as given above. The difference of approximately 12 years between a patrilineal and a largely matrilineal line of descent, at least in this study, resulted in an additional three or four steps over the course of 350 years.

Genealogy Charts: The charts in this study are generational.

However, because of the differences in the span of a generation in the various lines (20 to 30 years) the charts are not rigidly chronological. As an example of this feature, please see Chart I where Manual Jorge and his son Antonio Jorge de Vera, appear to be of the same generation. They obviously were not. This method of chart construction appeared best to illustrate relationships. Where known, birth dates or birth parameters are given.

Surnames: The surname period in a culture does not have a fixed beginning and an end. In Western society, the present norm is for surnames to denote patrilineal descent (from the father). Throughout most of Europe, this tended to become fairly fixed by the end of the fifteenth century but occurred later in Spain and was evolving during the first century of this study 1598-1698. During this period in Spain, and in the Spanish possessions, grandparental and maternal surnames were almost as common, making it possible for several members of the same nuclear family to have such surnames as Villanueva, Ortiz, Pacheco, Bohórquez and Baca. The determination of affiliation under these circumstances was indeed a challenge.

Early Spanish names are unique in many ways. They often included the surname of a person's father and mother with the father's name given first. The name, Antonio Jorge de Vera, would be an example of this. Often a person so named would have been referred to as "Jorge" but there was no general rule for designations.

Proper Names: Given names such as María (the Spanish equivalent of Mary) in this study reflects a long-standing Spanish custom of its use as a portion of almost every girls baptismal name. It is used here, however, only when the official record so designates. The same is true for men where the names José or Juan are fairly uniform prefixes. Too, some Christian names in this study are interchangeable. This is true of the names Ana/Juana, Luisa/Lucía and Hernando/Fernando.

Spelling: One should not place too much importance on the spelling of names in an age in which many people spelled their own names in a variety of different ways on different occasions. I have attempted to retain internal consistency by spelling a name the way it was most often spelled during the particular period of its discussion. An example is Chávez which was spelled Cháves until the late 1800s.

Spanish Words: The first time a Spanish word is used in the text it is italicized and its definition given. Because a literal translation would take away from their true meaning, I have omitted a glossary and instead the definition should serve as a guide to their use in context.

Pronunciation: Since this is a genealogical study of Spanish surnamed people, accents marks are used as consistently as possible throughout the text. For names of places italics are used for words that have not yet been incorporated into English such as *Río Abajo* but not, on the other hand, Rio Grande.

INTRODUCTION

The history of the Bacas and Luceros in colonial New Mexico begins with the 1598 Spanish colonizing expedition of don Juan de Oñate, New Mexico's first governor and captain-general. Spain, however, before embarking on the attempt at colonization, was involved in several authorized and unauthorized, intentional and unintentional explorations of this new land. This introduction details briefly the major efforts of exploration in this extraordinary place which made later colonization possible.

THIS EXTRAORDINARY PLACE

The Western Hemisphere had remained untouched for untold millennia while generations of ape men and men of the Paleolithic roamed the other continents. None of these earliest ancestors of modern men originated in the Americas. The most ancient human bones brought to light in the Americas were of men in their present form, Homo sapiens.

Perhaps as long as 40,000 years ago the forebears of the American Indian entered the still untouched New World. Archaeological finds have proven the presence of man in America at the time of the Ice Age mammals: the camel, mammoth, giant ground sloth, and primitive horse. These were here during the Pleistocene glaciations, the last of which is known to us as the Wisconsin. Thus, man has been in the Americas between 10,000 and 40,000 years. That these early men came across the Bering Straits is fairly certain.[1] They entered the continent long before there were boats large enough to have made an ocean crossing, which means they had to have come on foot. They entered during an iceless inter-glacial period or via ice-free corridors hundreds of miles wide which ran from the Arctic through Canada.[2]

The climatic changes during the Pleistocene were almost imperceptible, but the accumulation of climatic effects drove the people, plants and animals from one part of the world to another. The march from the Bering Straits to Tierra del Fuego took some 25,000 years. The imperceptible movements may have largely been north-south with east-west expansion occurring like ripples on a pond. However, it is simplistic to think of the oldest wave of migration as being on the edge of the concentric circles for this is not supported by archaeological evidence; a date of 29,000 B.C.E. years has been suggested for a site in California while dates of 8,000 B.C.E. are recorded for finds in South America.

These variances are also found in New Mexico, the site of three of the most important archaeological finds. One of these is at Clovis where there is evidence of hunters of 12,000 years ago butchering a mammoth. Still older appear to be the recent finds at Orogrande in southern New Mexico which may approach forty millennia. However, even now, in spite of many older artifacts having been found, the discovery of nineteen man-made projectile points at Folsom, one embedded between the ribs of an extinct bison, is perhaps the most important as it proved that people had been in North America much earlier than presumed.[3]

The prehistoric hunters of Clovis, Folsom, and Orogrande may have been the ancestors of the "Basketmakers," the earliest Ancient Puebloans. The descendants of these people are thought to be the Pueblo Indians whom Vásquez de Coronado found living in villages in New Mexico and present-day Arizona.

The report of the Vásquez de Coronado expedition lists seventy-one pueblos containing 30,000 people (likely a very low estimate), many of whom lived in the upper and lower regions of the Rio Grande. These communities, notes Burke, "were independent of each other and there was no tribal or political organization linking them into units larger than the individual village."[4]

The Pueblos of New Mexico (Indians from the pueblos) spoke seven different languages. The Zuñis spoke one. The others spoke a variety of languages gathered into two general groups, the Keres and the Tanos. The

Keres language was spoken by the Cochiti, Santo Domingo, San Felipe, Zía, and San Marcos, on the Rio Grande, and the Laguna and Ácoma Indians, located 50 miles to the southwest of the main group of Keresan speaking pueblos. The second major grouping was the Tanos which included Tewa spoken by the Nambé, Santa Clara, San Ildefonso, San Juan, Pojoaque, and Tesuque; Tiwa spoken by the Isleta, Alameda, Puaray, Paako, Quarai and Sandía near Albuquerque and the Taos and Picurís Pueblos north of Santa Fe; Towa spoken by the Jémez and Pecos; Piro spoken by the Alamillo and Senecu whose pueblos were between Socorro and El Paso, no longer in existence; and Tano spoken by the San Cristóbal, Galisteo and San Lazaro, also no longer in existence. Another vanished group was the Tompiros who lived far to the east of the Rio Grande in pueblos sometime referred to as the Salines and whose abandoned ruins are now known to us as Chilili, Tajique, Abo, Tabira and Las Humanas (Gran Quivira). It's important to note that a number of pueblos such as Zuñi that are spoken of as an individual entity are or were in fact a collection of villages inhabited by people who appear to have been closely related. There are an untold number of individual pueblos represented in the major groupings given.[5]

The Pueblos were collectively a group of reasonable, rational and responsible farmers who lived life in moderation. They had no excesses and were sober and industrious. As farmers, the Pueblos were tied to the earth, working extensive fields covering most of the arable land the length of the central and northern Rio Grande valley. Here they planted their several varieties of corn and beans and squash. Although it had become increasingly difficult to grow these, as well as their non-food crops, their cotton and gourds, due to the ever-shortening growing season, these village people worked to collect surpluses as a hedge against increasingly deteriorating climatic conditions. Winter temperatures were becoming more severe. They experienced excessive snowfall. There were late thaws and early frosts. And each year their great river, the Rio Grande, became a frozen water course.[6]

The Pueblos noted that these severe conditions had been so for six generations—certainly for the past fifty years. A period from AD 1550 to AD 1700 and some have said from AD 1450 to AD 1850 has become known as the "Little Ice Age."[7] Still the Pueblos had achieved a measure of equilibrium and were in harmony with the earth. They worked their fields that April of 1598 not knowing the harmony of things were about to be struck out of balance. They were now to experience six decades of winter and two of hell and their lives were to be changed forever.

This caustic statement has been rendered—*ocho meses de invierno y cuatro de infierno*, (Kessell)[8] and—*nueve meses de invierno, tres de infierno*, (Yeo)[9] in reference to New Mexico and Burgos, Spain respectively. Whatever the duration, they, of course, refer to a year of two seasons. With poetic license, I have used a variant of Kessell and Yeo's lament to describe the period between 1598 and 1680.

EXPLORATION: 1517–1592

An interesting aspect of the exploration of the geographic area which was to become New Mexico, is the way a number of the protagonists in these ventures were closely linked: Hernán Cortés to Pánfilo de Narváez to Álvar Nuñez Cabeza de Vaca to Estebánico to Friar Marcos de Niza to Francisco Vásquez de Coronado, covering the twenty-three year period from 1519 to 1542.

The first Spaniards who landed in Mexico came from Cuba in 1517. The Indians were awaiting them and they were driven back to their ships and returned to Cuba. The Governor of Cuba, Diego Velásquez, became very interested in this newly discovered civilization and organized a second expedition. The leader of this expedition, Juan de Grijalva, was ordered to establish a colony preparatory to exploring the interior. However, instead of doing this Grijalva sent one of his soldiers back to Cuba to ask for further instructions. This hesitation on the part of Grijalva so angered Velásquez that he chose a new leader. His man for this epoch making venture was his private secretary, an individual by the name of Hernán Cortés. Velásquez chose Cortés because he had displayed leadership potential and because he felt Cortés could be trusted.

Velásquez was correct about Cortés' leadership ability but completely misjudged his loyalty.

Before Velásquez could stop him the audacious Cortés was supplying his ships and enlisting Grijalva's crew. Thus, without Velásquez' complete approval, Cortés, with 500 soldiers and 11 ships, left for the Yucatan during February of 1519. This little army, with the assistance of thousands of Indian allies whom he recruited along the way, was successful in defeating the Aztecs, one of the most advanced civilizations in the Americas. However, to perceive the conquest as easy is naive. For although Cortés had been allowed to march into the Aztec capital unimpeded, the events leading to the conquest of this mighty empire and its people remains one of the least appreciated sagas in the history of the Americas.[10]

In the midst of his adventures Cortés bypassed Velásquez and had begun to communicate directly with the king, even sending to Spain some of the spectacular golden gifts received from the Aztec emperor, Moctezuma. Velásquez, infuriated, launched a large expedition to capture and execute Cortés. Placed in command of this army of retribution was Pánfilo de Narváez. Cortés became aware of these moves on the part of Velásquez and launched a small army of his own to intercept Narváez on the coast. Narváez, caught by surprise, was easily defeated, captured, and imprisoned by Cortés.[11]

Four years later Cortés was talked into releasing Narváez who briefly returned to Cuba before heading for Spain. Once there, he complained about his treatment at the hands of Cortés to anyone who would listen. Narváez, however, had a second agenda. He wanted the Spanish authorities to give him permission to seek out and colonize new lands. Eventually Narváez was authorized to colonize "Florida," meaning at that time the whole northern Gulf Coast to the mouth of the Rio Grande.[12]

Through its history the "great river" has had many names for the several reaches of its course among which are: *el Río de las Palmas* (Pineda, 1519); *Río de Nuestra Señora* (Alvarado, 1540); *Río Guadalquivir* (Rodríguez, 1581); *Río del Norte* (Pérez de Luxán, 1582); *Río Bravo* (Castaño de Sosa, 1590, and Oñate, 1598) and *Río del Norte y de Nuevo Mexico* (Map, in

Sigüenza y Góngora, 1700).[13] In this discussion it will be referred to as the Rio Grande, the name by which it is now known.

Pánfilo de Narváez with his contingent of 400 men set out from Cuba during the spring of 1528. Accompanying this group was Álvar Nuñez Cabeza de Vaca who functioned as treasurer of the expedition. Encountering stormy seas, Narváez was forced to seek shelter on Florida's West Coast. Here, against the advice of his men, he divided his forces into two groups, one to proceed by sea, the other by land along the coast to the mouth of the Rio Grande.

The people this group encountered, as well as the land itself, were very poor and hostile. Sick, facing starvation, and thoroughly discouraged, the land forces decided to construct boats to attempt an escape. They converted their weapons into tools and nails and wove ropes and riggings out of the manes and tails of their horses. Clothing was made into sails. Their food was a new horse killed every third day.[14] Finally, the men of the Narváez land expedition completed five very poor boats and, leaving the graves of forty men on the beach, they set sail for Pánuco, a distance of twenty-four hundred miles. They were never to reach their destination.

Although the men attempted to sail close to the shoreline, the five boats were blown out to sea and became separated losing approximately 100 men in the process. Narváez succeeded in bringing the remaining three boats within sight of land again, but he and his crew foundered in a landing attempt and drowned. The remaining two boats were again blown out to sea and became separated, neither crew knowing the fate of the other.

The boat commanded by Nuñez Cabeza de Vaca was driven up on the sandy beach of an off-shore island in Galveston Bay. There, Indians who provided them with food and water helped the soldiers. After a short stay, the group decided to relaunch their craft and sail westward. The men placed all of their belongings in the boat including their clothes which impeded their work and which they hoped to keep from being soaked. In the launching attempt, however, the boat took on water, overturned, and disappeared.

The survivors, naked and with no provisions, were later joined on the beach by the men from one of the other barks bringing the surviving group to eighty. This number was reduced to 15, and finally to four by sickness, starvation and loss of hope. The four hapless survivors were Nuñez Cabeza de Vaca, Alonso del Castillo Maldonado, Andrés Dorantes de Carranca, and his Moorish slave, Estebánico. They had lost everything but their lives.

For about a year, the four surviving members of the Narváez expedition remained on the island where they had been marooned. Eager to leave, however, they attempted another escape, this one successful and eventually reached the Texas mainland where each was to embark on a saga of major historical importance.

During the next six years, Alvar Nuñez Cabeza de Vaca and his men did whatever was necessary to survive, first working as slaves, then becoming traders. In time they chanced upon the roles that assured their survival in the new land. Essentially, they functioned as *curanderos* (healers), working their way westward with increasingly friendlier Indians. With reputations as healers, they began to be passed from one friendly group to another across Texas.

Where the party of Nuñez Cabeza de Vaca ultimately went is in question. Some historians believe they roamed as far north as Roswell, New Mexico,[15] while others maintain they skirted the southern fringe of the present state of New Mexico, but did not enter it. Nuñez Cabeza de Vaca himself, his account not published until 1542, had no idea. Almost certainly, they crossed the Rio Grande at present-day El Paso, Texas where the Indians told them of cities to the north with big houses and many people.[16] From there they continued westward, then turned south, eventually encountering in southern Sinaloa a group of four mounted Spanish soldiers looking for men to enslave. More than seven and a-half years had elapsed since the shipwreck on Galveston Island. This shipwreck influenced the history of the entire Southwest because of the interest in further exploration engendered by accounts of their ordeal.

Understandably, neither Nuñez Cabeza de Vaca nor his two

Spanish companions had any desire to return to this new land where they had endured such hardships. Alonso del Castillo Maldonado and Andrés Dorantes de Carranca settled in New Spain while Nuñez Cabeza de Vaca returned to Spain. In later years Álvar Nuñez Cabeza de Vaca led a party from the coast of lower Brazil to a new colony in Paraguay where he had been appointed governor. Thus, he is not the progenitor of the New Mexico family of this name.[17]

Estebánico was now the best man to go back.[18] Unfortunately, he had no choice in the matter since he was a slave and had become a possession of the Viceroy. The Viceroy was one link in an elaborate administrative structure that governed the Spanish colonies. Initially, the administrative unit to which control was entrusted was *El Consejo Real* (the Council of Castile). This body was charged with the responsibility of advising the king and queen on matters of state. In time the authority of this body was transferred to the *Real y Supremo Consejo de las Indias* (Royal and Supreme Council of the Indies) which sat in Spain. Its sub-part was an *audiencia*, a group of five judges (*oidores*) responsible for assisting with the political, financial, and religious administration of a territory. The *audiencia* also served as a court of justice for civil and criminal cases and was responsible to the king through the viceroy.

The first viceroy appointed in the Americas was don Antonio de Mendoza in 1529. However, he did not arrive in the City of Mexico until six years later. Mendoza was concerned that although Cortés had been made a *marquis* and given extensive estates, he would try to extend his influence by seeking a further assignment. Mendoza, therefore moved more quickly than he had intended to set up a full-scale expedition to *La Tierra Nueva*, (the New Land to the Europeans). This was the territory described by Nuñez Cabeza de Vaca, Estebánico and the other two Spaniards. His choice for this assignment was his friend Francisco Vásquez de Coronado. However, before he could send Vásquez de Coronado, he felt he needed more information to support the need for an expedition. For this preliminary assignment he chose a Franciscan priest, Marcos de Niza.[19]

Fray Marcos de Niza, a Franciscan priest of French or Italian origin, happily accepted this assignment and with Estebánico as his guide set out on March 7, 1539.[20] They were accompanied by a small group of Indians who acted as porters and who provided a measure of protection to the two principals. Where they went is not known, although, suspiciously, they were only gone for six months, hardly enough time to have reached the area Fray Marcos said he did and returned.

According to Fray Marcos, he and Estebánico had split into two parties with the elaborately costumed Estebánico and his two greyhounds moving ahead to scout and report back regarding the people he met. The code they devised for this communication was for Estebánico to send back a small cross if he sighted a moderately sized settlement, two crosses if a bigger one, and a large cross if he sighted a city. Day by day messengers came back to Fray Marcos with crosses, each larger than the one he had received the day before until one day, Fray Marcos received a cross as tall as a man![21]

Excitedly, Fray Marcos, with the main group, hurried to catch up to the scouting party only to find the remnants of this latter group moving toward them. The survivors related they had found a great city at the base of a hill (likely Zuñi). Estebánico, they said, had in his possession a rattle that he had obtained in his wanderings with Nuñez Cabeza de Vaca, a rattle that had apparently served him well in his work as a *curandero*. Estebánico sent this to the chief of the city as a token of friendship. The chief, they stated, insisted this was the rattle of his enemies and ordered the group to leave his territory. Estebánico refused and was killed.

Fray Marcos, coaxed two Indians from the scouting party to accompany him to the city. Fearing to approach too closely, however, he observed it from a distance, and built a mound of rocks on which he placed a small cross and named the immediate area "the new Kingdom of Saint Francis." He also took possession of the greater area, "Cíbola," for his king and viceroy. He then went east and planted two additional crosses and took even more land for Spain. With the remainder of his party, he then began retracing his steps toward Compostela and the City of Mexico.[22]

Some historians have speculated that Fray Marcos did not go

anywhere and did not find anything. The ruse perpetrated by Mendoza, they said, was for Fray Marcos to feign making a trip to *La Tierra Nueva* and to bring back a favorable report. The speculation further contends that Estebánico was not killed, but chose instead to stay in the north country rather than return to slavery.[23] The purpose of the ruse was to give Mendoza permission to place Vásquez de Coronado in the field in advance of Cortés.

Viceroy Mendoza, with permission from the Council of the Indies, had already appointed Francisco Vásquez de Coronado to lead this first large-scale operation in the North, an enterprise for which Vásquez de Coronado himself had put up approximately a million of today's dollars. On January 6, 1540, Vásquez de Coronado's large force began assembling at Compostela, the jumping-off point for many of these expeditions.

This expedition was composed of over 300 Spanish soldiers, six Franciscans, more than 1,000 Indian allies, large herds of cattle and sheep to be used as a walking food supply and some 1,500 pack animals and horses.[24] A few of the soldiers brought their wives and there were even some children, although this was not a colonizing expedition. The money, which Vásquez de Coronado had put up, was to pay for armor, food, and supplies. The soldiers were not paid, but hoped to receive Indian tribute.[25]

Accompanied by an advance party and with Fray Marcos as his guide, Francisco Vásquez de Coronado moved ahead of the lumbering force that slowly made its way across tortuous terrain. It soon became apparent that the easy trails and fertile land described by Fray Marcos did not exist. The group began immediately to doubt the truthfulness of the favorable report Fray Marcos had filed regarding his explorations. Extremely disappointed by the results of these early ventures, Vásquez de Coronado dispatched a report by armed escort to Compostela. At the same time he sent back Fray Marcos who had proven to be totally unreliable. Vásquez de Coronado sent him home not only because he was angry with him, but also because he wanted to save him from being killed by his bitterly disappointed soldiers.[26]

The advance party came first to Hawikuh, one of the villages among the six or seven towns at the pueblos of Zuñi. A splinter group then went to Hopi. At both locations they met with resistance from the Indians whose villages they visited. In both skirmishes the Spaniards prevailed, although Vásquez de Coronado was wounded slightly at Zuñi. Interestingly, because it reveals the character of the conquerors, the twenty-nine-year-old Vásquez de Coronado could not understand why the Indians would resist being overtaken. The rules of engagement under which he operated required he offer surrender to any group which mounted resistance. He begged them repeatedly to lay down their arms. They refused and their villages were sacked. The Spaniards were bent on exploring the interior and the Indians were equally bent on stopping them, if not by force of arms, then by guile.

Vásquez de Coronado then sent an exploratory group led by García López de Cárdenas west to the Colorado River, and these men became the first Europeans to see the Grand Canyon.[27] Hearing of the Pecos area from a party of Pecos Indians he met at Zuñi, Vásquez de Coronado also dispatched a second exploratory group to visit that region. This group led by Hernando Alvarado passed Ácoma and came to Tiguex where the Indians of this pueblo accepted the Spaniards in peace. They next went up the Rio Grande to Taos and then veered east to Pecos, the home of their guides. Here Alvarado's group was turned over by the Pecos to a Plains Indian who was living at Pecos. With the Indian whom the Spaniards called *El Turco* (the Turk), the scouting party moved out from Pecos onto the bison plains. Their guide directed them even farther onto the vast prairie toward a rich land called "Quivira" which *El Turco* said lay toward the east. He said he had been to this land before and had been given a gold bracelet which was subsequently taken from him by the people of the Pecos. When Alvarado returned to the Pecos Pueblo with his group, he was told *El Turco* had lied and there had been no such bracelet.[28]

Because the gold bracelet suggested the promise of riches at Quivira, Alvarado returned to Tiguex where he met Cárdenas whom Vásquez de Coronado had sent from Zuñi to prepare winter quarters for the expedition. Cárdenas had accomplished the housing of the Spanish soldiers by ordering the Indians of Tiguex (Tewa), a collective group of twelve pueblos near Bernalillo, to move out of one of the villages and seek shelter elsewhere.[29] These were the people who had received Alvarado in peace and now in return they were being displaced.

Despite the manner in which the conquerors treated the Pueblo Indians, these villagers, whom they perceived as a brave and modest, impressed the Spaniards. Said Pedro de Castañeda de Nagera, the chronicler of the expedition, in speaking of the Zuñi; "There is no drunkenness among them, nor sodomy nor sacrifices, neither do they eat human flesh nor steal, but they are usually at work."[30] Now, however, they were at work for the Spaniards who paid them back by taking their food, blankets, women and houses.

Vásquez de Coronado, responsible for the 1100 individuals in his party, wintered at Tiguex. It was truly a horrible period for all; Spaniards and Indians. Vásquez de Coronado's group, already in possession of one of the villages, made heavy demands upon the Indians among whom they lived. The Pueblo people retaliated by stealing the Spaniards' horses. Vásquez de Coronado saw this as an uprising he must put down if his expedition was to survive. It was now a war of retribution with Cárdenas sacking the fortified pueblo of Arenal near present-day Alameda. The town was destroyed in a quick and bloody battle.[31]

The war, however, was far from over. Many of the surviving warriors retreated to a pueblo named Moho (site unknown). The Spaniards lay siege to the place and after allowing the women and children to leave, killed most of the armed warriors as they tried to escape during the night.[32] This series of events, in this clash of cultures, established the basis for the difficult relationship which was to exist between the Pueblo Indians and the Spaniards for many years.

In the spring of 1541, Vásquez de Coronado's entire force was ready to move out onto the plains toward Quivira with *El Turco* as guide. The group now numbered about 1,500 including recently enslaved Pueblo Indians who acted as porters. Near present-day Amarillo, Texas, Vásquez de Coronado decided the terrain was becoming too rough for easy passage and with a contingent of about fifty, moved across the Oklahoma panhandle and into Kansas. He sent the remainder of the expeditionary forces back to Tiguex.[33]

Rather than the gold bedecked natives of whom the Spaniards had been told, the Plains Indians they found were a poor tattooed people living in grass huts. *El Turco* finally admitted that the task given him by the Pecos Indians when the Spaniards first arrived in their territory was for him to lead the Spaniards out onto the plains and to lose them. Furious at this infamy, the Spaniards killed him.[34] In bitter disappointment, the dispirited Spaniards returned for a second winter at Tiguex. Still feeling they had just missed finding the riches they sought, the Spaniards spoke of going back to Quivira the next year. These plans, however, were scuttled because Vásquez de Coronado suffered a fall from a horse and never fully recovered. During April of 1542, Vásquez de Coronado's group, after having carried out one of the most extensive explorations ever undertaken in the New World, began the long arduous march back to Compostela.[35] Their achievements were new extensive knowledge of *La Tierra Nueva*, and bitter relations with the people of the pueblos.

Difficult relations with the Indians appear to have stemmed from three sources: ignorance, greed, and the hostile feelings which the Spaniards had adopted toward other non-Christian groups. Although it may now be hard to believe, there was at this time some doubt in the minds of many otherwise intelligent people as to the exact nature of the aborigines they found in the Americas. Many Europeans argued they "were not really human beings, that they did not possess the power of reason" which separates men from the lower animals.[36] This perception, arising among the intellectuals from the teachings of Aristotle who spoke of the destiny of some men to be free and others to be slaves, resulted in the Indians being treated as less than human by many Europeans.

Too, because of the confusion of the intellectuals in these matters, they appeared unwilling or unable to alter this perception. Pope Paul III had attempted to correct the abuses by his edict of 1537, *Sublimis Deus*, in which he stated: "The Indians . . . are by no means to be deprived of their liberty or the possession of their property . . . nor should they be in any way enslaved."[37] Because Pope Paul attempted to correct behavior without touching the faulty thinking on which it was predicated he was unsuccessful. In truth, however, it probably would not have mattered whatever he had said or done, for few seemed to be listening.

Following the Pope's pronouncement, the Council of the Indies in 1542 issued its famous code of laws known as "The New Laws of the Indies for the Good Treatment and Preservation of the Indians."[38] "These regulations abolished slavery" of the Indians and "also prohibited the practice of the *encomienda*,"[39] the Spanish institution in which a subject people were commended to a privileged few for the collection of tribute. These pronouncements and regulations were not taken kindly because colonization was so dependent on the *encomienda* system.

Moreover, the Spaniards were not too far beyond their experience with the Moors, the Caucasoid Arabs and Berbers of northwestern Africa. These people conquered Spain during the 700's and were not expelled until 1492, not so coincidentally, the year in which Columbus "discovered" America. It was, in fact, Spain's expulsion of the Moors which allowed it to turn its attention elsewhere in its march toward nationhood. Some of these Moors were Arabic speaking Muslims of Spanish or Turkish descent. In the minds of the Spaniards, all were infidels. The displacement of these hostile feelings from one non-Christian group onto another occurred quite easily. The subjugation of the hostiles whom they encountered in the "new world" seemed to them quite justified.

In 1550, Charles V of Spain issued a directive, unique in the entire history of the world. He ordered that no further expeditions be sent out or territories conquered until it could be determined whether or not exploration could be accomplished and colonization undertaken without doing an injustice to those whose lands were to be invaded.[40] The new land was therefore to lie fallow for forty years after Vásquez de Coronado returned to New Spain in 1542. Her Catholic Majesties, Isabella, Charles V, and Philip II, meant well. The manner in which they resolved the question of "injustice" was to view the Indians as reasonable people who "deserved" to be Christianized. Once they embarked on this pursuit, they had to continue because they could not abandon those who had accepted baptism. Thus, the colonization and reconquest of New Mexico resulted from the perceptions of three devoutly religious monarchs who truly believed themselves responsible for these people they had discovered.

During the forty-year hiatus, the boundaries of New Spain moved ever northward. Silver was discovered at Zacatecas, and Durango and then at Chihuahua. New Mexico was still hundreds of miles away, but of primary importance, at least to the Franciscans, Dominicans, Augustinians, and Jesuits, the area held many thousands of souls awaiting conversion and baptism and these souls beckoned.

First to request permission to initiate missionary work in *La Tierra Nueva* during 1580 was a Franciscan lay brother named Agustín Rodríguez. The viceroy gave permission, but required that the missionary group be a small one. In addition to Rodríguez it contained two other priests, nineteen Indian servants, and nine soldiers under the command of Francisco Sánchez Chamuscado.[41] This expedition set out with both exploratory and missionary objectives in June of 1581 after a year of preparatory discussion.

The group made a circuitous trek up the Rio Grande to Socorro, Tiguex, and Jémez, and then back to Pecos and the bison plains. Against the advice of the party, one of the missionaries left the group at this point to return to New Spain and was killed along the trail. The remainder of the group then went west past Ácoma to Zuñi, and then back to New Spain, leaving at Tiguex Fray Rodríguez, the other Franciscan and several Mexican Indian servants. On the way home Chamuscado became ill and died. He was buried near Santa Bárbara.[42]

Almost immediately after Chamuscado's men arrived in Santa Bárbara, rumors of the possible murder of the two priests by the Indians with whom they were left prompted a rescue party. The command of this little force was entrusted to Antonio de Espéjo who mounted an expedition at his own expense as was customary during this period. In November of 1582 he left Chihuahua with fourteen soldiers and Fray Bernardino Beltrán.[43]

Upon their arrival in the north country, the rescue party learned the rumors were true, that the missionaries had been killed because the Pueblos with whom they were left saw them as sorcerers. The rescue party survived several skirmishes with the Pueblos, but did not attempt to avenge the deaths of the missionaries, as their second agenda was exploration. They traveled to Ácoma and Zuñi and then into what is now Arizona. Later they split into two very small groups, one returning to New Spain by following the Rio Grande, the second by following the Pecos River. Both groups returned safely with accounts of rich mineral deposits in the north country and great promise for exploitation of both this mineral wealth and the souls they found there. Espéjo is credited as the first to use the term *Nuevo Mexico* (New Mexico), likening the potential wealth of this new land to the richness of Mexico City.[44]

By 1586 plans were being made to colonize the northern territories.[45] But before an official colonizing expedition could be launched two unauthorized and illegal incursions occurred. Gaspar Castaño de Sosa, lieutenant governor of the state of Nuevo León, mounted the first of these. He recruited for colonization the entire population of the mining town of Almaden, today's Monclava. The mines at Monclava were beginning to play out and were no longer profitable. Castaño de Sosa decided to move the villagers north to establish a new colony. He notified the viceroy of his plans, but did not wait for authorization. With over 170 men, women, and children, he headed north. They crossed the Rio Grande at Del Rio, Texas, then continued north to the Pecos River, following it to the Pecos Pueblo. There they had a minor skirmish with the Indians. Castaño de Sosa then went north to Taos and south to the Rio Grande valley near the Santo Domingo Pueblo where he planted his colony.

Pleased with himself in having successfully transplanted Monclava, Castaño de Sosa sent a message back to the viceroy telling him what he had accomplished and asking for more soldiers, colonists, and supplies. Instead, the viceroy sent Juan Morlete to arrest him. Castaño de Sosa was sentenced, exiled and the colony dispersed. He was eventually exonerated and ordered back to become the first authorized governor of New Mexico. However, he was killed before he received word of his appointment.[46]

The second illegal incursion was conducted by two Spanish soldiers, Francisco Leyva de Bonilla and Antonio Gutiérrez de Humaña, who, with a small party including Indians from New Spain, had been sent out to punish some rebellious Indians in Nueva Vizcaya (present-day Durango and Chihuahua). Having accomplished this, they continued north. This small group marched up the Rio Grande and settled among the Indians at Bové, later the San Ildefonso Pueblo near Española. Leyva and Gutiérrez hunted for treasure and stayed among the Indians for about a year before moving east out onto the plains.

It is believed they ventured as far as the Platte River in Nebraska. Here in a fight over command, Gutiérrez killed Leyva. Later, some of the Indians from New Spain deserted. On the way back south, the group was attacked by Indians who set fire to the surrounding prairie, killing all except for one soldier, Alonzo Sánchez and a mulatto girl who was with the party. Why the Indians with whom they remained spared these two is unknown. Information regarding Sánchez and the group came back to the Spaniards via Jusepe (or Jusepillo) Gutiérrez, one of the Indians who had abandoned the group and who was later found by Juan de Oñate at San Juan.[47]

Thus, beginning with the exploits of Álvar Núñez Cabeza de Vaca who had neither intended nor wished to undertake his transcontinental trek, and extending to the treasure hunting of Francisco Leyva de Bonilla, who died among an unknown people on the bison plains, the stage was set for the colonization of New Mexico.

The Adobe Kingdom

1
COLONIZATION

D on Juan de Oñate had competed with numerous others for the assignment of colonizing New Mexico beating out Cristóbal Martín, Antonio de Espéjo, Francisco Díaz de Vargas, Juan Lomas y Colmenares, Francisco de Urdiñola and especially Pedro Ponce de León who was eventually to challenge his appointment. He was Juan de Oñate y Salazar who had illustrious credentials for the assignment. His Basque father, Cristóbal de Oñate, had been prominent among the conquerors of *Nueva Galicia* and was one of the founders of Zacatecas. His wife was the granddaughter of Cortés and great-granddaughter of Moctezuma. He was also thought to be immensely wealthy, an exceedingly important factor, for he would have to arrange the financing of the project with very little help from the government which made enormous demands on him.[1]

He was required, for example, to enlist 200 men and his contract specified exactly what these men had to carry. If his colonists did not have these arms and supplies, they had to be furnished by Oñate. He was also, as noted by Burke, required to furnish the livestock: "1,000 cattle, 3,000 sheep, 1,000 rams, 100 black cattle, 150 colts, 150 mares, and 1,000 goats."[2] Nothing was left to chance. His contract even specified the amount of writing paper, number of nails and everything imaginable to establish the baseline for a colony that would be founded at an enormous distance from its source of supply. He was to spend well over a million of today's dollars in accomplishing this.

By his contract Oñate had been made *adelantado* (leader of the march), which gave him the right to distribute land and Indian tribute, and granted him a government subsidy. He was to hold the title of governor and captain-general for two generations although he had asked for a four-generational right of inheritance. Oñate designated his nephews Juan and Vicente de Zaldívar as his assistants and they began recruiting soldiers and colonists in Puebla, Zacatecas and other communities on the northern frontier. Among the soldier/colonists recruited were **Francisco Cadimo**, **Juan de Vitoria Carvajal**, **Juan de Pedraza**, and **Francisco Vásquez**. Here too were the Martín Serranos, Robledos, and Romeros who passed inspection and swore to support the colonial effort and to respond to the commands of Oñate.

Things had moved slowly. King Philip II had issued the royal decree approving and authorizing an expedition to colonize New Mexico since April 19, 1583. However, Oñate did not sign his contract until September of 1595 and still the prospective colonists were not ready. He began to move northward with his group during early 1596, but then his contract was challenged. The crown had better offers. Did he have the means by which to support the colony? Did he have the correct complement of men, arms, and supplies? He underwent inspection after inspection, delay after delay. Meanwhile, the colonists were living off the provisions they needed for the long journey. Many had mortgaged all they owned for the venture, as had Oñate. He dared not tell them why they were waiting. He feared he would be unable to hold them.

In the end, the officials said, "If he still wishes to go and has the means, let him." Perhaps each of those who challenged his appointment had exhausted themselves. Ponce de León was in ill health and could no longer finance the expedition, however good his offer to the government had been.

Again Oñate stood inspection, but he no longer had the correct complement of colonists. In the two years of waiting many of his potential settlers had drifted off. This time only 129 men passed muster, 71 fewer than he was required to have. Oñate had exhausted his resources, but a wealthy relative came to his rescue and provided bond for another 80 soldiers and for shortages in equipment and supplies.[3] The inspection which had taken more than a month was finally completed and the expedition was free to leave.

When Oñate stood his final inspection at San Gerónimo, six of the 129 soldiers who stood with him were individuals who would become central in the lives of the Baca family. They were father and son **Juan** and Simón **Pérez de Bustillo**, the unmarried soldiers, **Asencio de Arechuleta**, **Hernando de Hinojos**, and the brothers, **Alonso** and *Pedro* **Varela**. As required of all, these men had provided information regarding themselves and were in return described for the record by the royal inspector, Juan de Frias Salazar.

The Varelas said that they were from Santiago de Compostela in Galicia, Spain. Alonso was described by the inspector as being "of good stature, with a chestnut beard, and 30 years old, the son of **Pedro Varela**."[4] Alonso's younger brother Pedro, of the same male parent and birthplace, was described as having a "good stature and a red beard."[5]

The 26-year-old Asencio de Arechuleta was the son of **Juan de Arechuleta** and a native of Eibar in Guipúzcoa, Spain. He was described as having "a medium build, black beard, and a slight wound on his forehead."[6] Thirty-six-year-old Hernando de Hinojos was a native of Cartaya, Condado de Niebla, Spain and the son of **Juan Ruiz**. His most distinguishing characteristics were "a good stature and a chestnut beard."[7]

The Pérez de Bustillo's, 40-year-old Juan and 22-two-year-old Simón presented themselves as the son and grandson of **Simón Pérez** of the City of Mexico. Simón and his father stood side by side at the scribe's table providing descriptive information about themselves while the inspector recorded it for purposes of identification. Simón was described as "of medium height, dark and freckled with a sparse beard," while his father was identified unflatteringly as an individual of "small stature, gray-bearded, having a wart on the left side of the face."[8]

Traveling with Juan and Simón Pérez de Bustillo, were Juan's wife, **María de la Cruz**, their seven-year-old foster son, Diego Santa Cruz, and daughters Ana seventeen, **Yumar** seven, **Beatriz** five and an infant named **Catalina**. As the girls observed these proceedings, they could not have imagined that Ana, Beatriz, and Catalina would eventually marry three of these rag-tag gentlemen: Asencio de

Arechuleta, Hernando de Hinojos and Alonso Varela (Jaramillo).

The expedition had picked up the livestock at Santa Bárbara. They left their encampment on the *Río Conchos* on February 7, 1598. In addition to the colonists and soldiers there were 80 wagons and carts and a herd of 7,000 head of stock.[9] The whole train stretched out along the trail for about two miles.

Traveling five or six miles a day, the force moved northward. Previous expeditions had followed the Conchos eastward to the Rio Grande. Oñate, however, sought a more direct route. He sent Vicente de Zaldívar with 16 soldiers to find a shorter way to reach the Rio Grande and the ford that they had to find there. Zaldívar was successful in developing a trail that would save the army weeks of travel.

Bravely, in two groups, with the first taking all the oxen, the second waiting for oxen reinforcements, the expedition struck out across the Chihuahuan desert to meet the Rio Grande 300 miles away. They arrived at the river about 25 miles below the present site of El Paso, Texas. Here on April 30, 1598, Oñate took formal possession of all the kingdoms and provinces of New Mexico in the name of King Philip II of Spain.[10]

The people of the expedition were ecstatic. After a two-and-one-half year delay and an extremely difficult march across tortuous terrain, they were about to cross into New Mexico. They stopped and took stock of their resources. They looked across the water barrier and saw a land much like that over which they had come. Before they crossed the river, however, they would count their blessings. A sermon was preached and there were festivities of every kind. A play written by one of the soldiers was presented. It depicted the way the Indians would welcome them and beg for baptism. The actuality would be quite different.

Continuing upstream several days later, the expedition crossed the Rio Grande at El Paso where the river emerged from between two mountains. The crossing must have consumed the better part of the day. After that they still had over 300 miles to go to get to the area of the Indian pueblo country where they intended to establish their colony.

Oñate now had them on the New Mexico side of the river. He

had successfully completed the first part of the passage. The second, he knew, would be more difficult. Leaving orders for the main contingent to follow him upriver, he culled a smaller group of 60 horsemen and with the commissary (the head of the Franciscans), he began to move quickly upstream. His purpose was to subjugate the Pueblo Indians and prepare for settlement. His experience among the hostile Indians of northern New Spain had taught Oñate that it was important to move quickly and decisively to make it impossible for the Pueblos to mount any kind of combined resistance. The Indians would know they were coming; the Spaniards could not take them by surprise.

The Spanish soldier at this time was considered one of the best in the world, second only to the Swiss. This superiority was attributed by some to his valor and vanity. He was "bounteously equipped with grand gestures"[11] as was well-demonstrated by individuals such as Cortés who burned his boats on the beach at Veracruz so as to block his own retreat.[12]

The Spaniards' weapons of war were very likely those of most European soldiers of the period. We know his implements of battle from the inventory of one of the better-equipped soldiers in Oñate's forces: "one set of coat of mail (flexible armor made of metal rings linked together), *cuisses* (thigh guards), and helmet with beaver (to protect the lower face and jaw) . . . one shield and hooked blade; one *harquebus* equipped with powder flasks; one personal sword; (and) one *jineta* (light) saddle... with bridle and spurs to match..."[13] The horse itself was protected by armor made of leather.

The *harquebus* carried by this soldier was an old instrument of war, still used by many soldiers of the day. Developed from the small hand cannon first used during the 1300's, it consisted of a short metal tube attached to a wooden stock. It was loaded through the muzzle with black powder and round shot and ignited by a wick which lit powder in a pan. Very inaccurate and short-ranged, it was possibly as dangerous to the man behind the barrel as to the man in front of it.

Some soldiers carried the musket, like the *harquebus*, a smooth-bored weapon loaded from the muzzle. The early ones were matchlocks, but soon flintlocks eliminated the need to light a wick making the weapon more serviceable. Flintlocks, however, were almost as inaccurate as the early muskets and considerably more expensive. Despite their limitations, these weapons were still far superior to anything carried by the Pueblos who were armed only with bows and arrows, clubs, and rocks.

What concerned Oñate was his plan to place his colony in the middle of a potentially hostile people. He had fewer than 200 men, they many thousands. He needed to secure the allegiance of the Pueblos.

Wishing to move the army faster, Oñate again divided his forces sending a smaller contingent under the command of Captain Pablo de Aguilar to reconnoiter the Pueblo's strength and position. Aguilar was specifically ordered not to let the Pueblos know of his presence. Ignoring these orders, however, Aguilar entered the first pueblo he found. Although we know that Oñate wanted to kill Aguilar for his insubordination, nothing else is known about the first meeting between the people of this southern-most pueblo and the *que-kos*. This was the Tewa expression for these "iron men," who brought "stone-oak" (iron). According to Burke, even today their term for a person of Spanish descent.[14]

For weeks the Pueblos had known the Spanish were coming with a large army and a smaller advance party moving ahead. The colonists were bringing with them the only three things that had been supplied to Oñate at government expense: three cannons with 30 *quintals* (3,000 pounds) of powder, 100 *quintals* (10,000 pounds) of lead for musket balls, and 10 Franciscans. Faced with such a material and spiritual force, it seemed the Pueblos would have little choice but to offer their allegiance.

Oñate pushed north stopping first at Teipana which he renamed Socorro for the assistance he was given there in food and information regarding the north country. Continuing on from pueblo to pueblo, Oñate made his presence known and moved on, reaching the pueblo of Santo Domingo on June 30, 1598. There, on July 7, Oñate met with a number of chiefs of the seven provinces. He met with them in a very large kiva (an underground religious or ceremonial chamber, first called a mosque and then an *estufa*, stove or hot house, by the Spanish), securing from each chief his loyalty and allegiance to Spain.

Oñate went on to explore many of the nearby pueblos, probably looking for the perfect spot to plant his colony, but then again began moving north. The site he finally chose (which may have been suggested to him by Captain Juan de Vitoria Carvajal who had been with the exiled Castaño de Sosa) was at the confluence of two major streams and was almost perfect. Unfortunately, the Indians thought so too and had at least two villages at this site. These were the pueblos of Yunge Oweenge (Caypa) and Okhe.[15] At Okhe, Oñate either moved in to areas unused by the Pueblos[16] or appropriated the entire pueblo for his own use as had Francisco Vásquez de Coronado at Tiguex a half-century earlier.[17] Oñate christened the site *San Juan Bautista de los Caballeros* (St. John the Baptist of the Warrior Knights). Walking, riding and carrying children, the main body of colonists were met above El Paso by Juan de Zaldívar who had been sent back to escort them. They arrived at San Juan on August 18, 1598. The march of seven months was over. This was to be their new home.

Who were these people and what were they doing here more than a thousand miles from their former homes in Spain and New Spain? Their motives are somewhat difficult to discern. Some, like Cristóbal Pérez, had little more than the clothes on their backs, while others, like **Hernán Martín Serrano** (I), married to **Juana Rodríquez**, had among other things, cattle, oxen, horses, plowshares, and even a millstone.[18] Perhaps Martín Serrano was interested in farming or ranching; others may have been looking for treasure, if not buried underground, then hidden in the veins of mineral wealth in this southern chain of the Rocky Mountains, or west in the mountains of present-day Arizona.

The pioneers seem to have come from every stratum of the rigid and complex social structure existing in New Spain at this time. There were the Spanish born in Spain called *gachupines* one of whom, **Pedro Robledo**, with his wife, **Catalina López**, had lived in New Spain for 20 years before coming north.[19] There were also the Spanish born in the New World called creoles and a few individuals such as Oñate's son, of both Indian and Spanish blood called *mestizos*. In addition, there were Indians of New Spain who accompanied the settlers to assist the missionaries and to work as servants.

All these settlers staunchly proclaimed their plan to establish a stable ranching and farming colony. Although, it is obvious Oñate at least had no such intention. He had invested a fortune to establish the colony, a fortune he could not possibly recoup by raising cattle. Among other possibilities, it is fairly certain he hoped to discover mineral wealth similar to that discovered at Zacatecas. Others in his party must have had similar aspirations, but they were to be sorely disappointed.

Some members of the expedition had more modest ambitions. These were the ones who had been promised land and the title of *hidalgo* (the lowest rank of Spanish nobility) for themselves and for their descendants. It was upon these homesteaders that the colony would eventually be founded.

Most certainly, Oñate had a mixed agenda. Exploration of the interior of North America had been prompted and sustained by fables, illusions, and a very imprecise understanding of the continent. First, and perhaps foremost, was the story of the "seven cities of Cíbola," seven legendary cities believed rich in gold, silver, and precious jewels. The Indian pueblos discovered by Estebánico and Marcos de Niza were first believed to be these cities.

When Vásquez de Coronado captured Zuñi and found no riches, this myth, although not completely dispelled, was at least replaced by "Quivira," a land of opulence and wealth. As stated in the introduction, their guide, *El Turco*, told them it was somewhere toward the east. Vásquez de Coronado understood Quivira lay in the middle of the present contiguous United States in central Kansas. Specifically, Vásquez de Coronado was looking in a level country for "a river two leagues wide" with fish "as big as horses," enormous canoes with sails and more than 40 oarsmen, and people immensely rich in gold.[20] What Vásquez de Coronado actually found were prairies beyond belief, gigantic herds of bison, and nomadic Indians.

The river of which *El Turco* spoke, if not completely a figment of his imagination, may have been the Mississippi. The river he described suggested to Vásquez de Coronado the "Straits of Anian" for which many had searched. These mythical straits were believed to be a sea passage through the Americas or around them to the north.

More realistically, Oñate was aware of the mines discovered by Espéjo. Too, he knew that toward the west somewhere lay the South Sea (Pacific Ocean). His immediate assignment was to establish his colony, distribute the missionaries among the Pueblos, explore beyond Quivira, capture and arrest Leyva de Bonilla whom he did not yet know was dead, open the mines discovered by Espéjo, and find a way to the sea with its potential for commerce with China.

SAN JUAN-SAN GABRIEL DEL YUNGE OWEENGE

For the first time the colonists had a real opportunity to appreciate their surroundings. With fall approaching, the days were still quite warm, even hot, the late afternoons and early evenings delightful. The Rio Grande, here lined with gigantic cottonwoods, which completely blocked the river from view, flowed clear and broad with a definite current, but without rapids or eddies. In the early mornings, many waterfowl lazed in shallow pools, flying just beyond reach if approached.

Dominating the view to the east was a range of mountains topped by a 13,102 foot peak, later to be named Truchas, meaning trout. The snow on its summit was both reassuring and worrisome. On the one hand, the colonists hoped the snow cover this late in the year would promise a constant flow from their river which, next spring, would be the source of water to irrigate their fields. On the other hand, the whitecap also reminded them that the days would be getting ever cooler until very soon significant snow would fall, perhaps as early as October. There was much work to be done.

Before the arrival of the main body, Oñate had already begun visiting the surrounding pueblos and on August 11, 1598, with the assistance of 1,500 Indians, he began work on an irrigation canal for the "City of San Francisco," the community he intended to build on the upper reaches of the Rio Grande.[21] Work was also begun on a church, "large enough to accommodate all the people of the camp."[22]

In the waning days of the summer of 1598 the colonists celebrated their arrival. A week was given to festivities which included a bull-fight on horseback, food and drink of every variety, and a very old play *Los Moros y Cristianos* (The Moors and the Christians) also performed on horseback.[23] This play, which was enacted for the 400 colonists, was probably also presented as a not-so-subtle message to their Indian guests. The play depicts a major confrontation between don Alfonso, leader of the Christians, and *El Gran* Sultan, leader of the Moors, who has one of his men steal a cross while he deceitfully asks to become a Christian. The cross is eventually recovered when the Christians, in a great show of force, storm the Sultan's castle, giving no quarter, accepting no truce. It is not likely the message was lost on its recipients.

By September 8, the church of *jacal* (vertical posts) was far enough along to dedicate and the following day the whole village assembled inside, cheek by jowl, for the first service. Following high Mass, at which all 10 friars assisted, Oñate gave religious responsibility for the kingdom of New Mexico to the Franciscans.[24] Then, having previously conferred with Commissary Alonso Martínez, Oñate distributed the pueblos and Indian provinces among the 10 friars.

The next day Oñate asked the leaders of the central and northern pueblos to meet with him in the main *kiva* at San Juan. Then, as he had done at Santo Domingo in early July, Oñate told the assembled leaders (except for the leader of the Ácoma who was conspicuously absent) why he was there. With the assistance of at least four interpreters, he stated that "he had come to this land to bring them to the knowledge of God and the King our Lord, in which lay the salvation of their souls and a safe and peaceful life in their republics, sustained in justice, secure in their properties, and protected from their enemies." He stated further, "he had not come to do them any harm."[25]

Although it was ordinarily cool in this gigantic *kiva*, the temperature rose as Oñate spoke. The leaders of the Tiwas, Puaray, and Keres looked around at those who sat on the stone bench that encircled the earthen room. The leaders of the Zías, Tewas, Pecos, Picurís and Taos looked back at them and at each other. They were not totally sure what was being asked of them, nor did they understand the theology being expressed: one God with the Roman Pontiff and Spanish King as his servants, and Oñate and the Franciscan priests as their representatives in New Mexico. What did it all mean? Whatever their confusion, there was one thing this *que-ko* made abundantly clear. They were to take the assigned missionaries to their villages and obey them, and if they failed to heed their friars or harmed them in any way, "they and their cities and towns would be put to the sword or burned alive."[26] Oñate stated, however, he wished these men to render allegiance to God and to Spain because they understood the correctness of the world he presented. He wished them, of their own free will, to become vassals.

One by one, these old men of the Pueblos who felt they had no choice but to render allegiance to the Spaniards, were asked to approach Oñate and the commissary, kneel before them, and kiss their hands. The old men left the oppressive heat of the *estufa* by means of a ladder leaning against the small entrance at the top. They were not weak men, but they gasped for air and faltered slightly in their walk as each was escorted away. All that remained now was for Oñate to establish the colony in more permanent quarters, then he could turn his attention to Quivira, the mines, and the pearls of the South Sea.

With winter approaching, Oñate's forces needed a more permanent site that they began to establish at the pueblo of Yunge Oweenge (Yuge-uinge: Village of the Ravine) across the river from Okhe.[27]

As noted in the opening of the main irrigation canal that fall, it may have been Oñate's intention to name his capital "*San Francisco de los Españoles*" (St. Francis of the Spaniards), perhaps a name suggested to him by the Franciscans, an order founded by St. Francis of Assisi. During the first year of the community, however, it became known as San Gabriel. It is not known if the Spaniards required the Yunge to leave their settlement, or took over a portion of the pueblo unused by the Indians. Archeological excavations at San Gabriel suggest the Spaniards built an extension onto the pueblo south along the river bank, but whether to accommodate themselves or others is not known. San Gabriel was to remain Oñate's capital through 1609.

ACOMA, THE FIRST RESISTANCE

In the middle of September, Oñate sent his trusted nephew *Sargento Mayor* Vicente de Zaldívar with the Indian Jusepe to the bison plains to see if he could capture the wild cattle. Zaldívar, assisted by 60 companions, constructed an enormous corral on the plains, but they were unable to get the bison to enter. They tried numerous times with disastrous results, many horses being gored. They captured some young calves, all of which died of shock before they could get them back to camp. Zaldívar determined the bison could not be captured or domesticated unless taken as newborns.

While Vicente de Zaldívar was on the bison plains, Oñate, left the colony in the hands of his commanding general, Juan de Zaldívar, and made his first attempt to reach the South Sea. The trust and reliance placed on these two men by Oñate is a recurrent theme throughout the early months of the colony. He asked Juan to follow him and act as his rear guard as soon as his brother returned from the plains.

In November, Juan de Zaldívar left Vicente in charge of San Gabriel and with thirty-one men, two of whom were Asencio de Arechuleta and Hernando's brother Sebastián Hinojos, left the capital with the intention of intercepting Oñate at Zuñi. Then tragedy struck.

Arriving at Ácoma on December 1, Captain Juan de Zaldívar camped at the base of the *mesa* on which the pueblo of Ácoma is built. He wanted to trade hatchets and other items for flour. The Ácome informed him it would take days to grind the grain. He camped a short distance away near water and on December 4, leaving some of the men with Captain **Gerónimo Márquez**, he and twenty-four men including four Indian servants, went to fetch it. He left Lieutenant Bernabé de las Casas and three men at the bottom of the *mesa* to guard the horses. Juan de

Zaldívar and the remaining sixteen soldiers then climbed the 400-foot escarpment.

Thrown off his guard by the friendliness of the Ácome, Zaldivar divided his men with instructions to follow the Indians throughout the village to gather the flour. Once they were divided, the Indians attacked them. Although the Spaniards fought bravely they were no match for the Ácome who greatly outnumbered them. Some of the Spanish soldiers who were with Zaldívar were repeatedly beaten to the ground, lanced and pierced through with arrows, beaten with rocks, and finally clubbed to death. Five managed to escape this onslaught by fighting to the edge of the cliff then jumping off. Twenty-year-old Pedro Robledo (II), died in the fall, but miraculously four, including his eighteen-year-old brother Francisco, survived when they landed in drifted sand at the base of the cliff. Three others who had escaped down the cliff trail leaving Sebastían Hinojos and the remainder of their fallen comrades on the summit joined them. The remaining desperately shaken troops under the leadership of Gerónimo Márquez hurriedly went into action. He divided the men into two groups. One composed of López Tabora and a few soldiers, left to reconnoiter with Oñate at Zuñi. Márquez then led the second group back to San Juan.[28]

Christmas 1598 was a sad one. Oñate had lost his most trusted assistant and nephew, *maese de campo* (commanding general) Juan de Zaldívar, Vicente de Zaldívar had lost his older brother, and the colonists had lost eleven of their own out of a force of 129. They were devastated. All knew they would not be safe unless and until the Ácome were severely punished for these killings. Oñate himself wished to lead the expedition, but was halted by Vicente de Zaldívar who begged to be allowed to go. With the approval of the Franciscans, one of whom was Oñate's cousin, Fray Cristóbal de Salazar, the colonists determined they had not only the right, but the responsibility to punish "this deliberate, premeditated, and treacherous" act.[29]

After church services on January 10, 1599, the colonists decided they must make an example of these murderous Indians. With 72 soldiers (about half of the colony's forces), Vicente set out to avenge the death of his brother. In a three-day assault, and with the loss of only one man, the Spanish forces succeeded in gaining the summit. Many of the people of the white rock, sensing they could not hold off these enraged soldiers, began killing themselves and their families, even as another people had killed themselves in a similar mountain stronghold in 73 A.D.[30] Nevertheless, the Spanish forces were successful in capturing over 500 men, women, and children.

Oñate met the victorious Spaniards and their prisoners at Santo Domingo. Here a trial was held and punishment handed down. As all the Pueblos watched, males over twenty-five years of age (which consisted of 24 individuals) were sentenced to have the toes of one foot cut off and to 20 years of servitude. Males between 12 and 25 escaped the mutilation, but were also placed into servitude for 20 years. All women and girls over the age of 12 were likewise condemned to 20 years of servitude and children under 12 were taken from their parents and placed in the care of Commissary Alonso Martínez and *Sargento Mayor* Vicente de Zaldívar. Then the impregnable fortress of Ácoma was burned and razed.[31]

There were to be other smaller resistances to Spanish rule over time, but for the most part, this brutal retribution served to keep the Pueblos in check for another 80 years.

Including his nephew Juan de Zaldívar, Oñate had lost eleven men. Was this the way it was to be? Would internal dissension and outward hostility eventually erode the mud foundations upon which his colony was being built? He needed more men.

In the spring of 1599 Oñate wrote a letter to the viceroy describing in some detail the potential bounty to be reaped by the colony, requesting "succor, favor and aid."[32] This he sent to Mexico City with Commissary Martínez, his cousin, Fray Cristóbal de Salazar, recruiters, and an armed escort. Viceroy Gaspar de Zúñiga y Acevedo, Count of Monterrey, gave his permission for the recruiting effort to begin. Recruitment took almost a year during which the fledgling colony hoped and waited.

In September of 1600, 73 soldier-colonists, many with their wives and families, left Santa Bárbara for San Gabriel. Two of these families were those of **Bartolomé de Montoya** and the 33-year-old Captain, **Cristóbal Baca** (I), progenitor of the Baca family in New Mexico. Cristóbal was the son of **Juan de Vaca**, a native of the City of Mexico. Juan (who may have been with Vásquez de Coronado) and Cristóbal would have been considered creoles, the grandson and son respectively of **Luis** or **Diego de Vaca**, two of the *gachupines* who arrived with Cortés.[33] Cristóbal would not have been considered either poor or wealthy. As an officer in the Spanish forces in New Spain, he had some leadership experience and ability, traits he hoped would serve him well in New Mexico where he and his family were to begin a new life.

Like Baca, Bartolomé de Montoya was there with his entire family. Montoya described himself as the 28-year-old son of **Francisco de Montoya**. His wife, **María de Zamora**, was the daughter of **Pedro de Zamora** and **Agustina Abarca**. Her father Pedro was the former *alcalde* of Oaxaca (a civil official, the closest equivalents of which are "justice" or "mayor"). Bartolomé himself was a native of Cantillana near Sevilla, Spain. His wife was from Mexico City. The couple had been married in Tezcoco and had by the time they joined the Oñate colony, three boys and two girls: Francisco, **Diego**, José, Lucía and the infant, **Petronila**.[34] Unlike many others of the period who would hark back to their grandparents for their surnames, Petronila would adopt her mother's surname as her own. She would become known as **Petronila de Zamora**.

Among those Oñate had sent from San Gabriel to recruit and guide the new colonists, was a chestnut-bearded soldier named Juan de Vitoria Carvajal. Carvajal's responsibility (along with Bernabé de las Casas, the nominal leader) was to get the soldiers, livestock, and supplies to San Gabriel as soon as he was able. Recruitment, a long and drawn-out affair, had taken as long as he had feared it might. He knew they should have started their trek in late spring or early summer, but here it was approaching fall and they had yet to leave Santa Bárbara. Carvajal considered his group a good one, equal to or perhaps even better than the one involved in the initial *entrada* (entrance). The group was diverse, mirroring the one that had entered New Mexico two years before. They ranged in ages from their early twenties to late forties; **Juan de Herrera**, at 20, was among the youngest. They were single and married, Spaniards and non-Spaniards who represented other homelands and nationalities. For example, some, like forty-year-old Captain **Juan López Holguín**, were from Spain (Fuente Ovejuna), others like Domingo Gutiérrez from a Spanish possession (La Palma in the Canary Islands), while others, like Juan Jorge were not Spanish citizens. Except for the differences in their military rank and the experience this may have brought them, they were here on equal footing, soldier-colonists coming to reinforce the fragile colony and to settle new land. Oñate's group had blazed the trail they would follow across the Chihuahuan desert to El Paso and they were prepared to make the desert crossing with the correct complement of oxen.

Day after unending day the train, under the command of Bernabé de las Casas, moved North at the fairly constant rate of six or seven miles a day. Traveling with Cristóbal Baca was his wife, **Ana Ortiz**, their four children, and their servant, Ana Verdugo. Some of the family walked, some rode horseback, and all were engaged in keeping the stock on the move. They never occupied the cart. The *carreta*, which held all their earthly possessions, was a means of carrying freight, household supplies, and provisions, not of transporting passengers. And so they walked and herded for 800 miles.

On Christmas Eve 1600, having been met at the Pecos Pueblo by a welcoming party, the reinforcement forces snaked their way up the Rio Grande Valley to San Gabriel. After a trip of approximately four months, they were finally home.

Home for the Bacas and for each of the other colonial families, however, consisted of two small rooms, one above the other at the pueblo of Yunge, and it was freezing.[35] With a fire built in their fire pit, the Bacas lay their blankets on the earthen floor and huddled together for warmth. They knew that their lives at San Gabriel were going to be hard, but there was no thought of turning back. Whatever New Mexico had to offer, they were going to make the most of it.

The colonists were in rather desperate straits. They had put in seed for their food-grains, wheat and barley. They had also planted cabbage, cantaloupes, lettuce, onions, radishes and watermelons, but the returns had been meager.[36] The reinforcement supplies helped, but just enough to keep them from torturing their Indian neighbors to force them to share their quickly dwindling supply. And, it would not stop snowing! The great joy created by the arrival of these reinforcements, could not completely dispel the gloom suffered by the colony that third dark winter. The land was beautiful but harsh and unforgiving.

Eventually, spring came to the high country and Oñate was again contemplating exploration. There had to be some way to make this land pay. His continuing plan was to follow in the footsteps of Vásquez de Coronado, Humaña, and Vicente de Zaldívar northeast to Quivira and beyond.

With the fields again planted, Oñate set out during June of 1601 with more than 70 soldiers, eight wagons and about 700 head of stock.[37] After five months of fruitless searching for Quivira, they uncovered absolutely nothing.

DESERTION

Thoroughly discouraged, the group returned to San Gabriel for what they anticipated was to be their fourth dismal winter. They had no inkling of what awaited them. They arrived to find the wind whistling through open doorways and silent streets. The village was nearly deserted. One of the very few families remaining was that of Cristóbal Baca.[38]

From all appearances, the summer had begun well enough, the sun bringing new promise for a good harvest and the potential for eventually moving the group to larger quarters. However, as soon as the expeditionary forces had disappeared over the horizon, many of the colonists, aided and supported by their Franciscan priests, had spoken of the poverty of the land and the general hopelessness of the situation.

Two town meetings had been held. The first, on September 7, had been used as a forum by the disenchanted colonists to present their arguments for leaving; the second, on October 2, had been used by those loyal to Oñate to offer a rebuttal. Those wishing to leave had prevailed. Lieutenant Governor Francisco de Sosa Peñalosa and Commissary Juan de Escalona, two of only three dozen or so remaining in the village, had been helpless to stop them. Captain Gerónimo Márquez, loyal to Oñate, had been chosen by the loyalists to accompany the defectors and to take favorable testimony back to New Spain in defense of Oñate.

This was not the first desertion that Oñate had experienced. During the first fall and winter, a party of about 45 made plans to desert, but had been discovered and their leaders arrested. Shortly thereafter, four soldiers had successfully escaped, but two of the four had been captured and executed. The penalty seems severe. However, soldier and civilian alike were under contract and failure to fulfill a contract was considered a very serious offense.

Oñate could not allow these new deserters to reach New Spain. The first thing he did was to start judicial proceedings against them. Next, he placed his nephew in command of an armed troop to overtake and arrest the retreating colonists, a group which had more than a month's head start. The hopes for the colony were constantly over the next horizon and forever out of view. Despite a Herculean effort on the part of Zaldívar to overtake them, they reached Santa Bárbara and viceregal asylum.

Although colonial law and justice were very precise and severe, the viceroy, never too pleased with Oñate, made what was likely the most sensible decision in regard to the colonists. If they did not want to return to San Gabriel, they would not be required to do so.[39] The remnants of Oñate's colony, just over 100 individuals, appeared abandoned by the Spanish authorities in New Spain.

But could Spain abandon them? Could the king and viceroy make the colonists come home? What about the Indians who had accepted baptism? Surely the authorities could not leave them there among their heathen brothers. How many of these newly Christianized Indians were there? It was a puzzle. Moreover, it was a puzzle not easily solved. The viceroy and the *audiencia* seriously considered abandoning the whole venture. Only 400 converts? Bring them back to New Spain!

The bad news reached the Council of the Indies and the king who ordered the new viceroy, Juan de Mendoza y Luna, Marquis of Montesclaros to study the matter and present his recommendations. Oñate sent Vicente de Zaldívar to New Spain to argue his case and request more troops: 300 at government expense, 100 additional at his. Bitterly stung by the criticisms of the Franciscans regarding his administration, he also requested they be withdrawn and replaced by another religious order. Replacement of the Franciscans would not be difficult for two-thirds of them had fled south with the departing colonists.

ONATE'S RECALL

It took two years for Viceroy Mendoza to sift through the mountains of conflicting testimony regarding Oñate's administration. During that time, the remnants of Oñate's colony lived and worked and battled the elements at San Gabriel. In 1603, despite Oñate's wishes, a few Franciscans were sent north to assist their brothers, and in 1605, twenty-four soldiers and two additional Franciscans arrived. The viceroy had also arranged a government loan to keep the colony going pending a final decision regarding its fate.

The Bacas, however, did not wait with bated breath, since they had already made their decision. Cristóbal, extremely critical about some of the friars whom he felt had fomented the desertion,[40] had no intention of leaving. Unless his recall was ordered, he and his family were going to make their home in New Mexico.

In fact, the Baca family was growing. When they had arrived, the family had consisted of Cristóbal, his wife Ana, three grown daughters,

Juana, **Isabel** and **María**, and a young son, **Antonio**. It was now obvious, however, that Ana, with a *muñeco* (a cord or sash) tied around her waist to keep the fetus in place, was going to have her fifth child. The conduct of her pregnancy was typical of the practice of the day. She had carried on with her household work and received no special favors, and, in fact, the pregnancy had been neither acknowledged nor discussed, for to do so would have been to invite bad luck. However, in the final days of her "condition," she was advised by the women of the village to restrict her intake of water lest the infant's head become too large for easy delivery and she was coaxed by her servant to observing additional dietary restrictions. Great precautions were taken to assure her emotional stability and protect her from fright. Nine days before the expected birth of the baby a novena to San Ramón Noñato was started.

At delivery Ana was assisted by a *partera* (midwife), her servant, and the three girls. Antonio was required to keep his distance and saw very little of his mother during the eight days postpartum she was required to stay in bed. Finally, although his mother was required to remain indoors for an additional month and to eat only the meat of male animals, Antonio was allowed to see her and his new brother, **Alonso**. They were to become thick and fast friends throughout their lives until separated by tragedy.

In 1604 Oñate made one final effort to save the colony and restore his lost prestige. Late in the year, he set out with thirty-one soldiers and two Franciscans to explore the lands to the West and to find the Pacific Ocean. Still not having any clear idea regarding the width of the continent, he hoped to find a harbor close to New Mexico which would assist in resupplying the colony with the goods it needed to survive. Knowing they could not cross the Grand Canyon discovered by Vásquez de Coronado's Cárdenas, the party went further south down the Colorado and Gila and after a trek of three months, took possession of the Gulf of California.[41] However, they had discovered nothing new and it was now apparent the sea was nowhere near their colony of San Gabriel.

Meanwhile, Viceroy Mendoza finally made his recommendation. He had not made a determination regarding Oñate's guilt or innocence regarding the charges brought against the captain-general by his retreating colonists. However, he did recommend that Oñate be recalled and replaced as governor until a special investigator could be assigned to sort out the affair.

Shortly after his return from the South Sea, Oñate realized that the enterprise was slipping through his fingers. He had first sent Vicente de Zaldívar to New Spain and then to Spain to argue his case, but now felt only he could turn the tide. In a desperate effort, he set off for the City of Mexico, but turned back at Chihuahua, perhaps because of ill health or persuaded by family and friends who told him he would probably not be allowed to return if he appeared before the viceroy.

On June 17, 1606, King Philip III, following the advice of Viceroy Mendoza and the Council of the Indies, requested Oñate's recall. Oñate resigned his position on August 24, 1607. His resignation was accepted during February 1608. He was told, however, to temporarily remain in New Mexico and was asked by the viceroy to serve under the newly appointed governor, his former captain, *Alcalde Ordinario* and *Encomendero* Juan Martínez de Montoya. Further insult was forthcoming from a committee of the *audiencia* appointed by the viceroy to study the case. The *audiencia* stated that although a commitment had been made to Oñate stating that the family would hold governorship for two generations, the contract was to be dissolved with neither his son Cristóbal de Oñate, nor any other member of the family being allowed to succeed don Juan de Oñate. The Oñates were in ruin. They were ordered home to face the charges against them.

The year 1608, in which Oñate's forced resignation was accepted, was the year of decision for the colony. Just shortly before 1608, there were only 400 converts in New Mexico made up of the domestics who worked with and for the Spaniards at San Gabriel, the former Ácoma prisoners, and a few others. Although Oñate was being recalled, the Franciscans were being asked to stay in place until a decision could be made regarding the converts. One of the decisions being seriously considered was to bring all, soldiers, civilians, and converts back to New Spain, and since they only numbered 400, this was a viable possibility. But, then, miraculously, the number rose from 400 to 7,000! Apparently, no one questioned these numbers as presented by the friars, although some believe they were exaggerated, perhaps greatly.[42] A group of 400 was one thing, of 7,000, entirely another. The Spanish authorities could not bring them home. The king, viceroy and *audiencia* had to make New Mexico work, but without the long-anticipated payoffs of Cíbola, Quivira, or "the mines."

The decision made was to maintain New Mexico as a royal colony with a governor, 50 married soldiers, and 12 priests to conduct missionary work. There was to be no further exploration. New Mexico was to be solely a missionary enterprise operated for the salvation of the Indians.[43] The decision set the course for the future lives of Cristóbal Baca and his family. It meant that they could remain in New Mexico.

As for Juan de Oñate, he was notified during the first part of 1609 that a new governor of New Mexico had been named. Oñate's small contingent left San Gabriel for the last time in late 1609 or early 1610. He arrived in Mexico City on April 30, 1610, exactly 12 years after he first saw the Rio Grande near El Paso.[44]

Oñate's later years were rather sad ones, although he achieved some measure of vindication before he died. In 1614 he was found guilty of 12 of the 39 charges brought against him, among which were, exercise of extreme cruelty toward the Ácome, the execution of the deserters, and the submission of false and misleading reports regarding mineral wealth. He was condemned to perpetual banishment from New Mexico and not allowed to enter the City of Mexico for four years. He was stripped of his titles and a considerable fine was levied against him. Oñate spent many years trying to get the verdict reversed. Petition after petition was sent to Philip III, his son Philip IV, and The Council of the Indies, which eventually recommended clemency. Finally, perhaps in 1624, the exact date is not known, he was restored to some degree of honor and prestige when he was named Royal Inspector of Mines and Lodes in Spain. He died on or about June 3, 1626.[45]

2
A NEW CAPTAIN AND CAPITAL

DON PEDRO DE PERALTA AND THE SETTLEMENT OF SANTA FE

Although, the viceroy appointed don Pedro de Peralta as governor of New Mexico during the first part of 1609, it took months for him to arrive at his new post. In addition to being given detailed instructions as to how he should conduct his administration, he was also directed to move his capital further south to a location in the midst of the pueblos, which stretched from Socorro to Taos, from Ácoma to Pecos.

Sometime during the spring of 1610, therefore, Governor Peralta and several settlers from San Gabriel selected a site 30 miles to the South of San Gabriel at the end of the Sangre de Cristo range. Why he chose the plain of Santa Fe, rather than one of the major river valleys remains an unanswered question. Although, it has been suggested that settlers from the disintegrating colony of San Gabriel began moving to the site, perhaps as early as 1608. Nevertheless, the formal establishment of the *villa* began after Peralta's appointment. It takes little imagination to see why Oñate would choose the area at San Juan-San Gabriel for the site, which he called San Francisco de los Españoles. The well-watered, highly fertile valley on a tongue of land formed by the junction of the Rio Grande with the *Río Chama* had many natural attractions, but the same could not be said of Santa Fe.

The plain of Santa Fe, which contains an area of approximately 100 square miles, is dry and barren, watered only by the little *Río de Santa Fe* which exits from the Sangre de Cristo Mountains at this spot and flows for a few miles across the plain at 7,000 feet above sea level, only to sink and disappear into the sand some distance from the Rio Grande. It is very unlikely the water supply was ever greater than that now found at the site.

Some have suggested the plain may have been the site of a populous Indian settlement or the centralized seat of government for several pueblos. While there is no native tradition or archaeological evidence to support this hypothesis that is not to say there were no Indian settlements here or that the plain was sterile.

No archaic sites (3000 B.C.E.-A.D. 600) have been found on the plain of Santa Fe. The closest site was discovered about 25 miles south of the present city of Santa Fe near Cochiti. There is, however, evidence of occupation on the Santa Fe plain through the Early and Late Developmental Periods (A.D. 600-A.D. 1150), during which the people of "the northern Rio Grande began to shift their economy from foraging to farming," although the evidence is scanty, perhaps because the population was small throughout the region.[1] In contrast, archaeological remains of the Coalition Period (A.D. 1150-A.D. 1325) are widely found throughout the northern Rio Grande region, some of which underlie parts of downtown Santa Fe. During this period people began to settle in larger villages, and it is the structures of this era which most of us would identify as "pueblos." Two of the better known sites are the one below the earliest floor level at the San Miguel Church, and the one ten feet below street level at the former Ft. Marcy barracks. More recently, discoveries have been made at *La Garita* Hill, below the City Hall Complex, and at the locale of an ancient pueblo now known as the Agua Fria School House site.[2] This latter pueblo, which may have contained as many as 1,000 rooms, was, in the early seventeenth century, known as "Pueblo Quemado." The land surrounding this Indian pueblo of the early 1300's was to become the home of several generations of Luceros (1617-1680/1693-1706?) as they established themselves on the Santa Fe plain.

It appears that the sites at Santa Fe were occupied only through the beginning of the Classic Period (A.D. 1325-A.D. 1425). It is from this period that evidence of such water-conservation techniques as dams and checked fields have been found, an indication of the degree to which the population engaged in farming.[3] From foragers to farmers, they had lived here sporadically for more than seven centuries, and then they disappeared.

Why? Likely because of a drought which devastated the region for the ten-year period 1415-1425. Periods of dry conditions affected small streams such as the Santa Fe long before they affected larger drainage areas and they did so for a more prolonged period.

Yet, Peralta must have had a reason for choosing this beautiful spot, precarious as it was. The plain at Santa Fe appears to have been chosen because there was no Indian presence closer than *La Ciénega* 12 miles southwest of Santa Fe where the Santa Fe River again comes to the surface in bogs referred to as the *bocas* (mouths). Peralta apparently did not wish to encroach on Indian land, and the plain, watered adequately by the Santa Fe River during periods of abundant rainfall and snow cover, would allow him to establish a truly Spanish settlement with room for expansion.

The pueblo on the ruins of which Santa Fe stands was called "Cua-P'ho-oge," or"Cua-Pooge" meaning "Mussel-Pearl-Place-on-the-Water,[4] or Kua' p'ooge or O'gha po'oghe meaning "the place of the shell beads near the water" or bead water place.[5] It had once served the Indians well. It would serve the Spaniards well also. The village was dedicated with the greatest of promise as *La Villa de Santa Fé de los Españoles* (the City of Holy Faith of the Spaniards)[6] or as it is better known, *La Villa de Santa Fe*. Peralta's instructions were to lay out six *vecindades* (districts) for the village and a square block for government buildings and other public works.[7]

This defensive compound, which may have been four or more times larger than the present compound known as the Palace of the Governors, was to contain structures for an arsenal, a jail, a chapel, the governor's residence, and offices built in a contiguous fashion around the perimeter, so as to completely enclose a large interior plaza.[8] The outer wall of the contiguous buildings, some areas of which were three and four stories high, contained neither windows nor doors to serve as defensive ramparts. The compound had one gate with a defensive trench and four sentry towers, two on the south wall, two on the north.[9] It was a rather impressive fortress.

Outside the defensive walls stood the homes of the settlers. Here

Cristóbal Baca and each resident was given "two lots for house and garden, two contiguous fields for vegetable gardens, two others for vineyards and olive groves, and in addition four *caballerias* (about 133 acres) of land; and for irrigation the necessary water."[10] Cristóbal was told he must live on the land for ten consecutive years or risk losing his property. Further, he had to receive permission for absences of more than four months or risk the reassignment of his grant to another.

Most of the homes for the settlers lay on the south side of the fortified compound with fields watered by the *acequia madre* (main ditch) that the settlers dug from the Santa Fe River. Those home sites on the north side of the compound had fields watered from a secondary ditch. Cristóbal Baca, perhaps with the assistance of Indians whom he hired, began making and laying adobe bricks while his family waited in San Gabriel. The Indians who worked with and for Cristóbal Baca and the other settlers were from New Spain. They were in New Mexico to assist the missionaries and to work as servants. These Indians lived in a separate section of the village southeast of the walled fortress.[11] Today, Santa Fe is the second-oldest still-inhabited European settlement in the United States after St. Augustine, Florida, founded in 1580.

ECCLESIASTICAL RESISTANCE TO CIVIL CONTROL[12]

When Vásquez de Coronado left New Mexico, three clerics, Fray Juan de Padilla, Fray Juan de la Cruz, and the lay brother, Fray Luis de Ubeda, elected to remain behind.[13] Although the *adelantado* was not required to support their folly, he was also helpless to stop them as they were not directly under his command. Vásquez de Coronado's difficulty points up the schizophrenic relationship that existed between Church and State in the Spanish colonial empire, and perhaps in Spain itself. On the one hand, the wishes of the Church were those of the State, while on the other, each marched to its own drum, tensioned and tuned separately, in different time, resulting in cacophony.

The difficulties between Church and State appear to have stemmed from two factors. The first was that the viceroy never defined precisely their respective jurisdictions. His admonition was for the governor to proceed "in consultation with the friars and persons of practical experience."[14] However, New Mexico was a very unusual colony in that it was a missionary effort under civil authority, functioning, or disfunctioning, at a distance of eighteen hundred miles from its central government. Here, the Franciscans were the Church, and the governor and his appointees were the State, each fighting over the Indians.[15] The Indians themselves were the second factor. Both Church and State wanted to have them, each for its own purpose, and it would be difficult to determine who misused them more.

The relationship between the first governor, don Juan de Oñate, and the Franciscans began amicably enough. Oñate waited at the San Pedro River for them to catch up and, in concert with Commissary Martínez, established missionary stations for the 10 friars who accompanied him, deeding missionary responsibility for New Mexico to the order in perpetuity. Unfortunately, forever was to last but two short years. Oñate had obtained the Franciscans' counsel on his right to make a just war on the Ácome, but his brutality toward these defeated people, his ironfisted control over his forces, his excesses and abuses of authority eventually drove a wedge between him and his former allies. They questioned his judgment and complained of his administration. He questioned their mettle and missionary zeal, and when it was done, he asked they be replaced. They were not. Instead, he was recalled and made to stand trial on the charges that they and the retreating colonists, leveled against him. The situation was to become worse.

Oñate's replacement, Governor Pedro de Peralta dutifully worked to establish his capital on the *Río de Santa Fe*. Peralta's ecclesiastical counterpart, who had arrived in New Mexico with him, was Friar Alonso de Peinado, Franciscan prelate of the New Mexico missions. Peinado chose not to establish his headquarters with Peralta, but instead decided to move farther south to the Pueblo of Santo Domingo, the centralized pueblo where Oñate had first met with the chiefs of the seven provinces.[16] There was no open schism between the civil and ecclesiastical leaders, but a symbolic, visual, and geographic separation of their responsibilities and functions. Amiable relations between the two administrative entities, however, were to last but one year.

During the summer of 1612, Friar Isidro Ordoñez, intending to assert missionary control over colonial interests, arrived at Santo Domingo with 12 new missionary recruits and bogus papers authorizing him as the replacement for Friar Peinado. Ordoñez' legitimate authority was actually as superior of the supply caravan, not as prelate, but he was successful in getting the extremely gullible Peinado to step down. Having established himself at Santo Domingo, Ordoñez moved on to Santa Fe to attempt to fool the governor into believing his appointment was real and to deliver orders which he stated he had received from the viceroy.

The orders that Ordoñez presented to Peralta stated that the governor should allow, perhaps even encourage, any soldier or civilian who wished to return to New Spain to ignore his contractual obligation and do so. Peralta was shocked and appalled. These orders were antithetical to those he had received from the viceroy only two years before. Then he had been told to do whatever he could to expand the sphere of Spanish influence, and to hold onto New Mexico at all cost.

Why would the viceroy now be asking him to abandon this approach? Peralta balked at making these "orders" known, but the heavy-handed Ordoñez announced them on his own, hoping the colonists would abandon New Mexico, leaving it exclusively the province of the Church. He was unsuccessful. However, if he had failed in his first attempt to get the colonists to abandon the Ship of State by making erroneous entries into their log, perhaps he could yet steal their navigational charts, compass, and quadrant. Let Peralta try to guide by the stars. If Peralta did not drive the Ship upon the shoals, then he, Ordoñez, would scuttle it!

Ordoñez did not have to wait long for his opportunity. During May of 1613, Peralta sent some of his men to the Taos Pueblo to collect the tribute that was his due. The willful Ordoñez, visiting the pueblo of Nambé through which the tribute collectors had to pass, stopped them enroute. Threatening them with excommunication, he demanded they return to Santa Fe to attend Mass on the Feast of the Pentecost. Literally not knowing which way to turn, the tribute collectors remounted their horses and returned to Santa Fe where Captain Pedro Ruiz, leader of the tribute collectors, conferred with don Pedro. The governor was furious. He demanded they get back on their horses and ride for Taos, telling them they could attend Mass at one of the missions along the way.[17]

On the afternoon of May 24, Peralta and Ordóñez met in the plaza and exchanged heated words regarding this incident. The governor lambasted Ordóñez for using the Church calendar to countermand his orders. Ordóñez complained bitterly that the governor had used his authority as captain-general to override his wishes, and his wishes were for these men to attend Mass in Santa Fe. In a final show of strength, Ordóñez produced from under his robes, a document naming him as the agent of the Holy Office of the Inquisition and angrily demanded Peralta recall the tribute collectors. When Peralta refused, Ordóñez excommunicated him, nailing the declaration on the door of the church.[18]

The laity was appalled and perhaps a bit frightened. A number of friends and advisors attempted to intervene on each side, trying to get one or both to back down. One of the friars, Luis Tirado, offered to conduct an absolution in private to spare Peralta the embarrassment of a public ceremony. Peralta refused. He wanted Ordóñez to retract the declaration and to acknowledge the error of the pronouncement, not absolve him. Finally, under truce, the two haughty Spaniards met and in a brief ceremony absolution was offered. Peralta, perhaps in an attempt to prevent a schism, accepted. The two men faced one another, each knowing it was not over.

Ordóñez took every opportunity to criticize Peralta, often in public. Peralta did not respond. Perhaps, interpreting Peralta's silence as a sign of weakness, Ordóñez then hatched a plot to publicly embarrass the chief executive. With Friar Tirado no longer trying to smooth things over, Ordóñez planned a series of Sunday Masses, one of which was to be a special Mass for the "captains and town officials."[19] On the appointed Sunday, Ordóñez and Tirado watched as the church filled with the most important individuals in the community. In preparation for attendance by the governor, Peralta's servants placed his canopied chair on its platform in the front of the church. While the congregation watched in horror, however, Friar Tirado stormed out of the sacristy and ordered that the chair be thrown out of the church.[20] It lay in the dirt when Governor Peralta arrived.

Showing great poise, Peralta had his men place his chair immediately within the entrance at the back of the church where he sat among the Indians. The emboldened friars, Tirado and Ordoñez, smiled to themselves and to each other as they began praying the Mass. After the gospel, read by Friar Tirado, Ordoñez approached the pulpit where he delivered a homily, proclaiming his power and authority as commissary and agent of the Holy Office of the Inquisition and stating, it seems, his intention to supersede the governor. Among other things, he said, "I can arrest, cast into irons, and punish as seems fitting to me any person without exception who is not obedient to the commandments of the church and mine."[21] He also stated, without naming the governor, that he was making these pronouncements "for the benefit of a certain person who is listening to me who perhaps raises his eyebrows."[22]

The next day, Ordoñez, apparently now expecting Peralta to accede to his every wish, asked him for the services of several soldiers and his syndic for the purpose of collecting the church tithe. Peralta refused, stating that the military duties of these individuals came first and, given the conflict between their military and ecclesiastical obligations, they were not available to him.[23] Ordoñez became furious. He branded Peralta a "Lutheran, a heretic, and a Jew"[24] and threatened to have him arrested.

That was it! Peralta had run out of patience with this madman. On Tuesday, July 9, the governor asked that several of his men-at-arms meet with him at the *casas reales* (governor's residence). There, the governor told them Ordoñez planned to have him arrested and he intended to strike first. With capes billowing behind them, and the sound of scabbards slapping against their thighs, the men marched noisily across the plaza to the *convento* (friary) where they confronted Ordoñez and several of the friars who had warned Ordoñez of their approach. The governor, wearing a coat of chain mail, sword and pistol, began bellowing at Ordoñez.

The scene would have been comical had it not been so bizarre and potentially deadly. Peralta's men were fully armed, while the friars had only their prayer books, except for Ordoñez who had grabbed a cane. A fierce scuffle ensued, the men flailing wildly at each other and grabbing onto one another's clothing. Ordoñez attempted to hit Peralta with his cane. Then Friar Tirado took a sword away from one of Peralta's men and thrust it at the governor tearing his cape.[25] Peralta had his pistol in his hand, with someone holding his wrist. The pistol fired and the acrid odor of burned powder filled the air. With the sound of the shot, the clamor stopped. When the smoke cleared, Friar Pedraza lay on the floor, writhing in pain. Luckily, his wound was superficial, but the sight of the priest lying bleeding on the floor cast the whole affair in a different light.[26]

One of Peralta's men had also been grazed by the shot, but neither his wound nor his status as one of the men-at-arms generated the degree of sympathy among the colonists as did the wounding of Friar Pedraza. As Friar Ordoñez rode off to Santo Domingo to gather his forces, he took with him some of the loyalty that had initially been directed to Peralta. Four days later, however, when he returned to enlist the colonists' support in arresting Peralta on charges of attempted murder, he was unsuccessful. Most of the settlers did not want any part of the insanity.

It was obvious to Peralta that he had to take action and since it was not clear who his supporters were, he decided to go to Mexico City to appeal to the viceroy for redress. Ordoñez heard of this move and decided to intercept him. Somehow, Peralta got by Santo Domingo, but Ordoñez put a posse together to track him down. In the middle of the night of August 12, they descended upon Peralta's encampment and arrested him.

Peralta and his men were dragged back to the Sandía Pueblo where, without approval of its guardian, Esteban de Pérea, they were placed in chains and put in cells.[27] Peralta's men were eventually released, but Peralta himself remained there until he escaped eight months later. During the period of Peralta's imprisonment Ordoñez ruled unchallenged.

Upon his escape, Peralta, still in shackles, managed to traverse the rugged country through snow and freezing temperatures. Finally, after three days and two nights on the plain, badly bruised, famished, for he had not eaten during the whole ordeal, and ill, he made it to a friend's home in Santa Fe where he went into hiding.

When Ordoñez learned of Peralta's escape, he ordered a search of the *villa*. When found, Peralta was dragged from hiding, put on a horse, covered with a pelt against the elements on this late March of 1614, and taken to Santo Domingo. Here a public spectacle was made of him before he was again taken to the Sandía Pueblo for incarceration. He was to remain there until April 6, when he was transferred to Zía.[28]

It is difficult to believe that Ordoñez was able to accomplish all this, and yet he did. The manner in which Peralta was treated was both pathetic and scandalous. Although he was charged with attempted murder, the real charge against him appears to have been that of obstructing the business of the Church. Another year passed during which Ordoñez held the colony in his grips. Then, news was received at Santo Domingo and Santa Fe that New Mexico's third governor had been appointed. He was the former admiral of the Spanish navy, don Bernardino de Ceballos.

Before Ceballos reached Santo Domingo, Ordoñez went out to greet him. The two men now measured each other. Ordoñez had the former governor in chains. How would Ceballos deal with this and with him?

It is somewhat difficult to characterize Ceballos' conduct toward Ordoñez. He did not reprimand him and certainly did not punish him. He merely informed Ordoñez that he would have Peralta released and accorded the honor due him while he conducted his *residencia*, the customary audit and review of the administration of the departing governor. However, it took Ceballos a month to have Peralta released from prison and during that time he began to hear testimony against him. There was little testimony in Peralta's favor for Ordoñez who was present at each of the sessions intimidated most of the colonists who may have spoken positively.

Peralta's *residencia* continued into August. Then, finally, in November, deprived of most of his possessions, he was allowed to leave New Mexico. Ceballos had earlier determined that Ordoñez lacked inquisitorial authority, yet, seemingly in collusion with Ordoñez, he had Peralta pursued and caught just above El Paso where his cart was ransacked in a search for information which might incriminate Ceballos and Ordoñez. Peralta had hidden his papers well, however, so was allowed to proceed. Sometime in the spring of 1615 he reached Mexico City where he reported to Spanish officials.[29]

Following Peralta's appearance in Mexico City a two-year Inquisition took place which reviewed the entire debacle regarding Peralta, Ceballos and Ordoñez. During these deliberations, a supply caravan was being put together for its trip north to Santa Fe. Counted among the escort was one Pedro Lucero de Godoy.[30]

From the time the Spanish government took on responsibility for supporting mission work in New Mexico, a supply service was maintained which had wagon trains scheduled to arrive in Santa Fe every third year. The round trip from Mexico City to Santa Fe and return usually took about a year and a half.[31] The leader of the Mexico City wagon train of 1616 was **Francisco Gómez** who was to become the most outstanding military leader in New Mexico. One of Gómez' responsibilities was to recruit soldiers for the escort. He interviewed and selected Juan Gómez Barragan and then the Lucero de Godoy cousins, *El Viejo* (the elder or old man) and *El Mozo* (the lad or young man). It seemed important to so differentiate them as each was named Pedro and each was a captain (leader). This may have bemused the 29-year-old Gómez. A 16-year-old captain? Well, they would wait and see. It was, however, this unlikely lad who was to become the progenitor of the Lucero family in New Mexico.

The supply train, bringing with it the first father *Custos* (head of a group of friars), with the Pedro Luceros de Godoy cousins in attendance, arrived in Santa Fe during January of 1617. Friar Ordoñez was to make the return trip to face trial and reprimand. Peralta, already in Mexico City, had been exonerated of the charges placed against him.

The *encomienda* system was an old one. As mentioned in the Introduction, it was a Spanish institution in which a subject people were "commended" to certain Spaniards in trust. Narváez had an *encomienda* in Cuba. In 1523, the king ordered Cortés to stop assigning them. It continued, and although Cortés himself was against the system, it was made legal in New Spain in 1526. In 1542, the Council of the Indies prohibited the practice of the *encomienda* beyond the lifetimes of the present holders of the privilege and yet it went on and on.

Oñate had assigned some in New Mexico, but how many and to whom is not known.[32] By the terms of his contract he was allowed to reward his followers by granting them Indian tributes. Peralta was also permitted to make new grants if they did not interfere with those made by Oñate.[33]

It is impossible to see how the Spaniard of 1500 reconciled the bipolar concepts of vassal and free man. On the one hand, Spain considered the Indians free men who could not be enslaved. This is why Oñate had placed a time limit of 20 years on the servitude of the Ácome. On the other hand, as vassals, they could be required to pay tribute, but only those Indians who rendered obedience and became Christians. It was an incredible concept! Common sense would suggest that the Spaniards would favor the "Christianized" Indians by not requiring tribute from them, but only from their non-Christianized brothers. However, that was not the way it worked. The Indians could not be forced to become Christians, and those who resisted were not placed in an *encomienda*. Thus, instead of treating the resisters badly, the Spaniards expected little of this latter group in terms of taxes or tribute.

The concept of the *encomienda* originated in about 1503 with Ferdinand V who hoped that by granting the proprietors of the new lands authority over the aborigines, he would assure both their spiritual and temporal welfare. Moreover, the Spanish would profit from the energies of the natives.[34] Thus, the Indians were commended to the care and protection of an *encomendero* who was given the right to exact their labor. The heads of Indian households were assigned to an *encomendero* who would hold the privilege for three generations. In return, the *encomendero* was required to defend the land at his own expense.

By viceregal decree there were to be only 35 *encomenderos* in New Mexico. These men were to be the backbone of the colony's defense. In return for the privilege of collecting tribute from specified pueblos, they were required to maintain horses and weapons and to respond to the governor's call to arms wherever and whenever needed. The *encomenderos* were, at least initially, also required to live in Santa Fe and were forbidden to live at the pueblo of their *encomienda*. The system, as noted by Kessell, was all inclusive. "When a woman or a minor" inherited an *encomienda*, "an *escudero* (shield bearer) was appointed as a substitute to render the military service." For this, the *escudero* was given "a share of the tribute."[35]

The law allowed tribute be collected "in local products" with the government reserving the right to collect tribute from "principal towns and seaports."[36] There being none of the latter in New Mexico, the governor appears to have retained certain pueblos for himself.

As the seventeenth century wore on, the tribute came to be fixed at one Spanish bushel of corn and a *manta* (a small cotton blanket) or, as a substitute, animal skins.[37] This tribute was customarily collected twice a year, in May and October and it was this tribute in May of 1613 that Peralta's men were trying to collect when they were turned back by Ordoñez.[38]

The amount of tribute required of each household does not appear to have been great, particularly in good times. However, "to keep from starving, Oñate and his men had collected tribute". . . "sometimes by violent means."[39] The Franciscans complained that the *encomenderos* "mistreated their Indians, gave them bad example, and severely hindered the work of making the natives Christians."[40] Likely, some of these complaints were accurate. Viceroy don Luis de Velasco stated in his orders to Peralta: "In as much as it has been reported that the tribute levied on the natives is excessive, and that it is collected with much vexation and trouble to them, we charge the governor to take suitable measures in this matter, proceeding in such a way as to relieve and satisfy the royal conscience."[41] Satisfy the royal conscience? Perhaps they could work on vexation.

While not a part of the *encomienda* system, per se, a related system called *repartimiento* caused an almost equal degree of trouble for the Indians. While the *encomienda* system was onerous to the Pueblos, it was at least systematized: tributes were collected May and October, May and October for three generations. It could at least be counted upon and planned for, even if in a grudging way.

Repartimiento was another thing altogether. Instead of allowing only a fixed number of individuals to exact tribute from the Pueblos as the *encomienda* system did, the *repartimiento* allowed any Spaniard to demand the Pueblo's labor. A colonist or public official could request a levy of up to 100 Indians to dig an irrigation ditch, reap a harvest, or construct a public work. Theoretically, at least, these Indians were supposed to be paid a daily wage and provided rations and law limited the term of their enlistment. Abuses, however, were flagrant. Some of the Spaniards, it is alleged, avoided paying the wages, held out on rations, demanded stints longer than that allowed by law, and, most importantly, took the Indians from their fields at harvest time.[42] The combination of these two systems put the lie to the term "free man." If these systems were not intended to win souls, neither did they do anything to win friends.

THE LUCERO PROGENITOR, PEDRO LUCERO DE GODOY

When **Pedro Lucero de Godoy** arrived in Santa Fé that January of 1617, he was but 16 or 17 years of age, yet counted as a man for some of this period, such as Cristóbal de Anaya Almazán, claimed to have begun soldiering at age 11.[43] Like Cristóbal Baca and the other settlers, Pedro Lucero de Godoy, *El Mozo*, was given two lots, two contiguous fields, and 133 acres of land, guaranteed to each of the early settlers of

Santa Fe to ensure development of the *villa*.

Soon after his arrival, Pedro Lucero de Godoy was to meet and marry **Petronila de Zamora**, mentioned earlier, who had come to New Mexico as an infant with her parents, Bartolomé de Montoya and María de Zamora, in the caravan of 1600. Although she later claimed to have married Pedro when but 11 years of age, she was, like Pedro, probably about 16. Keeping track of one's age was not a priority at this period of history. Like the Cristóbal Bacas, the Luceros de Godoy settled down to live on the plain. Pedro and his cousin of the same name continued to accept responsibility for the escort of the wagon trains of 1621 and 1631.[44]

Pedro and Petronila were to have at least two children, Catalina and **Juan**, each of whom was to lead a tumultuous life on the frontier. Petronila died at a very young age early in their marriage. A third child, also named Pedro Lucero de Godoy (II), may have been Pedro's son by Petronila or by his second wife Francisca Gómez Robledo.

Francisca was the sister of Francisco Gómez Robledo. They were the children of the Portuguese adventurer, Francisco Gómez, who had recruited the Pedro Luceros de Godoy for the caravan of 1616. One could say their father was responsible for the marriage of Francisca and Pedro for he was responsible for the lad's presence in New Mexico. He appears to have been responsible for much more as well.[45]

Gómez was apparently quite taken with the younger Pedro Lucero de Godoy. He may have recommended him to Governor Ceballos, Eulate or another governor as one who could be counted upon as a man-of-arms, willing and able to protect the colony at his own expense, for, sometime between 1616 and 1662, Pedro Lucero de Godoy became an *encomendero*. That the family of Gómez-Robledo was involved in his appointment is inferred from the site of Pedro's *encomienda*. Pedro Lucero de Godoy, who was to rise to the positions of *Maese de campo* and lieutenant governor of the kingdom, was given 24 houses of the pueblo of Pecos, the remainder being held by his brother-in-law, Francisco Gómez Robledo.[46] Although it is nowhere stated, it may also be inferred that the Pecos *encomienda* was originally held by the elder Francisco Gómez and inherited by his oldest son. Whatever the manner of possession, the Gómez-Robledos and Luceros de Godoy were families bonded both by military service and marriage.

LOVE AND MARRIAGE

The Baca children, especially the girls who were young women when they came to New Mexico, were soon marrying and establishing families of their own. Juana married Simón Pérez de Bustillo; **Isabel**, don **Pedro Durán y Cháves** (I); and **María, Simón de Abendaño**. Neither Juana nor Isabel could have had the slightest inkling that within two decades, they would be involved in arguably the greatest family tragedy to be suffered by the colony.

The girls, especially Isabel de Bohórquez had married well. Don Pedro Durán y Cháves (I), who for some unknown reason was always referred to by the honorific don reserved at this time for the governor, was an *encomendero* and held the highest military post in the kingdom. As a much younger man he had been a captain among Peralta's tribute collectors when diverted from his course at Nambé. By 1626 he was *Maese de campo* of all the royal troops in New Mexico with Pedro Lucero de Godoy and the Bacas, Antonio and Alonso, all serving under his command. While the Abendaños and the Pérez de Bustillos probably lived on the plain of Santa Fé, the Durán y Cháveses lived on their *estancia* (a large tract of land for raising livestock) at *Arroyo de Tunque* in the vicinity of the San Felipe Pueblo.[47] Although the exact site of his *encomienda* is not known, it was likely at the San Felipe Pueblo. He held extensive land in the Sandía jurisdiction "from the boundaries of the San Felipe Pueblo down through Bernalillo to Atrisco."[48]

Antonio Baca, too, was to marry into the family of Pérez de Bustillo. He married Yumar, the sister of Simón Pérez de Bustillo, husband of his sister Juana. These two star-crossed families were to become central in the issues of 1637-1641 that will be described in the next chapter.

The Pérez de Bustillo, Durán y Cháves, and Baca men were, first and foremost, soldiers. Pedro Durán y Cháves (I) rose through the ranks of *sargento*, (sergeant), *capitan* (captain), *sargento mayor* (major) on his way to becoming commanding general. He and his brothers-in-law served faithfully under several governors, one of whom was don Juan de Eulate who was to play a major role in both the lives of the Pueblo Indians and the Church.

NOTES ABOUT CHARTS I AND II AND III

The interconnectedness and interrelationships of the families who first settled New Mexico are phenomenal. The Bacas and Luceros de Godoy are but a few examples.

Chart I-(a) begins with the Baca progenitor, Cristóbal Baca (I), and his wife Ana Ortiz Pacheco. They are featured with their five children, four of whom are followed in this study; (b) Diego de Vera, first husband of María (Ortiz) Abendaño was tried by the Inquisition for the crime of bigamy. He was required to return to his wife in the Canary Islands and his marriage to María was annulled. María and Diego had two daughters. One, María Ortiz de Vera, married Manuel Jorge and then Diego de Montoya; (c) Manuel Jorge, first husband of María Ortiz de Vera, was the father of Antonio Jorge de Vera, husband of Gertrudis Baca, daughter of Antonio Baca. Antonio Jorge de Vera was likely the son of María Ortiz de Vera but this is not confirmed. Manual Jorge and María Ortiz de Vera had three known daughters. One, Juana, is shown in Chart III with connections to the Gomez Robledo family. María Ortiz de Vera's second marriage was to Diego de Montoya, brother to Petronila de Zamora, first wife of Pedro Lucero de Godoy. Luisa Montoya, daughter of Diego de Montoya and María Ortiz de Vera would also contribute to the Baca line; (d) Ana Moreno de Lara (Trujillo), wife of Cristóbal Baca (II), and Francisco de Trujillo, husband of Luisa de Montoya, were siblings, the children of Diego de Trujillo and Catalina Vásquez.

Chart II-(a) begins with the Lucero de Godoy progenitor, Pedro Lucero de Godoy, and his wives Petronila de Zamora and Francisca Gómez Robledo. Although only the descendants of the former are followed in this study, both are depicted to illustrate interrelationships. The chart is not chronological, rather, individuals are grouped as clans; (b) Francisco

Lucero de Godoy's wife, Josefa López Sambrano de Grijalva, will be found throughout the first part of this study in charge of the venerated statue of *La Conquistadora*.

Charts I and II-(a) Simón Pérez de Bustillo, husband of Juana de Zamora Baca, and Yumar Pérez de Bustillo, wife of Antonio Baca, were siblings, the children of Juan Pérez de Bustillo and María de la Cruz. Sibling exchange among these families was a very common practice. See Chart II for a connection with Francisca Varela Jaramillo wife of Antonio Lucero de Godoy (II); (b) Simón de Abendaño, husband of María de Villanueva Ortiz Baca, was probably the brother of Isabel Holguín, mother of Juana de Carvajal, second wife of Juan Lucero de Godoy. Juana was the sister of (María) de Carvajal Holguín, wife of Fernando Durán y Chávez (I); (c) María de Salazar, wife of Manuel Baca, Lucia Hurtado de Salas, wife of Fernando Durán y Chávez (II), and Isabel de Salazar, third wife of Juan Lucero de Godoy were apparently sisters adopted by Andrés Hurtado and Bernardina de Salas y Trujillo. Andrés Hurtado and Bernardina de Salas' biological daughter, Maria Hurtado, wife of Antonio de Montoya would further contribute to both the Baca and Lucero de Godoy lines; (d) Juana Hurtado, wife of Tomás García de Noriega, was the granddaughter of Andrés Hurtado. See Chart VIII for García connections.

CHART I
Parents of the First Century, Baca Family

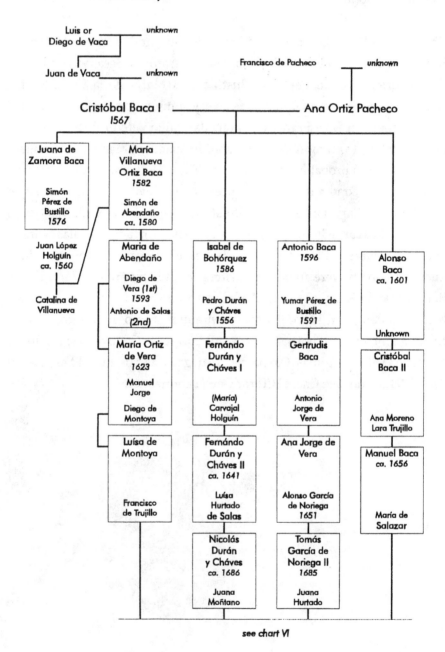

Luis or Diego de Vaca ——— unknown

Juan de Vaca ——— unknown

Francisco de Pacheco   unknown

Cristóbal Baca I
1567
———
Ana Ortiz Pacheco

Juana de Zamora Baca

Simón Pérez de Bustillo
1576

Juan López Holguín
ca. 1560

Catalina de Villanueva

María Villanueva Ortiz Baca
1582

Simón de Abendaño
ca. 1580

Maria de Abendaño

Diego de Vera (1st)
1593

Antonio de Salas (2nd)

María Ortiz de Vera
1623

Manuel Jorge

Diego de Montoya

Luísa de Montoya

Francisco de Trujillo

Isabel de Bohórquez
1586

Pedro Durán y Cháves
1556

Fernándo Durán y Cháves I

(María) Carvajal Holguín

Fernándo Durán y Cháves II
ca. 1641

Luísa Hurtado de Salas

Nicolás Durán y Cháves
ca. 1686

Juana Moñtano

Antonio Baca
1596

Yumar Pérez de Bustillo
1591

Gertrudis Baca

Antonio Jorge de Vera

Ana Jorge de Vera

Alonso García de Noriega
1651

Tomás García de Noriega II
1685

Juana Hurtado

Alonso Baca
ca. 1601

Unknown

Cristóbal Baca II

Ana Moreno Lara Trujillo

Manuel Baca
ca. 1656

María de Salazar

see chart VI

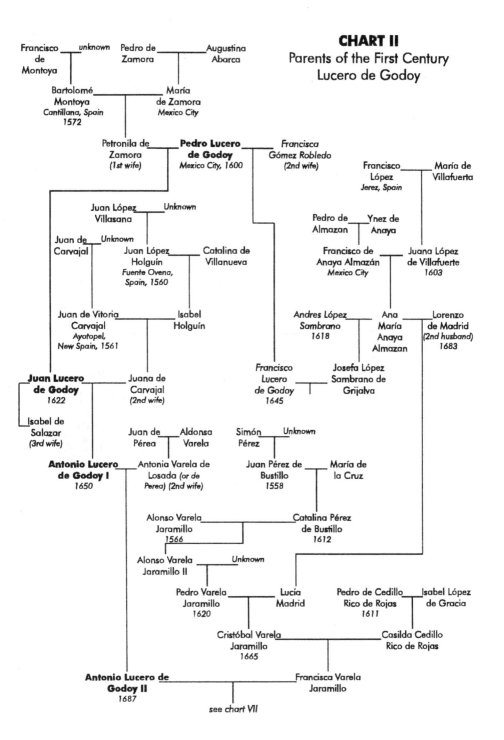

CHART II
Parents of the First Century
Lucero de Godoy

Francisco de Montoya —unknown— │

Pedro de Zamora —— Augustina Abarca

Bartolomé Montoya
Cantillana, Spain
1572

María de Zamora
Mexico City

Petronila de Zamora
(1st wife)

Pedro Lucero de Godoy
Mexico City, 1600

Francisca Gómez Robledo
(2nd wife)

Francisco López
Jerez, Spain

María de Villafuerta

Juan López Villasana —Unknown—

Pedro de Almazan —— Ynez de Anaya

Juan de Carvajal —Unknown—

Juan López Holguín
Fuente Ovena, Spain, 1560

Catalina de Villanueva

Francisco de Anaya Almazán
Mexico City

Juana López de Villafuerte
1603

Juan de Vitoria Carvajal
Ayotopel, New Spain, 1561

Isabel Holguín

Andres López Sambrano
1618

Ana María Anaya Almazan

Lorenzo de Madrid
(2nd husband)
1683

Juan Lucero de Godoy
1622

Juana de Carvajal
(2nd wife)

Francisco Lucero de Godoy
1645

Josefa López Sambrano de Grijalva

Isabel de Salazar
(3rd wife)

Juan de Pérea —— Aldonsa Varela

Simón Pérez —Unknown—

Antonio Lucero de Godoy I
1650

Antonia Varela de Losada (or de Perea) (2nd wife)

Juan Pérez de Bustillo
1558

María de la Cruz

Alonso Varela Jaramillo
1566

Catalina Pérez de Bustillo
1612

Alonso Varela Jaramillo II —Unknown—

Pedro Varela Jaramillo
1620

Lucia Madrid

Pedro de Cedillo Rico de Rojas
1611

Isabel López de Gracia

Cristóbal Varela Jaramillo
1665

Casilda Cedillo Rico de Rojas

Antonio Lucero de Godoy II
1687

Francisca Varela Jaramillo

see chart VII

83

CHART III
Gomez Robledo and other lines stemming from the first century

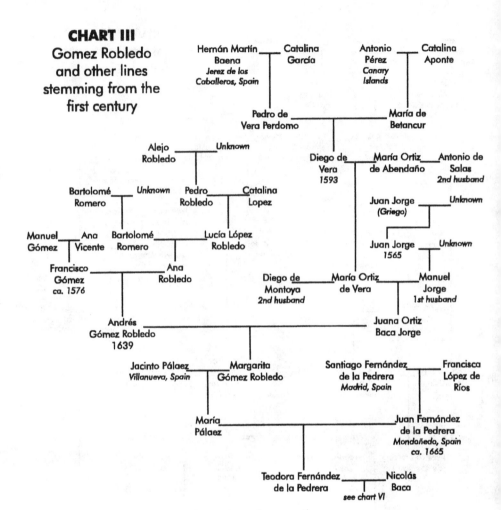

Hernán Martín Baena
Jerez de los Caballeros, Spain ⎯ Catalina García

Antonio Pérez
Canary Islands ⎯ Catalina Aponte

Pedro de Vera Perdomo ⎯ María de Betancur

Alejo Robledo ⎯ Unknown

Diego de Vera
1593 ⎯ María Ortiz de Abendaño ⎯ Antonio de Salas
2nd husband

Bartolomé Romero ⎯ Unknown

Pedro Robledo ⎯ Catalina Lopez

Juan Jorge *(Griego)* ⎯ Unknown

Manuel Gómez ⎯ Ana Vicente

Bartolomé Romero ⎯ Lucía López Robledo

Juan Jorge *1565* ⎯ Unknown

Francisco Gómez *ca. 1576* ⎯ Ana Robledo

Diego de Montoya *2nd husband* ⎯ María Ortiz de Vera ⎯ Manuel Jorge *1st husband*

Andrés Gómez Robledo *1639* ⎯ Juana Ortiz Baca Jorge

Jacinto Pálaez *Villanueva, Spain* ⎯ Margarita Gómez Robledo

Santiago Fernández de la Pedrera *Madrid, Spain* ⎯ Francisca López de Ríos

María Pálaez ⎯ Juan Fernández de la Pedrera *Mondañedo, Spain ca. 1665*

Teodora Fernández de la Pedrera ⎯ Nicolás Baca
see chart VI

3

ABSOLUTE AUTHORITY CORRUPTS ABSOLUTELY

S tudents of New Mexico's history may well ask where the officials of Spain and New Spain found these men who hoped to profit from the kingdom at whatever cost. In all fairness to the authorities in New Spain, it is likely that the colonization of New Mexico was seen by these officials as a thankless job with the only hope for profit being spiritual: to convert thousands of souls to the Catholic faith. Any other profits to be garnered from the northern province were meager. What was there? *Piñons*? *Mantas*? Skins? Slaves? In absence of other prospects, early colonial authorities turned greedy eyes toward the natives. Perhaps they could make these aborigines work for them and turn a mean profit. There were to be some excellent governors and church officials in New Mexico's future, but first there were Eulate (1618-1625), Rosas (1637-1641), López (1659-1661), and Peñalosa (1661-1664).

DON JUAN DE EULATE

E ulate came to New Mexico under the armed protection of Captain Francisco Gómez in a special caravan sent from New Spain to escort him to the northern kingdom. Enroute, the new governor, scandalized the friars traveling with him by his bawdy humor and irreverent comments regarding the Church and the religious.[1] He appears to have thrived on alienation from the Church and this became the dominant theme of his administration.

It must be remembered that New Mexico's very existence was predicated on missionary work. Civil authority was in place to support this endeavor. Eulate heard this mandate to bring Christianity to the natives, but chose the opposite course. He intended to reap the harvest of New Mexico even if this required severe pruning, thus changing the nature of the vineyard. If the clergy tried to erect a church, he threatened to halt its construction. If the settlers loaned the friars oxen to haul rock, soil, or timber, he threatened to fine them or worse, to kill them and their oxen. If the friars attempted to carry their work from their centralized missions to the more outlying provinces, he denied them military escorts even if offered by such cooperative *encomenderos* as Francisco Gómez. And, if the Indians themselves attempted to assist in mission repair or construction, he threatened to have them hanged unless they quit. He cowed, bullied, threatened, and harangued. If missionary endeavors did not come to a halt during his administration, it was not through lack of effort on Eulate's part.

Perhaps more important and more scandalous, at least to the friars, was Eulate's behavior toward the Indians themselves. He openly supported their non-Christianized behavior, approving their concubinage and native religious practices. And, while the Indians may have benefited from this support even if given merely to thwart the work of the religious, they did not benefit from his wickedness. He condoned their forced labor, enslavement, and even the kidnapping of orphaned Indian children by his henchmen, who then sold them to Spanish families as servants.[2]

Eulate was replaced by Governor don Felipe de Sotela Ossorio who, initially, sought to expand on the slave trade by sending out to the plains a large party of Indians to collect as many Plains Indian captives as they could. This approach was short-lived due to the protests of the friars, but Eulate had opened the door to slavery of the Indians. Eulate was to leave New Mexico in 1625 and his successor in 1630. During their stewardship the life of the colony moved haltingly forward.

One interesting glimpse into what life was like during this period occurred in 1634 when a company of Spanish traders, traveling under the protection of Captain **Alonso Baca**, ventured out onto the plains traveling as far as the Arkansas. During this trading expedition, Baca, who was accompanied by Francisco Luján, Gaspar Pérez, and Fray Andrés Juarez, had a most interesting adventure. The Apaches with whom they traveled invited them to an elaborate Indian ceremony in which they were to sleep with certain Apache maidens in the French manner of cementing alliances. As a result of this initiation rite, the three soldiers were made captains of the Apaches and entered into the tribe.[3] Gaspar Pérez supposedly left a son on the plains while the issue, if any, of Baca and Luján is not recorded. Both Luján and Pérez, but especially Francisco Luján, remained closely allied with the Bacas; their alliance, however, was not related to this colorful incident. Like much of what happened during this period, the Apache alliance held for just a brief period and Gaspar Pérez was never to see his son. Life was lived for the moment, and then it was gone.

After the departure of Eulate, the colonists and, especially the Indians, suffered through Governors Francisco de la Mora Ceballos and then Francisco Martínez de Baeza who attempted to turn the missions into trading posts and the missionaries into drummers.[4] Ceballos revived the *vale* (permission to take) which entitled the bearer to abduct Indian children, while Martínez de Baeza sought to turn the pueblos into cottage industries; nobody, however, Indian or colonist, was ready for the governor who followed them.

DON LUIS DE ROSAS

Luis de Rosas arrived in Santa Fe during April of 1637. He got his administration off to an injudicious start by allegedly accepting a bribe from the departing Governor Martínez de Baeza who wanted Rosas to give him a favorable report when Rosas conducted his *residencia*. Rosas complied and then took over his office with a vengeance. With Luis de Rosas, the struggle between Church and State, which had never been quenched, only removed from the flame, was rekindled, the banked embers brought to a blaze by cords of grievances on both sides.

According to the friars, Rosas was guilty of many sins. Like Eulate, he was accused of encouraging the Indians in their idolatrous practices to gain their favor and to obtain trade goods. It was alleged that he opened warehouses and sweatshops in the *casas reales* and had an insatiable appetite for *mantas*, hides, and tanned skins which he sold. He especially liked to use the trading fairs at Pecos, the *feria*, to barter with the Plains Indians for these commodities, behaving as though this ancient event was staged for his benefit. An aborted trading venture at Pecos resulted in a long string of incidents that were to further rend the already tattered fabric of the colony.

Rosas and a number of his men rode up to the Pecos Pueblo only to find that trading had begun prior to his arrival and only the dregs remained. Rosas was livid. How dare the Father Guardian allow them to start without him? He was threatening to arrest this friar when an aged missionary came to the Father Guardian's assistance. Rosas instantly diverted his anger from the Father Guardian to the 70-year-old Antonio Jímenez, whom he ordered seized and confined under the guard of four soldiers. It was only because the elderly friar feigned illness that he was not taken to Santa Fe for incarceration. Eventually, he and the Father Guardian were allowed to return to their quarters. But the conflict was far from over.

Back in Santa Fe, the four guards who had confined Friar Antonio Jímenez were confronted by Friar Domingo del Espiritu Santo who excommunicated them, stopping short of doing the same to the governor. Rosas hated Friar Domingo del Espiritu Santo but for the moment did nothing to retaliate. Several months later, however, Juan de Salas, the Franciscan provincial, reassigned Fray Juan de Vidania from Santa Fe to Picurís. The controversial Vidania was the one religious Rosas counted as his "esteemed" and "intimate friend."[5] To add insult to this injury, Salas put the hated Friar Domingo del Espiritu Santo in Fray Vidania's place. The governor then took Church matters into his own hands by reversing Vidania's assignment and having him returned to Santa Fe under military escort. To keep the peace, Salas backed down and officially reassigned Vidania to the *Villa de Santa Fe*.

Rosas' behavior continued to grow more outrageous and even when the friars were not his specific targets, his actions interfered greatly in their missionary work. On a missionary expedition to northern Sonora, which he joined for purposes of trade, for example, he so alienated the potential Indian converts with his incessant hawking, that he ruined any opportunity the friars may have had to place missionaries among them.

In 1638, on a slaving and trading venture out onto the plains, Rosas used Indians against Indians in his plan to bring back captives for private labor and for sale in *Nueva Vizcaya*. This latter venture was absolutely prohibited by his appointment and served to alienate the Apaches, the Indians who suffered this infamy and upon whose trade many of the Pueblos depended. Things were going from bad to worse.

The outrageous behaviors exhibited, however, were not one-sided. The *cabildo* (town council) in Santa Fe and some very prominent citizens praised Rosas as a military leader and explorer while lambasting the Franciscans.[6] Francisco Gómez, for one, complained that the Franciscans operated as though they were above the law with their faults and abuses remaining encapsulated and not known beyond New Mexico.[7] The *cabildo* was even more precise. It complained that the colonists were heavily burdened by the weight of three ecclesiastical authorities who accused them unjustly, judged their every move, and sold papal indulgences.[8] It contended that the citizenry were barred from the sacraments, excommunicated, and investigated by the Holy Office of the Inquisition at the slightest provocation. Also, the *cabildo* asked, why doesn't the Church reduce the size of its missions and get out of the livestock business?[9]

Then the hatred spilled over. When one of Rosas' men, an excommunicate, was murdered, Friar Vidania allowed him to be buried at the Santa Fe Church. His fellow Franciscans were aghast, and in the furor that followed, the governor had to rescue Vidania from his peers. He placed Vidania at his side as chaplain and under threat of death, banished the rest of the friars from the *villa*. He also closed the *convento*.[10] Now it was war!

The Franciscan missionaries retreated to their headquarters at Santo Domingo where a number of soldier-colonists joined them. They issued a proclamation that blamed the governor for many abuses including encouraging the Indians at Taos to disobey the missionaries.

This encouragement, they asserted, had led to the murder of Fray Pedro de Miranda by the emboldened Pueblos. The Franciscans vowed to go with their Father Custos if he was arrested and banished as promised by Rosas. Eventually, however, the friars voted to return to their missions, electing two priests to meet with Rosas and to attempt to reach a conciliatory agreement. When, under truce, these two delegates met with Rosas, he personally beat them and locked them up.[11] The friars now knew any hope they held for reconciliation was over.

The abuses of Governor Luis de Rosas took every form. The following, suggested by the play Peribanez and the *Comendador* of Ocaña by the Spanish dramatist Lope de Vega (1562-1635), presents one possible motivation for the authenticated historical events which come later. The dialogue, as well as the thoughts, feelings, and actions, of all involved, are conjectured to support the hypothesis being presented.

Rosas: Who is she? he asked, his lips pursed indicating the younger of the two women who stood at the church door speaking to the priest.

Aide: She is the wife of Nicolás Ortiz and the niece of Capitan Baca.

Rosas: She's lovely!

Aide: Yes, she's reputed to be one of the two most beautiful young women in the kingdom.

Rosas: Send a coach for her tonight. Tell her I wish for her to dine with me.

Aide: She is very beautiful, your Excellency, but quite unavailable. She's devoted to her husband Nicolás. But there are other . . . more available women, your Lordship, who would love to dine with you. We will get one of them.

Rosas: Devoted to her husband Nicolás? All the better. Love drives everything. She will not disappoint me.

María: Mama, what shall I do? You know his reputation. I'm afraid to go alone!

Juana: Feign illness. Send him a courteous note. He'll understand.

Aide: Please, Miss. He'll beat me if I come without you. It's now an invitation. He'll make it a command!

María: I must go Mama, or I will be ordered.

Rosas: And your husband, Nicolás, where is he now?

María: He's with the supply caravan. Thank God he didn't draw the assignment for the plains. It's very dangerous. The Vaqueros are especially fierce!

Rosas: Yes, already four of our men have been killed. He is very lucky to have this assignment . . . Still that could change. He could be assigned to the plains. Perhaps, if he was lucky, he would return safely. But, it's possible he could be assigned again and again until his luck ran out. It would happen eventually. No one's good luck lasts forever .... Finish your wine. You may go home now, but if you return, it will be because you ask to return. Please do not miscalculate, *Signorina*, he added as she entered the coach, I am the Prince. I can make anything happen.

María: Mama, what can I do? They're threats, hardly veiled at all. He'll have Nicolás killed!

Juana: I'll speak to your uncle Antonio. He'll know what to do. It'll be all right, you'll see.

María: No! Don't speak to my *Tio*! I forbid you speak to him! I'm shamed by the invitation. Don't speak to anyone. I must handle this myself!

Servant: Doña María. There's a footman with a message for you.

Note from Rosas:

I must have your request tonight. My man leaves tomorrow for
   Guadalupe del Paso with the new assignments. May Nicolás be
   well.

Juana: He won't be happy with once. He'll ruin you.
María: I have no choice Mama, I must go.

The coach entered the gate of the fortress at dusk and did not emerge
again until dawn. It was to make this sad journey many times. As the
commander, or *comendador*, Governor Rosas felt that he could do as he
pleased. This deed, however, would not go unpunished, as later events
would demonstrate.

Why Rosas took the next step is not known, but perhaps it was
his intent to drive the Franciscans from the kingdom by staging raids at
their missions. Whatever the reason, Rosas' men robbed the *conventos* of
San Ildefonso, Santa Clara, Nambé, Sandía, Quarai, and Socorro and drove
off the stock. The Pueblos were appalled and afraid. At Taos, the villagers
abandoned their pueblo and moved out onto the plains with the Apaches.[12]
Other Pueblos also fled. At Santo Domingo, the Indians and missionaries,
along with 73 of the colony's 120 soldiers, led by Antonio Baca, put up
fortifications against the hated Rosas.[13] He was literally tearing the colony
apart.

Then, almost miraculously, Rosas was replaced. Governor don Juan
Flores y Sierra y Valdez took office during the spring of 1641, after which
the Franciscans had Friar Vidania arrested and the anti-Rosas faction won
control of the *cabildo*. Then, fate intervened for a second time. After only a
few months in office, the new governor died. The *cabildo*, afraid that Rosas
would leave the kingdom before his *residencia* was completed, placed him
under arrest.

Around that time, Nicolás Ortiz returned home. He had been gone
with the supply caravan for over a year. The fact that María was pregnant
was apparent to him and to everyone else. He experienced every emotion

possible from blame to guilt to rage. He didn't know what to do and was inconsolable.

The Pérez de Bustillo family was devastated to an even greater degree. María was Nicolás's wife, but also their child. She had shown such promise; the family had looked at her with such expectation. Juana, the mother of María, perhaps more than anyone, felt the most guilt. She should not have listened to her daughter. She should have moved positively to intervene many months ago while the situation could still have been stopped. Each family member engaged in the same soul-searching with each being able to ascribe a portion of the blame to him or her self.

Antonio Baca was María's double uncle. He was married to **Yumar Pérez de Bustillo**, his sister Juana to Simón Pérez de Bustillo. Juana and Simón were María's parents. Responsibility for leadership fell to Antonio Baca and he seized it. Baca, the Pérez de Bustillos, and many of the other colonists appear to have felt that Rosas was a pig and a menace to all of them whatever his status. He had once tried to resign his post, but the viceroy had refused.[14]Would he now be reappointed governor? He had to be pulled down. It was long overdue. Nicolás and the family appear to have felt justified in killing him.

The family met at Antonio's home. Present, in addition to Antonio's brother, Alonso, was María's adoptive brother, Nicolás Pérez de Bustillo, and two of María's first cousins, Juan de Arechuleta and Juan Ruiz de Hinojos. Also present were **Diego Márquez** brother of Juan Márquez who was married to María's first cousin, María de Arechuleta, and the first cousins, Cristóbal Enríquez and Agustín de Carvajal. With Carvajal was his brother-in-law, don Pedro Durán y Cháves (II). As Antonio Baca's nephew, Durán y Cháves, the son of don Pedro Durán y Cháves (I) and Isabel de Bohórquez, had an even closer tie with the family. Of the 20 men in attendance, 13 were related to María through blood or marriage. Unintentionally, she had led her family into a cul-de-sac, with the family apparently feeling, it had no way out.

The plan was for María to arrange a liaison with Governor Rosas, now under house arrest at the *casas reales*. What she was told of their plans is not known. The assassins were to wait until the household had retired for the night, leaving but one guard at Governor Rosas' door. They would overpower the guard and force entry. Only four would be required for the work inside the governor's apartments. Nicolás was promised a primary role. It was January 25, 1642, and it was snowing outside.

The plan went without a hitch. Antonio Baca, accompanied by his nephews Nicolás Ortiz and don Pedro Durán y Cháves (II), and a fourth captain, **Luis Martín Serrano** (I), entered the *casas reales* with their ten masked compatriots. They broke off into small groups as they proceeded through the darkened passages. Their target was Rosas. They didn't want to hurt anyone else.

Sitting at the bedroom door, and quite unaware that disaster was about to strike, was Antonio de Salas. As the stepson of Pedro Lucero de Godoy (*El Viejo*) he was known to all. They fell upon him and he watched helplessly as Martín Serrano broke down the door.

In the subsequent trial, with Francisco López de Aragón acting as lawyer for Nicolás Ortiz, it was determined that Nicolás may have been justified in the murder, but they could make no such judgment regarding his accomplices. The motives of the others, they judged, sprang from politics, not passion. Their crime was sedition. Those who the authorities were able to place at the scene of the murder were sentenced to be executed.

Despite the pleas of the Baca, Pérez de Bustillo, Márquez, Arechuleta and Hinojos families, the sentences were carried out on July 21, 1643. Alonso Baca, Agustín de Carvajal and four of their compatriots were ordered executed, but somehow escaped the sentence. The other eight, with Antonio Baca determined to be the leader, were beheaded. The colonists were stunned. It was as though they had collectively been kicked in the stomach. They had lost eight of their best and brightest and for a Rosas! What a waste!

With the relatives of the executed men bringing charges against the government, the 24-year-old Nicolás Ortiz was first tried and acquitted in Santa Fe then sent to Mexico City for a final verdict. While traveling through the State of *Nueva Vizcaya*, he was arrested by the governor of this province who had been asked by Spanish officials through Francisco de Olivera to intercept him. The governor of Parral took it upon himself to secure a verdict. Ortiz was retried and sentenced to hang. He escaped from prison, however, and disappeared. María and her child, with death scattered before them, were to remain in New Mexico.[15]

> The hypothesis presented suggests that María was an unwilling participant in her relationship with Governor Rosas. This hypothesis is supported by what is known of Governor Rosas' character as well as by the fury with which her family responded. On the other hand, it is possible for the same events to be interpreted as proof of other theories. Nicolás Ortiz, for example may have been responding with the fury of a jealous husband, seemingly placing the blame for the events on Rosas rather than on both María and the governor. The murder may also have resulted from a sense of violated honor, with the family responding to defend it. A further possibility is that the fury displayed by María's family may have reflected the heroic response of a community to the cruel tyranny of Luis de Rosas. Perhaps the community, as represented by the family, believed that it would be pardoned for its actions, as had the residents of Fuente Ovejuna, Spain, in the popular play by the dramatist Lope de Vega, in which the citizens killed their *comendador* for behavior identical to that displayed by Rosas.[16]

While the Bacas were heavily involved in the Rosas affair, the Luceros de Godoy somehow managed to stay out of the fray. It is likely that Pedro, if not neutral, would have been counted among Rosas' men along with his father-in-law Francisco Gomez, since both he and Francisco were *encomenderos* and as such were required to support the crown. Francisco saw this as his absolute mandate. Just as he had stuck by the Oñates, Francisco Gómez gave his "first allegiance to the king's man regardless of who he was."[17]

Pedro Lucero de Godoy was now 43 with numerous adult children:

Catalina, married to *Encomendero* Diego Pérez Romero; María, married to Lazaro de Mizquia; Ynez, married to Juan de la Escallada; Luisa, married to Pedro Montoya de Esparza; Juan; Pedro and Francisco. Thus, the extended Lucero family by itself accounted for at least four of the thirty-five *encomenderos* in the kingdom. They functioned on the side of royal authority, especially as kin to Francisco Gómez who had been appointed by the dying Governor Flores to the position of interim governor. Although not accepted by the hostile city council because of his support of Governor Rosas when he was in power, Gómez is nonetheless listed as New Mexico's twelfth governor and is on record as having served with the *cabildo* in this capacity.

Who would test the colonists next?

CHART IV - Principals in the Rosas Affair

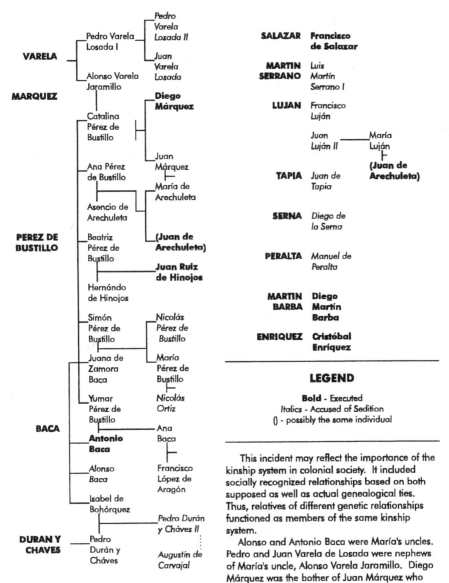

VARELA

Pedro Varela Losada I
— Pedro Varela Losada II
— Juan Varela Losada

Alonso Varela Jaramillo

MARQUEZ

Catalina Pérez de Bustillo
— **Diego Márquez**

Ana Pérez de Bustillo
— Juan Márquez
— María de Arechuleta

Asencio de Arechuleta

PEREZ DE BUSTILLO

Beatriz Pérez de Bustillo
— **(Juan de Arechuleta)**
— **Juan Ruiz de Hinojos**

Hernándo de Hinojos

Simón Pérez de Bustillo
— Nicolás Pérez de Bustillo

Juana de Zamora Baca
— María Pérez de Bustillo
— Nicolás Ortiz

Yumar Pérez de Bustillo
— Ana Baca

BACA

Antonio Baca

Alonso Baca
— Francisco López de Aragón

Isabel de Bohórquez
— Pedro Durán y Cháves II

DURAN Y CHAVES

Pedro Durán y Cháves
— Augustín de Carvajal

SALAZAR Francisco de Salazar

MARTIN SERRANO Luis Martín Serrano I

LUJAN Francisco Luján

Juan Luján II — María Luján
— **(Juan de Arechuleta)**

TAPIA Juan de Tapia

SERNA Diego de la Serna

PERALTA Manuel de Peralta

MARTIN BARBA **Diego Martín Barba**

ENRIQUEZ **Cristóbal Enríquez**

LEGEND

Bold - Executed
Italics - Accused of Sedition
() - possibly the same individual

This incident may reflect the importance of the kinship system in colonial society. It included socially recognized relationships based on both supposed as well as actual genealogical ties. Thus, relatives of different genetic relationships functioned as members of the same kinship system.

Alonso and Antonio Baca were María's uncles. Pedro and Juan Varela de Losada were nephews of María's uncle, Alonso Varela Jaramillo. Diego Márquez was the bother of Juan Márquez who was married to María's first cousin María de Arechuleta. Juan de Arechuleta, Juan Ruiz de Hinojos and Pedro Duran y Chávez II were María's first cousins. Augustín de Carvjal was a brother-in-law to María's first cousin, Pedro Durán y Cháves II. Of the remaining co-conspirators, Francisco and Juan Luján were brothers. María Luján, possibly, married to the executed Juan de Arechuleta was Juan Luján's daughter. The relationship of the others, if any, is not known.

Between the administrations of Governors Rosas (1637-1641) and López (1659-1661), at least eight individuals were to occupy the governor's chair. The last of these relatively benign administrators was to offer one of the most colorful and scandalous incidents yet experienced by the colony. One must remember the colony was very small and not only did everybody know everyone else, but many, if not most, were related. An affair, especially another one involving a sitting governor and the wife of one of his men-at-arms, could not go unnoticed.

Governor Juan Manso, 27 or 28 years of age, came to his post in 1656. He was the younger brother of Friar Tomás Manso, administrator of the mission supply service and a former holder of the office of custodian in the Franciscan order. The governor's lady was the exquisite, Margarita Márquez, wife of *Encomendero* Gerónimo de Carvajal who held one half of the *encomienda* of Awátobi. The Carvajals lived at their *estancia* located at *Nuestra Señora de los Remedios de los Cerrillos* near Santa Fe. It was there that don Juan and doña Margarita apparently conducted their affair.

The whole event was one that could only happen on the frontier, far from anything that made much sense. The affair between don Juan and doña Margarita seems to have been of long duration. What her cuckolded husband had to say about it all is nowhere written. Two children were involved, a girl and a boy, both of whom may have been Margarita's by Juan Manso. The first, being a girl, only caused don Juan to wince. At her baptism, faked by Friar Sacristan apparently because it would be unseemly to so use the sacrament, Manso was named as Godfather and his involvement with this child evidently ended at this juncture. The second child, however, was another thing altogether. Don Juan could not just pretend to baptize him and let him go. Instead, with doña Margarita and Fray Sacristan, he hatched a second plot. They waited until Señor Carvajal was gone from the *estancia* to have the child "die," his death "attended" by the honorable friar. Then after burying a doll or a bunch of rags, they hid the child at the *estancia* of Luis Martín Serrano (I) at *La Cañada de Santa*

Cruz. The child was subsequently spirited off to New Spain, transported there by the wife of Tomás Pérez Granillo in 1656. There he was to be raised in the house of the Mansos.[18] The plot only came to light when the repentant friar confessed his part in this scheme and hanged himself.

The colonists could only click their tongues and shake their heads. This provided them with entertainment in their wait for don Bernardo López the next governor.

There are two postscripts to these colorful events. Governor Manso was later to return to New Mexico as *alguacil mayor* (chief constable) of the Holy Office of the Inquisition. In 1673, he fell off his mule and was killed.

And the unbaptized child? It is believed it was she who later attempted to poison her husband, don José de Cháves, but only succeeded in making ill another Cháves who drank the potion by mistake.

DON BERNARDO LOPEZ DE MENDIZABAL

Difficulty between Governor López and Friar Juan Ramírez the Franciscan *procurator general* and the Father Custos began even before they left Mexico City for Santa Fe. López demanded that a large number of the wagons be allocated to him for his personal goods and for supplies that he hoped to sell in New Mexico. One can almost envision the two authorities throwing rocks at one another as the caravan rumbled northward. So severe was their wrangling that 10 of the 24 friars who accompanied them deserted enroute.[19] These friars refused to become embroiled in their pettiness.

When Governor López and Friar Ramírez arrived in New Mexico in midsummer of 1659, each took over from his predecessor. López eventually jailed former Governor Juan Manso while he conducted his *residencia*. Governor López opened a general store in the *casas reales* where he sold everything from shoes to saddles. López haggled with the former governor over the price of the cows he had bought from him and over the ownership of Apache captives.[20] The friars, following the lead provided by Ramírez, refused to pay López any respect and López refused to formally receive Ramírez. It was an authentic Spanish standoff.

Soon, López, like so many of those who preceded him, sought to win over the Indians at the expense of the missionaries.[21] Don Bernardo sought to separate the Pueblo Indians from the missionaries under the pretense of a reform. First he sought testimony from the Pueblo Indians regarding their friars in an attempt to discredit them. He then attacked the free use of Indian labor by the missionaries and raised the Indian wage from half a *real* to one *real* a day plus rations.[22] He demanded that the missionaries pay for the Pueblo Indians they used as interpreters, sacristans, bell ringers, organists, herdsmen, cooks, porters, and field hands.[23] The friars had previously claimed these Indians as unpaid assistants. He forbade the Indian servants from baking the friars' bread, carrying the missionaries' messages, or interpreting for the religious. And since few of the missionaries spoke the language of those with whom they worked, they were struck mute. Worse, at least as far as the friars were concerned, López decreed the Indians could resume their ceremonial dances.[24]

That was the last straw for the Franciscans. They threatened to abandon the colony if something was not done about López. They dispatched their complaints to the viceroy, while López prepared his countercharges. Don Bernardo was accused of being a crypto-Jew as evidenced by his taking a bath on Friday night in preparation for the Jewish Sabbath. More seriously, however, he was accused of having sexual relations with his slaves, an offense punishable by a life sentence on a slave galley. He was also accused of blasphemy and heresy.

In the cavernous depths of the *casas reales*, López composed his tale of truths, half-truths, innuendoes, and lies. He first asked Tomé Domínguez de Mendoza (II) to carry his version to New Spain. However, somehow, Domínguez managed to refuse his governor on the grounds that the reports contained too many falsehoods concerning both friars and citizens. Whether or not he couched his refusal in these terms is not known, but the governor accepted Domínguez' explanation and looked elsewhere for a courier. The governor then asked two of his men-at-arms, the uncle, Francisco Gómez Robledo, and his age-mate nephew, **Juan Lucero de Godoy**.

According to later testimony, the two men found themselves in a quandary, although Gómez appears to have been more willing than Lucero to act as courier for this questionable assignment. Whatever the case, Gómez and Lucero, feeling they had no choice, left Santa Fe for the *Estancia de San Antonio* in southern New Mexico where they were to pick up the packet of dispatches.[25] They left the *estancia* on November 16, 1660, for what they anticipated was to be a ride of over 1,800 miles.

Leaving New Mexico and entering New Spain, they were confronted with a further dilemma. On the trail, they met Friar Alonso de Posada, newly appointed to the position of religious custodian of New Mexico. He asked them what they were about. They told him they carried messages from the governor to the viceroy concerning difficulties in New Mexico. He advised them to speak to don Diego de Peñalosa Briceño y Verdugo, the incoming governor of New Mexico whom they then met at Zacatecas. Peñalosa later said that Gómez and Lucero told him they carried reports for the viceroy from the governor and *cabildo* on the subject of Indian labor "in order that his Excellency might provide a remedy for the abuses (committed) by the friars."[26] Governor Peñalosa told the couriers he was going to New Mexico to remedy this situation and if this was the extent of the message, they should deliver the reports to his person and return with him to Santa Fé.

For Gómez and Lucero, this was not a decision easily made. To whom did they owe allegiance? Ecclesiastical authority? Civil authority? Old or new? And to whom and for what were they responsible? After much deliberation, Lucero and Gómez turned over the dispatches and reports to Governor Peñalosa, although Gómez later intimated this was done without his consent.

This incident may have driven a small wedge between Juan and Francisco. Clearly, Gómez' natural inclination, as that of his father before him, was to complete his mission. Governor Peñalosa and his nephew interfered, and even in retrospect, this caused him pain. Lucero's stance, however, was somewhat different. He felt that the report by Governor López was false and therefore should not have been delivered. The intervention of his new superior, Governor Peñalosa, made this a possibility. Governor Peñalosa had the papers in his possession and Gómez and Lucero were back home.[27] But what a homecoming.

Custos Posada reached the colony three months before Governor Peñalosa. Once Peñalosa arrived, he and Posada began to bring López to ruin. Peñalosa amassed more than 70 formal complaints against the former governor, but it was Posada, acting with the authority of the Inquisition, who really brought López to his knees.

The Holy Office of the Inquisition in Mexico City ordered the arrest of four prominent individuals closely allied to former Governor López: Nicolás de Aguilar, *alcalde mayor* of the Salinas district; *Encomendero* Diego Pérez Romero, former *alcalde ordinario* (municipal magistrate) of Santa Fe; Cristóbal de Anaya Almazán, *alferez real* (royal standard bearer), inspector and captain of the militia; and *Encomendero* Francisco Gómez Robledo.[28]

The Luceros de Godoy were shocked. Three of the accused were kinsmen: Diego's wife was Catalina de Zamora, daughter of Pedro and sister of Juan Lucero de Godoy, Cristóbal was an uncle to the wife of Francisco Lucero de Godoy, and Francisco Gómez Robledo was Pedro's brother-in-law and Juan and Francisco's uncle. They knew Diego was a lout, but the others were considered honorable men.

When Francisco Gómez Robledo was arrested he was asked to name a person of his choice to assist in the attachment of his property, one of the legal requirements for one accused of a crime. He requested "the local depository of the royal treasury," his brother-in-law, Pedro Lucero de Godoy.[29] The Holy Office of the Inquisition then began proceedings against him. Gómez and the others were placed in prison at Santo Domingo while Friar Posada and *Alguacil* (Constable) Manso seized Gómez' property, selling at auction enough to pay for his imprisonment and pending trip to Mexico City for trial.[30] While the four sat immobile in jail, the governor and the Father *Custos* began wrangling over who had control over the *encomiendas* of Romero, Gómez, and Anaya as Cristóbal's father, **Francisco**

de Anaya Almazán, died soon after his arrest. While Posada impounded the properties of the accused simply because he had been commanded by the Inquisition to do so, Peñalosa impounded them so he could dispense them and use the proceeds for his own purposes.[31]

CHART V
A Lucero Clan
Interrelationships and the Inquisition

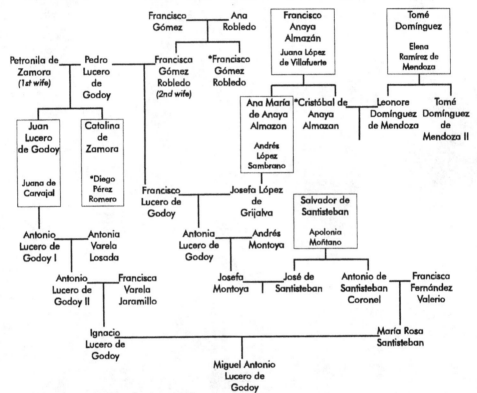

*Those arrested by the Inquisition

Francisco Gómez Robledo, Cristóbal de Anaya Almazan and Diego Pérez Romero were arrested by the Inquisition in 1662 and taken to Mexico City for trial. Cristóbal's father, Francisco de Anaya Almazan died in 1662. His death was attributed to his sorrow for his son's arrest. Earlier, Governor López de Mendizabal had asked Tomé Domínguez de Mendoza II to take his defense to Mexico City. Tomé refused. The packet was then taken to New Spain by Francisco Gómez Robledo and his nephew, Juan Lucero de Godoy.

During October of 1662 the south-bound supply train carrying don Bernardo López de Mendizabal, his wife, doña Teresa de Aguilera, Francisco Gómez Robledo, Cristóbal de Anaya Almazán, Nicolás de Aguilar and Diego Pérez Romero moved out, going first from Santa Fe to Santo Domingo and then from Santo Domingo to Mexico City. Doña Teresa was allowed to ride in a carriage, but the others were shackled and treated to the further indignity of being made to ride among the bales of skins that were going to New Spain to pay for their imprisonment.

Don Bernardo died in prison before a verdict was reached, and the charges against his wife were eventually dropped for lack of evidence. Francisco Gómez Robledo, accused of having Judaic leanings, earned a verdict of unqualified acquittal, and, after "three years, four months and fourteen days of his life" and the loss of several thousand pesos, he was allowed to return to New Mexico.[32] Aguilar, was found guilty of persecuting the friars and, after participating in an *auto de fé*, (a public inquisitional ceremony) he was banished from New Mexico for 10 years and forbidden to ever hold public office again.[33]

Anaya was released on the condition that he stand up at Mass on a given Sunday and recant his supposedly heretical remarks. He rode home on a white horse wearing a red scarf to symbolize his "dismissal with honor."[34] Diego Pérez Romero, accused of heresy, was made to participate in the same *auto de fé* with Aguilar and was subsequently banished from New Mexico. He later requested his wife Catalina join him in New Spain to marry off his sister to Alonso Lucero. However, Catalina had apparently had enough of Diego and chose instead to remain in New Mexico.[35] Since Catalina refused to join him, Diego later married a second time. This second marriage was illegal, divorce not being recognized in New Spain. He was, therefore, charged with polygamy, sentenced to 200 lashes and made to participate in his second *auto de fé*, meaning he had to walk barefoot, wearing the penitent's garb and carrying a green candle. He was also sentenced to six years labor as a galley slave, but died in jail before the sentence could be carried out.[36]

DON DIEGO DIONESIO DE PEÑALOSA BRICENO Y VERDUGO

Relations between Peñalosa and Posada had been cool since their falling out over tribute from the Gómez, Romero, and Anaya *encomiendas*. When Posada impounded at Parral (*Nueva Vizcaya*) goods that Peñalosa had taken from López, however, Peñalosa went from cool to explosive. In his fury he made imprudent and slanderous statements regarding the Inquisition and the inquisitors.[37] Friar Posada moved to Pecos to stay out of his way.

From that point on, things steadily and rapidly deteriorated. Through the years there had been a remarkable sameness in the difficulties between Church and State, López sounding like Rosas and so on, all the way back to Eulate. But now Peñalosa was about to add a new twist, violation of the right to sanctuary. During 1663, Peñalosa got into a fracas with don Pedro Durán y Cháves (II), nephew of Antonio and Alonso Baca, and one of the four masked men who had accompanied Nicolás Ortiz the night Rosas was murdered. The disagreement between Peñalosa and Durán y Cháves was not over politics, but over livestock.[38] Peñalosa ordered him arrested. At Santo Domingo, Durán y Cháves escaped and sought sanctuary at the church. Peñalosa had him dragged from the church and jailed in the *casas reales*. Posada felt he could not ignore this. One's right to sanctuary had to be honored.

Posada first made a polite request by letter asking that Peñalosa release Durán y Cháves. Peñalosa refused. Posada then wrote a second letter to which Peñalosa did not respond. Posada retaliated by initiating legal proceedings against him. Posada issued an order that the governor release Durán y Cháves or suffer excommunication. However, in a last effort to avoid a complete break with Peñalosa, he also dispatched one of his aides to Santa Fe to make two personal appeals. Still there was no response.

"He's going to excommunicate me? Well, we'll see about that!" That may have been Peñalosa's reaction when he read Posada's communication. It was Peralta/Ordoñez all over again. Governor Peñalosa commanded several of his *encomenderos* to join him on a hill outside of Santa Fe. None of the *encomenderos* knew the others were coming, nor did they know why they were being summoned. Present, among others, was Captain Diego Lucero de Godoy (I), astride a beautiful mount.[39] He was sent ahead to scout and to report back to the governor. Missing the larger party on the trail, however, he was later to be joined at the Pecos *convento* by Peñalosa, his lieutenant governor, Manso de Valdés, Francisco de Madrid (II), Diego Gonzáles Lobon, and Juan Griego (II).

When the whole party reached the *convento*, the governor himself requested entry to the building to "drink a bit of chocolate"[40] after which he engaged in a harangue with Posada which must have consumed hours. He searched Posada's room for something with which to accuse him, all the while demanding to know who would dare to excommunicate the governor and threatening to garrote a *custos* or pontiff who tried. Then, in the dead of night, and after numerous fits and starts, he forced Posada to accompany him to Santa Fe. There, for nine days, Peñalosa kept *Custos* Posada, agent of the Inquisition, his prisoner while the colony held its breath.[41]

One can only imagine how this episode would have ended had the two men continued to hold to their positions. Posada, who apparently felt there was absolutely nothing to be gained by an impasse, told the various friars who had closed their churches to Peñalosa to admit him and to administer the sacraments to him. The governor then released *Custos* Posada and the colony collectively breathed a sigh of relief.

These events occurred during September and October of 1663. In March of 1664, don Diego Peñalosa left New Mexico for New Spain. He passed his first night on the road at the home of doña Margarita Márquez and her husband *Encomendero* and *Alcalde Mayor* Gerónimo de Carvajal. After this short stay, his entourage again moved out for the City of Mexico. There he was astounded to find himself placed under arrest by the Inquisition.

The charges against Peñalosa ran to 237 articles and took two days to read.[42] Among many other things, he was charged with opening Inquisition mail, a reference to the reports he took from Lucero and Gómez at Zacatecas. It took almost two years for the Inquisition to reach its verdict and his punishment was harsh. He was sentenced to appear in a public *auto de fé*, a large fine was levied upon him, he was subjected to lifetime "exclusion from civil or military office" and banished "from New Spain and the West Indies."[43]

Peñalosa left New Spain a bitter and ruined man vowing to make the inquisitors and Spain pay. Back in Europe, appearing as the self-styled Count of Santa Fe, he first approached the crown in England and then in France, trying to sell his services and his knowledge of the Spanish possessions. What he offered were blueprints to invasion. He was successful in engaging the French in these pursuits, which later resulted in the French-led expedition of La Salle. Peñalosa eventually died in France as an expatriate and foreign agent.

4
EXPULSION

Although a growing colony in terms of numbers, New Mexico was weak and failing. Because it had so little fat, it was now losing muscle and bone. By 1670 there were approximately 2,000 men, women, and children spread up and down the Rio Grande Valley with perhaps 1,000 of these living in the *Villa de Santa Fe*. Pedro Lucero de Godoy's sons, Pedro, Juan, and Francisco each lived here. Juan lived one league southwest of Santa Fe at the Pueblo Quemado and Francisco on the Ciénega Road. The Lucero *estancia* was built on land of a prehistoric pueblo. This *"pueblo quemado"* (burned pueblo) was recently rediscovered in 1988. Diego Lucero de Godoy (I), believed to be a brother of the three mentioned above, had his home in Taos, while Juan's son, Juan de Díos Lucero de Godoy, is believed to have lived on a grant of approximately 31,000 acres just above the original colony's home at San Gabriel.[1]

Following the Rosas tragedy, the remnants of the Baca families, except for Ana, appear to have moved to the *Río Abajo* district, the area of the Rio Grande below *La Bajada* (The Descent), the demarcation between *Río Arriba*, (Upper River), and *Río Abajo* (Lower River). Ana appears to have been the one Baca who remained on the plain living on her *Estancia del Alamo* near Santa Fe. All of them, Luceros and remaining Bacas now sat there wondering if it would ever rain again.

The colony was starting to come apart, each factor like a thread loosening in a badly worn garment: the ongoing feud between the Church and State; the abuse of the Indians, including the suppression of the Indians' religion; the subsistence economy; the distance from their supply source; the ambivalence on the part of the Church and State about supporting the colonial and missionary endeavor; the increasing hostility of Indians outside the kingdom; and now the absence of rain for a prolonged period of time. Some of these were isolated factors, but most were interlinked and interwoven, so as to cast a blanket of discontent and discord on the populace.

Which factor was of most importance? Perhaps the drought. Because of the effect the drought had on hunting and foraging, the Navahos and Apaches attacked the Pueblos over and over again. Among themselves, the Pueblo Indians must have raged: "We pay tribute for them to protect us. Why do they not protect us? They are fighting amongst themselves. They only wish to enslave us. We must get the balance back into our lives, then all will be well."

Although the Spaniards were almost as badly hit by the drought and by attacks from hostile Indians outside the kingdom, they still found time to hunt down and punish those Pueblo Indians who were returning to their idolatrous ways.[2] The Spaniards broke the Indians' clay, stone, and wooden idols and cast them down with disdain. The Pueblos hid the ones they could, whether they were whole or in pieces, and resumed their former religious practices with few, if any, changes.

The last two governors, López and Peñalosa, had been dealt with severely by the Inquisition. Perhaps the governors who followed were too cooperative with the Church. Or perhaps, in the same way that some Indians felt Christianity and its ministers were responsible for their misfortune, the Spaniards felt their misfortunes resulted from the Indians' open return to their idolatrous lives. At any rate, Governor don Juan Francisco de Treviño linked arms with the friars in an open assault on paganism. Treviño had just taken office in 1675 when Fray Andrés Durán, father guardian of the San Ildefonso Pueblo, provided him with his test case.

Fray Andrés Durán made incredible charges against the Indians. He claimed the Indians had bewitched him, his brother, sister-in-law, and an Indian interpreter, Francisco Gutier, who was living at the mission.[3] More seriously, however, these Indians were also accused "of having killed seven friars and three Spaniards,"[4] although by what means is not reported. Incredibly, 17 alleged sorcerers were rounded up and taken to Santa Fe for trial. Four of the Indians were reported to have pleaded guilty to the charges brought by Durán. Three were hanged, one each at Nambé, San Felipe and Jémez. The fourth hanged himself rather than subject himself to the authority of the Spaniards. The remainder were sentenced to be whipped and sold into slavery.[5] They were lashed, but were rescued from servitude by a delegation of their heavily armed Indian brothers who threatened severe consequences if the sentences were carried out. Instead, the ransom the rescuers offered of eggs, chickens, tobacco, and beans was accepted and the remaining 43 released.[6]

Among those released was, Popé, an Indian of the San Juan Pueblo. Popé, an alleged sorcerer, was a shaman whose own sense of power came from his averred access to the spirit world. By his assessment, he had the power to cure and to harm. There was no question which he would use against his oppressors.

After his release, Popé returned briefly to San Juan before moving to Taos. These were two of the fifteen or so pueblos of the Tanos Indians. Although the San Juan and Taos Indians were Tanos who spoke different dialects, Popé was apparently accepted at each of the northern and central pueblos he visited. Three lieutenants whom he recruited along the way assisted him in his work of fomenting rebellion. They were Alonso Catiti, a *coyote* (one with a Spanish and an Indian parent) Indian leader from Santo Domingo,[7] Jaca from Taos, and Luis Tupatú, a native of Picurís who was living at Pecos.[8] The message of Popé, Catiti, Jaca, and Tupatú was everywhere the same: we must throw off this Spanish yoke and live as Indians!

REVOLT

The Spaniards knew trouble was coming, they just did not know from whom or from what quarter. For more than four years Popé and the others moved and lived among the Pueblos, group after group, pueblo after pueblo, threatening, cajoling, persuading. When would they be ready?

Popé did not know of Chief Metacom (King Philip) of the Wampanoags and of his mission to drive out the Plymouth colonists, but their aims were similar: liberation from the white invaders in their land. The Wampanoags, however, had a federation. The Pueblos had never united for anything. Could he make them act as one?

* * *

The clatter of hooves against cobbles was deafening as the escort party rode through the village of *Guadalupe del Paso*, to meet the wagon train coming from Mexico City. In command of the escort party was Captain Pedro de Leyva, lieutenant governor for the Salinas Pueblo district. Captain Leyva was an old soldier of 67. Although not of a *conquistador* family, he could still count himself a native, having lived in New Mexico since 1637. Well liked and well respected by all who knew him, he was a soldier one could count on. With the senior Leyva, were two of his sons, Pedro and José. Both José and his father had left families at Galisteo as they rode south to *Guadalupe del Paso*.

Also with the Leyva escort party were two soldier-colonists from Taos, Domingo de Herrera and Diego Lucero de Godoy (I). Both had large families at Taos. Domingo's family consisted of his wife, mother-in-law and seven children. Diego's family was even larger. He lived in a *casa corral* or *plazuela*, a single-family version of the fortified village, in which contiguous rooms surrounded and enclosed a small courtyard.[9]

With Diego in his fortress-home was his large extended family of 32 persons including his sons and servants. Although an imposing fortress, with walls more than three feet thick, it would not be sufficient to keep them from harm.

On this day, the mounted men sat on their horses looking south for the wagon train, when one of them noted a lone rider approaching from the north hell-bent-for-leather. He came with devastating news. The colony, their families, were under attack.

* * *

One of the mysteries of the Pueblo Indian Rebellion is how Popé communicated with the scores of pueblos involved. Initially, the means that Popé chose was a device similar to the *quipu* used by the Peruvians as an arithmetical and mnemonic aid. This device, as employed by the Incas and others, consisted of a main cord from which smaller cords of different colors hung at various distances.[11] In the Peruvian version, each color had a meaning with numbers expressed by tying knots in the smaller cords. Pope's *quipu*, which three spirits, Caudi, Tilini, and Tleume,[12] reportedly instructed him to make, was a cord of maguey fiber. Although a single cord with knots of one color, it was sufficient to accomplish its singular purpose of telling the Pueblo Indians the Spaniard's days were numbered.

The date for the rebellion was set for August 13, 1680. The *quipu* was passed from pueblo to pueblo to synchronize the countdown. With each day, the Pueblo Indians grew more anxious until some could no longer contain the secret. At Pecos, Galisteo, and Taos, the Spaniards began to hear word of the plan. Then two of Popé's messengers were betrayed to the Spanish by some of the Pueblo Indians whom they visited. Both Governor Otermín and Popé himself heard of this, which provided warning for the governor and required Popé to move up the date. How Popé informed the Pueblo Indians of the change is not known. Certainly his method of communication was superior to the governor's, for the colonists, especially those furthest removed from Santa Fe, were caught almost totally off guard.

Pedro Hidalgo, an armed escort who had accompanied Friar Juan Bautista Pio[13] from the *Villa de Santa Fe* to the Tesuque Pueblo for Mass, was the first to warn Santa Fe of the rebellion. Pio's Indian congregation had hidden in a nearby ravine and ambushed him as he searched for them. Some hours later, Nicolás Lucero de Godoy (son of Juan or Francisco Lucero de Godoy), and Antonio Gómez Robledo (son of Francisco Gómez Robledo) rode into Santa Fe with news of what was occurring in the north. They had been sent by the *alcalde mayor* of Taos to warn the villa of the conspiracy.[14]

Lucero and Gómez, like their fathers, were men who could be counted upon to get the message through. They rode the 60 miles from Taos to Santa Fe through increasingly hostile territory. When they found the Camino Real (Royal Road) blocked by Pueblos lying in wait for fleeing colonists, they began to pick their way through the mountains, eventually reaching *La Cañada de Santa Cruz* and then Santa Fe. At Santa Cruz they found a soldier garrison had been attacked, with two men killed. When Lucero and Gómez left their families in Taos that morning, they thought they had three days to prepare. Lucero and Gómez now found the Taos, Picurís, and Santa Clara Pueblos in full rebellion and knew that the day of infamy had arrived ahead of schedule.

Governor Otermín, too, had felt the colony had time to prepare. Some later said he had as much as 20 days' warning provided by the Pecos Indians through their *Encomendero* Francisco Gómez Robledo. He had not moved to devise a plan of defense, however, until the ninth. The repairs to the fortress walls and gate had only been completed eight days before, and this was serendipitous, not an aspect of planned defense.

Now Otermín acted decisively. He sent messengers to all the outlying districts warning the embattled colonists to defend themselves. Those who could attempted to gather at two defensive sites, at the *Villa de Santa Fe* for those in *Río Arriba* and at the pueblo of Isleta for those from Cochiti to Socorro in the *Rio Abajo*.

Governor Otermín had to determine the extent of the revolt. After conferring with Nicolás Lucero de Godoy and Antonio Gómez Robledo, he asked Antonio's father, *Maese de campo* Francisco Gómez Robledo, and a squadron of soldiers to ride to *La Cañada* and to determine "the extent of damage and atrocious murders . . . at Tesuque, Cuyamungue, Pojoaque, and the rest of the pueblos on the way to Taos."[15] After assembling their gear, the men left that evening.

When the Gómez party returned two days later, they had chilling news. All the pueblos from Tesuque to San Juan were in open rebellion. A large group of warriors had amassed at Santa Clara. Many friars had been killed. And all the colonists not now behind the fortress walls had either been killed or captured.

The messengers returning from the southern reaches of the Río Arriba carried similar messages: friars were dead, roads were closed, colonists were killed or captured. The exception was at *Los Cerrillos* where *Sargento Mayor* Bernabé Márquez (son of **Diego Márquez** executed in the Rosas affair), and the Márquez family were managing to hold the Pueblos at bay from their fortified *plazuela*. Otermín sent a squadron of soldiers to help them and to bring whatever other survivors and livestock they could to the *villa*.

Governor Otermín had ordered the officials at the armory to distribute "*harquebuses*, blunderbusses, swords, daggers, shields, and munitions"[16] to all males who did not have arms so they could defend the capital. He had the trench or dry moat, which was located in front of the gate, lengthened so as to encircle the walls of the fortress. He ordered embrasures be cut into the top of the walls so as to permit gun placements on the roof. Two small canons, on their carriages were set outside the walls, positioned to fire at street entrances to the plaza. And in final preparation, he requested that the friars consume the host, close their *convento* and church, and bring all vestments and sacred objects to the *casas reales* for safe keeping.

Likely, the most important of these sacred objects was the famed statuette of *La Nuestra Señora del Rosario* (Our Lady of the Rosary) to become known to the colonists as *La Conquistadora* (Our Lady of the Conquest).[17] Even more than Our Lady of Remedies, who graced the royal standard carried by Oñate, *La Conquistadora* came to represent New Mexico, her poor, fragile, and devout Catholic kingdom. Whether *gachupina* or *criolla*, this lovely statuette of unknown origin had been brought to New Mexico in 1625 by Fray Alonso de Benavides. First given the title of Our Lady of the Assumption and then The Immaculate Conception, the statue would be washed and dressed with loving care by the ranks of her confraternity to mark the major feasts of the Virgin and to remind the people, of their origins as a colony. The care of their most sacred object and historical symbol was entrusted to a non-combatant, Josefa López Sambrano de Grijalva, wife of Francisco Lucero de Godoy.[18]

Still there was no news from the *Río Abajo*. Otermín had sent three messages to Lieutenant General **Alonso García** in command of the southern forces, but each of the messengers, including Lucas de Gamboa, had been killed and the messages not received. It probably would not have mattered for García and those at Isleta were also under attack. The Spanish forces had been divided into two groups, each believing the other doomed.

Small groups of Pueblo Indians began arriving at the *Villa de Santa Fe* ahead of the larger forces that were approaching from the South and the North. A small group of Tanos began burning and looting in the *Barrio de Analco* and around the church of San Miguel. One of these, an Indian named Juan, rode into the plaza to confer with Governor Otermín and to urge his surrender. Otermín, of course, refused, offering instead to pardon the Indians if they would lay down their arms and return to their pueblos. The Pueblo Indians jeered and scorned this suggestion.

On the advice of his council of war, Otermín decided his forces should attack the rebels in the south *villa* before the Pueblos from Pecos, Galisteo, and La Ciénega who were advancing from the South could reinforce them. The soldiers were attacked as soon as they left the gate, requiring that Otermín himself lead reinforcements to drive the Indians off. The troops outside the wall then attacked those rebels holed up in *Analco* and San Miguel, burning the houses in the south *villa* so the rebels could no longer use them for shelter. They also rounded up the livestock before retreating behind the fortress walls. As they did so, the Indians from the Taos and Picurís pueblos arrived to mount an attack on them from the North.

Their situation was desperate. They were surrounded on all sides by hostile Pueblo Indians now reinforced by Apaches from the plains who were furious at the unscrupulous conduct of *Maese de campo* Francisco Xavier who before the Pueblo rebellion had proved himself treacherous. He along with a group of frontiersmen had seized a number of Apaches who had been trading at Pecos under promise of safe conduct. All the Indians knew these Spaniards could not be trusted and they were determined to be rid of them.

One can only imagine the conditions inside the *casas reales*. Within the walls were approximately 1,000 men, women, and children, (including Indian servants), and some 5,000 head of livestock (cows, horses, and sheep). The noise was deafening. The stench of excrement, human and animal, rose in the August heat like a heavy vapor from a swamp. Worse, however, was the miasma of fear that pervaded everything. This, combined with the odors of filthy bodies and gaping wounds, sickened all.

Most sickened were they who had lost their families. Juana, daughter of Francisco López de Aragón, married to Sebastián de Herrera Corrales, was massacred at Taos, where she had gone for a visit. Killed with Juana was her mother Ana Baca, daughter of Antonio Baca. **Antonio Lucero de Godoy** (I) had lost his wife, two children, and four servants. Francisca Gómez Robledo, wife of the late Pedro Lucero de Godoy, was killed. The Gómez Robledos also lost **Andrés**, Francisco's brother, the only officer to be killed in defense of Santa Fe. And the list went on and on.

Crying out with joy at finding a friend or loved one, the families attempted to regroup and to make a niche for themselves amid the squalor. They lived like this for six sweltering days, in fear and in expectation of the next assault.

The anticipated attack occurred on Friday, August 16, when approximately 2,500 Indians from all the northern pueblos stormed the fortress. Using captured arms, they were a formidable force. They were finally beaten back, but not before they set fire to a portion of the building. The fire, however, was put out and the Indians did not breach the walls.

Because of the shortage of feed and the lack of water for their livestock, some of the animals died, the stench of the bloated bodies only adding to the putridity surrounding the trapped Spaniards. Then the Indians cut off the *acequia* which brought water near the fortress. It was now only a matter of time. Governor Otermín assembled all in the plaza within the *casas reales*. After two days without water, they had little choice. They decided it was better to fight their way out than to die there in their own filth.

THE FORCED EXODUS

On the morning of August 20, 1680, after being trapped behind the walls for 10 days, Otermín led a small group of armed troops into the plaza where some of the Pueblos had encamped. Taken by surprise, the rebels were routed with a loss of about 300 Indians. They retreated, allowing the colonists to take their stock out of the fortress for water and feed. However, if the Spaniards had retained any hope of staying in Santa Fe, the sight of their ruined *villa* crushed it. The colony was lost. They had no choice but to retreat again to the fortress before the Pueblo Indians had a chance to regroup.

After securing a vote from his council of war, Governor Otermín made plans for the colony to begin its retreat south. He did so with the knowledge that his might be the first colony, a European power had lost to native conquerors. It was important to Otermín that he go on record as obeying the combined will of his people. He did not want it said that he had acted in his own interest, but rather, in theirs.

Having first distributed the clothing and livestock among themselves, the group of 1,000 men, women and children marched in full military formation, through the gate of the *casas reales* trying to look brave and in command of its destiny. The immediate plan was to rendezvous with Alonso García at Isleta. The colonists marched in a column, with the women and children in the center, the men flanking them on all sides, front and rear. With the women and children was Josefa López de Grijalva, clutching the statuette entrusted to her care. She prayed that *La Conquistadora* would protect her family and all the colonists from harm.

As they marched, they looked over their shoulders fearing sight of the enemy, but also in fear of what they would find relative to the other colonists. As they came upon Galisteo, Francisco de Anaya Almazán (II) looked for his wife, Francisca Domínguez, and his children, one of whom was a small infant. He did not find them—and was probably spared the agony—because as he was searching his home, his wife lay naked in the field with her head bashed in and their infant lying at her feet.[19]

The Hurtados kept looking behind them hoping by some miracle to see their beloved Juana and María, from whom they had been separated, running to catch up. Not knowing where they were or what was happening to them was somehow even worse than knowing they were dead. What would the Indians do to them? At Cochiti, Santo Domingo, and San Felipe, the situation was the same, the outlying *estancias* destroyed, the people dead or gone. At the Narrows, south of San Felipe, the retreating colonists found the naked bodies of Cristóbal de Anaya Almazán, his wife, six children, and numerous others of their household, heaped like cordwood at the front door.[20]

The colonists from Santa Fe walked and walked. The mystery was they had not been attacked. They wondered anxiously what they would find at Isleta, but when they got there, they found nothing. It was an odd time. They didn't know whether to be fearful or furious: "God damn it, they left us." "My God, what has happened to them?" "García better have a damn good explanation for this one!" These were probably typical exclamations as the colonists stood, dumbfounded and frightened, in the deserted village.

Finding nothing at the island pueblo, the Rio Grande which encircled it now in flood, the retreating colonists gathered their resources and continued south with almost nothing between them and *Guadalupe del Paso* almost 300 miles away. Correctly guessing that those from the *Río Abajo* had retreated south before them, Governor Otermín sent out a scouting party with orders for Lieutenant Governor Alonso García and his retreating group to stop and wait for him.[21]

When García received this report, he had reached a location below Socorro, and with a small group of his 1,000 survivors, retraced his steps to meet Otermín at Socorro.

This meeting between Governor Antonio de Otermín and Lieutenant Governor Alonso García was not a friendly one. García's partly gray hair looked even grayer as he stood in the August sun receiving harsh words from his superior. He was later to stand a court-martial by Governor Otermín for not having come to the aid of the colonists in Santa Fe. He was to be exonerated of these charges, however, and his superiors may even have commended him for his valor in having made several trips to the area between Isleta and Santo Domingo where he successfully rescued many. But for the moment, he could only stand there, his naturally protruding eyes filling as he received the upbraiding from his superior. To some extent, Governor Otermín was merely expressing his grief, and, García was unfortunate enough to be the scapegoat.

The amassing of 2,000 colonists was a very rare occurrence. This large group was a pathetic sight, exhausted, hungry, ill equipped. The 1,000 survivors from Santa Fe had only two wagons carrying their pitifully inadequate food supply. Foodstuff from the people of the *Río Abajo* supplemented their provisions. Nonetheless, it was a sad army that now had to cross the 300-mile *Jornada del Muerto*, the Dead Man's Route, in order to reach the relative safety of *Guadalupe del Paso*.[22] Franciscan Friar Francisco de Ayeta and the members of the Leyva escort were the first to receive mixed reports from the North regarding the Indian revolt. As these reports came from the *Río Abajo*, the enormity of the tragedy and the condition of the *Taosenos* were still not clear. Diego Lucero de Godoy (I) and Domingo de Herrera were not to discover they had lost their entire families (a total of 43 persons) until the whole group reassembled at El Paso. Meanwhile, Friar Ayeta wasted no time waiting for the survivors to arrive. He mounted a relief column of supplies, armed men, and friars to meet the exiles on the road. Never were the colonists so happy to see the blue-robed friars as they were when they caught sight of them approaching from the south.

5
EXILE: 1680–1693

REGROUPING

Not all had acted honorably on the torturous march south. Tomé Domínguez de Mendoza (II), whose *estancia* had been below the Isleta Pueblo, was accused of burying plowshares and other agricultural implements as a means of lightening his wagons, although he knew these would be needed by the exiled colony. He and a number of the Pedro Durán y Cháves (II) clan were later indicted for profiteering on the misery of the colony. Others, such as Antonio de Carvajal and Cristóbal Enríquez (II), were accused of taking an undue share of relief supplies. For the most part, however, the group demonstrated exemplary behavior.[1]

It was not until the colonists reached *La Salineta* above El Paso that they were able to stop and fully assess the damage. Catalina Bernal and Ana de Sandoval y Manzanares were representative of the many widows who were left with young children. There were so many devastated families! The initial determination was that the colony had suffered the loss of 380 colonists and 21 Franciscans, but the exact number will never be known. On the other hand, the census taken by Governor Otermín determined that the survivors numbered 1,946 with approximately 300 Pueblo Indians who had cast their lot with the retreating Spaniards and joined them in exile.[2] Undoubtedly, additional survivors had continued running, escaping into New Spain, out of reach of both colonial authority and Indian revenge.

The Albizuses were perhaps a bit better equipped than were many of the other families. Colonists from the *Río Abajo*, they were at least able to pack some bedding and a canvas with which to construct a rude tent. The chestnut-haired Antonio Albizu needed the help of his son to secure to the wheels of his wagon the ropes of the canvas which flapped uncontrollably in the desert wind. He hated his inability to grasp the wildly flapping sheet, but his lame finger restricted the complete use of his good hand.[3] While his wife, Gregoria Baca, searched among the survivors for her sister **Gertrudis** and for her cousins, one can imagine what was in Antonio's mind. He was probably thanking God his children were older and able to assist during this grueling period. It would be horrible, he must have thought, to have young children who were completely dependent upon you for their survival. It was bad enough to suffer one's own hunger, thirst, and fear, but to have to suffer these also for your children, whom you had a responsibility to protect, would be unthinkable.

Gregoria and Gertrudis were the only children of Antonio Baca to escape the onslaught,[4] and they could only find a single surviving first cousin among the impoverished crowd. **Cristóbal Baca** (II), son of their uncle Alonso, was there with his wife, **Ana Moreno de Lara**, and his six adult children.[5] Some of his children had their own families with them, and they were scattered throughout the encampment. The survivors were no longer a colony. Each family was wondering what the next move would be and was badly in need of direction.

Almost immediately, Governor Otermín attempted to provide that direction for his exiled people. In early October, he moved his group across the Rio Grande where he established them in three camps below the mission of *Guadalupe del Paso*. Here the colonists began to erect rude shelters. And here Governor Otermín received new orders from his viceroy to retake Santa Fe and to reestablish a Christian enclave among the Indians.

The viceroy's orders revealed his distance from the reality of the situation. He could issue his directives, but both the undertaking and accomplishment of these were another matter. Otermín had some difficulty mounting an expeditionary force for the return to New Mexico. Many felt they had been totally demoralized; others had lost everything. When Diego Lucero de Godoy (I), for example, packed his gear at Taos for the trip to El Paso as a member of the Leyva escort party, he had no idea he would never return. He was one of those who had lost it all. For him there was nothing to go back to but memories. He preferred to remember his smiling and laughing children as they cantered alongside him when he left his *estancia*, to the bitter reality of returning to the beautiful but desolate place they had called home, to the place where he would never hear their voices again. No. He was not going back. There was nothing there but the reminder of what was forever lost.

Diego was not alone. A number of colonists petitioned to return to New Spain, while others crept away in the night. Although some were caught and required to return, others, like Diego, eventually received permission to move south and did not return to New Mexico.

On November 5, 1681, however, after more than a year in El Paso, the governor was able to put a group of 146 Spaniards into the field, the majority of these being colonists from the *Río Abajo* who had not suffered the full fury of the rebellion. They were accompanied by four or five friars, twenty-eight servants and 112 Indian allies.[6] This force, which included *Sargento Mayor* Ignacio Baca, left El Paso during November, perhaps with the intention of retaking New Mexico, although how Otermín expected to accomplish this with his very small force is uncertain.

As they marched north, they found the pueblos of the Piro deserted and burned them. Continuing north, they took the Indians of Isleta by surprise and easily moved into their village. Here the Isletans, who had not taken part in the rebellion, perhaps because this pueblo had been the southern outpost for the colonists of the Río Abajo, greeted them rather amiably. Beginning again, the Spaniards absolved the people for any part they may have played in the rebellion, baptized their infants, and began destroying their idols. Had they learned nothing?

Establishing Isleta as his base of operations, Otermín sent Indian scouts to the Indians of the northern pueblos, telling them to stay in their villages and to prepare themselves to be placed under Spanish rule once again. Hearing nothing from them, Otermín ordered one of his cavalry officers to mount a scouting party to move north and determine what was going on. This officer was Juan Domínguez de Mendoza, brother of Tomé, who had lightened his wagons in order to more easily make the trip south into exile.

From Isleta, the 52-year-old Domínguez moved north finding pueblo after pueblo deserted except for an occasional wizened old man or woman, too old or feeble to have gone into hiding with their people.[7] Finally, at Cochiti, the scouting party met the Pueblos, a large force assembled and waiting for them on a fortified *mesa*.

This was the first encounter between the Pueblos and the colonists since the latter had fled down river more than a year before. In the colonists' absence, the Pueblos, under the fierce direction of Popé, had burned and razed the churches, desecrated and destroyed Christian religious objects. They had also been ordered to burn Iberian seed (the seed of those agricultural products introduced to the Americas by the Spaniards). The Pueblo Indians were, of course, forbidden to speak Spanish and had been required to scour their bodies in the river with yucca root soap to erase their Christian names and to remove any vestige of baptismal water or holy oil. They had also been required to ignore their Christian-sanctioned marriages and to take new wives. Except for the destruction of Iberian seed, an act, which the Indians refused to carry out, Popé's dictates had been obeyed almost to the letter even though they caused great consternation among many of the Pueblo Indians. In destroying everything Spanish, many of the Pueblos could see that they were losing much that was beneficial.

In one very interesting way, Popé took over where the Spaniards had left off. Popé now collected the *encomienda* tribute previously directed to the Spaniards. Not only did he require that the Pueblo Indians give up their sheep, cattle, and fruit trees, but he also required they pay taxes. His leadership was to last less than a year.[8] Thus, when the large group of Pueblo Indians met Domínguez on that fortified mesa near Cochiti during the winter of 1681, it was not Popé with whom the colonists parlayed, but Alonso Catiti and he was just as bright and crafty as Popé.

In a series of meetings between the two groups, Catiti played for time. Pretending to sue for peace with the Spaniards, he offered to negotiate with the Indians of the other pueblos while planning the Spaniards' slaughter. His scheme was quite simple. He planned to have some attractive young women of the Cochiti enter the Spanish camp to entertain the soldiers. Then, when the soldiers were engaged with the Indian women, the Indian men would drive off the soldiers' horses. Catiti felt that, on foot and 60 miles from their main force at Isleta, the hapless Spaniards could be picked off at leisure. Had the plot not been betrayed to one of Domínguez' men by a former servant, Domínguez' small group would surely have been cut off and cut down by both the Pueblo Indians gathered at Cochiti, and those arriving from the north. Instead, Domínguez and his mounted troops in deep snow through which they trudged, began a retreat south to Isleta. When Domínguez and his group met Otermín and the remainder of the soldiers on the trail, the total group decided to quit New Mexico, taking with them to El Paso 385 of the Isleta people.[9]

If Otermín's intention had been reconquest, he was unsuccessful; the *entrada*, however, was not without accomplishment in that it taught the Spanish conquerors some hard truths about the people they had conquered and converted. For example, if the Spaniards had labored under the misconception that their leaders had forced the Pueblo Indians into rebellion they found this to be untrue. They also found that the Pueblo Indians were not waiting for their return with open arms.[10] The Spaniards would have to wait at El Paso for reinforcements and new leadership during which time some of their members would desert, and others would be allowed to leave; marriages would be consummated, and children born; and many of their company would die. It would be 12 long years before the colonists would return to the homes they had been forced to abandon.

Originally settled into three camps at El Paso, the colonists, and their Indian allies, eventually established several scattered settlements in the vicinity of Guadalupe del Paso. These were *El Santisimo Sacramento* (later to be called *Corpus Christi de Ysleta*), *San Pedro de Alcantara*, and a third site, which was later to become the capital of the colony in exile.[11] In El Paso Governor Otermín brooded about what lay ahead. Apparently feeling that New Mexico was a lost cause, or that it offered little even if reconquered, he tried to resign his appointment so he could get on with the rest of his life. His request to step down was refused, however, and he was required to serve out his term on the Diablo Plateau.

At the conclusion of his tenure in 1683 Otermín was replaced by General don Domingo Jironza Petriz de Cruzate. Governor Jironza, a veteran of many military campaigns in Europe, began immediately to organize the dispirited colonists into a group hoping to renew a sense of purpose. He gathered them in from their scattered camps, consolidated them, and directed them in their building of a new town. They called this new settlement *El Real de San Lorenzo*, for the saint on whose feast day (August 10) the Pueblos had initiated their rebellion.

Life at *San Lorenzo*, although not impossible, was very difficult. While Jironza was building his adobe palace, the colonists constructed rather rude shelters made of tree branches plastered with mud. They seemed totally disinclined to build more permanent homes, hoping perhaps that they would eventually be allowed to return to New Spain or to New Mexico. (The destitute condition of these settlers is best described in a chronicled visitation by Attorney General Juan Severino Rodríguez from September 11 to 14 in 1684. His descriptions are given in Appendix I.)

During the cold January of 1683, **Juana de Carvajal**, wife of **Juan Lucero de Godoy** died at San Lorenzo.[12] Fifty-nine-year-old Juan, former secretary of government and war, may have wondered if it had all been worth it. At the rebellion of 1680, he had been *alcalde mayor* of Santa Fe. Although not a position of privilege, this post as a superior civil official with executive, legislative, and judicial responsibilities placed him and his family in a position of some respect. At *San Lorenzo*, they were nothing. They spent their days fighting off the Texas Indians who were bent on finishing the job of annihilating the Spaniards that had been left incomplete by the Pueblos. All felt the pangs of hunger and hardship, but Juana succumbed to them. Surrounded by her adult children and many grandchildren, she passed from life, never again to see her Pueblo Quemado.

Life went on though for Juan Lucero de Godoy and for the other members of the colony. Despite the hardships presented by the Indians and the sparse farming and grazing land at *San Lorenzo*, some of the colony even decided they would make their permanent homes there. They farmed and built a small church for their *Conquistadora* and thanked God they were still alive.

The Spaniards now had new forces driving them. Competition was coming at them from all sides: the English, the Dutch, the French, and the Portuguese. In 1685, Frenchman Rene Robert Cavelier Sieur de la Salle, apparently working on information furnished to the French by the exiled Diego de Peñalosa, former governor of New Mexico, attempted to establish a colony on the Texas coast. He began also to move westward in search of gold and silver. Four years later, the Spaniards would mount an expedition led by Alonso de Leyva to destroy the French colony, but in the meantime, it seemed imperative to Spain that it retake New Mexico. This was the directive that was given to Governor Jironza by the Spanish government. The Spanish officials, however, gave him nothing with which to accomplish their order. The colony of *San Lorenzo*, therefore, merely waited, regaining its strength, preparing for the next opportunity to move north.

The next opportunity came in 1689 when Governor Jironza put together a small force for what must have been a reconnaissance expedition. This group had approximately the same number of men in it, as did the group led by Otermín eight years before. They marched quickly up the Rio Grande Valley to meet a group of northern Pueblo Indians massed at the stone pueblo of Zía above present-day Bernalillo. The Indians at Zía greatly outnumbered the Spanish and, in addition, had sent north for further reinforcements. Despite being outnumbered ten to one, however, the Spanish forces won a decisive victory, killing 600 of the Keres people, and taking 70 prisoners to be sold as slaves. The *quekos* then moved south with their prisoners, but all knew they would be back.

By this time, at the age of 65, Juan Lucero de Godoy had married his third wife, Isabel de Salazar, the adopted daughter of *Encomendero* **Andrés Hurtado** and **Bernardina de Salas**.[13] Ironically, had it not been for the Indian rebellion, Juan might never have met Isabel, for the Hurtados were a family of the *Río Abajo*. Isabel's father held the *encomienda* of Santa Ana and the neighboring pueblos. Her sister, **María de Salazar**, was married to **Manuel Baca**, son of Cristóbal Baca (II). Thus, Juan Lucero de Godoy and Manuel Baca became brothers-in-law.

On February 22, 1691, don Diego de Vargas Zapata y Luján Ponce de Léon ascended to the governorship of New Mexico in exile.[14] It is approximated that **Antonio Lucero de Godoy** (II), son of **Antonio Lucero de Godoy** (I) and **Antonia Varela de Losada** was born some four years earlier. Thus, Juan, Antonio (I) and Antonio (II), son, grandson, and great-grandson of Pedro Lucero de Godoy, waited at *San Lorenzo* for don Diego de Vargas to take them back to New Mexico. Placing their trust in this unlikely-looking hero, a strutting aristocrat who spoke with a lisp, they could not in fact have chosen a greater champion.

Don Diego de Vargas had all the credentials for the job. The last legitimate son of the illustrious house of Vargas of Madrid, [15] he was a nobleman of 20 years' service to the crown. He had served gallantly in New Spain and was here seeking fame and fortune. He wanted the assignment, although he later came to hate New Mexico, and he paid for his appointment. He would probably have preferred to climb onto his horse and ride north by himself, but good sense dictated that he plan his campaign well. Otermín and Jironza had failed to retake the kingdom. He must not also fail, for New Mexico was needed as a northern buffer to the mines in New Spain. He had promised the viceroy, Gaspar de la Cerda, the Conde de Galve, he would retake New Mexico; moreover, he was impatient to get out of the El Paso district which he despised.

As with everything else on the frontier, it took forever to get going. There were problems of supply, recruitment, and continual Indian depredations. Finally, however, on August 10, 1692, the twelfth anniversary of the Pueblo Rebellion, don Diego de Vargas was ready to go.[16] Each of the two previous expeditions had numbered about 150 individuals, but his initial party appears to have been even smaller consisting of only forty mounted soldiers, ten armed civilians, fifty Indian auxiliaries and two Franciscan Friars. The energies and skills of the former colonists, however, were concentrated totally on a single objective: the retaking of New Mexico.

His plan was a two-stage affair. First, don Diego had his supply carts, pack mules, and artillery units move out from the *presidio* (military post) to await him at Mount Robledo. Then, he, his mounted men and Indian auxiliaries marched out of the plaza of *Guadalupe del Paso* on August 21, amid the cheers and tears of the wives and families being left behind.[17]

Moving quickly, this party marched up the Rio Grande unimpeded, arriving at Santa Fe less than four weeks later. Through the gloom of the early morning of September 13, 1692,[18] the Spaniards could just make out the shadowy form of the *casas reales*. But, as it began to grow light, they saw that what had once been their governor's palace with its attendant buildings, was now a multi-storied Indian pueblo!

On the march north, the officers and men of this expeditionary force had been amazed at the impact their governor had on the hostile Indians of the pueblos they had encountered. Although delicate-looking, their 48-year-old governor and captain-general had completely won over the people, pueblo after pueblo, with his soft voice, sincerity and strength of personality. Could he do the same here?

The small force worked its way to the walls of the *casas reales*. Don Diego de Vargas had told the soldiers that, under penalty of death, they were not to fire unless they saw him unsheathe his sword. Then, from outside the walls, the group, speaking as one man, uttered the loud cry, "Glory to the Blessed Sacrament of the Altar!" The startled Indians inside the *casas* raced to the rooftops to see a splendidly dressed Spaniard standing below. Through his interpreters, one of whom was his armorer and captain of artillery, Francisco Lucero de Godoy, Vargas told the Pueblos that "he had come in peace to pardon them and to accept their renewed obedience to God and King.[19] The Spaniards could just hear the Indians shouting obscenities at them over the din of their trumpet calls and drum rolls. Then the arrogant and daring don Diego de Vargas divided his very small force. Outnumbered again, ten-to-one, the Spaniards nevertheless surrounded the *casas reales*, brought up two field pieces, and got themselves into position to do battle if necessary.

With some apprehension, the Spaniards watched while armed

Indian warriors from some of the other pueblos gathered on the hills nearby. Then, as the Pueblos had done to them some 12 years before, the invading forces cut off the *acequia* bringing water before the fortress and waited, Vargas directly in front of the one door leading into the interior. Some hours later, and without a shot being fired, the Indians capitulated, sending their leaders out to make peace. Don Diego dismounted and embraced these men as respected compatriots. The next day, Vargas, resplendent in the dress of a man-at-court, watched while the Franciscans absolved the Pueblos of their sins, celebrated mass, and baptized the many children of the Tanos and Tewas born since 1680.

Then, at pueblo after pueblo, don Diego and his small force repeated the ritual repossession of the kingdom. Most remarkably, at Pecos don Diego, after waiting for many days for these fearful and recalcitrant Pueblo Indians to return to their homes as requested, did not burn the pueblo. He also chose not to destroy their *kivas*, and he freed the Pecos people whom he had captured. He then erected a large cross in their plaza and withdrew to confer with the Tewas and Tanos of the other northern pueblos, and accept their surrender.

While waiting at the Pecos Pueblo, Vargas had captured three very old women, two of whom he felt must have been over a hundred years old. With them was a young man for whom these old women had apparently cared who identified himself as the son of Cristóbal de Anaya Almazán. It was his father who had been imprisoned by the Inquisition and killed by the Indians along with the rest of his family at his *estancia* at Angostura during the Indian revolt in 1680. The youth, Francisco de Anaya Almazán, was placed in the care of his uncle, Francisco Lucero de Godoy.[20]

There were other colonial survivors of the 1680 rebellion also found at this time. Francisco Márquez, nephew of Pedro Marquez, rescued Pedro's wife and daughter during this bloodless *entrada*.[21] Martin Hurtado found his mother, Juana Hurtado, and sister, Maria Naranjo, at this time.[22] Juana and María were the sister-in-law and niece respectively of Juan Lucero de Godoy and Manuel Baca. José Domínquez de Mendoza found his sister Juana, her four daughters, and one son.[23] Two daughters of José

Nevares de Leyva, spared when their mother was killed at Galisteo while their father was gone with the Leyva escort party, were found at San Juan by Juan Olguín, a relative.[24]

Lucía de Madrid, eldest adopted child of Ana María de Anaya Almázan and Lorenzo de Madrid, might have been the Lucía that was made captive in 1680. She was single at the time but when discovered by her brother, José de Madrid, twelve years later, she had two children, one about twelve.[25] And perhaps most tragically (as the particular speaks to the life of these women in captivity), when Petrona Pacheco, wife of Cristóbal Nieto was discovered by Roque de Madrid, she had six children, three more than she had before her captivity.[26] All—soldiers, armed citizens, Indian auxiliaries, Franciscans, and these newly repatriated women with their young children—began the long march south to *Guadalupe del Paso*, triumphant, but cautious. It had been too easy.

Although don Diego de Vargas felt the *entrada* had been too simple, as future events would demonstrate, he was hopeful the Pueblos were as they presented themselves, repentant, and at least willing, if not eager, to again accept Spanish domination. As so correctly noted by one authority, it had been a ritual repossession and merely a symbolic reconquest.[27] He was back in the miserable hole of El Paso and the Pueblos were still there in his remote adobe capital in Santa Fe. In October of 1692, when he wrote to Viceroy Cerda and to his well-placed son-in-law in Madrid, he spoke of the difficulties he had endured, figuring that his victory would be well-received and would eventually result in his promotion to a more lucrative assignment.

RECONQUEST

Back in *Guadalupe del Paso*, Vargas began to plan for the second phase of his reconquest of New Mexico, occupation. Generously supported by the Conde and the crown, he threw himself into the tasks of recruitment and supply for the recolonizing effort. He had come back to El Paso in December of 1692 with the intention of returning to New Mexico as soon as possible. The timing of the contiguous reconquest and recolonization was crucial. He could leave no gap, no void within which the Pueblos could place a wedge. It would be like a chink in the armor of his venture through which the first well-placed arrow could be driven home. He had to move fast, but fast meant leaving in mid-fall of 1693. Many argued against this move, but the impatient Vargas insisted in putting his expedition on the trail.

Don Diego de Vargas had said he needed 550 families[28] and 100 soldiers, but when his crew forded the river at El Paso for the trip north, he had but seventy families.[29] (See Appendix II.) This time Josefa López de Grijalva had time to prepare the beloved statue of the Virgin for her journey. *La Conquistadora* had been entrusted to Josefa's care 13 years before and she had carried her into exile, wondering if either would ever return. Now, having taken her from her throne in the small church at *San Lorenzo*, Josefa dressed her in the figured, white French silk provided by her husband, Francisco Lucero de Godoy.[30] She attempted to affix a silver crown to the Virgin's head, but gave this up as futile, since the statuette would have a long trip in a two-wheeled cart, making the retention of her fragile crown improbable. Then, kissing her softly and wrapping her in one of the soft cotton blankets of her children, she carefully placed her in a box to be loaded onto a freight wagon. She would see her in Santa Fe.

In the Vargas party was the family of José de Valle and Ana de Ribera. They were traveling with an orphan, **Bernardino de Sena**, son of **Agustín de Sena** and **María Ynez de Amparano**.[31] Here, also, were the Gallegos, the Gonzáles, the Garcías, the Herreras, the Jaramillos, the Leybas, the Montoyas, and the Zamoras. They were all, like the Luceros de Godoy and the Bacas, returning to their homes in New Mexico. The Lucero contingent consisted of old Juan with his third wife, Isabel de Salazar, and her mother, Bernardina de Salas y Trujillo. Returning with Juan, were four of Juan's adult children, Antonio (I), Nicolás, Juan de Dios, and Pedro (III), each with a family of his own, and Juan's half-brother Francisco and his family.

The Baca family had been severely depleted. Alonso, the surviving son of Cristóbal (I), had died long before the Indian rebellion. Cristóbal (II), Alonso's only male child, also had died by 1687. Cristóbal's offspring, like their granduncle Antonio who was beheaded in the Rosas affair, appeared ill fated. **José** had been married to **Josefa Pacheco** at *Guadalupe del Paso*. On July 3, 1687, he got into a fight with his brother-in-law Silvestre Pacheco and was killed by him.[32] His wife Josefa and daughter **Juana** were now returning with Vargas. Ignacio, the second son of Cristóbal (II), had been a *sargento mayor* at the *presidio* of *Guadalupe del Paso*. As the assistant *alcalde* of *El Real de San Lorenzo*, he had been required to arrest Pacheco, who had murdered his brother.[33] Ignacio had died by 1689, but his widow, two sons, and five daughters were returning with the reconquest. Thus, of the male Bacas, it was only Cristóbal's third son, Manuel Baca, who was returning with the recolonization forces. He, like Juan Lucero de Godoy, was going back with his sons, Antonio, Juan Antonio, **Diego Manuel,** Cristóbal (III) and Gregorio.

The brothers-in-law, 34-year-old Manuel Baca and 69-year-old Juan Lucero de Godoy, forded the cold river at El Paso that morning of October 1693, each convinced it was too late in the year for the arduous trip which awaited them. The group, in addition to the settlers, consisted of approximately 100 soldiers, many Indian allies, 17 Franciscans, 18 wagons, 1,000 mules, 2,000 horses and 900 cattle.[34] The train was stretched out along the trail for several miles. Soon, the journey, which had begun with such promise, turned into a nightmare. The colonists had not prepared well enough, if preparing well enough was ever possible, and winter had come early with its freezing wind and driving snow. Their carts began falling apart. They began to run out of provisions and had to trade their belongings for food as they moved upriver. Perhaps as many as 30 women and children died and were buried in nameless graves along the trail.[35]

The colonists arrived in Santa Fe in mid-December, 1693, and camped on frozen ground outside the high city walls that had been built in their absence. Then, on December 16, don Diego de Vargas staged a glorious *entrada* with the intention of initiating a formal transition of the custody of the *Villa de Santa Fe* from the Indians to the Spanish.[36] With the

Tanos and Tewas filling the plaza and the roofs of the *casas reales* to the north, don Fernando Durán y Cháves (II), aboard a magnificent charger, cantered regally into the plaza.[37] The royal ensign for the occasion, Durán y Cháves, was the only one of his large family to return to New Mexico. He carried the royal banner with Oñate's Our Lady of Remedies blowing stiffly in the morning chill. The infantry and then the cavalry, marching in ranks and falling into parade formation in front of their reconstructed pueblo-fortress, followed him. Once the troops were in place, all awaited the entrance into the plaza of their captain-general, don Diego de Vargas.

When don Diego de Vargas rode into the plaza, he was greeted with resounding cheers from his people and subdued hurrahs from the Indians both inside and outside their new pueblo. He entered the plaza with the civil, military, and religious officials to whom he now planned to entrust the *villa* and the missions of his kingdom. Vargas issued a full pardon to the Pueblo Indians and promised them peace and good care. The Spaniards, leaving a few of their company to oversee the Indians' departure, retired to their encampment to give the Indians time to gather their belongings and depart for their former homes in the Galisteo basin where they were supposed to be going. The only problem was the Indians didn't go.

It had been naive to think the Indians would meekly uproot themselves at the bidding of their "conquerors." The Spaniards went on hoping, however, while they huddled around their campfires outside the *villa* walls. Perhaps they thought the Pueblo Indians needed more time. The Spaniards continued to wait in the blue cold. Malnourished and totally exposed to the elements, 21 Spaniards, including many infants, died of exposure and had to be buried beneath the snow, the frozen ground refusing to accept their bodies in a proper burial.[38]

Don Diego de Vargas conferred with the Indians. He even asked for their assistance in replacing the roof on the chapel of St. Michael that had been burned in the rebellion 13 years earlier. The Tanos and Tewas said they would help, but this would have to wait until the weather was better and timber could be brought from the mountains.

Don Diego thought back to his late November encounters with the

Pecos Indian, Juan de Ye, at San Felipe, and to his more recent meeting with him at his encampment outside Santa Fe. In the latter discussion with Juan de Ye and four other Pecos, ably interpreted by Francisco Lucero de Godoy, Vargas had learned of a plot to annihilate the entire expedition.[39] He had decided at that time to proceed as if he had not heard that this was their intent, hoping the Pueblo Indians would see the futility of this move. This was a measure of his confidence in the Spaniards' ability to best the Pueblo Indians in a fight. But the plan of the Indians was being carried forward. Vargas had sent foray after foray to the distant pueblos to trade meat for flour, *maize* and beans. The food they obtained, however, was not enough; moreover, cold and illness were decimating his ranks. His people pressed him for action. He could wait no longer.

On December 28, 1693, after spending a freezing Christmas in the snowdrifts, which piled against his tent, Vargas received word from the blind interpreter, Agustín de Salazar,[40] that the rebels inside the pueblo-fortress were poised for an attack. At the request of Vargas, Juan de Ye went to his pueblo to ask his people to join the Spaniards against the hated Tanos and Tewas.

The next day, hearing that the Pecos were waiting in the hills for his word, Vargas sent Francisco Lucero de Godoy to fetch them. Within hours, Lucero was back with 140 Pecos.[41] Vargas' decision not to destroy their *kivas* or pueblo the previous year was paying off.

Early the next morning, the little statue of *La Conquistadora* was set up on a makeshift altar outside the *villa* walls. Then the companies of cavalry and infantry were assembled before her in full military formation. They knelt in the snow and recited the Act of Contrition in a loud voice, and as one man. Given absolution by one of the friars and with words of encouragement from Vargas, the cavalry mounted and the infantry began to fall into ranks behind the horses which now fouled the snow over which they had to march. While tears streamed down the cheeks of their wives and children, the men began to move toward the wall where they would re-form for a charge on the fortress. Many of the men had difficulty seeing, their vision clouded by frozen tears.

The Spaniards charged the fortress and were met by a hail of arrows, stones, and obscenities. Over and over they attacked the walls, but the moat and the height of the palisades, proved to be formidable barriers. Still, they were able to take the parapet above the main entrance, burn the gate, and enter the first of two patios constructed within the compound in their absence. They secured the houses encircling this patio, began to build ladders, and then turned their attention toward a second group of Tewas from the northern pueblos who attacked them from the rear. With the help of the Pecos Indians, they were successful in repelling this attack with great losses to the Tewas. As night fell, the Spaniards held the first patio and were poised to attack the second.

The soldiers did not wait long. In the dark of early morning, they attacked the remaining Indians in the second half of the compound. The surprise ensured their victory. Caught totally off guard, and experiencing the full fury of these men whose children were freezing in the snow, the rebels ran, albeit hurling arrows and stones in the direction of the Spaniards as they fled. Seventy, who refused to surrender, were captured and executed in the plaza that morning.[42] Some 400 women and children who had been abandoned by their retreating warriors, were distributed among the colonists and soldiers and placed into servitude for 10 years.[43] Although the Pueblo-Spanish war was to continue sporadically for at least another four years, the Spaniards could celebrate. With a cross erected over the main entrance of the pueblo-fortress, and Oñate's banner flying from its rooftops, they again had Santa Fe and their exile was over.

6
RAPPROCHEMENT: 1693–1706

ESTABLISHING SETTLEMENTS AMID THE RUINS

I t was difficult to look at the *villa* of Santa Fe and not be struck by the devastation: solitary walls supporting nothing, surrounding nothing, sheltering nothing. The Pueblo Indians were responsible for some of the devastation, but much was of their own making, for they had burned the south *villa* to render it useless to the Pueblo Indians during the siege of Santa Fe in 1680. Too, the *casas reales* had taken on a new appearance and function having now many additional walls, segmentation, storage pits, *kivas*. It bore only a slight resemblance to the structure within which they had originally sought shelter, and if it were to become theirs again, much of it would have to be dismantled. They immediately set upon this task and upon that of rebuilding their homes, but they kept sentries posted and made sure their *harquebuses* were within easy reach. They possessed Santa Fe, but the country beyond it was not theirs.

It was impossible to tell who could be counted upon as friends. Some of the Keres people (the Zía, Santa Ana, and San Felipe) appeared to be theirs, but fragmentation and factionalism among the Indian tribes was ever-present, with alliances forming and then disappearing like eddies in a moving stream. Even the Pecos, those Pueblo Indians who had assisted them in retaking Santa Fe, were not solidly in their camp. Their chief, Juan de Ye, appeared to have his people under his control, but their allegiance was fragile, wholly dependent upon his leadership and strength of personality. Ye's purpose in befriending the Spaniards was to reestablish and support the pueblo of Pecos as the gateway to the plains. The Spaniards, he reasoned, sought to bring balance and peace to their kingdom, each of which was good for trade. And for the Pecos

Indians, trade with the Apache Farones and the other Indians of the plains was essential to maintaining their way of life.

Juan de Ye attempted to intercede on behalf of the Spaniards, asking the people of the other pueblos to come down out of the hills and reoccupy their villages. He asked them to lay down their arms, accept baptism, and engage in trading. He was enormously helpful to the Spaniards, but he was to pay with his life, for the Pueblos of Taos saw him as the king's man, and eventually killed him.[1]

Don Diego de Vargas sought to have the missionaries reestablish themselves at the various Indian pueblos, ignoring the fact that the Spaniards were not in control of the territory. The friars were justifiably afraid, but their demands for military support were excessive; had Vargas acceded to their wishes, he would have had no army with which to defend the kingdom. Therefore, without the armed support they had demanded, the missionaries worked in fear to establish themselves in the pueblos to which they were assigned. They also worked in hope, however, that they could do their work and still be safe.

On June 23, 1694, the 70 families under Vargas' leadership received their reinforcements.[2] This second group of more than 200 colonists included 67 families who had formerly lived in the city and valley of Mexico and who were known as the *Españoles Mexicanos*.[3] This group included **Salvador de Santisteban**.[4] and three French survivors of the massacred LaSalle colony, Jean L'Archeveque (Archibeque), Jacques Grole (Santiago Gurule), and Pierre (Pedro) Meusnier. They had voluntarily surrendered to the Spanish in Texas in 1689.[5] The colonists should have been happy, but they were not. Now there were more mouths to feed.[6] Don Diego de Vargas sought to establish the additional colonists in a new community 22 miles north of the *Villa de Santa Fe*. The new colonists were housed at the pueblos of San Lazaro and San Cristóbal vacated, by the Indians, as requested by Vargas. Although the Martín Serranos, Martín Barbas, and others had lived here prior to 1680, it became, in 1695, only the second community to be chartered by the Spanish government.[7] Like the *Villa de Santa Fe*, it had an official name which was considerably longer than its pedigree: *La Villa Nueva de Santa Cruz de los Españoles Mexicanos del Rey Nuestro Señor Carlos Segundo* (The New City of the Holy Cross of the Spaniards of the City and Valley of Mexico of the King Our Lord Charles the Second). However, most Spanish records refer to it as *La Villa Nueva de Santa Cruz de la Cañada* (Cañada meaning Ravine).

During the same year, Vargas founded a third community south of Santa Fe which even in 1695 was referred to as Bernalillo. Here, as in *La Villa Nueva de Santa Cruz*, several families had already been living prior to 1680. The families included those of Cristóbal Baca and don Fernando Durán y Cháves (II) from whose son, Bernardo, the community apparently took its name.[8]

On May 9, 1695, a third contingent of colonists arrived in Santa Fe.[9] This group from Zacatecas represented the final organized effort to introduce colonists into New Mexico. From this point on, others would arrive either singly or in family units. As the century drew to a close the settlers had once again begun to spread up and down the Rio Grande Valley. From Santa Cruz to Santa Fe to Bernalillo, the colonists were busy re-establishing themselves, seemingly challenging the Pueblos to make their move.

The colonists, and especially the friars at Nambé, Picurís, Taos, Jémez, San Ildefonso, Santo Domingo, San Cristóbal, and Tesuque told Vargas of a gathering storm of harassment, threats and ridicule from the Indians.[10] Vargas, however, sought to ignore these signs, displaying again that trait which so distinguished him: if he conducted himself as if nothing ominous were happening, perhaps it would not. Unfortunately, it did.[11]

On Monday, June 4, 1696, the Indians of the northern pueblos struck again, driven to a synchronized frenzy by Diego Xenome of Nambé who had spent the previous winter traveling from pueblo to pueblo in an attempt to incite revolt. This time the pueblo leaders were less successful in their rebellion, their people less united in their desire to separate from the Spaniards. However, the Jémez, Tewa, Tano and Tiwa pueblos of the north joined forces for this their final concerted attempt to drive out cross and crown.

At San Ildefonso, San Cristóbal, and Jémez, the Pueblo Indians succeeded in killing their blue-robed friars. In addition, 21 Spanish settlers were killed. Among them were Juana de Anaya Almazán, widow of Ignacio Baca, and three of her children, Alonso (II), Rosa, and Leonor, wife of Pedro Sanchez, all murdered at San Ildefonso. A second son, Andrés Baca, was killed at Nambé, tragically ending this line of Baca men.[12] Of the three surviving girls, Margarita Baca would become in 1716 the wife of Diego Lucero de Godoy (II), thus initiating the first of the Lucero-Baca unions in the eighteenth century.[13] At least one other would follow.

For the next six months, Vargas initiated campaign after campaign in his attempt to bring the recalcitrant Pueblo Indians into the fold. He was only partially successful as whole pueblos remained abandoned with the Indians unaccounted for. However, the rebellion had not only stalled, but backfired. The rebels had demonstrated that they no longer had the ability to act as one, whatever their feelings toward the occupying forces. Moreover, Spain had made a commitment to New Mexico. Whatever it took in terms of men, arms, or provisions, New Mexico would be saved.[14] Spain would hold New Mexico against all outside influences. Spain could not foresee that when the break with New Mexico finally came, it would be its Spanish colonists who would provide the impetus.

For four years don Diego de Vargas sought to put the colony firmly on its feet. He ruled with an iron hand and many resented him. Although, he had done much to publicize his successes, the crown had not rewarded him with a promotion. He then tried for a second five-year assignment as governor and captain-general. He had waited too long, however, and Spain had already replaced him.[15]

Vargas then refused to relinquish control. He challenged the appointment of his successor, and managed to hold his replacement at bay for 16 months. His successor, don Pedro Rodríguez Cubero, immediately hated this haughty nobleman who had challenged his right to hold office. Vargas may have delayed his putting on the mantle of authority, but now Governor Rodríguez Cubero would have his day.

Governor Rodríguez Cubero, who had arrived in Santa Fe on July

2, 1697 as New Mexico's new governor, was responsible for conducting his predecessor's *residencia*.[16] The charges brought against Vargas by the six-member *cabildo* were serious: the misuse of royal funds, the abuse of authority, the exercise of favoritism, and the fomentation of sedition among colonists and Indians.[17] The charges of abuse of authority appear to have stemmed from Vargas's initial plan to bring the colonists back to Santa Fe in the dead of winter, and his refusal to heed the friars and colonists when they attempted to warn him of the impending rebellion of 1696.[18] His arrogance, it was felt, had cost them many lives. Governor Rodríguez Cubero's response to these charges was to jail Vargas.

In retrospect, it is amazing that no one seemed to notice that governorships inevitably ended this way. One could not rule on the frontier and stay out of trouble. The Spaniards were always fighting off Indian depredations and holding other European powers at bay, but in the final analysis, they appear to have been their own worst enemy.

Vargas sat in jail for eighteen months, five of which he spent in irons. During this time, Fray Francisco de Vargas pleaded his case to the viceroy who reported the situation to King Charles II. Although King Charles did not exonerate Vargas, the king ordered Vargas' release and, his reappointment as governor. In addition, he honored him with the title of marquis (*Marqués de la Nava de Barcinas*).

Released in 1700, Vargas left New Mexico for the City of Mexico to answer the charges placed against him and to reacquaint himself with his youngest son whom he had not seen in 27 years. For three years he was to remain there, protesting his innocence and seeking his exoneration.[19] In 1703, perhaps assisted by the new viceroy, the *Duque de Alburquerque*, Vargas returned to New Mexico as governor and captain-general. Here on November 10, 1703, at the age of 60, he took office for the second time.[20]

Had old Juan Lucero de Godoy been alive when don Diego de Vargas reacceded to the governorship of New Mexico, he would have been 79 years old, his son and grandson, Antonio (I) and Antonio (II), 53 and 16 respectively. Early in the eighteenth century, there is a record of Antonio (I)'s asking for the Santa Fe land that "had belonged to his father."[21]

Therefore, it appears, each of the Antonios, like old Juan, initially lived on the family's lands at Pueblo Quemado.

THE INITIATION OF A CLAN

The Bacas, on their return to New Mexico in 1693, first settled at Santa Fe, but were back on their lands in Bernalillo as early as 1699. Here Manuel Baca, the only surviving male of this family, resettled the land owned by his father, Cristóbal Baca (II). In 1703, Manuel Baca was 44, the father of a large family. He had five sons, Antonio, Juan Antonio, **Diego Manuel**, Cristóbal (III) and Gregorio. He also had four daughters two of whom had been unimaginatively named María Magdalena. (This propensity is noted among many Europeans of the period. Many families used the same name several times, hoping that fate would have done whatever it wished with the buried namesake. In this instance, however, each of the two women lived into adulthood.)

Although the Bacas had extensive lands at Bernalillo, the children, at least, were soon on the move. Antonio, married at Bernalillo but later moved to Santa Fé.[22] Cristóbal (III) appears to have moved to San Juan, [23] while his older brother, **Diego Manuel**, with his wife, **María de la Vega y Coca**, lived at La Cañada de Guicú (present-day La Ciénega).[24] Thus, of Manuel Baca's male children, only Juan Antonio, remained on his father's lands at Bernalillo. It was from here that he was later to become responsible for the Alcaldía of Cochiti.[25]

While Manuel Baca's four daughters were more elusive, each appears to have remained in the Río Abajo. Josefa, Manuel's unmarried daughter, had an estancia at El Sitio de San Ysidro de Pajarito near Isleta where, as a single parent, she raised a number of her own children.[26]

It is remarkable that Manuel Baca's moderately sized family was so quickly to become a horde—literally, a disorderly swarm. The five male Baca children had at least twenty-eight offspring, while the incredibly independent Josefa, added six more. Although each of the lines of descent for Manuel Baca's many children is a story unto itself, only two lines will be followed here. The first of these lines is that of Diego Manuel Baca of *la Cañada de Guicú*.

In 1726, Diego Manuel and a group of rowdy traders from Santa Fe were involved in a brouhaha at the Pecos trade fair. Diego Manuel was responsible for inciting a riot when he asserted that the fair was conducted for the benefit of the citizenry, not for public officials. He and his fellow traders then set up shop on their own. They refused to follow the rules of trade as set by the *alcalde* and paid exorbitant prices in horses and tack for captive Indians.[27] Diego Manuel seemed not to care that he could achieve greater financial success by adhering to the prices as established by the Spanish authorities. The principle of asserting his independence appeared to take precedence over obtaining a bargain.

Diego Manuel's stubbornness and talent for leadership (so apparent in Diego Manuel's father, Manuel, and great-granduncle, Antonio Baca) were to become family traits. Diego Manuel's grandson, **Diego Pedro**, and fully a century later, his great-grandson, **Celso Baca**, would demonstrate the traits of strong determination and stubborn persistence. The intractable Diego Manuel, who died in 1727, had three children: Manuel, **Juan Esteban**, married to **Teodora Terrus**, and **Nicolás**, who married **Teodora Fernández de la Pedrera** in 1747.[28] The son of Nicolás and Teodora Fernández, **Diego Pedro Manuel Baca**,[29] born in 1748, established two Baca lines of descent followed in this study. He will be met again later in this narrative.

New Mexico was to have Vargas back for only a short time. Five months after his return, while he was pursuing Apaches who had stolen stock from the various ranches at Bernalillo, he took ill. He was taken to the *estancia* of don Fernando Durán y Chávez (II) in Bernalillo where he died on April 8, 1704. In compliance with his wishes, he was buried in the church at Santa Fe "in the main chapel beneath the platform where the priest stands."[30] Unfortunately, the site of this church and of his burial is unknown.

With Bernalillo now well established, the colonists sought to extend their land holdings into the Rio Grande Valley both north and south of Santa Fe. In 1706 don Francisco Cuervo y Valdez, although not authorized by King Philip V of Spain, founded the fourth community in New Mexico at a site then known as the *Bosque Grande de doña Luisa* (the Great Woods of doña Luisa)[31] where the *estancia* of **Francisco de Trujillo** had been prior to the revolt of 1680.[32] With Nicolás Lucero de Godoy (believed to be one of old **Juan's** sons and a brother of **Antonio Lucero de Godoy** (I)), **Juan's** sons, **Antonio** (I) and Pedro (III) **Lucero de Godoy**, **Bernardina de Salas y Trujillo** (old Juan's third mother-in-law, daughter of **Francisco de Trujillo** and doña **Luisa de Montoya**), **Cristóbal Varela Jaramillo**, and 28 other families,[33] Governor Cuervo y Valdez established *San Francisco de Alburquerque*. The *villa* was named to honor Viceroy don Francisco Fernández de la Cueva Enríquez, *Duque de Alburquerque*, and the name-saint of Francisco de Trujillo. Later, however, fearing that King Philip might assume that Cuervo y Valdez was glorifying his own name in so-calling the community, the governor renamed the *villa*, *San Felipe de Alburquerque*.

Perhaps the governor's deed had been self-serving. It didn't matter. Most of these early governors would prove to be itinerant fellows—here today, and gone tomorrow. What did matter were the land, and the people who would make New Mexico their permanent home. The parent's of Bernardina de Salas y Trujillo were gone, as was her husband, *Encomendero* **Andrés Hurtado**. Governor Cuervo had made it possible for her to again have her *merced* (land grant). Her acquisition of the Lucero de Godoy family—through the marriage of her adoptive daughter, Isabel—had almost been her own accomplishment. Her son-in-law, Juan, had brought her back to New Mexico. Now her new grandsons, **Antonio** (I) and Nicolás **Lucero de Godoy**, would take her home.

CHART VI - Parents of the Second Century, Baca Family

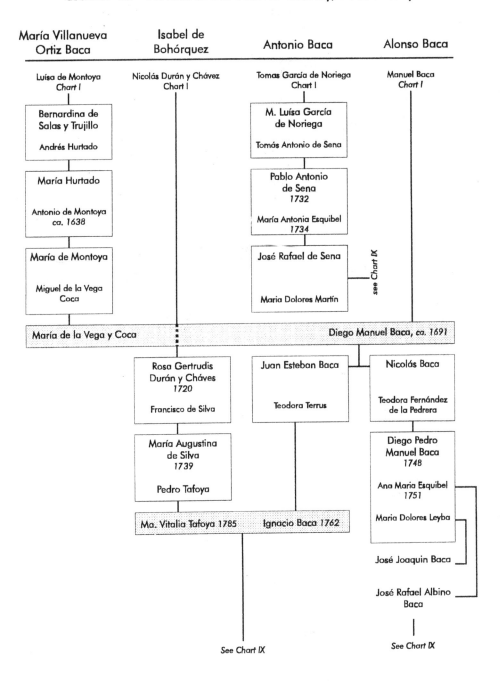

María Villanueva Ortiz Baca   Isabel de Bohórquez   Antonio Baca   Alonso Baca

Luísa de Montoya
Chart I

Nicolás Durán y Chávez
Chart I

Tomas García de Noriega
Chart I

Manuel Baca
Chart I

Bernardina de Salas y Trujillo

Andrés Hurtado

M. Luísa García de Noriega

Tomás Antonio de Sena

María Hurtado

Antonio de Montoya
ca. 1638

Pablo Antonio de Sena
1732

María Antonia Esquibel
1734

María de Montoya

Miguel de la Vega Coca

José Rafael de Sena

Maria Dolores Martín

see Chart IX

María de la Vega y Coca   Diego Manuel Baca, ca. 1691

Rosa Gertrudis Durán y Cháves
1720

Francisco de Silva

Juan Esteban Baca

Teodora Terrus

Nicolás Baca

Teodora Fernández de la Pedrera

María Augustina de Silva
1739

Pedro Tafoya

Diego Pedro Manuel Baca
1748

Ana Maria Esquibel
1751

Maria Dolores Leyba

Ma. Vitalia Tafoya 1785   Ignacio Baca 1762

José Joaquin Baca

José Rafael Albino Baca

See Chart IX   See Chart IX

145

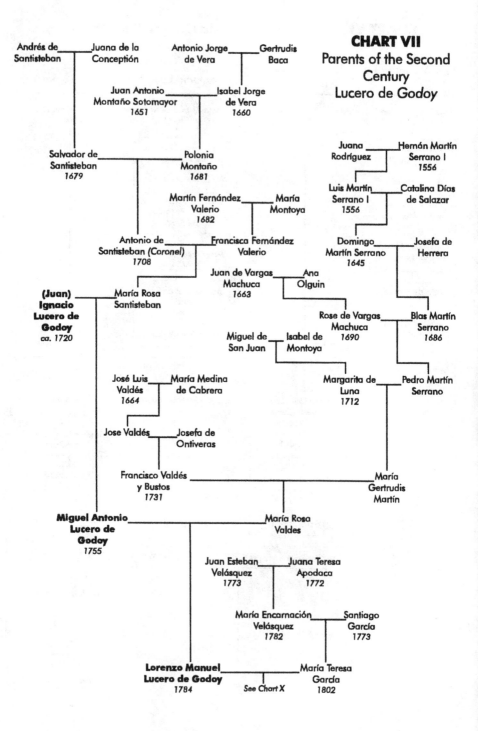

CHART VII
Parents of the Second
Century
Lucero de Godoy

Andrés de Santisteban ____ Juana de la Conceptión

Antonio Jorge de Vera ____ Gertrudis Baca

Juan Antonio Montaño Sotomayor 1651 ____ Isabel Jorge de Vera 1660

Salvador de Santisteban 1679 ____ Polonia Montaño 1681

Martín Fernández Valerio 1682 ____ María Montoya

Juana Rodríguez ____ Hernán Martín Serrano I 1556

Luis Martín Serrano I 1556 ____ Catalina Días de Salazar

Antonio de Santisteban (Coronel) 1708 ____ Francisca Fernández Valerio

Domingo Martín Serrano 1645 ____ Josefa de Herrera

Juan de Vargas Machuca 1663 ____ Ana Olguin

(Juan) Ignacio Lucero de Godoy ca. 1720 ____ María Rosa Santisteban

Rose de Vargas Machuca 1690 ____ Blas Martín Serrano 1686

Miguel de San Juan ____ Isabel de Montoya

José Luis Valdés 1664 ____ María Medina de Cabrera

Margarita de Luna 1712 ____ Pedro Martín Serrano

Jose Valdés ____ Josefa de Ontiveras

Francisco Valdés y Bustos 1731 ____ María Gertrudis Martín

Miguel Antonio Lucero de Godoy 1755 ____ María Rosa Valdes

Juan Esteban Velásquez 1773 ____ Juana Teresa Apodaca 1772

María Encarnación Velásquez 1782 ____ Santiago García 1773

Lorenzo Manuel Lucero de Godoy 1784 ____ See Chart X ____ María Teresa García 1802

146

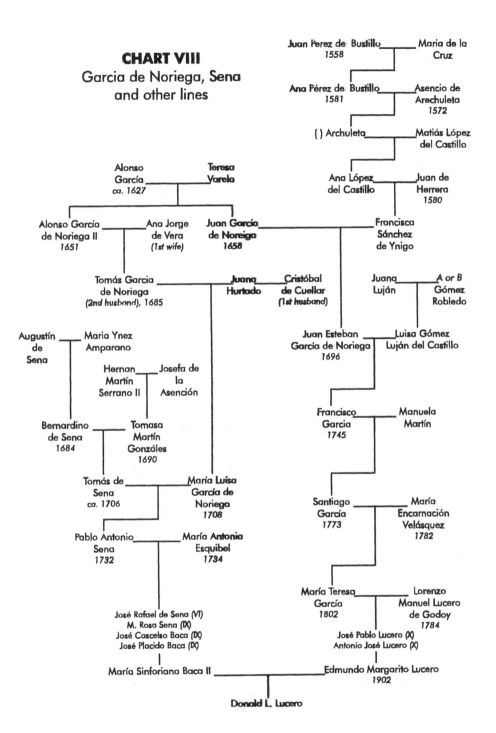

CHART VIII
Garcia de Noriega, Sena and other lines

Juan Perez de Bustillo 1558 — Maria de la Cruz

Ana Pérez de Bustillo 1581 — Asencio de Arechuleta 1572

( ) Archuleta — Matiás López del Castillo

Alonso García ca. 1627 — Teresa Varela

Ana López del Castillo — Juan de Herrera 1580

Alonso García de Noriega II 1651 — Ana Jorge de Vera (1st wife)

Juan García de Noriega 1658 — Francisca Sánchez de Ynigo

Tomás Garcia de Noriega (2nd husband), 1685 — Juana Hurtado

Cristóbal de Cuellar (1st husband)

Juana Luján — A or B Gómez Robledo

Augustín de Sena — Maria Ynez Amparano

Juan Esteban García de Noriega 1696 — Luisa Gómez Luján del Castillo

Hernan Martín Serrano II — Josefa de la Asención

Bernardino de Sena 1684

Tomasa Martín Gonzáles 1690

Francisco Garcia 1745 — Manuela Martín

Tomás de Sena ca. 1706 — María Luisa García de Noriega 1708

Pablo Antonio Sena 1732 — María Antonia Esquibel 1734

Santiago García 1773 — María Encarnación Velásquez 1782

José Rafael de Sena (VI)
M. Rosa Sena (IX)
José Cascelso Baca (IX)
José Placido Baca (IX)

María Teresa García 1802 — Lorenzo Manuel Lucero de Godoy 1784

José Pablo Lucero (X)
Antonio José Lucero (X)

María Sinforiana Baca II — Edmundo Margarito Lucero 1902

Donald L. Lucero

7
LAND GRANTS AND SETTLEMENTS: 1706–1794

LAND HOLDINGS

For the most part, the land holdings in New Mexico fell into three rather indistinct and blurred categories. These were: grants to a community, usually for grazing purposes; grants to an individual as a reward for some outstanding service, such as helping to defend against the nomadic Indians or settling a new area; and grants to Pueblo Indian groups.[1]

Of the 43 major land grants awarded during the seventeenth century and the first half of the eighteenth, most were awarded to individuals or small groups seeking land in the northern half of the state (specifically, within the present six contiguous counties of Río Arriba, Taos, Sandoval, Santa Fe, Bernalillo, and Valencia). Among these grants were the ones awarded to **Sebastián Martín Serrano**, Diego Lucero de Godoy (I), and **Antonio Lucero de Godoy** (II). Also included was the very small one awarded to José Antonio Lucero de Godoy in Santa Fe, although it was hardly in the same league as those just cited. Other equally large grants with which these Baca and Lucero families were to be associated would be made to other individuals during the last half of the eighteenth century and first half of the nineteenth.

TRANSITION OF THE LUCERO DE GODOY/MARTINEZ LAND GRANT, C 1630–1680

Diego Lucero de Godoy (I) had been given a grant of approximately 61,000 acres in an area west and north of the Taos Pueblo Grant between Arroyo Hondo and Ranchito. The boundaries were: "on the east, an arroyo nearest the pueblo; on the west, the *Río del Norte*; on the north, the mountains which were the source of Lucero's River; and on the south, a line extending to the junction of the Taos and *Del Norte* (Rio Grande) Rivers." (See H. Dunham in Bibliography.)

As mentioned earlier, Diego had lived there with his large extended family prior to the Pueblo Indian rebellion of 1680, and during the revolt he was in *Guadalupe del Paso* with the Leyva escort party. The Indians attacked his *estancia*, killing 32 persons of his household. Like the other retreating colonists, he then made his home at *San Lorenzo*. He did not return with Vargas in 1693, having obtained permission to move south to New Spain.[2] Since his land was thus abandoned, the grant was re-awarded to Antonio Martínez on October 26, 1716, and so passed out of the sphere of Lucero control.

SEBASTIAN MARTIN LAND GRANT, C. 1703

The Martín Serranos were an old *conquistador* family. **Hernán Martín Serrano** (I), the progenitor of this extensive family, was one of the original Oñate colonists who settled New Mexico in 1598. **Luis Martín Serrano** (I), one of Hernán's two sons, was one of those who had accompanied Antonio Baca and Nicolás Ortiz in the assassination of Governor Rosas. **Pedro Martín Serrano** was representative of the third generation of this family. Pedro's grandfather, Hernán, had lived in Santa Fe. Luis and his son Pedro resided in *La Cañada de Santa Cruz* prior to the revolt of 1680 and long before Santa Cruz became the second chartered community in New Mexico. While Luis had been *alcalde mayor* and captain of the Tewas jurisdiction, he is perhaps best remembered for having hidden Governor Manso's son while arrangements were being made to take the child out of New Mexico. He is known as well for his intrigues involving Governors Rosas, Manso, and López, who disliked him because of his friendship with the friars. His son Pedro is best known as the father of **Sebastián Martín Serrano**.

The Martín Serranos lived at *La Cañada* on the northern fringe of the Santa Clara Pueblo. Each member of the family knew well the land from the Taos Pueblo south to *La Ciénega* in the *Río Arriba*. They also had long had their eyes on the land above the San Juan Pueblo and just north of the site of the colony's initial home at San Gabriel. It was not hard to see its potential. Each year new soil was deposited along the flood plain as the Río Grande River overflowed and receded. Throughout history, the river carved new channels for itself as it rolled back and forth through the broad valley. The land had originally been registered to Joseph García Jurado, Sebastián de Polonia and Sebastián de Vargas, the latter, a master blacksmith and the lieutenant *alcalde mayor* of the Pecos Pueblo.[3] These men had never occupied the land, however. Thus, like Diego Lucero de Godoy (I), who had abandoned his holdings at Taos, Sebastián de Vargas and his partners, lost all rights to the land above the San Juan Pueblo, making it available for further disposition.

In 1703, just before the return to New Mexico of don Diego de Vargas, the brothers Sebastián and Antonio Martín Serrano registered this unoccupied land for themselves, four additional brothers, and their brother-in-law, Felipe Antonio Sisneros.[4] The grant was certainly sufficient to sustain this large group. With the lands of the San Juan Pueblo as its southern boundary, the grant extended north to the Embudo (Funnel) Creek, the spot where this stream flows through a narrow pass to enter the Río Grande. The grant incorporated land on both sides of the Río Grande, its shallow holdings on the west bank and extensive holdings on the east embracing a gigantic, if somewhat distorted, parallelogram of over 50,000 acres.

Sebastián Martín Serrano, representative of the fourth generation of this important family, was an interesting gentleman. Made a captain in 1708, he earned fame as an Indian fighter, being involved in campaign after campaign, chiefly against the Apaches. Twenty-nine when he requested the grant, he was thirty-eight when he revalidated the grant on May 23, 1712, although both he and his brothers continued to reside at least part of the time at Santa Cruz. In fact, he became Santa Cruz' *alcalde* in 1714.[5]

Eventually, Sebastián Martín Serrano and his family moved a short distance upriver from Santa Cruz to an area immediately above the San Juan Pueblo. There Martín Serrano found the ruins of a four-room adobe structure, believed by some to have been the pre-revolt home of Juan de Díos Lucero de Godoy. The existing walls may have been incorporated into the four-room *plazuela* with defensive towers which Martín began constructing on the site.[6] This home was to grow to enormous proportions. By 1763 it was a compound of 24 rooms surrounding an interior courtyard.

Felipe Antonio Sisneros and Sebastián Martín Serrano were kinsmen. Felipe Antonio was married to Josefa Luján, Sebastián to María Luján. The women were the daughters of don Fernando Durán y Cháves and Elena Ruiz Cáceres, formerly of Taos. What had happened to these women as young children is unclear. Either they had been captured by the Taos Indians and rescued in 1692, or they had escaped with relatives when their mother and other members of their family had been killed. With their father and brother Cristóbal, who had been away from Taos when the Indians attacked, they were the only members of this family to survive.[7]

Felipe Antonio, married to Josefa, was as prominent as his brother-in-law Sebastián. Following the reconquest, he became *alcalde mayor* of Galisteo. However, very shortly after he and the Martín brothers requested their grant, he became *alcalde mayor* of Zuñi where he was killed by the Apaches during early August of 1706.[8] At Felipe's death, Sebastián bought Felipe's portion of the grant from his widow, his sister-in-law, Josefa Luján, for the purchase price of 150 pesos. As payment for the portions that belonged to the Sisneros children, Martín gave them "a little Indian of six or seven years of age, a cow and a young ox," [9] hardly a fair remuneration for 25,000 acres. Although no longer owners, the Sisneros family, along with their Martín relatives, continued to occupy the grant.

In 1727, the Sisneros children sued their uncle for the return of their half of the grant, claiming that the award had actually been given to their father, who had in turn given half to Martín with the stipulation that he colonize it. The children were successful in having returned to them a small parcel immediately north of the San Juan Pueblo.

Within the sphere of the Martín Serranos, were two additional individuals of importance to the Lucero and Baca families. The first of these was one associated with the Luceros. He was **Domingo Martín Serrano**, believed by some, including Fray Chavez, to have been the son of Luis (II) or **Hernán** (II), the uncle or granduncle of Sebastián Martín Serrano.[10] Others such as Margaret Buxton have placed Domingo as the fifth, previously unidentified brother of Sebastián, and thus one of the original Martín Serrano grantees.[11] In this study (because of the short time span between their ages—12 to 18 years) he is placed as the brother of Luis Martin Serrano (II) and Pedro Martin de Salazar. Whatever his actual tie, he is among the Martín Serranos initially closely associated with the Sebastián Martín Land Grant.

The second Martín in this group was a woman associated with the Bacas. She was Tomasa Martín Gonzáles, daughter of *Encomendero* **Hernán Martín Serrano** (II) (brother of Sebastián Martín's grandfather) and of his third wife, **Josefa de la Asencion Gonzáles**. Tomasa, of the same generation as her first cousin, Pedro Martín Serrano, father of Sebastián, was later to marry **Bernardino de Sena**. Thus, the Martín Serranos were to contribute to the genealogy of both the Baca and Lucero families.

CANADA DE COCHITI LAND GRANT, 1728–1800

Antonio Lucero de Godoy (II), who was born in 1687 at *San Lorenzo* while the colony was in exile, first lived on the land of his father and grandfather at the Pueblo Quemado in Santa Fe. Early in the eighteenth century he is found in the new *Villa de Alburquerque* where his father, Antonio Lucero de Godoy (I), and grandmother, Bernardina de Salas y Trujillo, had been among the original settlers. Here, on September 27, 1712, he married **Francisca Varela Jaramillo**, daughter of **Cristóbal Varela Jaramillo** and **Casilda Cedillo Rico de Rojas**. The Varela Jaramillos, a family of the *Río Abajo*, had first lived at Bernalillo and then, like the Luceros de Godoy, were among Albuquerque's first settlers.

Around 1720, probably at Albuquerque, (**Juan**) **Ignacio Lucero de Godoy** was born to Antonio Lucero de Godoy (II) and Francisca Varela Jaramillo. On August 2, 1728, Antonio (II) initiated a petition to don Juan Domingo de Bustamante, governor of New Mexico, asking for land north of the Cochiti Pueblo Indian Grant.[12] Thus, in addition to two tracts of land which Antonio (II) had purchased from his father-in-law in Albuquerque, Antonio (II) now received a long, narrow portion of land within the Cochiti Canyon. The grant, which may have been given as pasturage for the horse-herds of regional militias, was described as being bounded on the north by one of the old pueblos of the Cochiti,[13] on the east by the Rio Grande, on the south by the present Cochiti Pueblo, and on the west by the Jémez Mountains. Antonio (II)'s grant which may have exceeded 100,000 acres, was certified at a later date by Juan Antonio Baca, chief *alcalde* of Cochiti. Juan Antonio apparently acceded to this position following the removal of his father, Manuel Baca, from the office.[14]

Following tradition, Juan Antonio Baca and Antonio Lucero de Godoy (II), perhaps accompanied by others, would have ridden to the Cochiti Pueblo where Baca would have formally introduced the people of the Cochiti to their new neighbor. Then, riding south from the old pueblo into the Canyon of the Cochiti, they would have made a cursory review of the tract before dismounting, and proceeding with a formal ceremony of acceptance.

Antonio Lucero de Godoy (II) and his wife, Francisca Varela Jaramillo, moved with their children to their *Cañada de Cochiti* land grant sometime after it was awarded to them in 1728. The settlement was to become a sizable one, with Luceros and others registering births, marriages and deaths here through at least 1790. The communities which developed on land grants such as the Cochiti, constituted a folk society, bound together by custom and tradition. One of the less appealing aspects of living on the land as a farmer rather than in the *villas* as, for example, a blacksmith or adobe maker, was that the farmer had to provide water for the fields.[15] Farming was either *de temporal* (with rainfall) or *de regadio* (under irrigation). The fields at Cochiti were *de regadío*. This required opening waterways from the *Cañada Bonito* Creek. Once opened, these waterways, the *acequia madre* and *contra-acequias* (secondary ditches), required a communal effort to maintain them. The annual project of opening and cleaning the waterways, the rite of spring, was appropriately called *la fatiga* (the fatigue).

The *Cañada de Cochiti* was a community that developed on a land grant and, as such, probably did not have a *junta del agua*, a group responsible for the determination of water use and supply. Here, as on other single-family holdings, Antonio (II) most likely requested that the community perform the labor of opening the waterways, an effort in which both he and all adult males participated.

The tie that bound the community together, however, was the *compadrazgo*. In the 50-odd years *La Cañada de Cochiti* survived as a village, everyone was eventually related to everyone else. Christenings required *padrinos* (godparents), who became *compadres* and *comadres* (literally, co-fathers and -mothers) with the parents. The *comadres* especially cemented relationships beyond those of the nuclear family. All eventually became one enormously convoluted family.

(**Juan**) **Ignacio Lucero de Godoy** grew up on his father's lands at Cochiti. Around the year 1740, he married **María Rosa Santisteban**. Ignacio was one of at least three Lucero men at Cochiti to marry women of this surname. This was a very familiar practice among siblings which further connected the individuals in these families as *cuñadas* and *cuñados* (sisters- and brothers-in-law).

During June of 1755 the second of their six children, **Miguel Antonio Lucero de Godoy**, was born to Ignacio and María Rosa. Although far from uneventful, their lives at Cochiti were neither remarkable nor spectacular, echoing, for the most part, the tenor of the times.[16] They attended *prendorios* (engagement parties), *casorios* (weddings), *bautismos* (baptisms) and *enterios* (funerals). They planted, harvested, and tended their stock. But in the mid-eighteenth century, a prolonged and severe drought caused Ignacio and many of the others occupying the grant to cast their eyes northward in search of land less subject to the vagaries of an inadequate water supply. They looked to the land held by Sebastián Martín Serrano.

As noted previously, the heirs of Felipe Antonio Sisneros testified that their father had given half of his grant to Sebastián Martín Serrano with the stipulation that he colonize it. The Martín Serranos had lived on the grant since 1703, but with difficulty because of repeated raids by nomadic Indians who attacked each of the outlying plazas, *estancias*, and *ranchitos* throughout the colony. In order to hold the land against the nomadic Indians who had driven them from the grant in 1747, Martín Serrano needed colonists. He, therefore, invited potential settlers to his frontier outpost which he named *Puesto de Nuestra Señora de la Soledad del Río del Norte Arriba* (Outpost of Our Lady of Solitude of the Upper River of the North), the name of the chapel he had built there.

The first actual attempt at resettlement occurred in 1750. Eventually, the settlements of the *Plaza del Alcalde*, *La Soledad* (present-day Los Luceros), *La Villita*, and *La Joya* (present-day Velarde) were each established within the original grant.[17] Exactly when the family of (Juan) Ignacio Lucero de Godoy moved to the Sebastián Martín grant is unknown, but this appears to have occurred sometime after 1771. The American Revolution was perhaps five years in the future when Ignacio settled at La Joya, with plazas and *placitas* beginning to dot the *Río Arriba*, especially in the area of Abiquiu, Chama and San Juan. In the *Río Abajo*, there were, by 1790, at least 50 additional plazas.

As for the *Cañada de Cochiti* Land Grant, it was never completely abandoned. A much smaller grant of 19,112 acres was approved by the United States Congress and awarded to its heirs in 1883, and several families were still living there as late as 1920.

THE PIEDRA LUMBRE LAND GRANT, 1766

In the galaxy of the Martín Serranos at *La Soledad*, were grandfather **Domingo**, son **Blas**, and grandson **Pedro Martín Serrano**, the latter, the grantee of the *Piedra Lumbre*. (This is either *piedra de alumbre*, "alum rock," or *piedra de lumbre*, "rock of fire," perhaps so-named because of the abundance of flint on the land.) As noted previously, some historians have speculated that Domingo was the brother of Sebastián Martín Serrano, although it appears more likely that he was of the previous generation and was Sebastían Martín Serrano's uncle.

The *Piedra Lumbre* Land Grant of almost 50,000 acres went through several hands before coming into the possession of its final owner, Pedro Martín Serrrano. The grant, which spanned both banks of the Chama River, ten miles west of Abiquiu, was first given to Captain Antonio Montoya and then to Domingo de Luna, the latter a lieutenant of the militia of Tomé. Domingo de Luna was married to Josefa Lucero de Godoy, daughter of Miguel Lucero de Godoy (II) and Rosa Baca. This was the second of the Lucero-Baca unions in the 1700s.[18]

The chain of ownership of the *Piedra Lumbre* land grant is convoluted, but appears to be traceable to Jacinta Peláez (daughter of **Jacinto Peláez**, *La Majada* grantee), first married to Antonio de Luna and then to Captain Antonio Montoya. It appears that Antonio de Luna, who died August 9, 1729, was the father of Domingo de Luna. When Domingo's stepfather, Antonio Montoya, died in 1745 (the same year Domingo married Josefa Lucero de Godoy), Domingo de Luna apparently became heir to the grant. The grant to Domingo de Luna was made in 1760. In 1766, Domingo de Luna transferred the grant to **Pedro Martín Serrano**, lieutenant of the militia company of Chama.[19] Pedro, who was married to **Margarita de Luna**, took possession on February 27, 1766. They followed the custom when one was given possession of a grant. The *alcalde* of Santa Cruz took Pedro to meet his neighbor, Gerónimo Martín, and the grant was then his officially.

Among the Martín Serrano/Luna children, was **María Gertrudis Martín** who was to marry **Francisco Valdés**. This is the third of the many connections with the Martin Serrano family in this study. (Please see Chart VII, VIII and X.) One of the children of the latter couple was **Maria**

Rosa Valdes who would contribute to the Lucero genealogy as described below.

When 28-year-old **Miguel Antonio Lucero de Godoy** of San Juan (apparently the Martín Serrano community of *La Soledad*)[20] married **María Rosa Valdes** at the Santa Clara Mission on August 26, 1783, he was, in the eyes of his era, an old man. Although both he and his wife were heirs to the land grants that had been bestowed upon their grandfathers, they elected at some point to make their home at the *Plaza del Río de Chama* where they appeared on the census of 1818. The *Piedra Lumbre* Land Grant was eventually abandoned because of war with the Navajos.[21]

Miguel Antonio and María Rosa lived in the *Río Arriba* throughout the 35 or more years of their marriage. After the death of María Rosa, Miguel Antonio and his adult children journeyed down river and over the mountains to a new community being built as a gateway to the eastern plains. It is in this new settlement that they will appear later in this narrative.

SETTLING IN, 1704–1821

For contemporaries ignorant of and unsympathetic to the circumstances under which the New Mexico colony was founded, the settlers must have looked like a pathetic group hovering on the brink between subsistence and starvation. It is true that they had very little in terms of food or material goods, but what they had, for the most part, was sufficient for the simple lives they led. Many of the original settlers from both Spain and New Spain, were individuals born to the pastoral traditions of the arid Iberian provinces of La Mancha and Extremadura, the poorest parts of Spain.[22] As rural stockmen, they came to New Mexico in search of grazing land for their sheep, cattle, and horses. They did not come to farm. They were not there to create a new society but to transplant an old one, and they had no intention of being anything other than Spanish in the pastoral mold. As a people, they were narrowly specialized in the extreme. There were no artisans, educators, or men of the professions among them.

Because the settlers had no artisans, they built their homes in the basic Moroccan style that they saw replicated in the Indian villages into which they had moved at Tiguex and San Gabriel. These houses had thick adobe walls for insulation against the weather. Dirt-topped roofs, some of which leaked when it rained, provided additional protection against both cold and heat. Rooms with leaky roofs often had coarse muslin pasted on their ceilings with a mixture of flour and water. A cord was attached to the muslin directing the flow of water to the floor where it was collected in a bucket.[23] Windows were sheathed with mica or sheets of selenite, a translucent material. To provide some aesthetic satisfaction, and perhaps also to provide additional light to the interior of their homes, the settlers whitewashed their walls with a thin lime or gypsum solution which rubbed off on one's clothing unless the walls were subsequently treated with a wheat flour paste, or covered with calico.

The colonists had very little furniture. As they had done in Spain (a vestige, perhaps of their long and close association with the people of North Africa), they sat on the floor or on low stools. Clothing was kept in chests and other household items were kept in a *trastero*, a sort of upright chest resembling a cupboard. Most homes did not have separate sleeping quarters and few had beds. During the day the families in most homes placed their folded mats and blankets on a long built-in shelf that was sometimes also used for seating. They had neither tables, except for very low "coffee" tables, nor chairs. The chair thrown out into the street by Friar Tirado when Peralta was governor was a symbol of status and was government property.

The smooth earthen floors, some hardened with ox blood, were partly covered with a coarsely woven black and white wool carpeting known as *jerga*. For heating and cooking, there was a corner fireplace. Baking was done in a cone-shaped adobe oven that stood in the yard or in an enclosed patio. Ironically, history would later view these beehive ovens as inventions of the Pueblo Indians.[24]

The homes of the more privileged differed very little from those of their less privileged counterparts. The 1662 Santa Fe home of Francisco

Gómez Robledo would have been considered one of the former, but it was hardly a stately mansion, consisting only of "a *sala* (salon), three rooms, and a patio, with its kitchen garden at the rear."[25] Individuals of privilege were rather identified by the number of stock they owned, the size of their compounds, the number of their servants, and the amount of raw material they could provide for the creation of products. Their homes often had sleeping quarters separate from other rooms, and some had *camas altas* (beds with mattresses raised above floor level). Except for a separate room in which the Indian servants made bedding, clothing, floor covering and other necessities, however, the homes of each of the colonists were virtually identical.

Treasured articles were items made of metal such as metal griddles (*comales de fierro*), serving and cooking spoons, kettles (*cazos grande*), and dippers, plus articles of clothing made from materials unobtainable in New Mexico.[26] These items, which were often mentioned in wills, were cherished possessions to be bequeathed from one generation to another. The colonists required little, and what they had was the minimum and the simplest. If something wore out, they replaced it if they could, the privileged sooner than their poorer counterparts. What they could not make, they had to get elsewhere and elsewhere was many hundreds of miles away.

While a few of the colonists lived in fortified *plazuelas* which they built on their large grants, most of the settlers lived in small communal groupings called plazas or in single family *ranchitos* scattered from Albuquerque north to Taos, up and down the two major river valleys, the Chama and the Río Grande. The settlement pattern was unlike that found in many European villages which were walled for protection. In these communities the villagers went out each morning to tend their fields, returning to the safety of their walled villages in the evening. In contrast, the New Mexico colonists vigorously resisted attempts made to centralize them within fortified villages. Even at Albuquerque, Bernalillo, Santa Fe, and Santa Cruz, the colonists wanted to live near their fields where they could keep the bears and other wildlife from destroying their crops. More importantly, most were ranchers who could not live in the *villas* despite the protection this provided them from the Indians. In spite of these roadblocks, however, communal life began, little by little, to take hold, especially on some of the large grants where colonization was essential to hold the land.

8
THE PUEBLO LEAGUE, THE PLAINS INDIANS
AND THE *GENIZARO*

THE PUEBLO INDIANS, 1694–1794

During the century between the return of the Spanish colonists and the expansion of their settlements onto the eastern plains, the Pueblo Indians were just trying to hold their own. After their last united attempt at revolt in 1696, they helped the Spaniards rebuild their churches and embarked on a life of peaceful coexistence, supported by the determinations made by Governor don Juan Ignacio Flores Mogollón who took office in 1712.

In the beginning the governor's attitude toward the Indians was anything but benevolent. In fact, his first decision was to make war on the Pueblo Indians or, if not on the Indians themselves, then on those things which tied them together as a people and made them what they were. He decided to destroy their *kivas*, to forbid their dances, to ban the ornamentation they wore, to require that they dress like their European conquerors, and to make them give up their Spanish weaponry. Although this was the course he embarked upon initially, somewhere along the way he unaccountably appears to have had a change of heart. In what was arguably one of the more enlightened decisions made during the first hundred years of the colony, he and the friars decided to let time make changes for them. Although the Spaniards made no specific commitments in this regard, both Church and State appear to have decided not to force cultural change.[1] The Pueblo Indians were allowed to stand by and watch their friars argue with the Spanish authorities, incorporate their Indian heritage into their practice of Christianity, and still remain Indian.

In terms of the Pueblos' land, there were also some important determinations made. Appropriately, the "*encomienda* system did not survive" the Pueblo Indian Revolt of 1680.[2] Too, after 1693 a move was initiated to contain each Pueblo group within defined boundaries. Although Governor Jironza (or one of his successors) probably did not initiate this move, it had some support in Spanish law.

Prior to 1700 the Pueblo Indians seem to have possessed whatever land they historically occupied or used whether contiguous to their pueblos or located elsewhere. However, sometime after 1700, and before 1846, a method was devised by which each pueblo eventually came into possession of a legal minimum of four leagues of land. The process by which this occurred is obscure.[3]

In 1683 an ordinance, based on the *Nueva Recopilación de Las Indias* of May 28, 1567, was given to Governor Jironza. This ordinance, as well as more detailed instructions given him on June 4, 1687, instructed him that if he was successful in restoring New Mexico to the Spanish crown he was to assign to the Pueblo Indians the grounds and boundaries of each pueblo as well as any land they might need for settlement, farming or pasture.

It is doubtful that Jironza, a governor in exile, ever made these grants. Nevertheless, sometime during the eighteenth century a doctrine evolved which established for each pueblo a given league. And, in the nineteenth century several of the Pueblo Indians spoke of their title, and some even produced bogus documents supporting their claim. Their verbal testimony and forged documents were later used to establish legitimacy, securing for them at least a portion of the ancestral lands that were their rightful inheritance.

Among these Pueblo Indian groups were the Ácoma, Cochiti, Galisteo, Jémez, Laguna, Pecos, Picurís, San Cristóbal, Sandía, San Felipe, San Juan, San Lazaro, Santa Ana, Santo Domingo, Zía and Zuñi.[4] The Jémez Pueblo grant may be viewed as representative of these awards, since all the grants (each of which was known as a "pueblo league") had similar proportions. The Jémez Pueblo had an area of approximately 27 square miles (or more than 17,350 acres). The boundaries that enclosed the pueblo were set at "north one league, east one league, west one league, south one league, to be measured from the four corners of the church in the center of the pueblo."[5] Reportedly, the pueblos of Santo Domingo and Santa Ana produced Jironza documents supporting their claims.

The demise of the *encomienda* system and the status of the Pueblos as landholders reinforced the fact that the Pueblos, although a subject people, had rights as well as responsibilities. Still, the abuse inflicted upon the Indians continued through the eighteenth century and beyond.

THE PLAINS INDIANS, 1730–1785

After re-establishing their adobe kingdom in 1693, the colonists had to maintain it, a tall order when faced with the combined onslaughts of war, conquest, famine, and death. Although the Spaniards did not always know which Indian group was harassing them, they did know that Indians were an increasing aggravation and danger to them and their struggling colony. Initially, the Spanish classified all the hostile Indians as "Apaches," (the Zuñi word for enemy) but they began to differentiate among them as time went on.

Within the Apache tribe they identified distinct groups: the Carlanas, the Chipaynes, the Cuartelejos, the Faraones of the Sandías and the plains, the Limitas, the Mescaleros, the Natages, the Palomas, the Trementinas and the Jicarillas. The Jicarillas, they thought, were friends, but who could tell anything for certain? The various groups of Apaches would come to trade at Pecos and Taos and, on their way out, would steal cows and horses. If confronted by a superior force, they would sue for peace, but once peace was made, it meant absolutely nothing to them. For the Apaches, at least, amnesty seemed out of the question.

The Spanish knew the Comanches (the Ute word for enemy) were foes. An offshoot of the mountain Shoshoni, the Comanches had come out onto the plains as soon as the Spanish horse had become available to them. A short-legged and ungainly people when on the ground, they became supremely skilled riders on horseback. In battle, they eluded arrows and bullets by hanging against the sides of their horses or even underneath them. They appeared to possess a sense of almost mystical superiority as riders, and considered not only whites, but also other Indians, inferior beings.[6]

Although raids by the Comanches began about 1730, the truly devastating attacks began in the mid-1740s when the Comanches struck at both the pueblos of Pecos and Galisteo. Again in January of 1748, the Comanches attacked the Pecos Indians a second time. During the six-year period from 1743 to 1749, perhaps as many as 50 Pecos Indians were killed in these attacks with untold numbers killed elsewhere.[7]

In 1749, the Comanches attacked the Galisteo Pueblo, requiring that the Spaniards erect fortifications around it and around the Pecos Pueblo as well, since it guarded the entrance from the plains. The hostilities continued and in 1751 the Comanches, with a force of over 300, attacked Galisteo, despite the squad of *presidial* (military housed at the *presidio*) soldiers stationed there.[8] The attacks went on and on with both the Pueblo Indians and the Spaniards seemingly unable to stop them.

In 1768 the *Marques de Rubi*, a Spanish official in New Spain, recommended the Indians be pacified by whatever means. This recommendation, directed specifically at the Apaches, was the most brutal Indian policy yet considered by the Spaniards toward any Indian group. It clearly demonstrates the Spaniards' sense of futility about solving the hostile Indian problem by more benign means.[9] While the Indian regulations of 1772 were not as extreme as the measures recommended by Rubi, the instructions of 1786 by the king to the Spanish officials presented a compromise. The Spaniards decided to try to resolve their dilemma by pitting one Indian group against another. The policy toward the Indians was convoluted. It was as if the Spaniards were saying:

> Trade with them. Accustom them to things Spanish. Make them want more. Raise their awareness. Encourage their use of liquor. Give them the old muskets. Force them to rely on us for ammunition and repair. If you promise them something, keep your word. Treat them gently. Do not abuse them. Try to convert and

educate them. Overlook their faults and lesser offenses. Use force if you must, but inflict the fewest possible injuries. Do not enslave them. Cajole, persuade, and gift them. Offer them protection. If all else fails, kill them![10]

And, truly, King Charles III of Spain did not want them killed.

The Spaniards' difficulties, however, were enormous and did not end with the Apaches. The beleaguered settlers also had to contend with the Kiowas, the Navajos, the Utes, the Comanches, and beyond them, the French.

Lt. Colonel Juan Bautista de Anza took the reins of office as governor during 1778. Already considered a hero for his work on the Sonoran frontier, he was perhaps the one man equal to the tasks of "pacifying, developing, and defending"[11] New Mexico, New Spain's most vulnerable buffer against forces which were attempting to intrude from the north, east and south. Working directly under Teodoro de Croix, first *commandant general* of the *Provincias Internas*, (Internal Provinces) Anza set out to solve the Indian problem.

Setting out from the San Juan Pueblo in mid-August of 1779, Anza went north into present-day Colorado and then east across the Arkansas River. There he found a large group of Comanches north of present-day Pueblo, Colorado.[12] With approximately 600 men, including 200 Ute and Apache auxiliaries, he chased the Comanches across the plains, killing 18 of them when they stopped running and turned to confront him. He then returned to the Comanches' original campsite to meet *Cuerno Verde* (Green Horn), one of their leaders who he knew was coming to rendezvous with his people following a raid in New Mexico. Anza killed this famed leader, thus setting the stage for the eventual capitulation of this group six years later.[13]

For many reasons, perhaps the two most important of which were the death of their leader *Cuerno Verde*, and the desire of their members for access to trade, the Comanches eventually decided to come in out of the cold. With each of the three major branches, the Jupe (the people of the timber), the Yamparika (root eaters), and the Cuchanec (the bison eaters),[14] now willing to sue for peace, the Comanches, as the Spaniards requested, even began to parley with the Utes, their hated enemy.[15] What Anza and the Spaniards got from this peace was the assurance that not only would the Comanches no longer wage war against them or their Pueblo auxiliaries, but that they would make war on the Apaches.[16] The Indians of the Plains had been divided. Perhaps now they might be conquered.

THE *GENIZARO*

Through time, one of the benefits of trade for the Pueblo Indians had been the children and young women brought to the fairs at Pecos by the Indians of the Plains. For the most part, these non-Christian captives were individuals captured by such Indians as the Apaches in their wars against other Indians such as the Comanches, the Navajos, the Pawnees, the Utes and the Wichitas. Occasionally, a Spanish child or Christian Indian would appear among these human *piezas*,[17] but for the most part, they were potential slaves waiting to be "ransomed." Everyone wanted them, the Pueblos, the colonists, and the friars. They were sought after as domestic servants, wedding gifts, *convento* servants, and as instruments of barter and trade as demonstrated previously when Sebastián Martín Serrano gave a *genizaro* child to the children of Felipe Antonio Sisneros as partial payment of a debt. These captive Indians were baptized and given the surnames of their Spanish masters. As a class in New Mexico, these former captives were called *genizaros*, a Spanish term used to denote a detribalized Indian who had been pressed into domestic service.

Occasionally, a *genizaro* would marry a Hispano or Pueblo Indian, but for the most part *genizaros* married other *genizaros*. The Hispanic settler, no matter how lowly his station, demonstrated to himself and to others that he had arrived by bringing the *genizaro* into his home as a servant. For, as correctly noted by Kessell, *genizaros* "were as sure a symbol of status as a fine horse."[18] They were to become both prize and problem, [19] however, for when they married, they won their freedom, and then they, like everyone else, wanted land.[20]

9
TO THE CENTRAL PLAINS: 1794–1810

THE PECOS RIVER AND VALLEY

The Pecos River, which was alternately known as the *Río de las Vacas* in reference to the bison the Spaniards found there, was originally referred to as the *Río Salado*. Castano used the latter term in apparent reference to the brackish waters he found further south. The river in the area of Pecos is most certainly not brackish.

The Pecos River begins in the Sangre de Cristo Mountains northeast of Santa Fe at an elevation approaching 13,000 feet. Beginning as snow melt and scattered springs, the river in the first hundred miles of its course is a beautiful mountain stream, crystal clear and bone-chillingly cold. It eventually flows through eastern New Mexico and western Texas in its 900-mile languid roll to the Rio Grande. Among its major tributaries in New Mexico are the Hondo, Gallinas, Felix, and Black Rivers. One of its smaller tributaries is the *Río de la Vaca* which parallels the Pecos as it flows through the Sangre de Cristo Mountains and onto the plains. Here two geological features, the Glorieta Mesa and Tecolote Range, distinguish the routes of the Pecos and the *Río de la Vaca*. The Pecos River, the largest branch of the Rio Grande, has provided sustenance for scores of hunters, gatherers, and subsistence farmers for tens of thousands of years. It was here, in the region defined by its exit from the mountains that a new staging area was provided for the embarkation of the settlers onto the plains.

Prior to 1680, the Pecos Pueblo had been the *encomienda* of the Gómez Robledos and the Luceros de Godoy. Their *encomienda* may have encompassed a second, very small pueblo approximately 20 miles southeast of the Pecos Pueblo and probably inhabited by Indians of the same stock. The *encomendero*, whoever he was, appears to have built a small trading post here where he apparently did business with the Pueblo Indians allotted to him.[1]

Also on the site below the Pecos Pueblo are the ruins of the summer houses of the Pecos Indians, built to shelter them while they tended the crops they had planted there.[2] All this, however, was prior to 1700 and the onslaught of the Apaches, Kiowas, Navajos and Comanches.

SAN MIGUEL DEL BADO GRANT, 1794

The man worked with a shovel, directing the water he had diverted from the Pecos River to the small field of corn he had planted in the river bottom. To work his field, he had to come in from Santa Fe to the hut which he had built in the *barranca* (ravine). As he worked, he was forever looking over his shoulder, for he had no business being where he was; he was a squatter. But the land! Deep black earth it was, begging for the plow. He had to have it.

Late in 1794, Lorenzo Márquez, speaking for himself and 51 other squatters,[3] made a petition for the land which they had cultivated and coveted and which held such promise.[4] The petitioners did not so much misrepresent themselves as stretch the truth. They felt their chances of obtaining the land would be enhanced if they emphasized the presence among them of *genizaros* who wished to establish a community. In fact, there were *genizaros* in their midst, but they comprised only a quarter of the group.[5] For the most part, the petitioners were from Santa Fe where each was a land owner. They claimed, however, that urban sprawl and the scarcity of water required that they expand into new territory. Governor Fernández Chacón agreed for practical reasons. Various plagues had decimated the Pecos people who now numbered a mere 150.[6] Such a pueblo could no longer be considered a buffer between Santa Fe and the plains. A settlement placed some 20 miles downriver from the pueblo, however, would be a good replacement.

The grant that the group requested was enormous. The northern boundary was the *Río de la Vaca* from *La Rancheria* to *El Aguas Caliente*. The southern boundary was the *Canyon Blanco*. The eastern boundary was *La Questa* and *Los Cerritos de Bernal*, while the western boundary was *El Paraje*, commonly known as *Gusano*.[7] The area requested encompassed 315,000 acres.

The day after the petition was admitted, Antonio José Ortiz, *alcalde mayor* of Santa Fe, rode out of the *Villa de Santa Fe* toward the spot below the Pecos Pueblo where the trail from the plains crossed the Pecos River. There, at the site that the colonists were to name *San Miguel del Bado* (St. Michael's Ford or Crossing), he met the settlers who had already staked out some of the uninhabited land. He read them the conditions under which they were to be granted the land. Among these was the requirement that the grantees always keep land available for future homesteaders with most of the land held in common. The grantees were also told that the few Pecos Indians who remained were to have the use of a small portion of the land but without any rights of inheritance. It was further stipulated that the building and maintenance of their plaza and irrigation system were to be conducted as communal affairs. In a symbolic expression of ownership, the settlers pulled up grass and threw rocks and the initial stage of ownership was completed. If they could hold the land for five years, they were told, it would be theirs.[8]

Now they had to contend with the difficulties involved in doing that, for although the Spaniards were at peace with the Comanches, the settlers still had to deal with the Apaches and the bears. In 1760, for example, a bear mauled one of the Indians at the Pecos Pueblo as he sat beneath a tree resting from his work in a cornfield. This attack, which ultimately resulted in his death, followed four days of festivities at the pueblo during which this Indian, with bogus miter and crozier, played at being a bishop. In this manner, he bestowed blessings, said Mass and even served communion. By his own assessment the bear attack was God's punishment for his outrageous behavior.[9] However, whether God's punishment or otherwise, the bear attacks continued. One of these resulted in the death of two settlers at San Miguel in 1804.

The settlers knew that making the land theirs was not going to be easy. Only 25 of the 52 had firearms; the rest, *genizaro* and Spaniard alike, had only bows and arrows.[10] The settlers had to be able to defend themselves because the civil authorities were not able to provide them with more than a token complement of *presidial* soldiers. Alcalde Ortiz told them that they had two years within which to obtain firearms; those who were unsuccessful would lose their land. Few of those without firearms were able to obtain them but, despite this threat by Ortiz, they were allowed to keep their land.

The settlers were given permission to stay at the Pecos Pueblo located approximately 20 miles northwest of their site while they built their homes.[11] It is likely that the men took advantage of this opportunity, but they probably left their families in Santa Fe.

Despite the difficulties of living under the constant threat of an attack by the Plains Indians, the settlers were still there in 1803, their numbers now increased by the addition of six families. They had held the land for nine years and had moved from one level of land ownership to another. In recognition of their new status, Governor Chacón sent Pedro Bautista Piño, justice of the peace of the second precinct of Santa Fe, to officially distribute the available farmland to them.[12]

Beginning in the north along the irrigation canal that the settlers had dug, Justice Piño began to mark off 60 parcels of land of various sizes but equal desirability. Most of the parcels were of 50 to 65 *varas* in width with a few parcels of 100 to 130 *varas*. The largest parcel contained 230 *varas*.[13]

All of the parcels, according to Piño, were distributed by the drawing of lots. When the parcels were distributed, one was held aside for the justice of the precinct, and the products of the final parcel were set out for the payment of three Masses for the blessed souls in Purgatory.[14] The settlers were told to mark off their property with mounds of stones to avoid boundary disputes. Among the original grantees were Diego Baca who received 65 *varas*; **Diego Pedro Manuel Baca**, 49 *varas*; **José Ramon Baca**, 65 *varas*; and José Antonio Lucero, 65 varas.[15] Two days later, Justice

Pino repeated these proceedings three miles upriver at *San José del Bado*, before returning to the comfort and safety of his home at Santa Fe.

Eventually, and in stages, the settlers built a large village containing two enormous plazas with defensive walls and sentry towers. Barracks were built so soldiers could be stationed there and the villagers began to construct a small chapel.

In 1804, the priest in residence at the Pecos Pueblo supported the request of the settlers down river at San Miguel to have their own church.[16] This priest was Fray Francisco Bragado y Rico who, before his assignment to the Pecos, had been a priest at Chama where he had officiated at the marriage of one of Miguel Antonio Lucero de Godoy's children. It may have been through Fray Bragado's influence that this Lucero family eventually moved from the *Plaza del Río del Chama* to *San Miguel del Bado*.

Miguel Antonio Lucero de Godoy and **María Rosa Valdes** lived at Chama from sometime after their marriage in 1783 through at least 1818. Four of their children are known to have been born there or at one of the other communities of the San Juan. They were **Lorenzo** in 1784, Gregorio in 1793, María Dolores in 1798 and José de Jesus in 1800. María Rosa, mother of the aforementioned children, died in 1811. Sometime after 1818, and approximately 25 years after the founding of San Miguel, Miguel Antonio and his adult children made the trip down river to Santa Fe and across the mountains to *San Miguel del Bado*, the community which was to be not only their home, but also that of a multitude of Bacas.

PUERTOCITO AND LAGUNITA

In 1808 a large group of settlers mustered at San Miguel to seek out the Apaches who continued to menace them. The 148 men, only 47 of whom carried firearms,[17] set out on a mission of search and destroy. Although they did not take many Apache captives, inflict many casualties, or recover much stolen stock, they had collectively demonstrated their intention and ability to hold their land and herds. They also showed they were capable of mounting the force necessary to accomplish this. This was their land, and not only were they going to keep it, but they were going to get more of it if they could.

Sometime during the initial period of the *San Miguel del Bado* settlement, 1803-1821, a number of splinter *placitas* (even smaller communal settlements) became established within the grant, both up and down the river from San Miguel and in a neighboring river valley. Two of these were the *placitas* of *Puertocito* (spelling also given as *Puertecito* meaning little pass), where the present-day Sena is located and *Lagunita* (Little Lake or Pool). Both settlements were to become future homes for the Lucero family as they moved away from San Miguel in the mid 1850s. Many other *placitas* were established within the grant either then or later. Among them were Pueblo, Pueblito, Garambullo, La Fragua, La Questa (the present Villanueva),[18] and El Cerrito.

LAS DISPENSAS/LAS VEGAS GRANDES, 1819

Although the Spanish government had been relatively successful in establishing free standing and contiguous land grants in New Mexico for over two centuries (ambiguous boundaries notwithstanding) its ability to do so declined in direct proportion to the waning of royal authority. This weakening became increasingly apparent as the creole Spaniard and *mestizo* of New Spain began to make bids for independence. Confusion appeared to reign after 1810, and chaos after 1821. After 1825, however, as future events would demonstrate, all hell broke loose.

Further requests for land in the vicinity of San Miguel had come as early as 1813. Francisco Trujillo, Bartolomé Márquez, and Diego Padilla requested a grant that lay in an area approximately 19 miles north of San Miguel at a place called *Las Ruedas* (The Circles).[19] Although this petition was not granted, the request unleashed a greed for more and more land. People began to move both with and without official authorization onto land and river valleys adjacent to *San Miguel del Bado* and then the boundary disputes began.

In 1819, while Antonio Ortiz was legally obtaining title to a large land grant along a branch of the Canadian River northeast of San Miguel, a second group of citizens from San Miguel was moving its sheep to previously discovered pasturage in the foothills of the Rocky Mountains. The villagers had long been aware of the spot known as *Las Dispensas*. There were many things about the site that made it ideal.

The term *Las Dispensas* was first applied by Castañeda, the chronicler of the Vásquez de Coronado expedition and literally meant a storeroom or storehouse for food. One of Vásquez de Coronado's soldiers in 1541 said regarding the site: "There we found something we prized more than gold or silver, namely, much *maize*, beans, and chickens larger (than) those in New Spain, and all better and whiter than I have seen in my whole life."[20] It is at this location that the Río Gallinas leaves its picturesque canyon among the foothills of the Rocky Mountains to emerge upon the plains and continue its course toward the Pecos River. At its exit from the mountains, the river winds around the south side of a natural oval amphitheater formed by the bordering cliffs that are covered with scrub oak and pine trees. In this basin, 6,500 feet above sea level are many hot springs that keep the riverbanks free of snow in even the cruelest weather. From the hot springs, the Gallinas flows for approximately 15 miles through lush meadows before it enters a second canyon on its path toward the east.

In 1819, the springs and abundant water, plus a salt lick on the northern fringe of the lush meadows, made the area a haven for game in every season. So abundant was the game, that the Indians made a pact among themselves to hold the area as a preserve where they would hunt only during the winter when their need was the greatest. The settlers initially honored this pact, but the 163,921acre grant given to Antonio Ortiz in 1819, made it only a matter of time before someone requested the even more desirable *Las Dispensas*.

First to request the land were eight sheep ranchers from *San Miguel del Bado*. One of these had spoken favorably of the land to 66-year-old Luis María C. de Baca of Peña Blanca who was seeking grazing land for his cattle. (C. de Baca is the New Mexico form of the name, "Cabeza de Vaca." The more commonly used form is simply "Baca.") C. de Baca's home was at

La Caja del Río also known as Santa Cruz. This former village, the grant of **Nicolás Ortiz Niño Ladron de Guevara** (III), lies beneath the waters of the Cochiti Reservoir near present-day Peña Blanca.

C. de Baca, who had been unable to hold his grant in the Jémez Mountains due to the Indians' continual plundering of his stock, joined the residents of San Miguel in their petition. The application for the group was approved in 1820, but only C. de Baca settled on the grant. The only settler on a grant of close to a half million acres, C. de Baca made a second petition on behalf of himself and his 17 sons. His petition for the grant, which he called *Las Vegas Grandes* (the Great Meadows) *en el Río de las Gallinas*, was approved in 1823. Although the grant was a perfect location for the cattle ranch that C. de Baca had started there, it was also impossible for one family to hold because of its exposure to the plains. Again, C. de Baca could not protect his stock against marauding Indians. Vowing to return, the diminutive Luis C. de Baca, (only 5' 4" in his well-worn boots), moved his cattle off the meadows and back to Peña Blanca. After his departure, others from San Miguel continued to graze their sheep on the meadows, but the game preserve, which was the next gateway to the plains, remained relatively untouched for a decade.

THE SENA CONTINGENT

By 1810 the population of San Miguel was over 550, perhaps third in size and importance to Albuquerque and Santa Fe. Although this village was only 30 miles from Santa Fe, in many respects it was in a different world. The *Villa de Santa Fe*, which had long lost its defensive walls, was, if not peaceful, at least relatively safe from the ravages of marauding Indians and the wildlife which wreaked havoc in the outlying plazas, *estancias*, and *ranchitos*.

At the *villa*, the aged **Bernardino de Sena**, was Santa Fe's most respected citizen. He had been the orphaned child who had arrived in New Mexico in 1693. With his foster parents, he had first settled at Santa Fe and then at Pojoaque, a small village 18 miles northwest of Santa

Fe resettled by the Spaniards in 1703. From the time of his marriage to **Tomasa Martín Gonzáles** in 1705 until his death in 1765, the 81-year-old patriarch of this family lived at Santa Fe where he had acquired considerable property including the plaza which now bears his name.[21] The Sena Plaza was on land originally given to Captain Diego Arias de Quiros who had accompanied don Diego de Vargas when he retook New Mexico in 1693.[22]

More important to Bernardino than the wealth and property that he had acquired, however, was his religion. He was devoted to the Church and was instrumental in acquiring funds for the restoration of St. Michael's Chapel. He also functioned as *mayordomo* (chief steward) of the Confraternity of *La Conquistadora* and served as syndic to the Franciscans. Syndic was the title given to the individual authorized, as Cristóbal Baca (I), Juan de Vitoria Carvajal, Pedro Lucero de Godoy (I), and **Diego de Trujillo** once had been, to collect tithes, and to handle the money and property for this religious order.[23]

When Bernardino de Sena died in 1765, he was buried in St. Michael's Chapel vested in a Franciscan habit. Sena's only son, **Tomás Antonio**, was to accede to his father's prestige and property. The Senas were one of the few pioneer families to engage in mining. Tomás Antonio and two others registered a mine, the *Nuestra Senora de los Dolores* (Our Lady of Sorrows), in 1762. The mine was located south of a hill called "Turquoise."

In 1776, while the American colonists were initiating their break with England, Tomas was being elected to the office of *mayordomo* of the Confraternity of *La Conquistadora* in his adobe kingdom thousands of miles away.[24] Tomas Antonio, married to **María Luisa García de Noriega**, was also to hold the posts of *alcalde mayor* of Galisteo[25] and Pecos.[26] It was of him that Governor Tomas Veles Cachupin spoke when making his recommendations to his successor, Governor Francisco Antonio Marin del Valle. Regarding Tomas de Sena, Cachupin stated that he, "because of his kindness, is greatly loved by the Indians. If he should be separated from them . . . you could not find anyone who would wish to serve in that office."[27] Like his esteemed father, the blacksmith and armorer, Tomas de Sena was dearly loved.

Tomas Antonio and María Luisa García had 14 children. One of their seven sons, **Pablo Antonio**, was born about 1732 and was a contemporary of Miguel Antonio Lucero de Godoy. He would contribute to the Baca genealogy through his son, **José Rafael**, and granddaughter, **María Rosa Altagracia Sena**.

COMANCHEROS AND CIBOLEROS

After Governor Anza was successful in initiating what would turn out to be a generation of peace with the Comanches, a group of plains traders and hunters began to establish themselves at *San Miguel del Bado* to engage in commerce with the Plains Indians. These hunters were called *cíboleros* and the description of them by Gregg cannot be improved upon:

> These hardy devotees of the chase usually wear leather trousers and jackets, and flat straw hats; while swung upon the shoulder of each hangs his carcage or quiver of bows and arrows. The long handle of their lance being set in a case, and suspended by the side with strap from the pommel of the saddle, leaves the point waving high over the head, with a tassel of gay parti-colored stuffs dangling at the tip of the scabbard. Their fusil (musket or firearm), if they happen to have one, is suspended in like manner at the other side, with stopper in the muzzle fantastically tasseled.[28]

These strangely attired mounted Spaniards, residents of San Miguel, would each year go out onto the plains in large parties followed by oxen-driven carts. They would hunt bison on horseback, traveling as far as present-day Amarillo, Texas, trade with the Comanches at some prearranged spot, and return to San Miguel with their cache of *charqui* (jerked meat), horses, and mules, the latter sometimes stock stolen from other ranchers. In addition to conducting commerce with the Indians, they kept their eyes on the horizon and their ears pressed to the ground. Perhaps it was they who heard the first faint rumble of something coming from the east.

10
ENCROACHMENT AND INDEPENDENCE: 1739–1821

LEAKS ALONG THE BORDER

There had been some seepage of foreigners here and there along the canal that was the Spanish frontier at the Arkansas River. The most notable incursion was the one made by a small group of Frenchmen including the Mallet brothers in 1739.[1] By maintaining vigilance along the watercourse, however, the Spaniards had been able to check the influx of foreigners and retain the Spanish integrity of the frontier/channel. The Spanish authorities in New Mexico could have shot these Frenchmen when they first appeared. Instead, the colonists had welcomed them with open arms, entertained them, and perhaps even packed them lunches as they sent them on their return trips to Illinois and Louisiana. The reason for this cordial treatment was that the Spanish colony wanted the French goods. The authorities in Spain, however, required that the colony trade only with New Spain. If trade was to be a factor in the maintenance of the New Mexico colony, they felt it should benefit the mother country. Thus trade with the outside was illegal and would be severely punished. Foreigners who violated the trade embargo were to be treated as unwelcome intruders, spies or even as members of an invading army.

Additional French traders appeared in New Mexico in 1744, 1750, and 1752, but the Spanish authorities treated these intruders more harshly. These interlopers were arrested, their goods confiscated and sold, and the prisoners packed off to *Nueva Vizcaya*, Mexico City and Spain.[2] The Spanish colonists might want and need goods which they could not manufacture themselves, but for the time being at least, they would have to continue to get these from the government-run stores in Chihuahua.

ZEBULON M. PIKE, 1806

On July 15, 1806, Lt. Zebulon M. Pike with a party of 22 set out from St. Louis, sent by the American government to escort 51 Osage and Pawnee Indians back to their own lands and to arrange a peace between the two tribes.[3] Upon Pike's arrival at a Pawnee village on the Republican River in mid-America, he learned that an enormous expedition of Spaniards had been there looking for him. The Pawnee had been told to turn him back, but had failed in their mission.

Pike's group continued westward and, surmounting the incredible obstacles presented by Colorado in late November, explored a considerable portion of the southeastern part of this state. During February of 1807, Pike erected a small fort near Colorado's present southern boundary where he was finally taken into custody. The Spanish viewed his intrusion as an invasion by American forces which gave Spain the right to capture him. The Spanish troops took all his maps and papers away from him and started him on a long march south. He was taken to Chihuahua and then Natchitoches on the Louisiana border where he was released. Although he was kept from making and keeping notes, his observations were later incorporated into the report he published in 1810. So keen was the interest of others in the region he had traversed, his report quickly went into print where it was published in English, French, German and Dutch.[4]

The Spaniards may have had second thoughts about not having shot him, but it hardly mattered. Foreigners would be coming at the Spanish colonists from all directions. The floodgates had been opened.

MEXICAN INDEPENDENCE, 1810–1821

With the American Revolution of 1776 and the French Revolution of 1789 as models of successful revolts against royal authority, the creole Spaniards of New Spain grew defiant. They decided they had enough of trying to meet the demands of royal authority while living like second-class citizens.

Their first attempt at independence in 1810, occurring thousands of miles away in the cities of Guanajuato and Guadalajara, caused hardly a ripple in New Mexico. The settlers at *San Miguel de Bado*, having little connection with New Spain, probably shrugged their shoulders and continued hoeing. Of more immediate concern to them was the departure of their priest, Father Francisco Bragado, who had gotten into some sort of dispute with their deputy justice, Manuel Antonio Baca. Although there had been some attempt at reconciliation, the two having met with *Custos* José Benito Pereyro who attempted to arbitrate, the bad blood remained and Father Bragado left as soon as his replacement arrived.[5]

The rebellion in New Spain, however, did not quiet with the execution of the priest, Miguel Hidalgo y Costilla, who had led the first attempt to achieve independence. A second priest, José María Morelos y Pavon, replaced Father Hidalgo as rebel leader, but he too was caught and executed.[6]

Although the unrest continued, conservatives in New Spain who disliked the reforms promoted by Morelos were somewhat successful in controlling it. Nevertheless, when a liberal revolt swept Spain in 1820 forcing King Ferdinand VII to accept a constitution, the anxiety of New Spain's conservatives intensified. Afraid social reforms such as those promulgated by Morelos would follow in the colonies, they persuaded the viceroy to send the Spanish military leader, Agustín de Iturbide, to crush the revolutionaries now being led by Vicente Guerro. Instead, Iturbide and Guerro agreed to make Mexico independent. With few Spanish forces remaining loyal to the crown, little actual fighting ensued, and Mexico became independent by late 1821.

Although the New Mexican colonists had, since the founding of the colony in 1598, been "Spanish" in their self-identification, their colony had developed and in some ways degenerated in complete isolation from Spain, New Spain, and the rest of Spanish America.[7] The colony was a cultural island, as it were, created in the seventeenth and eighteenth centuries and then separated from the mainland by tectonic forces which drove it from its cultural roots.

From its San Gabriel beginnings, the Hispanic colony of New Mexico had little connection with New Spain that later evolved into present-day Mexico.[8] This was due to geography and the conditions under which New Mexico was maintained. The colony's umbilical cord, the mission supply train, sufficed to support the missions, but provided little commercial or social intercourse between the colonists and the people they had left behind. With the reconquest of 1693, the psychological break was complete. Many of the colonists who returned to New Mexico from El Paso had never known any other home. Their great-grandfathers were part of a forgotten past. They would venture into New Spain to obtain what was unobtainable at home, but then they returned to New Mexico. In many respects, the people of Mexico and New Mexico were growing up in different worlds.

When Mexico secured its independence from Spain in 1821, the message went out that its independence was to be celebrated throughout the country, including in its outlying provinces. As Simmons notes, the New Mexicans were cut off "by distance and poor roads from events in the south." They had played no part "in the winning of independence from Spain." Yet, "once it was an accomplished fact, they made a show of enthusiasm."[9]

Word of the change in political status did not reach remote Santa Fe until September 11, when a trail-worn rider rode into the capital with a special packet.[10] The New Mexicans were told in October they were to begin staging events marking Mexico's independence. The people complied, but not until January of 1822. They celebrated by staging processions and patriotic dramas, playing music, ringing church bells, firing artillery salvos, giving patriotic speeches, and watching the dancing of Pueblo Indians.[11] They also had a grand ball at the governor's palace. While the celebration, with all of its attendant hoopla was described by Governor Facundo Melgares as a genteel affair, an American, Thomas James, in speaking of these same activities referred to "licentiousness of every description" and "unrestrained vice" at dice and *faro* tables.[12]

If there was any elation at the break with Spain, the reasons lay in the possibility for free trade. The New Mexican colonists had been at the mercy of Chihuahua merchants for so long that the removal of the barriers to trade with the outside world was viewed by the majority of the people as the most promising benefit of independence.[13]

When Mexico became independent, Santa Fe was a city of about 5,000. It was the provincial capital of an area that today is comprised of New Mexico, Arizona, and parts of Colorado and Utah. The distance from San Miguel to Santa Fe had, figuratively speaking, increased to about a thousand miles, and Mexico City might as well have been a million miles away.

WILLIAM BECKNELL, AND THE SANTA FE TRAIL, 1821

When Mexico achieved its independence from Spain in 1821, Miguel Antonio Lucero and his son Lorenzo, like the other residents of San Miguel, were just trying to meet the requirements of everyday life. Miguel was an older, robust gentleman of 66; Lorenzo Manuel was 37. During the previous decade, while Napoleon was suffering a major defeat on the Russian steppes, **Lorenzo Manuel** married the very young **María Teresa García**. In line with her very young age at the time of her marriage, possibly eleven years old, María Teresa gave birth to at least ten children. This large family was living at *San Miguel del Bado* when William Becknell, a Missouri farmer and speculator, and a group of about 20 men, were discovered in Mexican territory by a troop of Mexican soldiers as they patrolled the borders of the province.

It is unlikely the encounter between Becknell and the soldiers was accidental. Becknell's intent, he said, was to trade with the Plains Indians,[14] although his real intent appears to have been to bring trade goods into Santa Fe. Although trade with Spain had been illegal, Mexico's New Mexico colony was now free of Spanish domination. Becknell appears to have been loaded for bear and gambling on a cordial reception by don Facundo Melgares, governor of the newly liberated province of New Mexico.[15]

Miguel Antonio and Lorenzo Manuel must have wondered who

Becknell and his men were as they were brought into San Miguel from the plains. The goods lashed to their pack animals must have further piqued their interest. From *San Miguel del Bado*, Becknell and his men were escorted to Santa Fe where they were allowed to make a small fortune in gold, silver and furs by selling their trade goods.[16] Both Becknell and the Mexican colonists benefited from this initial trading venture. Upon leaving Santa Fe, Becknell was invited to return. He did so, mounting three expeditions the following year.

Now the traders came with wagons rather than pack animals. Some were farmers who had mortgaged their land to outfit a single wagon; others were businessmen who controlled several wagons that carried cotton goods, hardware items, costume jewelry, and everything else imaginable. One of the most sought-after commodities was empty bottles which served as receptacles for the colonists who had none. The traders would buy liquor in Missouri, drink the contents while on the trail, and sell the empty bottles for more than the full bottle had cost them in Independence. It was insane, but highly profitable.[17]

Westward-bound wagons were made ready for the trail in Franklin, Westport, and Independence, Missouri. Singly, wagons of the Conestoga type would journey to Council Grove, Kansas, where large caravans would assemble each spring as soon as there was sufficient grass to sustain the oxen, mules and horses pulling the wagons.

Each type of draft animal had its strengths as well as its weaknesses. Oxen did not stampede, but they were poor grazers and had delicate feet. Mules were hardier but could be stampeded by a storm or an Indian attack. Horses were good animals but were not up to pulling loads approaching three tons across difficult terrain. Often, a wagon went out drawn by oxen and, unless sold along with its draft animals and contents in Santa Fe, returned drawn by mules bought there for the return trip. These were the mules for which Missouri became famous.[18]

The trip from Independence to Santa Fe covered a distance of approximately 800 miles. Once the trail entered New Mexican territory, it passed first through the verdant meadows, which were to become present-day Las Vegas, and then through the small community of San Miguel, where the trail crossed the Pecos River, before reaching its destination, the *Villa de Santa Fe*. Josiah Gregg, on the trail in 1831, provided this description of the Gallinas meadows:

> From there [the Canadian River] to the Gallinas [which Gregg said meant Turkey River], the first of the *Río del Norte* waters, the road stretches over an elevated plain, unobstructed by any mountainous ridge. At Gallinas Creek, we found a large flock of sheep grazing upon the adjacent plain, while a little hovel at the foot of the cliff showed it to be a *rancho*. A swarthy *ranchero* soon made his appearance, from whom we procured a treat of goat's milk, with some dirty ewe's milk curdle cheese, to supply the place of bread.[19]

Gregg's description of the Gallinas meadows may have described the *rancho* of don Luis C. de Baca as it was before C. de Baca was harassed from the site by the Plains Indians.

From the meadows where the village of Las Vegas would be founded four years later, Gregg continued toward Santa Fe via San Miguel:

> Some 20 miles from this place [Las Vegas] we entered San Miguel, the first settlement of any note upon our route. This consisted of irregular clusters of mud-wall huts, and is situated in the fertile valley of Río Pecos, a silvery little river which ripples from the snowy mountains of Santa Fe . . . from which city this frontier village is nearly 50 miles to the northeast."[20]

Gregg's ultimate destination was Santa Fe. He provided this description of his first view of it and his thoughts as he approached the village:

> A few miles before reaching the [capital] city, the road again emerges into an open plain. Ascending a table ridge, we spied in

an extended valley to the northwest, occasional groups of trees, skirted with verdant corn and wheat fields, with here and there a square block-like protuberance reared in the midst. A little further, and just ahead of us to the north, irregular clusters of the same opened to our view. Oh, we are approaching the suburbs, thought I, on perceiving the cornfields, and what I supposed to be brick-kilns scattered in every direction. These and other observations of the same nature becoming audible (from others in the caravan), a friend at my elbow said, "It is true those are heaps of unburnt bricks, nevertheless they are houses . . . this is the city of Santa Fe."[21]

During the first 20 years of the Santa Fe Trail's existence, 1821-1841, an average of about 80 wagons and 150 persons used it each year. In these early years the commercial venture was largely the enterprise of Midwesterners. By the 1850s, however, the commerce, to a remarkable extent, became an enterprise conducted by Las Vegans,[22] merchants in Santa Fe, and at least one Mexican official. By the late 1860s, more than 5,000 wagons were using the trail each year.

During the initial years of the Lucero's residence at San Miguel, the Santa Fe trade was becoming a considerable enterprise. In 1824, just three years after the initiation of trade, 25 wagons left Missouri packed with merchandise worth $35,000. These goods were then sold in Santa Fe several months later for $190,000. Although the margin of profit never again reached this level, these early train masters had proven what a tremendous boon trade with the isolated province of New Mexico could be. Thus, year after year, enthusiastic groups of aspiring traders would gather on the eastern frontier of the United States for the trip west.

From the various communities of the Missouri frontier, the wagons came. Four abreast, through tall-grassed prairies and short grassed plains they rumbled toward New Mexico. The trail, through the land of nomadic Indians who pursued great herds of bison, was soon to become a two-way trail. For the people of the new state of Missouri, desperate for cash, the

New Mexico colonists offered a new market ready to be tapped. For the Hispanic settlers, the trail pointed toward Quivira, toward Pawnee Rock on the broad horizon of central Kansas, and beyond.[23]

11
PERMANENT SETTLEMENTS: 1821–1835

ANTON CHICO, 1822–1823

By 1821, the settlers of *San Miguel del Bado* numbered 735. Now, more secure in their land and in their community, they began to graze their stock in the valley to the south and in ever-increasing numbers, went out to the plains to hunt. At Pueblo, Puertocito, and La Questa, the villagers built their homes and searched farther and farther afield for grazing land. In 1822 Salvador Tapia and 16 others requested a grant contiguous to San Miguel on its southern boundary. The Indians drove off this original group, but the people of San Miguel persevered. A second group from San Miguel led by Manuel Rivera and 36 other men, received approval to occupy the same grant on May 2, 1823. Manuel Baca, the constitutional justice of the precinct of San Miguel, placed the land on the Pecos River below San Miguel in their possession. Among the conditions attached to the grant, officially named Sangre de Cristo, was one which we have heard before: the settlers had to equip themselves with firearms and arrows.

The community that formed on this grant became known as Antón Chico.[1] The grant was abandoned in 1830 and resettled in 1834. It was to become the home for many of the Bacas as they moved away from San Miguel in the 1830s.

TECOLOTE LAND GRANT, 1824

Additional settlers, seemingly unwilling or unable to effect a clean break with the parent community, moved northeast to a location about midway between San Miguel and *Las Dispensas*. The Tecolote Grant of

65,000 acres was given to Salvador Montoya and five others on November 19, 1824, and settled on April 23, 1825.[2] They too were eventually driven off by the Indians and temporarily retreated to San Miguel.

AGUA NEGRA LAND GRANT, 1824

During 1824, Antonio Sandoval, a resident of *Los Padillas*, a community about nine miles south of Albuquerque, requested a grant of land by the Pecos River southeast of San Miguel and near present-day Santa Rosa. He asked for a section one-league square to include the *Agua Negra* (Black Water) spring. At one time the name attributed to the area was *Agua Verde* (Green Water). The land requested was north of the *Los Esteritos* Land Grant given to José Leandro Pérea and his wife, Dolores Cháves. Doña Dolores was the niece of Ursula Cháves, wife of Antonio Sandoval.[3] When the grant was laid out, the plat was measured one league in each of four directions from the spring (similar to the so called Pueblo League), giving don Antonio four times as much property as he originally requested.[4] Don Antonio Sandoval and his well-connected wife, Ursula Cháves, apparently ran cattle on the grant both before and after its award, although they may have continued to live on their *estancia* at *Los Padillas*. The land grant was to figure prominently in the history of the Baca family who would, in 1865, challenge the Sandovals for control of the grant.

Doña Ursula, who appeared at the *Alcaldia* of Isleta to inquire about their petition, first paddled and then swam in a sea of New Mexico governors. She was the sister of the former governor, Francisco Xavier Cháves, 1822. Another close relative, don Antonio José Cháves y Castillo, became governor in 1845. To make the picture complete, the measurement error that gave don Antonio and doña Ursula their huge grant was made by don Francisco Sarracino, the *alcalde* of Isleta, who became governor in 1833.[5]

By late 1818, after having been gone from San Miguel for eight years, Father Francisco Bragado was back.[6] Although only 50, he had aged a great deal, the difficult years on the frontier having taken their toll. On his return, he and **Miguel Antonio Lucero**, newly arrived from the Chama region, reestablished their long friendship. The two never lacked topics to discuss or argue about as they smoked endless cigarettes while sitting in the shade of the portal at the home of one or the other. Father Bragado was largely responsible for don Miguel's being in San Miguel, and their friendship spanned many years.

In 1825, at only 57 years of age, Father Bragado died. Father Teodoro de Alcina, Juan José Salazar, and the aging Miguel Antonio Lucero attended his death and the events that followed. A sign that was recorded by Father Alcina accompanied the death of Father Bragado. Fully 26 hours after his death, Father Bragado's face bled profusely from a cut that he had just received while being shaved by don Juan Salazar. The blood, "as fresh as if he were alive," [7] ran to the tip of his beard where it collected as though waiting for Father Bragado to wipe it away. The event was striking enough for Father Alcina to request an attestation and to have a record made of the event in front of the *alcalde*. Although don Miguel didn't know what to make of the occurrence, he may have figured that his old friend Father Bragado was reluctant to go, and was merely hovering between this world and the next. Miguel Antonio was too old to be frightened about this sort of thing. What really scared him was the prospect of getting married again.

The marriages of Miguel Antonio Lucero and of his son, José de Jesus, occurred on February 22 and 23, 1827, respectively. The actual circumstances surrounding the marriages are conjectured, but are likely fairly accurate for they are based on the customs and traditions of the times. Miguel Antonio Lucero's second marriage two years after Father Bragado's death was certainly not forced upon him, although he had been strongly encouraged by his children who felt he needed a wife. The intended was probably no beauty, for had she been, she would have been married at 14 or 15. She was a good woman, however, and the idea for a marriage was apparently a mutually beneficial one.

Miguel Antonio would have liked his old friend Father Bragado to have performed the ceremony. Here he was, at 72, a nervous bridegroom. Thank God he didn't have to accompany his prospective father-in-law on a trading expedition to Chihuahua to prove himself worthy of Guadalupe's hand. And, although he was a *pretendient* (prospective groom), he didn't have to go calling on the family to get better acquainted, as was the custom, for the family was well known to him.

His prospective bride was Guadalupe Martín, daughter of Tomas Martín and María Petra Romero. Both the Martíns and Luceros were by this time *vecinos* at the plaza of *Puertocito*, a settlement downriver from San Miguel, but within the *San Miguel del Bado* grant. Miguel Antonio had met Guadalupe through his son, José de Jesus Lucero, who was engaged to Juana Nepomucena Martín, Guadalupe's sister. The December-May marriage arranged by José, made sense to both families and approval was gained from Guadalupe's parents.

Once official *novios* (engaged partners), Miguel Antonio and Guadalupe had to formally visit Father Juan Caballero who had replaced Father Bragado. Although Father Caballero knew don Miguel, he had only been in the village of San Miguel for about a year and was not as well acquainted with him as his predecessor had been. Father Caballero met the *novios* in the small office that he had set up in a nave of the church. There he formally questioned each of the participants on subjects such as their lineage and marital history. Miguel indicated that he had been a widower for 16 years and had lived the life of a rancher at Cochiti, San Juan, Chama, San Miguel, and *Puertocito*. Guadalupe informed Father Caballero of her lineage and the fact that she had lived her whole life at San Miguel and Puertocito where her father, like all the men of the village, was a stockman. Her history was both uncomplicated and unspectacular. Her age was not given, but she was likely in her late teens or early twenties, although she may have been somewhat older. She may have blushed and looked uncomfortable when talking about the responsibilities of marriage, duties to the Church, and so on, but both she and the 72-year-old Miguel Antonio managed to get through it. Father Bragado, Miguel probably thought, would never have asked such personal questions, nor would he have had to do so. He had known Miguel for a hundred years! Father Caballero, a gentleman in keeping with his surname, had only one request to make of the *novios* and of José de Jesus and Juana whom he had yet to interview. He felt it only proper for Miguel to marry first. It was decided, therefore, that there should be at least one day between the two ceremonies.[8]

The laws of the Church required that banns be read at Mass on three successive Sundays. Sometime during this period, the couple and their families conducted a *prendorio*, the folk equivalent of an announcement party.[9] Since Juana María and José de Jesus Lucero were also being married, the *prendorio* was conducted for both couples with the four no doubt exchanging silver rosaries as *memorias* (remembrances) of the occasion. Between the *prendorio* and the wedding, Miguel made courtesy calls on the Martín family, bringing with him on each occasion a lamb, chicken, or other item of food as a *diario* (gift). By custom he was required to do this until the date of the marriage. As a counter-gift, Guadalupe's father, Tomás Martín, gave to Miguel Antonio 350 ewes, seven cows, four oxen, ten mares and four mules. As dotal property, these would be retained by Guadalupe and would help her attract a husband of similar social status should the aged Miguel Antonio precede her in death.

The wedding preparations for the Martín family were enormous. The villagers of the valley numbered over 800 and all were invited. Several days before the wedding, two wagons of provisions, provided by don Miguel, arrived at the Martín ranch and both the immediate and extended Martín families began preparing the huge quantities of food necessary to feed the guests, some of whom would be staying overnight.

There being no impediments to the marriage, Miguel Antonio and Guadalupe were married in the chill of February 22, 1827. The marriage was performed in the church in San Miguel with Antonio Gonzáles and José Archibeque acting as witnesses. Miguel Antonio, in faithfulness to the very ancient traditions by which his people conducted their lives, gave his new wife 14 *reales* neatly wrapped in a work scarf and tied into a small bundle. He had paid for her trousseau and had also bought her wedding dress which Guadalupe's father had purchased in Chihuahua.

On the day of the wedding a large bridal party wound its way up the Pecos Canyon, proceeding from the Martín ranch at *Puertocito* to San Miguel. The young Guadalupe, somehow looking much prettier on this day, entered the church on the arm of her godfather. Miguel followed, accompanied by Juana Martín, the maid-of-honor. These were followed by Guadalupe's parents, her relatives (none of whom had thought Guadalupe would ever marry), and all others from the village who could fit into the church. The four principals sat within the sanctuary during the wedding ceremony and the Mass that followed.[10]

The fiesta was an all-day affair, beginning with a light breakfast after which guests began to arrive to offer their congratulations. Miguel and Guadalupe sat stiffly in the *sala* of the Martín home accepting the good wishes and the silver coins pressed into Guadalupe's hand as the guests passed by. A sit-down dinner was provided for the bridal party and special guests, with everyone else invited to pass to the tables laden with candy, raisins, wine and all manner of meats and pastries.

During the afternoon, musicians played, and in the evening there was a dance. The dance began with a march around the room led by the newly married couple, now looking more comfortable and even appearing to enjoy themselves. The dance went on and on until the singing of the *entriega*, the turning over by some designated person.[11] These were verses of advice and songs of parting for the godparents who were returning the children to the care of their parents, and for the parents, who were, in turn, giving their children to the care of their son-or daughter-in-law. The ceremony was both a sad and a joyful one. Miguel Antonio and his new bride were two of those staying at the Martín ranch. Miguel was happy that he didn't have to go home, although he may have wondered aloud whether or not he had the strength to go through it all again the next day.

Although Guadalupe didn't have the opportunity to serve a bride's apprenticeship in the home of her in-laws, as did many young brides of the era, she was a good wife, and Miguel an attentive and dutiful husband. The marriage was fruitful with Miguel Antonio and Guadalupe becoming the parents of at least two children. The aged Miguel became a father for the fifth and sixth times in 1827 (Juan Cristóbal) and in 1837 (Manuel) at the age of 82.

THE MEADOWS, 1833–1835

While don Antonio Sandoval was running his cattle on his grant on the Pecos below Antón Chico, the settlers of San Miguel decided to try again to settle the land at *Las Dispensas/Las Vegas Grandes*. Don Luis María C. de Baca and don Salvador Montoya had been driven from their grants at *Las Dispensas/Las Vegas Grandes* and Tecolote, but their settlements had not been populous. *Las Dispensas/Las Vegas Grandes* had been settled by a single (albeit enormous) family and Tecolote by only six families.

With sufficient numbers a self-selected group from San Miguel hoped to place themselves in an advantageous position and to establish a new community where the other two groups had failed. On April 6, 1835, 29 of them, men only at first, traveled the 22 miles from San Miguel to the lush meadows of the Gallinas River to a spot approximately six miles below the hot springs. They immediately set out to plant crops, hoping to bring their families from San Miguel as quickly as possible. Although the crops flourished, a hailstorm dashed their hopes of success that first year and forced them to retreat to their homes at San Miguel.

In the spring of 1836, this time with their families, the prospective settlers returned. They built temporary log huts, dug a series of irrigation ditches to water their crops, and began to work on an adobe church. The church and their grant were both named *Nuestra Señora de los Dolores de Las Vegas* (Our Lady of Sorrows of the Meadows).[12] The settlers, accompanied by Constitutional Justice José de Jesus Ulibarrí y Durán, from San Miguel, laid out a large plaza on the west bank of the Gallinas River and then built an adobe wall around it so that it could be used as a corral for their cattle. The settlers' first flat-roofed log and adobe homes were built in a contiguous fashion to form a rectangular defensive enclosure with the plaza as its center. Thus, The Meadows, home to the Paleo Indians of 10,000 B.C.E and the Pueblo Indians by at least A.D. 1200, became a permanent settlement by the winter of 1837-1838.[13]

12
CULTURAL CONFLICT: 1835–1845

In one corner of (the small, square room) stood the little fireplace, like a square stove, open on two sides, and filled with small sticks of pine set upright and burning, filling the room with all heat and comfort. Round the whole room was a pile of blankets, striped red and white, answering the purpose of sofas. High up on the walls were various small looking glasses, pictures of saints, wooden images of the Savior, and wooden crucifixes, interspersed with divers roses of red and white cambric. These, with two or three wooden benches which served for both chairs and tables, completed the furniture of the room. The description of a New Mexican home of 1834.[1]

TAOS: WHERE CULTURES MET

Taos, first settled in 1617,[2] was the very early home of Diego Lucero de Godoy (I) and don Fernando Durán y Cháves among others. Don Fernando was the father of Josefa and María Luján, the latter the wife of Sebastián Martín Serrano. He is memorialized in the Taos Valley by the name by which the river (*Río de don Fernando*) is known. He is also remembered by a much later association, don Fernando de Taos, the name by which the community of Taos was originally known.[3]

Taos became a community of some importance in the 1820s with the influx of the mountain men. During this period, every well-dressed man east of the Mississippi wore a tall beaver-skin hat. They were the rage, and every gentleman had to have one. Needed for these hats was the beaver's short, soft under fur that serves to keep it warm by trapping air and acting as a protective barrier. The fur trade brought the mountain man south and west over the Santa Fe Trail to Taos in search of these animals whose pelts were selling at six to eight dollars apiece in St. Louis.[4]

Home to the mountain men of the 1820s, Taos had also drawn the Frenchmen of the previous century who sought to make their fortunes there in illegal trading. Something in the brooding canyons and snow-capped peaks of Taos gave rise to a fierce sense of independence in many of its citizens, both Indian and white. This propensity for non-conformist thought and action was to put a number of its illustrious citizens at the forefront of many controversies and movements affecting New Mexico during the first half of the nineteenth century. The lives of Kit Carson and Padre Antonio José Martínez best illustrate this affinity for conflict and rebellion.

CHRISTOPHER (KIT) CARSON

Kit Carson had arrived in New Mexico in 1826, a runaway from his apprenticeship as a saddler in Missouri.[5] Almost immediately, he moved to Taos where he made his home when not on the trail. During his incredible life on the frontier, Carson met the very young and beautiful Josefa Jaramillo. He was introduced to her while visiting his friends Charles and Ignacia Bent. Josefa was Mrs. Bent's younger sister. The Jaramillo women were the daughters of don Francisco Jaramillo and doña María Apolonia Vigil. As noted by Estergreen, the Jaramillos and Vigils were "two of the most prominent Spanish Catholic families in the Southwest."[6] Kit was instantly smitten. In order to marry Josefa, however, he had to convert to Catholicism.

Following the necessary instructions and preparations, Padre Antonio José Martínez baptized him on January 18, 1842. After an engagement of almost a year, Kit married the 15-year-old Josefa on February 6, 1843, at the Guadalupe Catholic Church in Taos. The marriage was performed by Padre Martínez and was witnessed by George Bent, one of the numerous Bent brothers, his wife, Cruz Padilla, José María Valdez, and Manuel Lucero. Manuel appears to have been Manuel Salvador Lucero, son of Julian Lucero and Barbara Antonia Sisneros.[7]

Historian Marc Simmons refers to Manuel as the founder, in 1859, of the "Lucero Plaza" on the "upper reaches of the Rio Grande."[8] Actually, Los Luceros, was the *estancia* of the Martín-Serranos, and under the name of *La Soledad*, had existed at this site since as early as 1703.

PADRE ANTONIO JOSE MARTINEZ

Padre Antonio José Martínez was an extremely controversial figure in the history of New Mexico. He was born in the *Plaza de la Capilla* of the Abiquiu demarcation on January 17, 1793, the son of Antonio Serverino Martínez and María del Carmen Santisteban.[9] Born into land and wealth, Antonio José Martínez married María de la Luz Martín in 1812. A year later, his wife died while giving birth to their daughter. The Martínez-Martín marriage gave Antonio José two of three historical and genealogical ties to the Lucero family. A brother, José Santiago Martínez, was married to María de la Luz Lucero, while his wife's brother, José Vicente Martín, was married to María Salome Lucero. Each of the Lucero women was a direct descendent of Diego Lucero de Godoy (II) and Ana Martín, who were themselves very prominent residents of the *Río Arriba*. Ties to the Lucero family, however, had little if anything to do with Padre Martínez' major role in a number of historical events. It was this involvement that caused him to be painted as both saint and sinner.

On March 10, 1817, at 24 years of age, Antonio José Martínez, who had suffered the loss of his wife, entered the Tridentine Monastery in Durango, Mexico, where he studied for the priesthood.[10] Before he was able to complete his formal studies, however, he became ill, and returned to live with his parents in northern New Mexico.[11] He was ordained as a priest in 1822 at age 29.[12] His daughter, named after her mother, died around 1825 at the age of 12.[13]

The kindly, passionate, brilliant, socially involved Martínez was to cut an enormous swath in New Mexico. He was to become its "most significant" nineteenth century educator when he opened one of the first New Mexican coeducational schools at Taos in 1826.[14] He was the first to make use of a printing press to publish at his own expense both religious and educational material.[15] As a political activist, he pleaded first with Spanish, then Mexican and finally American authorities, for a humanitarian and civilizing policy toward the Indians.[16] He expressed ecological concerns in his fear for the extinction of the bison.[17] He railed at the trickery being used to take land from the Indians. Most of all, he was a "champion of the people,"[18] both Indian and white, who he felt were being taxed to death by both their government and their church.[19] He expressed all of these opinions openly and loudly, making such a nuisance of himself that he eventually "shot himself in the foot." We will meet Martínez again in stories dealing with the Chimayo Rebellion, the doctrine of Manifest Destiny, and with his fellow priest and religious superior, Jean Baptiste Lamy.

GOVERNOR MANUEL ARMIJO

Although not from Taos, the infamous and extremely controversial Governor Manuel Armijo had close links to Padre Martínez, the mountain men, and the Santa Fe trade. A Lucero descendent, this man was nothing if not an enigma.

Manuel Armijo, portly and handsome, gained a reputation for being arrogant, charming, quick-tempered, incredibly independent, and tough.[20] There were several events in his long political career, however, which seemed to reveal him as a coward and the antithesis of the above description. In fact, he was a good administrator, a clever politician, and, if not a man for all seasons, at least the man for this one, the final autumn of New Mexico as a Hispanic province.

Manuel Armijo was the first governor to serve New Mexico for three terms (1827-1829, 1837-1844, 1845-1846),[21] and his tenure included what was arguably New Mexico's most turbulent period. He appears to have risen from obscurity. As legend has it, he gained his wealth by stealing sheep from his employer, then turning around and selling the stolen stock back to him.[22] So clouded is his background, however, that one cannot truly distinguish fact from fiction.

He was the son of Vicente Ferrer Durán de Armijo and Barbara Casilda Durán y Cháves of Albuquerque. His grandparents were Salvador Manuel Durán de Armijo (II) and Francisca Alfonsa Lucero, whose uncle was Antonio Lucero de Godoy (II) of Cochiti. In actuality, Governor Armijo's grandfather was not a poor man. According to his grandfather's will, his grandfather stated that he "had been a poor soldier who by hard work had acquired plenty of worldly goods."[23] He appears to have left a considerable estate and his grandson may not have had such impoverished beginnings as were popularly attributed to him.[24] If Armijo stole sheep, it may have been out of greed, rather than need.

Governor Armijo first came to power in 1827, six years after the founding of the Republic of Mexico and at the initiation of the Santa Fe-Missouri trade. He became heavily involved in the overland commerce created by the opening of the Santa Fe Trail and this involvement greatly influenced his official policies. He is said to have exacted his own tariff on the trade goods requiring $500 for each wagon, no matter what it carried. As Gregg describes it, the tariffs were divided into three portions, one for the officers, a second for the merchants and a third for the government.[25] These duties were initially collected at the customs house in San Miguel before customs was moved to Santa Fe.

Another step taken by Governor Armijo was to issue licenses to the mountain men allowing them to trap in New Mexico. If the trappers were caught without a license, their pelts and traps were confiscated. For the trapper this meant not only losing the implements of his trade, but a year's production as well. Worse, the granting of licenses was erratic; sometimes the licenses were available to the trappers, while at other times they were not. Although Armijo had close ties to the foreign community, many of its members, Missouri trader as well as mountain man, hated him.

The name by which Armijo was known reflects the contempt in which some in the foreign community held him. When out of earshot, he was referred to as "His Obesity." His first term of governor ended in 1829 and, after next losing a job as a customs official, he appears to have gone angrily home to Lemitar. The New Mexicans, however, had not heard the end of Manuel Armijo.

Following Armijo's first term as governor, New Mexico had three benign administrators, José Antonio Cháves, Santiago Abreau, and Francisco Sarracino. In 1835 Colonel Albino Pérez acceded to the governorship. A brassy, aristocratic outsider, he was thought to be disdainfully aloof and was, if possible, even more disliked than Armijo. He appears to have alienated everybody, New Mexico's small upper class by his haughty manner, and the rural poor by his decision to levy new taxes and to abridge their right to self-government.

General discontent among the populace turned to fury when the government brought suit against a group of farmers to collect a debt of 100 pesos. The fury spilled over into the streets when the mob became an army bent on displacing Pérez and establishing a popular government. Although there were some whites among this group, most of the rebels appear to have been Indian. Governor Pérez gathered a force of about 150 militia to meet the insurgents, but the governor's forces were defeated and scattered. In the aftermath, the governor and 16 of his civil and military officials were captured and executed by the insurgents.[26]

The American residents, who cowered behind barred doors as these events unfolded, could only listen as the insurrectionists decapitated Governor Pérez, carried his head through the streets and then kicked it around like a football. The Americans, as well as those who had been associated with the governor, feared that they would also be executed. Instead, the insurgents chose a Taos Indian named José Gonzáles as provisional governor, appointed Indians to most government offices and seized the property of deposed officials. The mob asked that their grievances be redressed, then disbanded and went home to their fields for the fall harvest.

This insurrection of August 9, 1837, known as the Chimayo Rebellion, propelled former Governor Armijo back into power. The

Missouri merchants in Santa Fe put up 400 pesos to finance and support a counterrevolution to be led by Manuel Armijo. Armijo was also aided by wealthy ranchers from the area of the *Río Abajo* near his home in Lemitar seven miles north of Socorro. With a company of dragoons (mounted soldiers) recently arrived from Mexico, he marched north to capture Interim Governor Gonzáles who was later executed by firing squad. Although it was alleged that both Governor Armijo and Padre Martínez were involved in fomenting the rebellion, this was never proven. However, Padre Martínez would most certainly have been in sympathy with the rural people who railed against taxation,[27] while Manuel Armijo may have been using the situation to his own advantage. Certainly, Padre Martínez, if involved, would not have supported the execution of Governor Pérez. The rebellion, however, took on a life of its own, and once initiated, appears not to have been directed by anyone.[28]

ARMIJO AND THE TEXAS-SANTA FE EXPEDITION

During his second term, Governor Armijo had to contend with the Texans. In 1841, Texas President Mirabeau B. Lamar, with the announced intention of mounting a trading expedition, sent a mixed company of soldiers and traders to visit, or perhaps to capture, Santa Fe. The expedition, whether of trade or conquest, appears to have been part of Governor Lamar's grand scheme to create a Texas Republic extending from the Gulf of Mexico to the Pacific Ocean. There were, however, a number of factors which worked against the expedition and which eventually resulted in its defeat.

Contemplating New Mexico from a distance of more than 600 miles, Governor Lamar may have felt that three factors assured his success in a trade or military expedition mounted with or against New Mexico. First, Governor Lamar appears to have felt that Texas had claim to at least half of New Mexico by virtue of Texas' treaty of independence from Mexico. Second, the Pueblo-led Chimayo Rebellion of 1837 may have persuaded Governor Lamar that New Mexicans would view his armed citizens as protectors. Third, and perhaps most important, was Governor Lamar's view that New Mexico would be enthusiastic about formulating a trade agreement with Texas. Obviously the New Mexicans were interested in trade with the outside since they were already actively involved in a lucrative foreign trade with Missouri. Therefore, why would they not also be interested in trading with the Republic of Texas?

The Texas declaration of independence from Mexico was probably the most important negative factor presaging the failure of the Texas-Santa Fe expedition. Texas' declaration had not been recognized by Mexico and a state of war continued to exist between Mexico and its former Texas colonists, who were called the *empresarios* (promoters). The Texans' belief that they were welcome in Santa Fe was folly and contributed to their downfall.

Ultimately, however, the Texas-Santa Fe expedition was defeated by the *llano estacado* (the staked plain), the torturous country through which the Texas army had to pass on its way to Santa Fe, rather than by the New Mexican people themselves.[29]

Cursed with poor leadership, and having little idea of how to reach Santa Fe, a force of 300 Texans set out from Austin on the 600-mile march. Traversing the waterless staked plains, they were harried by the Indians and allowed by their leaders to eat their scanty provisions although bison and other game were fairly plentiful. In the end, their pitiful condition and divided command were betrayed to Governor Armijo when two deserters wandered into Taos. Armijo used this to his full advantage. He tricked the embattled Texans by somehow getting word to them that an army of several thousand awaited their arrival. After paying a bribe to one of the Texan leaders and allegedly promising the Texans safe conduct, Armijo asked the Texans to lay down their arms and surrender. Governor Armijo then sent two scouting parties out onto the plains to round them up. With inadequate supplies, poor horses, and little ammunition, the Texans offered no resistance. Although the Texans had allegedly been offered safe conduct, some were apparently shot during their capture.

When the scattered parties of Texans began to be brought in from the plains, they were housed in the jail, in private homes, and in the public buildings of Antón Chico and San Miguel. The prisoners were specifically not taken into Santa Fe because it was believed that there were many Americans there who would wish to liberate them.

During the two weeks it took to roundup all the Texans, a small group of prisoners were housed in a room adjoining the church at San Miguel. One of these prisoners was George Wilkins Kendall. Although there had been some consideration given to executing all of the prisoners, the ones kept in San Miguel were really treated quite well. The parish priest kept them supplied with coffee and a child named Juan Sandoval brought them the tools needed for carving corncob pipes. They were, however, bedeviled by voracious bedbugs and menaced by the Mexican officer who was in charge of them. A tall distinguished-looking man of good build, light skin and tidy beard, Captain Damasio Salazar was charged with the responsibility of marching them south into Mexico. Apparently, he would rather have had them shot, and according to Kendall, dealt with them in an extremely cruel manner. Thus came to an abrupt end, the kind treatment the prisoners received at San Miguel under the benign authority of don Gregorio Vigil who later became its *alcalde*. They were roped together and forced to march into Mexico where they were chained and placed in labor details. Governor Armijo ordered four of the prisoners released. These were apparently those who had collaborated with him.

The inhumane handling of the Texas prisoners left a very bad taste in the mouths of many Texans regarding Governor Armijo and New Mexico. These negative feelings resulted in a retaliatory strike by the Texans during February of 1843. Under the direction of John McDaniel, a group ambushed the trading caravan of Antonio José Cháves of Santa Fe. In this attack Cháves was murdered. Ultimately, the Americans punished these crimes, which had occurred in Kansas within U.S. territory. In 1846, however, the Americans during another invasion and acting for their Texas compatriots, would come looking in San Miguel for Captain Salazar.[30]

By all reports, Governor Armijo's first loves were rich food, pretty women and gambling. It is debatable, however, whether the woman reputed to have been Armijo's mistress, María Gertrudis Barceló (known as *La Tules*, a diminutive for Gertrudis), was pretty. Susan Magoffin described her in 1846 as "a stately dame of a certain age, the possessor of a portion of that shrewd sense and fascinating manner necessary to allure the wayward inexperienced youth to the hall of final ruin."[31]

Gertrudis was the daughter of Dolores Herrera and Juan Ignacio Barceló, newly arrived from Mexico. They lived at Tomé, five miles northeast of present-day Belen, the site of the pre-revolt *hacienda* of Tomé Domínguez de Mendoza (II).[32] Here the Barcelós became associated with the Sisneros. So close did Gertrudis become to the Sisneros family that she was asked to be the godmother, a position usually given to a close member of the family, for José Manuel Cecelio Sisneros, son of don José Miguel Sisneros and doña Juliana Cháves, grandson of Hermenigildo Sisneros and María Rita Juliana Lucero. The baptism took place February 3, 1822, at Tomé. [33] Although the child's parents lived at Tomé, the Sisneros family was originally from the area of *La Soledad* above San Juan where Hermenigildo, as the grandson of Felipe Antonio Sisneros, was associated with the Sebastián Martín Land Grant and Los Luceros. The next year Tules married Manuel Sisneros.[34] The young couple, however, determined to seek their fortune elsewhere.

La Tules and her husband, Manuel, initially began their business enterprises by running card games in the various mining camps of the *Río Abajo*. By 1835, they had moved to the *Río Arriba* where they established themselves in Santa Fe. Here they parlayed their winnings into the ownership of a lavish bar and gambling casino. To what degree her husband assisted her in amassing her fortune is unclear. However, later, as a childless widow, she became a very successful businesswoman and like Governor Armijo was involved in the Santa Fe trade.

Upon their arrival in Santa Fe, many of the members of the Anglo-

American community who came from the Eastern American states and territories, were appalled to find a woman engaged in running a gambling hall and living in what they considered a man's world. They did not understand the Hispanic people or their culture and were very scornful of them.[35] Although Gertrudis was literate in English, as many of the Hispanic women were not, the newly arrived members of the Anglo community thought of *La Tules* as coarse and crude, having only the trappings of refinement. *La Tules*, they insisted, must be a woman of loose morals!

Gertrudis Barceló was the most expert *monte* dealer in Santa Fe. Through her wealth and influence, she became doña Gertrudis Barcelo, a title of honor and respect, and functioned as one of Santa Fe's leading citizens. One of the roles she played was as a bank for the American army during the American occupation of New Mexico in 1846. With the promise that one of the American supply officers would escort her to a military ball in Santa Fe, she agreed to lend the U. S. Army $1,000 which it used to pay some of its soldiers. Shrewd lady that she was, however, she made sure that she got to the ball before she handed over the money.[36]

Although Gertrudis Barceló was unique, she is important for what she reflects regarding Hispanic society in general and the status of women in particular in Spanish and Mexican New Mexico.

Women had always retained legally inalienable rights over the dowries they received when they married. These seldom included land rights as these were to be provided by her husband's family. However, eventually, over time, wives began to develop a legal identity separate and distinct from their husbands. As individuals with their own legal identity they acquired new legal rights; the freedom to enter into binding contracts and the right to draw up independent wills. As evidence of these increasing legal rights, Juana Baca was given a grant as early as 1703. In addition, Elena Gallegos in 1714 was permitted to keep land bequeathed to her by Diego de Montoya, and in 1746 Josefa Baca was allowed to claim a land grant. In their new roles as heiresses and grantees, women invited settlement on the lands. Women also inherited *encomiendas*, and although they were required to have an *escudero* perform their military obligation, they were, in fact, *encomenderas*. As owners of property and livestock, women achieved status. Their lands became known by their name, as previously mentioned the Great Woods of doña Luisa Montoya, and they became independent powers to reckon with.

The increased spirit of women's independence was most markedly manifest in the marketplace. Not only did women sell in the plaza the produce from their gardens or the goods that had been brought via caravan from Chihuahua or Independence, but, also, some had their own businesses, rental properties and flocks of sheep. Thus, in an era in which most wives of the world were mere chattel, the women on the New Mexico frontier obtained rights unavailable to women in other cultures.

Although Catholicism contributed greatly to the customs, traditions, and family practices of New Mexico, due to the shortage of priests, couples were sometimes unable to legitimize their conjugal relationships, baptize or confirm their children. This was especially true during the Mexican period (1821-1846). As noted by Lecompte in her wonderful account of Santa Fe as a Mexican town, "men and women lived together and raised children in relationships sanctified by society if not by the church."[37] It is important to note, however, that great importance was always placed in the sacraments by the Church and by the people. This was clearly indicated in 1833 when Bishop José Antonio Zubiria finally visited Santa Fe. He was given a royal welcome and during his visitation validated the great number of baptisms, confirmations, and marriages which had occurred since the expulsion of the Franciscans in 1828.[38]

As an illustration of the pervasiveness of common law marriages, consider the family lines in this history. Manuel Baca had four daughters in addition to the five sons who are discussed in this study. One daughter, Josefa Baca, although unmarried, had numerous and prominent "Baca" descendants.[39] At least one of the two lines of Bacas followed here, emanates from her.

Geographically distant from either a centralized government or a source of supply, New Mexicans were forced to pool their resources and depend on each other for support and mutual assistance for almost two-

and-a-half centuries. This isolation and need for mutual aid developed among its people a strong sense of independence and inter-dependence and caused a considerable blurring of its classes. The fierce independence and pride in their identity as a people would soon serve them well as an army, on the far reaches of the kingdom, amassed to attack them.

13
OCCUPATION AND REBELLION: 1845–1847

Early in the seventeenth century the Puritans ridiculed the Indians of New England for their supposed failure to improve the land. The Puritans did not understand that the Indians' culture required that they remain mobile so as to take advantage of the land's diversity. This was possible for the Indians as long as they owned nothing that could not be transferred on their backs. Thus, the Indians did not have fixed villages, create wealth or acquire surplus property. The Puritans failed to see that the Indians' land use was as legitimate as theirs. Rather, they viewed the perceived failure, not as an aspect of the Indians' chosen way of life, but rather as due to their laziness. Such people, they said, who moved so much and worked so little did not deserve to lay claim to the land they inhabited. The land, they felt, was waiting to be occupied by a more productive people. Although the term 'Puritan' ceased to be applicable after 1660, its tenets remained as an aspect of the American psyche.

In 1812 the United States, which believed that the British were encouraging Indians to attack American pioneers moving west, declared war on Britain. Although little was gained in this struggle, the United States emerged from the war with a strong spirit of nationalism, increased feelings of self-confidence and a greater sense of unity. Following the War of 1812 many people began to believe that the United States because of its economic and perceived political superiority, and growing population, should rule all of North America—a throwback to that Puritan notion of 1620. They believed that God had destined them to own and occupy all of the land from one ocean to the other and from pole to pole. "Their mission, their destiny made manifest to spread the principles of democracy and Christianity to the unfortunates of the hemisphere."[1] This ideology of conquest would be used to justify the occupation of another people's lands.

The American occupation of New Mexico in 1846 had more remote antecedents. In the Transcontinental Treaty of 1819, the United States signed an agreement with Spain recognizing all of the land south and west of the Arkansas River as belonging to Spain. The Arkansas River, with its genesis in the Colorado Rockies, flows through south central Colorado, continues across Kansas, and bisects Oklahoma and Arkansas on its way to the Mississippi. The land defined by this northern boundary included portions of present-day Utah, Colorado, Kansas, Oklahoma, and Arkansas, as well as all of the present states of the American West: Texas, New Mexico, Arizona and California. The history of one of these latter states, Texas, was to shape the destiny of New Mexico.

In 1820, Moses Austin, a Missouri banker, asked Spanish officials for permission to establish a colony of Americans in Texas. His son, Stephen Austin, carried out the colonization. By 1835, the number of American colonists in Texas numbered almost 25,000. One short year later, these colonists revolted against Mexico, issuing a declaration of independence on March 2, 1836, a declaration which was made a reality on April 21, when the Texas troops defeated General Antonio López de Santa Ana at San Jacinto. Although Santa Ana (who had gained power by overthrowing Mexico's constitutional government) signed a treaty with Texas, the treaty was never approved by the government of Mexico.

When Texas declared independence, it claimed the Rio Grande all the way back to its source as its western boundary. Historically, however, it had no right to this territory that included about half of present-day New Mexico. After approximately 10 years as an independent republic, Texas became the twenty-eighth state when annexed by the United States on December 29, 1845. In annexing Texas, the United States government accepted responsibility for settling the boundary disputes between its new state and Mexico.

Settling the claim to Texas and establishing a permanent boundary between the United States and Mexico fell to President James Knox Polk whose views were decidedly expansionist. His plan was for the United States to purchase from Mexico all land lying north of a line drawn from El Paso to the Pacific Ocean.[2] Mexico, however, wanted no part of such a scheme. The Mexican government, which had broken off diplomatic relations with the United States upon its annexation of Texas, refused to receive the emissary sent by President Polk. President Polk's response was to send a 4,000-man "Army of Observation" under the command of Brigadier General Zachary Taylor to a point in the disputed territory between Texas and Mexico. President Polk was exerting enormous military pressure to force purchase negotiations. For Mexico, the situation was desperate. Its nationhood was at stake. The sale of these lands in the north, it was felt, would lead to a rebellion among its citizens. Mexico didn't want war with the United States but felt it had no choice.[3]

GENERAL STEPHEN WATTS KEARNY

Old Colonel Kearney, you can bet
Will keep the boys in motion,
Till Yankee Land includes the sand
On the Pacific Ocean

Oh what a joy to fight the dons,
And wallop fat Armijo!
So clear the way to Santa Fe!
With that we agree, O!
—A ditty composed by Ebednego Smith, one of the men in
Kearny's command.
From Hamele, *When Destiny Called*, page 24.

The move by the United States into the disputed Texas-Mexican territory began during April of 1846. In May, the same month in which the United States declared war on Mexico, Colonel Stephen Watts

Kearny mounted an army of 300 regulars and over 1,000 raw Missouri frontiersmen, who volunteered to assist in the conquest of New Mexico and the entire Southwest. The expedition, labeled the "Army of the West," left Fort Levenworth, Kansas, for Santa Fe in June of 1846. They stopped at Fort William,[4] commonly known as Bent's Fort, the huge adobe trading post on the Arkansas River owned by the Bent brothers and Ceran St. Vrain. While there, Kearny studied the plan of invasion provided him by Major Richard B. Lee who had recently returned from Santa Fe. Among other things, the document told Kearny that "by a cautious approach and a night march," the army could advance undetected perhaps even as far as San Miguel del Bado.[5] In fact, however, the New Mexicans, alerted by their border patrols, knew that the Americans were coming and Colonel Kearny hoped to use this knowledge to his best advantage.

While the American army was packing its gear in preparation for leaving its encampment on the Arkansas, three riders with an escort of dragoons left ahead of the milling forces. Two of these men were Captain Phillip St. George Cooke and James Magoffin, a prominent Santa Fe trader. A Mr. Gonzáles, a United States-Chihuahua merchant, accompanied them.[6] This embassy was sent ahead under a flag of truce to penetrate the New Mexican defenses and to meet with Governor Manuel Armijo of New Mexico. On August 12 they arrived in Santa Fe where the governor very graciously received them. Captain Cooke described him as "a large fine looking man" dressed handsomely in "a blue frockcoat, with a rolling collar and a general's shoulder straps, blue striped trousers with gold lace, and a red sash."[7]

Cooke and Magoffin delivered to Governor Armijo a letter from Colonel Kearny, stating that the United States owned New Mexico by virtue of the annexation of Texas, and he had come to take possession of it. Although Governor Armijo disputed the historical claims to the territory as presented by Kearny, he offered to negotiate. Governor Armijo first met with James Magoffin in the governor's small, plain office furnished with two calico-covered sofas pushed up against one of the walls. Armijo and Magoffin sat at a small table which served as the governor's desk and was placed in the center of the room. The *jerga*-covered earthen floors and four chairs were the room's only other furnishings. The two men talked for what must have seemed like hours to Captain Cooke who awaited them. Eventually, the governor and Magoffin sent for Captain Cooke and the talks continued.

What occurred in the governor's office can only be conjectured by later events. The circumstantial evidence indicates that Governor Armijo was offered a bribe to abandon New Mexico, but this was never proven. What is known for certain is that Armijo's second-in-command, Colonel Diego Archuleta, was offered a position with the American army and promised control over that part of New Mexico lying west of the Rio Grande.[8]

On August 14, Captain Cooke and James Magoffin completed their business in Santa Fe. Cooke, accompanied by Dr. Henry Connelly who presented himself as a commissioner sent by Governor Armijo, left the Mexican capital to meet Colonel Kearny who in the meantime had continued his march from Bent's Fort and was approaching Las Vegas. On that same day Kearny's Army of the West set up an encampment on one of the highest hills overlooking the village of Las Vegas. As the army had approached, the women and children of the village had been sent to hide among the rocks and trees of the mountain escarpment, known as the *creston*, which bordered the village on the west. Their priests and civil officials had told the villagers, numbering about 550, that the American army would brand the women on their cheeks and commit other atrocities. Some townsmen apparently believed these reports, but others visited the members of the army to satisfy their curiosity, and also to sell them bread, cheese, cream, and mutton, taking care, as one soldier put it, "to demand a very high price."[9]

The next morning, August 15, 1846, Kearny received Captain R. H. Weightman who brought news from his superiors that he had been brevetted a brigadier general. Thus it was General Kearny who climbed to the roof of one of the houses on the north side of the plaza at Las Vegas to speak to the 200 men of the village assembled below. With *Alcalde* Juan de

Díos Maese, and two of the *alcalde's* aides at his side, the general read his proclamation:

> Mr. *Alcalde*, and people of New Mexico: I have come amongst you by orders of My Government, to take possession of your country, and extend over it the laws of the United States. We consider it, and have done so for some time, a part of the territory of the United States. We come amongst you as friends—not as enemies; as protectors—not as conquerors. We come among you for your benefit—not your injury. Henceforth, I absolve you from all allegiance to the Mexican Government, and from all obedience to General Armijo. He is no longer your Governor. I am your Governor. I shall not expect you to take up arms and follow me to fight your own people who may oppose me; but I will now tell you, that those who remain peaceably at home, attending to their crops and their herds, shall be protected by me in their property, their persons, and their religion; and not a pepper, nor an onion shall be disturbed or taken by my troops without pay or by consent of the owner. But listen! He who promises to be quiet and is found in arms against me, I will hang.[10]

> From the Mexican government you have never received protection. The Apaches and Navajoes (sic) come down from the mountains and carry off sheep and even your women, whenever they please. My government will correct all this. It will keep off the Indians, protect you and your persons and property; and I repeat again, I will protect you in your religion. I know you are all great Catholics; that your priests have told you all sorts of stories, that we should ill-treat your women, and brand them on the cheek as you do your mules on the hip. It is all false. My government respects your religion as much as the Protestant religion and allows each man to worship his creator as his heart tells him best. The law protects the Catholic as well as the Protestant; the weak as well as the

strong, the poor as well as the rich. I am not a Catholic myself. I was not brought up in that faith; but at least one-third of my army is Catholic, and I respect a good Catholic as much as a good Protestant.

There goes my army. You see but a small portion of it. There are many more behind it, resistance is useless. Mr. *Alcalde*, and you two captains, the laws of my country require that all men who hold office under me shall take the oath of allegiance. I do not wish, for the present, until affairs become more settled, to disturb your form of government. If you are prepared to take oaths of allegiance, I shall continue you in office and support your authority.[11]

Thus, without a shot being fired, the *alcalde* and his aides took the oath of allegiance and the citizens of Las Vegas were the first to see their new governor. There had been no fighting and, at least for the moment, things were calm. With mixed feelings at being a subjugated people, the Las Vegans could only hope that the American army would restore the Santa Fe-Missouri trade which had been halted in anticipation of the American invasion and would help them bring the Plains Indians under control.

Cooke has given us a detailed description of a typical Las Vegas home in 1846:

There is some mixture of stone in the structure of the houses; that material being here very convenient and suitable; but the village, with its small fields, scarcely fenced, differed little from those of our Pawnees in appearance; these dwellings are smaller and square instead of round; fine mountain streams are near, and all conducted—as usual—by the main canal of irrigation, through the place. While my horses were fed, we sat down to dinner; it was composed of a plate, for each, of poached eggs, and wheaten tortillas; seeing some cheese on a small pine table, I asked for a knife to cut it; the old man went to a hair trunk, and produced a very common pocket knife. The room had a smooth earthen floor; it was partly covered by a kind of carpeting of primitive manufacture, in white and black or natural coloring of the wool; it is called *Jerga*; around the room, mattresses, doubled pillows, and coverlids, composed a kind of divan; the walls were whitewashed with gypsum, which rubbing off easily, a breadth of calico was attached to the walls above the divan; there was a doll-like image of the Virgin, and two very rude paintings on boards and some small mirrors; the low room was ceiled with puncheons, supporting earth; there were several rough board chairs.[12]

MANUEL ARMIJO AND THE DEFENSE OF SANTA FE

The American army left a squadron of soldiers in Las Vegas as a rear guard and continued out of the village through the *puertocito* ("little door," later to become known at Kearny's Gap) to Tecolote. There Kearny met and conferred with Cooke and Connelly who had recently arrived there from Santa Fe.

At San Miguel, Kearny stopped long enough to read his proclamation and then he and the army continued toward Apache Canyon, a declivity approximately 30 miles east of Santa Fe, through which any caravan or army approaching from the east had to pass. General Armijo reportedly was waiting in the canyon, massing his resistance. Just outside the canyon, however, General Kearny was met by a young boy, mounted on a small horse, who reported that Armijo had made a military retreat and had withdrawn down the Rio Grande where he would await orders from his government.[13] Kearny was free to enter Santa Fe.

Speculation regarding the collapse of the defense of Santa Fe has been endless. Much of this speculation surrounds the person of Governor Manuel Armijo who, some have said, had previously demonstrated himself to be a coward. Certain incidents were usually cited as evidence. During Armijo's first term as governor, for example, he ordered the arrest of a group of American trappers who, in total disregard of Armijo's authority, were cleaning the pelts of their illegally trapped beavers in the plaza in front of the governor's palace. When these trappers began loading their weapons, however, the governor withdrew the command for their arrest and the trappers, amid the jeers and cheers of their compatriots, escaped with their contraband.[14] On a second occasion, Governor Armijo led a small army of New Mexicans out onto the plains to confront a group of Texas pirates who were operating on the Arkansas in Mexican territory against the Santa Fe-Missouri caravans. At the first sign of a confrontation, however, he ordered a retreat. This latter incident resulted in the loss of his military command, and eventually led to his resignation as governor during his second term.[15] In each of these instances, Governor Armijo seemed to sense that his poorly equipped and ill-trained militia were no match for the well-armed and aggressive Texas and Missouri frontiersmen whose firepower greatly exceeded anything he could bring against them.

At the time of the American invasion, Governor Armijo's forces consisted of fewer than 200 *presidial* soldiers and a militia of perhaps 4,000. Although these citizen-soldiers were well intentioned, they constituted a pathetic army. The uniforms of the *presidial* soldiers were tattered and haphazard with no one sporting complete dress. Although the uniform does not make the soldier any more than clothes make the man, the soldier does need the will to fight and weapons that are at least equal to his enemy's. There were at this time, perhaps fewer than 250 operable muskets in the whole of New Mexico.[16] Most of the militia were armed with clubs, lances, bows and arrows.[17] Although the militia men were willing to fight, it is unlikely that the same could be said of the *presidial* soldiers[18] who knew they were outranked, outclassed and outgunned. Many of these latter men were in the military because they had neither land nor other employment. Military service offered them provisions and shelter with a salary initially paid in grain. It is true that some had not been paid in 20 years,[19] but even so, the *presidio* at least provided them with food and a roof over their heads.

With the initiation of the Santa Fe-Missouri trade during the Mexican period, the Mexican government allowed Santa Fe to keep the customs receipts it collected. Armijo then paid his *presidial* soldiers out of these duties. When income was low, however, the *presidial* troop was disbanded. Thus, there were times when New Mexico had 200 paid soldiers, and times when it had none. The *presidial* soldiers, when employed, led the American caravans into Santa Fe, prevented smuggling, acted as a ceremonial guard for the governor, led the militia in campaigns against the Apaches and Navajos, and killed stray dogs.[20]

The real soldiers in New Mexico were its private citizens. Gone were the days of the *encomenderos* who were paid by Indian tribute to defend their country. The citizens who made up the militia were requisitioned by their *alcalde* for three-month enlistments.[21] They had to furnish their own mounts, weapons, and supplies, but received neither salary nor provisions. Some who could afford it paid others to take their enlistment, but for the most part, the citizen-soldier stood ready to defend his country. When the call went out for the militia to muster in Santa Fe to counter the impending invasion by the American army, as many as 4,000 packed their saddle bags, grabbed whatever weapons they owned, and responded.[22] The New Mexico militia and soldiers appear to have outnumbered Kearny's forces by more than two to one. Had they made a stand at Apache Canyon, they undoubtedly would have done great damage to the American army when it invaded Santa Fe. Armijo had been told by Captain Cooke, however, and by a recently arrived Santa Fe trader, that Kearny's army numbered twice the 1,500 actually in Kearny's command. Armijo rode out to Apache Canyon where he had ordered his army to make its stand. There he conferred with his command. Although, the consensus of his men was to fight, Armijo, again, must have looked at his ragged, albeit eager men clutching their worn muskets, clubs, lances, bows and arrows, and decided it was futile. He had artillery, as did Kearny, but he knew that these Americans his army faced, would have their way. In the end, he saw armed resistance as a useless sacrifice of life, disbanded the militia, and sent them home.

Governor Armijo first fled to Albuquerque and then south to Chihuahua, accompanied by 70 Vera Cruz dragoons, who had been sent north to support the defense of New Mexico. Armijo was later tried by court martial, acquitted, and retired to his home in Lemitar where he died in 1854. He is buried in the San Miguel Church in Socorro.[23]

KEARNY ENTERS SANTA FE

When General Kearny entered Santa Fe on August 18, 1846, one of those who witnessed his *entrada* was don Juan Sena, descendant of Tomas de Sena. At this time, he was the owner of the compound that was to become known as the Sena Plaza. Sena owned and operated a store on the east side of the plaza and was very involved in the Santa Fe-Missouri trade. Sena's *tienda*, which boasted the only wooden plank floor in Santa Fe, was considered to be "the second best store in town."[24] As Kearny rode into the plaza with his troops, don Juan must have wondered what this new conquest would mean to him, his family and the citizens of New Mexico.

Although Acting Governor Juan Bautista Vigil y Alarid received General Kearny with respect and dignity, he did little to ingratiate himself with Kearny who was there to replace him. While a few New Mexicans received the American military with a real show of affection and admiration, most of the citizens accepted the change in national affiliation with sullen resignation, still others with tears. Many were afraid that the conquerors would misinterpret their values of courtesy, generosity, honesty, and hospitality[25] as signs of weakness. Many of the newly subjugated people knew that these armed men perceived them as simple peasants and realistically feared the way they would be treated.

General Kearny remained in Santa Fe for about a month during which time he established a civil government. In accordance with previous plans, he placed in command citizens known to and, it was hoped, respected by, the New Mexicans. As governor, Kearny appointed the well-known Taos resident and trader, Charles Bent.[26] Bent was, of course, co-owner with his brother and Ceran St. Vrain of Bent's Fort where Kearny's army had garrisoned prior to the invasion of New Mexico. As secretary, a position equivalent to lieutenant governor, Kearny appointed a second prominent

New Mexican, Donaciano Vigil, an individual with a distinguished civil and military career who had formerly been stationed at San Miguel.

To assert the supremacy of the invading forces, Kearny built a fort on a site overlooking the plaza of Santa Fe. This "star-fort," so-called because of the configuration of its parapets, was named Ft. Marcy to honor Secretary of War William L. Marcy. The fort was deliberately designed with its 17 guns trained on the community below. This was done so that "every house in Santa Fe could be leveled on the least appearance of a revolt."[27] Although no shot was ever fired from the fort, the imposing edifice served successfully to intimidate the residents of the city and hold them in check.

When General Kearny left Santa Fe for California on September 3, 1846, he must have felt that Santa Fe and New Mexico were safely under America's wing. Leaving New Mexico in the hands of Colonel Alexander W. Doniphan who was later followed by Colonel Sterling Price and a regiment of Missouri volunteers, Kearny and the remainder of his army went off to carry the war into present-day Mexico and California.

The conquest of New Mexico, led by the point men, Captain Phillip Cooke and James Magoffin, had been easy. Kearny could not have imagined that the peace he had established would soon give way to a furor. Put mildly, many New Mexicans hated the occupying forces. The citizens of New Mexico especially hated the volunteers of the Second Missouri Regiment who had been left behind. Never had the New Mexicans, among whom "courtesy was the first rule of conduct," [28] seen a more unruly, uncouth and undisciplined mob. Many New Mexicans could not imagine living under the rule of these men from Missouri whom they perceived as barbarians.

With General Kearny now out of gunshot range, a group of New Mexicans who believed themselves to be members of the Mexican resistance began plotting how they could rid themselves of the invading army. Led by ex-Colonel Diego Archuleta, Manuel Cortez, Pablo Montoya, and Tomas Ortiz,[29] the insurgents plotted to kill or drive from New Mexico all Americans and all New Mexicans who had accepted positions in Kearny's territorial government. The revolt was originally planned for December 19, but was postponed to December 24 because it was felt that the rebels would be better able to gather undetected in Santa Fe, San Miguel, and Taos if the Americans were busily engaged in Christmas festivities. The wife of one of the conspirators who was fearful of bloodshed betrayed this plan to the American military authorities. Several of the conspirators were arrested.[30] Governor Bent asked for New Mexicans to exercise restraint and to support their new government instead of fomenting unrest against it.

GOVERNOR CHARLES BENT AND THE TAOS REBELLION

With the arrests of the insurgents and with the appearance of calm restored to the capital, Governor Bent left Santa Fe on January 14 for Taos to gather his family and return to Santa Fe. Sheriff Stephen Louis Lee, Prefect Cornelio Vigil, Circuit Attorney James W. Leal, and two others accompanied him. The party reached Taos on January 18, 1847.[31] The night after their arrival it was snowing and bitterly cold outside when a mob descended upon the jail at Taos and demanded the release of one of its inmates. Sheriff Lee was all for letting the mob have his prisoner, but Vigil protested. Both Lee and Vigil were killed. The mob next sought Attorney Leal who, when found, was marched naked through the streets. When he stumbled and fell, he was shot through with arrows and scalped alive. The mob then descended on the home of Charles Bent.

At the Bent home was Bent, his wife Ignacia and their children, Teresina and Alfred; Ignacia's sister, Josefa Jaramillo Carson; a Bent stepdaughter, Rumalda Luna Boggs; Pablo Jaramillo, brother of the Jaramillo women; and Narcisse Beaubien, son of Judge Charles Beaubien. Dawn was just breaking in Taos when the mob began pounding on the door. Ignacia and Josefa, sensing the danger, begged Governor Bent to leave by the back door. Instead, Governor Bent opened the front door to be met by a mob screaming for his head. The governor tried to reason with the horde while buying time for his family who, using a large iron spoon and a fireplace poker, were trying to dig a hole in a wall of a back room through which to enter the house next door.

The governor was shot in the face. Governor Bent with his hand pressed tightly against his cheek, and the blood pouring from between his fingers, stood there in shock, but still capable of speech. He offered to go with the mob if they would spare his family. He was shot again and again, but he was still alive as the Indians tried to scalp him. With his 10-year old son, Alfred Bent, trying to give him a gun, the mortally wounded governor managed to reach the hole in the wall and was pulled through. Some of the mob attempted to follow, while others climbed to the top of the house next door where they dug through the roof and ceiling and finished off the governor. The women and small children escaped. Given away by the Bent's servant, however, Pablo Jaramillo and Narcisse Beaubien were discovered hiding in the hay loft and were hacked to death.[32]

The rebellion spread through Taos to Mora above Las Vegas, where other Americans were killed. At Santa Fe, Albuquerque, and Las Vegas, the American troops gathered to march north to Taos and Mora and put down the rebellion. Colonel Sterling Price, whom General Kearny had left in charge of the military forces in New Mexico, received news of the revolt on January 20.[33] He called for a volunteer company to be organized under Ceran St. Vrain who, with Price, mounted a force of 353 men to march on Taos. Four days later at Los Luceros reinforcements from various quarters arrived bringing the army of reprisal to almost 500 men. (Ironically, the great house at Los Luceros had also been used by Mexican Colonel José María Cháves of Abiquiu as a training center for the troops amassed to meet General Kearny's army at Apache Canyon. However well trained Cháves' men might have been, Kearny never saw them.)

Tomás Ortiz and Pablo Montoya led the insurrectionists, numbering between 1,500 and 2,000 men. The Americans encountered them first on the afternoon of January 24 near Santa Cruz. The battle was indecisive and the insurgents scattered. Battles then followed at Embudo, Trampas and Chamisal with the rebels finally retreating to the adobe church at the Taos Pueblo. Here, the rebels were shelled until they surrendered. With perhaps as many as 150 of the insurrectionists killed in this final assault alone, the back of the movement was broken.[34] Many were accused of treason and brought to trial. (At one time there were more than 80 prisoners in the Taos jail.) Although, it was questionable as to whether those accused were in fact United States citizens or simply Mexicans fighting to dislodge the invading forces. Pablo Montoya and five others were hanged.[35] While a group of grieving widows, their dead husbands strapped to their backs, slowly trudged toward the Taos Pueblo, the American soldiers remounted their horses for their triumphal ride back to the village of Taos. These sad events brought the Taos rebellion to a conclusion. The hostilities, however, were far from over.

14
THE TERRITORIAL PERIOD: 1846–1912

A TURBULENT NEW MEXICO

W hen General Stephen Watts Kearny left Santa Fe on September 3, 1846, he left the "Territory of New Mexico" in the very capable hands of Colonel Alexander W. Doniphan, Governor Charles Bent and a cadre of civil officials each of whom was to exercise power under the Organic Laws of the Territory of New Mexico. These laws, which became known as the Kearny Code, divided governmental functions into the three traditional branches. Executive powers were given to the governor who was to serve for two years unless replaced sooner by the president of the United States. Legislative authority was vested in a House of Representatives representing New Mexico's counties, and a Legislative Council representing its districts. The General Assembly, established by the Kearny Code, was scheduled to convene in Santa Fe on the first Monday of December 1847, and every two years thereafter. Also established by the Kearny Code were a superior court, and the positions of secretary of the territory, marshal, United States district attorney, treasurer, and auditor of public accounts. Kearny, claiming presidential authorization, filled these positions he had created then left New Mexico for present-day California to continue the war against the Mexican forces there.

It was soon apparent, however, that General Kearny had exceeded his authority by establishing a permanent government in New Mexico. As long as a war was in progress with Mexico, the jurisdiction of New Mexico occupied by the military could not be considered permanently annexed to the United States.

The instability of New Mexico's government had been confirmed during December of 1846 and January of 1847 when Governor Bent was murdered. The military campaign led by Colonel Sterling Price to put down the Taos insurrection forcefully reiterated the fact that New Mexico's government was military-led. Moreover, although Secretary Donaciano Vigil was allowed to assume authority as governor, he did so as a civil officer subordinate to Colonel Price, the military commander. With the military essentially in control of the citizens of New Mexico, there was a question as to whether Colonel Price would allow a General Assembly in Santa Fe during December of 1847 as directed by the Kearny Code. The Taos insurrection had suggested that the New Mexicans were not ready for self-governance. The question was—would they be allowed to try?

Many New Mexicans voiced their resentment at the power the military had over their lives and expressed a sense of futility at establishing a civil government with no authority. Nevertheless, the General Assembly did meet in Santa Fe that December. One of its major pieces of legislation was one calling for a convention to study the permanent annexation of New Mexico as a Territory of the United States. In December of 1847, however, New Mexico was still a Mexican Territory under the military occupation of the United States, and the United States was still at war with Mexico.

On February 2, 1848, the United States and Mexico signed the Treaty of Guadalupe Hidalgo. As a result of the treaty, the United States obtained the land that today makes up the states of California, Nevada, and Utah, most of New Mexico and Arizona, and parts of Colorado and Wyoming. This treaty fixed a portion of the boundary dispute between the United States and Mexico, but only brought the boundary dispute between Texas and New Mexico to the fore without solving it.[1]

When the Texas forces had captured Mexican General and President Antonio López de Santa Ana in 1836, he was forced to sign a treaty recognizing Texas' independence.[2] The new Republic of Texas, as devised by this treaty, included parts of present-day Colorado, Kansas, New Mexico, Oklahoma, and Wyoming, land to which the Texas *empresarios* had no historical claim. With the Treaty of Guadalupe Hidalgo establishing peace between the United States and Mexico, Texas wanted its territory. Getting it, however, was not going to be easy. Not only did Texas have to contend with the prior claim by New Mexico for the same land, but also with much larger issues affecting both the territorial ambitions of Texas and the progress of New Mexico toward statehood. The following presents in brief some of the issues and remote antecedents that affected not only those territorial claims, but also New Mexico's quest for statehood, and the future of the United States.

THE ISSUE OF SLAVERY

In the late 1700s, a boundary dispute arose between Pennsylvania and Maryland. The two states agreed to settle their dispute by having the land surveyed. This survey, which was conducted from 1763 to 1767, employed the services of two English astronomers, Charles Mason and Jeremiah Dixon. The Mason-Dixon line, when completed, not only divided Pennsylvania from Maryland, but also Pennsylvania from a part of West Virginia, and Maryland from Delaware.[2] Before the American Civil War, this line plus the southern boundary of Pennsylvania were considered the boundary between the south and the north and between slave and non-slave states.

In 1818, the Territory of Missouri applied for admission to the Union. At the time of this request there were 11 states that permitted slavery and 11 states that had abolished it. The admission of Missouri was crucial, for it would upset the balance of 22 senators on each side of the slavery question. On the east side of the Mississippi, the Mason-Dixon Line and the Ohio River easily determined the boundaries for free vs. slave states, with slavery being permitted south of the line. There was, however, no such natural or historical boundary west of the Mississippi. Missouri could not be authorized to establish a constitution (required of potential states prior to their admission) and upset the balance of slave and free states.

In 1820 the United States adopted what became known as the Missouri Compromise. With Maine requesting admission as a free state, the Senate authorized Missouri to draft a constitution and, except for the state of Missouri itself, banned slavery north of Missouri's southern boundary. Later attempts to extend this line by law across the continent failed. The line, however, at 36° 30' north latitude became the North-South, free-slave boundary in the western United States until repealed by the Kansas-Nebraska Act of 1854. This Act allowed the settlers of the Kansas-Nebraska Territory, which lay north of the previously agreed-upon boundary for slave states, to decide the issue of slavery for themselves. The Kansas-Nebraska Act of 1854, an act which may have hastened the American Civil War, thus rekindled the bitter quarrel over the expansion of slavery, which had died down with the Missouri Compromise of 1820.[3]

NEW MEXICO, ISSUES AND DISPUTES

New Mexico could not have chosen a worse time to come before the community of states seeking parity. There was at this time almost continuous quarreling among the different sections of the country, each of which was demanding special national legislation. The Northeast wanted a protective tariff for its industries. The West wanted free land for settlers and federal aid for roads and other improvements. The South, which saw slave labor as an integral part of its economy, feared national legislation against slavery. It resisted measures that would strengthen the national government and opposed the demands of other sections.

In 1847, New Mexico began its long, arduous march toward statehood, a journey none could have imagined would take over 60 years. New Mexico's major block in the sectional issue was Texas, a state with over 183,000 slaves who worked the cotton plantations largely in the eastern half of the Texas territory. Texas, a slave state, claimed the New Mexico territory as far as the Rio Grande. This claim encompassed every major settlement in New Mexico from Taos to Albuquerque, including New Mexico's capital, Santa Fe, in spite of the fact that some of these New Mexican settlements had existed more than a century before the founding of Texas. If Texas prevailed in its claim, slavery would be extended to the Rio Grande. There were many in the United States and in New Mexico who saw this possibility as unacceptable.

On March 15, 1848, the Texas legislature created Santa Fe County which incorporated all of the disputed territory. With encouragement from some American authorities, Texas sent Spruce M. Baird to the city of Santa Fe to serve as a judge in the newly created Texas judicial district of Santa Fe.[4] Baird stayed in New Mexico for a time while he tried to get someone to recognize his authority. Ignored by the powers in New Mexico who were trying to establish their own government, however, Baird returned home.

Undaunted, the Texans tried again. In 1849, the Texas legislature reorganized Santa Fe County into four counties: *Presidio*, El Paso, Worth, and Santa Fe, taking in territory which extended from what is today southeastern Texas northward into central Colorado, and southern Wyoming as well as land both north and south of the Oklahoma panhandle. In this new organization, Santa Fe, Taos, Las Vegas, San Miguel and Albuquerque remained in Santa Fe County. The state of Texas then tried to hold elections within Santa Fe County, and when it was unable to do so, threatened to send armed men to occupy the disputed territory, although it did not.

In the midst of this conflict, New Mexico continued in its efforts to join the Union and to deal with Texas on an even footing. With peace established between the United States and Mexico, New Mexico moved to request its permanent annexation to the United States.

NEW MEXICO SEEKS TO JOIN THE UNION

On February 10, 1849, the General Assembly met in Santa Fe to further explore union with the United States. Elected president of this body was Father Antonio José Martínez, the brilliant cleric considered by many to be a natural leader. In attendance among others were individuals whom we have met before: Francisco Sarracino, former governor of New Mexico under Mexican rule; Donaciano Vigil, present civil governor of New Mexico; Judge Charles Beaubien, appointed by General Kearny to the superior court of New Mexico; and Gregorio Vigil, former *alcalde* at San Miguel. This group requested the speedy organization of a territorial civil government and declared its desire to outlaw slavery within its borders.

During September of 1849, the Assembly met again with Father Antonio José Martínez once more acting as president. In addition to Father Martínez and Gregorio Vigil, the Assembly also included Manuel Antonio Baca, former county prefect at San Miguel; Ceran St. Vrain of Taos; and Salvador Lucero of Río Arriba. The body again requested territorial status, but the impediments to this soon became evident. With the sectional issue over slavery so volatile, Congress could not allow New Mexico's admittance as a free state and upset the balance of states on each side of the slavery question. In addition, New Mexico was not the only player in the game of "states"-manship, and with every move of each of the other players, New Mexico stood to lose some of its territory. Attempts were made by other westerners to take portions of New Mexico to establish the territories of Arizona, Pimeria, and Montezuma, and the state of Deseret (Utah). Each of these initial attempts at partition was unsuccessful. New Mexico countered with moves of its own.

During 1850, the citizens of New Mexico called for a constitutional convention. This convention was marred by dissension over whether to seat one of its delegates, Diego Archuleta, who was believed by many to have been a principal in the murder of Governor Charles Bent. Archuleta, however, was eventually seated and the convention began to hammer out a document which reasserted two major stands: first, New Mexico's territory as recognized by the Transcontinental Treaty of 1819 would remain intact with Santa Fe as its capital, and second, under no condition would slavery be accepted.

Upon the submission of its constitution, New Mexico, at least in theory, could have entered the Union as a state. In reality, things were not so clear-cut. The dispute with Texas, the sectional issue, and the attempts by Congress to quell the secessionist movement gaining momentum in a number of the Southern states were all complicating factors. Congress, therefore, made two determinations regarding New Mexico, one in its favor and one against it. First, the Congress established what remains today the boundary between Texas and New Mexico.

Ironically, in this compromise, Texas was financially compensated with 10 million dollar's worth of stock for land it never owned. Second, New Mexico was admitted as a territory, and the question as to whether it would allow or disallow slavery was left undecided. It had taken four long years for New Mexico to achieve this status as a territory. It would take another half century for it to be admitted as a state.

NEW MEXICO AND THE AMERICAN CIVIL WAR

The initial decade of New Mexico's quest for statehood (1846-1856) was the saddest and most disruptive in America's history, with the issues of slavery, sectional strife, and secession from the Union eventually leading the nation into civil war. On April 12, 1861, the Southern forces of the United States shelled Fort Sumter in the harbor of Charleston, South Carolina, thus initiating the war between the states. This war, although fought mainly in the East, Midwest, and South, spilled over into New Mexico which became a border territory fought over by Confederate Texans against Californians, Coloradans, and New Mexicans.[5] When the New Mexicans heard that the Texans were again planning to invade New Mexico, as many as 4,000 volunteered to repel the invasion. One volunteer group, organized under the command of Colonel Kit Carson, was destined to play a major role in the Union's campaign against the Confederate States of America.

During July of 1861, a Confederate force of Texans invaded New Mexico. This force, under the command of Lieutenant Colonel John R. Baylor, occupied the little village of Mesilla and seized Fort Filmore, the southernmost federal post in the New Mexico territory. As a result of this successful occupation, the Confederate Congress in January of 1862 organized the Confederate Territory of Arizona which incorporated all of New Mexico below Socorro.[6] The Confederacy, however, had greater plans for the Southwest. Fort Craig, Santa Fe, and Fort Union, 26 miles north of Las Vegas, were all that stood between the Confederacy and the gold fields of Colorado and California. This gold would help the South finance its war.

During the same month that the Confederacy successfully lopped off a third of present-day New Mexico, Confederate President Jefferson Davis sanctioned a second invasion of the beleaguered territory. The Confederate army, composed of over 3,000 tough undisciplined Texans under the command of Brigadier General Henry H. Sibley, marched up the Rio Grande to encounter Union forces who awaited them at Fort Craig. The Confederate forces, however, decided against a frontal attack at Fort Craig, and, leaving the Union army behind its embattlements, continued north. Sibley's movement was a ruse to allow his army to cross to the east bank of the Rio Grande. He thus severed the Union supply-line northward and forced the Union army, under the command of Brevet Colonel Edward Canby, to come out to meet him. The ensuing battle was a disaster. Colonel Canby had in his command regular troops, militia, and New Mexico Volunteers. Although, he later attempted to blame the loss on the citizen-soldiers, this assessment is both misleading and unfair. Mistakes were made by all parties, but it is obvious that the militia and volunteers exhibited loyalty and courage in the Union defeat.[7] However, the battle at Valverde succeeded only in slowing the Confederate advance. The Texas army was successful in taking Albuquerque and Santa Fe and continued its relentless march north.

With most of the New Mexico volunteers concentrated at Fort Craig, Governor Henry Connelly requested assistance from the Colorado territory. The Colorado volunteers first marched to Fort Union and then on to Glorieta Pass and Apache Canyon, the narrow declivity deserted by Governor Armijo during the American invasion of the previous decade. After a three-day battle at Glorieta Pass, the Confederate army held the field but the Union forces were successful in destroying the Confederate supply wagons. With the loss of his supplies, General Sibley was forced to break off the battle. He retreated down the Río Grande Valley and withdrew from New Mexico just ahead of the "'California Column" which had marched east across the desert to engage him. With the Confederate forces driven out, New Mexico could now return to its own sectional issue—how to deal with the Indians.

Although the American Civil War continued to rage in the East, Midwest, and South, New Mexico decided to concentrate its forces to solve at least one aspect of the Indian problem. The American army had been trying for 16 years to make good on its promise to end Indian depredations. It had been totally unsuccessful, with the Apaches and Navajos continuing their plundering seemingly at will. It was during this 16-year period that the *Piedra Lumbre* Land Grant and a number of others in the area of Chama and Abiquiu were abandoned.

In desperation, the American military command in New Mexico appointed Colonel Kit Carson to wage war on the Navajos. It was the intent of the military to place the Navajos on a reservation. The army first attempted to do this by establishing a lasting treaty with these Indians.

When one side or the other broke treaty after treaty, however, the Indian problem began to appear insoluble. The army then decided to starve the Indians into submission. A combined force of American and New Mexican troops and Indian auxiliaries, destroyed the Navajos' crops and fruit trees, and either rounded up the Navajos' extensive flocks of sheep, or killed them. Many of the Navajos tried to bring the war to a close. They had made similar pleas to end hostilities on previous occasions, however, only to return to their depredations once the army had withdrawn. The American forces, therefore, continued to press their advantage. The burning of cornfields and the killing of sheep went on. Eventually, however, the pleas of the Navajos to bring the war to a close were heeded. Approximately 8,000 of these thoroughly demoralized people were amassed in Navajo land, in present-day western New Mexico and eastern Arizona, for the long walk to their new homes on the Pecos River.

The suffering endured by the Navajos on their forced march to the *Bosque Redondo*, an area on the Pecos defined by a massive grove of cottonwoods, is beyond the scope of this book. Suffice it to say that they were brutally treated. Those Indians who were ill or aged and unable to maintain the pace, were shot.[8]

The suffering of these captured Navajos was not greatly alleviated when they reached their new home about 49 miles below present-day Santa Rosa. A licensed trading post had been established in the area of the *Bosque* in 1851, and Fort Sumner was built there in 1862, the year of the Confederate defeat at Glorieta Pass. It was to this fort, named for General Edmond Vose Sumner, commander of the 9th Military Department in New Mexico, that Colonel Carson was bringing his charges.

At Fort Sumner, the Navajos were put on a reservation with a group of Apaches, their Athapascan-speaking brothers and sisters of the distant past.[9] By this period in their respective histories, however, they were two distinct tribes with different customs and languages. Whether long-lost kinfolk or not, they didn't like each other. Worse, though, was the fact that, in spite of the reservation's being a large one, it had little arable land and the Indians had few implements by which to dig irrigation canals or turn the soil. With only 50 spades and their bare hands, however, the Indians were successful in digging an *acequia* which was twelve feet wide and six miles long.

Because there were no communities near the reservation, residents from Santa Fe, San Miguel, Puerto de Luna and Las Vegas sold corn, wheat, and mutton to the American army so that it could feed the Indians in its charge. These military contracts were to lead to the establishment of a number of ranching enterprises on the Pecos River both north and south of the *Bosque Redondo*. One of these ranches, owned by a Baca, would become central to the history of this family on the eastern frontier.

DISUNION AND DISDAIN[10]

Although the New Mexicans appeared to be a fairly homogeneous people, with religion, land, and history as common denominators, it is, in fact, questionable to what degree they shared the same aspirations for statehood. They had directed their own lives for 250 years without major interference from centralized authority. Tenacious and extremely individualistic, they had learned to fight together to hold their land, but their identity as a people suffered inevitable fragmentation. It was, in fact, in the areas of collective expression that the New Mexican experienced the most difficulty: social cohesion beyond the extended family and the village, democratic government and economic organization. In individual drive, stubborn will, and indefatigable energy, they were the match of any people, but whether they had the ability or even the desire to subordinate their personal ambitions to a collective end is debatable. Moreover, the difficulties the New Mexicans were experiencing due to their failings were compounded by the behavior and attitude of the non-native New Mexican toward them.

The American people in contact with New Mexico since the early 1800s had often been critical and even intolerant of Spanish ways. In the beginning, these foreigners were very few in number, and their negative attitudes seldom had any major influence on the way the citizens of New Mexico conducted their lives. However, with the opening of the Santa Fe Trail in 1821 and the conquest of New Mexico by the United States in 1846 came a more open expression of the ethnocentric attitudes held by both the Hispanic settlers and by many Anglo-Americans both inside and outside the territory.

Many individuals who entered the territory, and also many who viewed New Mexico from thousands of miles away, thought their own way of life, values, folkways, and even their language were superior to those of the New Mexicans. They spoke of New Mexico, its land, and its people, in the most pejorative of terms. Anglo-Americans sometimes expressed these attitudes through verbal aggressiveness, proselytizing and discrimination.

The following provides some examples of these attitudes, most of which were expressed in the popular press during the decade 1870-1880. Regarding Santa Fe and its citizens:

> Santa Fe is "a Mexican city of 6,000 people, and of the lowest class on God('s) earth." Marsh Giddings, Territorial Governor from 1871–1875 [11]

Regarding the territory and its people:

> A "very considerable portion of the population of the Territory do not [even] speak the English language." Representative Clarkson Potter of New York State, 1874 [12]

> "These people of Mexican descent' [are] almost wholly ignorant" of the English language. The people "are aliens to us in blood and language . . . popular ignorance prevails like a pall throughout the whole territory, with few and insignificant exceptions." The Cincinnati Commercial, 1875 [13]

> The New Mexico Territory "is thinly populated, the towns scattered over its vast area are few and ill-regulated, and a large part of the people is ignorant and utterly destitute of enterprise and public spirit." The New York Times, March 5, 1875 [14]

Newspapermen and politicians who, except for Territorial Governor Giddings, had never been to the territory expressed these editorial comments. However, even Susan Wallace, wife of Territorial Governor Lew Wallace, thought that New Mexico was full of cutthroats and that the land was most unappealing. A letter to her cousin in 1879 expresses these views of New Mexico, its land and its people:

> New Mexico is a "land of sagebrush and cactus . . .[the villages look] like nothing so much as a collection of brick kilns." And regarding the potential for statehood: ". . . the Americans would bear the taxes and the Mexicans hold all the offices—it is not in the interest of the white men to bring that about." Susan Wallace, March 4, 1879 [15]

There was little doubt about it: as far as many Anglo-Americans were concerned, New Mexico was a valueless nuisance, its people slovenly, ignorant, and ungovernable. In addition, many viewed the territory as unprotectable. Many seemed to feel that perhaps, as suggested by General William Tecumseh Sherman in 1874, the United States should prevail upon Mexico to take back the territory.[16]

In the political arena, the ethnocentric attitudes held by many Anglos resulted in a patronizing attitude toward the native New Mexican. Worse, however, in regard to the confusing issue of land ownership, ethnocentrism resulted in contemptuous exploitation, fraud, deceit and even violence. Apart from slavery and the sectional issue, ethnocentrism was to be the major factor impeding New Mexico's progress through the next century.

* * *

It was an ironic twist of fate. The colonists, separated from their cultural roots by the Treaty of Guadalupe Hidalgo in which the Mexican government had ceded the Southwest to the United States for $15 million dollars, became strangers in their own land. They had two choices. They could either leave their lands and retreat behind the new political border or they could remain in the occupied territory and be assimilated. Approximately 2,000 of the settlers chose the former, but most of the new-Americans chose to stick it out. Although the Mexican government did its best to protect them in terms of their previous customs in language, law, and religion, it failed. Its former citizens, whom it had been forced to cut loose, were cast adrift, awash in a sea of hostility.

15
TERRITORIAL VIOLENCE, CORRUPTION AND SCHISM

TERRITORIAL VIOLENCE

I t is important to note that some of the criticisms to which New Mexicans were subjected had a basis in fact. During the 1700's the Church's primary concern on the Spanish frontier was for the conversion and religious education of the Indians. No provisions were made for the education of its colonists. This would have to await greater prosperity and protection from the Indians outside the kingdom who continued to menace them. Over time, however, this defense and protection increased, but the kingdom, province, and territory remained very poor. New Mexico continued to lack an economy sufficient to support the needed schools. Thus in 1827, there were only eighteen schools in the whole of the territory and five years later this number had dwindled to six.[1] In 1847 New Mexico had only one public school and although the wealthy were able to employ tutors or obtain their education outside the territory, the masses remained illiterate.

In addition, elections were rife with fraud, and political shenanigans were both comical and deadly. Political representatives on both sides of the aisle came to their meetings armed and ready for just about anything. Political seats were taken away from representatives without cause, while other representatives were literally locked out of their legislative chambers. Worse, however, was the violence that New Mexican politics appeared to generate.

During the territorial elections of 1851, an American soldier named Burtinett and a large group of drunken Anglos tried to close down a polling place at *Los Ranchos* near Albuquerque in an attempt to secure the election for their candidate. In the resulting melee, Burtinett was shot and killed. Following this incident, William C. Skinner was sent to Albuquerque to prosecute the case. He, too, was shot and killed in a confrontation with Juan Cristóbal Armijo whom Skinner had threatened to "cowhide or whip."[2] Again in 1871, nine men were killed and forty or fifty wounded in a politically motivated conflict in the southern community of Mesilla. This latter incident resulted in the following description of two of New Mexico's cities, neither of which, ironically, had been involved in the fracas. Santa Fe was described as "the heart of our worst civilization," and Albuquerque as "younger, but with all signs of ignorance and sloth."[3]

Although these two incidents, separated by an intervening period of 20 years, can hardly be seen as representative of the difficulties New Mexico had in resolving its differences, they illustrate some of the dilemmas. These struggles became even worse in the final decades of the century.

THE SANTA FE RING

The exploitation of New Mexicans reached its zenith during the 1880s over the confusing issue of land ownership. This difficulty had its roots in the distribution of land and the way land tenure was granted and passed on during the 300-year period, 1598-1898. Into the morass came a few shrewd Americans whose intention it was to make hay while the sun shone, and in New Mexico, the sun shone all the time. Prominent among these individuals, most of whom were lawyers, were Territorial Governor Samuel B. Axtell, United States District Attorney Thomas Catron, and Catron's former classmate at the University of Missouri, Stephen B. Elkins.

Governor Axtell arrived in New Mexico on July 30, 1875, and immediately got himself embroiled in a private feud that would later become known as the Lincoln County War. The "War" pitted two rivals against one another: Lawrence G. Murphy, who controlled all the business enterprises in Southern New Mexico's Lincoln County, and a newly arrived lawyer in Lincoln named Alexander A. McSween. McSween, with the financial backing of John Henry Tunstall and cattle baron, John Chisum, sought to challenge Murphy's financial monopoly in Lincoln County by building a store and acquiring a bank. Matters came to a head when Murphy's partner, Emil Fritz, died leaving a $10,000 insurance policy. Attorney McSween was employed by the Fritz heirs to collect on the policy. Once he had done so, however, McSween refused to release the money to the heirs citing the many unforeseen expenses encountered in its collection. The Fritz heirs then sued. As a result of the suit, McSween's property, as well as the property of his partner, John Tunstall, was seized by Sheriff William Brady. During the process of seizure, John Tunstall encountered the sheriff's posse on the road and was shot and killed.[4]

Because of Lawrence Murphy's influence in Lincoln County, Tunstall's friends and cowhands (one of whom was William Bonney, better known as "Billy the Kid,") were thwarted in their attempts to seek legal justice. Some of Tunstall's allies took matters into their own hands and shot and killed Sheriff Brady and one of his deputies on Lincoln's main street in full view of its townspeople. In this debacle, Billy the Kid killed several of his mythic 21 victims. These killings, and others that followed, ultimately led to a bloody confrontation with approximately 40 men on each side. The shoot-out lasted five days (July 15-19, 1878) and resulted in numerous deaths. (It is really very difficult to tell who were the good guys and who the bad in the Lincoln County War and the shoot-out of 1878. L. G. Murphy's protégé, James J. Dolan, had drawn County Sheriff William Brady, District Judge Warren Bristol, and the outlaw gang of Jessie Evans into his camp. On the other side of the fence were McSween's gunmen, who called themselves the Regulators. This latter group, one of whom was Billy the Kid, rode under the command of Justice of the Peace John B. Wilson and Lincoln Constable Atanacio Martínez. Neither side wore white hats; each masqueraded as an arm of the law. When a troop of U. S. soldiers from Fort Stanton rode into Lincoln on July 19 to put an end to the hostilities, their leader, Colonel Nathan Dudley, apparently judged the former Brady bunch to be the less tarnished of the opposing sides and supported them in resolving the conflict.)[5] Billy the Kid escaped unharmed, however, to carry his own New Mexican career to its inevitable conclusion.

The Lincoln County War of 1876-78, which had begun as a personal feud, eventually pitted armed sheepmen, ranchers, homesteaders, and squatters against one another, all vying for land and water rights. The war became so heated that President Rutherford B. Hayes sent General Lew Wallace to New Mexico as territorial governor to restore order. (Governor Wallace stayed in New Mexico where, while residing in the governor's palace, he wrote part of his widely read novel, Ben Hur.)

In the Lincoln County War and the Colfax County War which followed, Governor Samuel Axtell proved himself to be a weak and unprincipled man. The problems in Lincoln County consumed several years during which Governor Axtell and United States Attorney General Thomas Catron obstructed justice by intervening a number of times on behalf of the Murphy faction. Why Axtell and Catron shielded Murphy and the deceased Fritz is unknown, although it has been suggested that they did so to cover up some irregularity in Murphy's government contracts to supply the Mescalero Apaches or the military post at Fort Stanton.

Axtell's role as an obstructionist was to come into play for a second time during the decade, 1877-1887, when there was an attempt to evict settlers from a land grant which had been purchased in 1870 by a group who sought to develop it. An English-Dutch company had bought the Maxwell Land Grant, named for its owner, Lucien B. Maxwell, Kit Carson's friend and business partner. At issue was the largest land holding in the Western Hemisphere.

In 1841, Mexican Governor Manuel Armijo had given 1,714,764.93 acres of land in northern New Mexico and present southern Colorado to Charles Beaubien and Guadalupe Miranda of Taos. Lucien Maxwell married Luz Beaubien and, after Beaubien's death in 1864, bought out the remaining heirs.[6] In Beaubien's conduct of the grant, he allowed individuals to settle the land according to the old feudal system by which he received a token payment and a share of the settler's produce. Maxwell continued this arrangement. However, when Maxwell sold the enormous grant to a group of investors, and they in turn sold it to the English-Dutch company, the feudal system under which the settlers had occupied the grant did not transfer with new ownership. The settlers, all of whom had occupied the land for many years, suddenly became squatters. The company moved to evict the settlers, and a group of ambitious and unscrupulous lawyers helped them. After four years of intermittent bloodshed, the syndicate, aided by its lawyers and hired Pinkerton gunmen, prevailed. These lawyers and their political cronies, such as Governor Axtell and Territorial Representative Stephen Elkins, became known as the Santa Fe Ring.

The men of the Ring saw the confused legal status of the land grants as a perfect opportunity for self-aggrandizement and they were incredibly successful. The members of the Ring purchased, patched, and plundered; they manufactured wills and titles, and involved themselves in all manner of unscrupulous activity to gain control over the Spanish and Mexican land grants. Thomas Catron, a former Confederate artillery captain who had come to New Mexico in 1867, was by 1883 the nation's largest landowner. In the intervening 16 years, Catron had managed to acquire 240,000 acres of the Mora Land Grant above Las Vegas, and 593,000 acres of the Tierra Amarilla Land Grant in northern New Mexico and present-day southern Colorado. In addition, Catron also had five other grants and extensive land holdings elsewhere.

Catron's law partner, Representative Elkins, upon winning congressional confirmation of the Mora Land Grant for its heirs, appropriated a large portion of this grant for himself. The Ring, however, did not confine its activities to the northern part of the state. Elkins was also able to secure a land grant north of Albuquerque, and later, as Secretary of War in the Harrison administration, used his influence to block a re-survey of this grant to determine whether valuable mineral land had illegally been incorporated into it.[7]

Through all of this, New Mexico limped toward statehood, with many Hispanics believing that statehood was being pushed by Catron, Elkins, and their constituents of the Santa Fe Ring, to better their own financial and political positions. How the territorial period played itself out at the local level will be explored by looking at events occurring in three communities: Taos, Santa Rosa, and Las Vegas. These events may be viewed as representative of life on the New Mexico frontier during the period from 1850 to 1912.

THE MARTINEZ—LAMY SCHISM

When Fathers Jean Baptiste Lamy and Joseph Projectus Machebeuf, friends and fellow priests, left their homes in France for a missionary expedition to the New World, they could not have imagined the land or the people whom they would encounter. The year was 1839 and the men were on their way to America as part of the effort by Bishop John Baptiste Purcell of Cincinnati, Ohio, to recruit young priests for missionary work in the United States.[8]

Fathers Lamy and Machebeuf spent their first 12 years in America in the Midwest, with Machebeuf stationed in Ohio, Lamy in Ohio and then Kentucky. They were not, however, to remain in the Midwest; in time, destiny would call both of them to serve elsewhere.

On July 23, 1850, as the result of a synod in Baltimore, Father Lamy, much to his own surprise, was appointed by Pope Pius IX as vicar apostolic for the Vicariate of Santa Fe, a position he neither sought nor much wanted.[9] Bishop Jean Baptiste Lamy had no choice but to go to New Mexico. If he had to go, however, he would take his friend Machebeuf with him as his vicar general.

A vicariate for New Mexico was an old idea whose time had come. Prior to the establishment of the New Mexico vicariate in 1850, Santa Fe and New Mexico had been under the authority of the Bishop of Durango 1,500 miles away. Fray Alonso Benavides, as early as 1630, had argued for the establishment of a New Mexico vicariate, noting that it took almost a year for one to make the round trip from Santa Fe to Durango.[10] It had never come to pass, but now with New Mexico established as a territory of the United States, the issue of placing a bishop in this vast area re-surfaced anew, and this time was acted upon.

Lamy and Machebeuf entered Santa Fe on August 9, 1851, and

were welcomed by Territorial Governor James Calhoun and several thousand people from Santa Fe who had ridden five or six miles out of town to meet them.[11] It did not take long for this auspicious beginning to turn sour. Although Vicar Forane (Rural Dean) Juan Felipe Ortiz, who was responsible for the administration of the Church in New Mexico, welcomed Bishop Lamy, he informed him that neither he nor his clergy recognized him as their bishop. Ortiz informed Lamy that Bishop José Antonio Laureano de Zubiría y Escalante of Durango, had been in Santa Fe a few short months before Lamy's arrival. Bishop Zubiría had used this occasion to discuss with Ortiz Zubiría's understanding that the Mexico bishopric would continue to exercise Episcopal authority over New Mexico despite the change in political boundaries.[12] Lamy, Ortiz stated, might have his miter and crozier, but he didn't have a vicariate.

Led by Vicar Forane Ortiz, the priests in his charge stood defiant and refused to recognize Bishop Lamy. While pressing Bishop Zubiría to clarify his authority over the New Mexico territory, Lamy also tried to secure Church property for which he claimed responsibility. One of these properties was a very old military chapel, now much in disrepair, which the U.S. military had ungraciously appropriated for use as a storehouse. This ancient chapel with its stone *reredos* (altar pieces) was an historic and architectural treasure known as *La Castrense* (meaning "of the military"). While awaiting confirmation of his appointment as bishop of New Mexico, Bishop Lamy began a campaign to get the United States authorities to relinquish its jurisdiction over the chapel. In this campaign, both Lamy and Machebeuf incurred the wrath of Chief Justice Grafton Baker, presiding judge of the New Mexico Supreme Court, who threatened to have them hanged. Although New Mexico's clergy refused to recognize Lamy's authority over them, the laity rushed to support him in his bid for the chapel. Citizen support was so vociferous, in fact, that Justice Baker was forced to make a request of the American commandant at Fort Marcy for military protection. Bishop Lamy won this skirmish, bringing the laity to his side and obtaining the ancient chapel, but he still had to contend with the priests who refused to accept him. This unfortunate beginning was to lead to many years of difficulty for Bishop Lamy, culminating in a schism between him and a number of the religious responsible to him.

Bishop Zubiría was made aware of Lamy's presence in Santa Fe by Father Antonio José Martínez who, in a letter to Bishop Zubiría, expressed his disappointment over losing the relationship with his revered superior.[13] The association between Father Martínez and Bishop Zubiría was of long-standing. Bishop Zubiría had recognized the superior abilities of this secular priest and had appointed Martínez to a number of important posts. For example, Bishop Zubiría gave Martínez permission to "grant dispensations" to blood relatives wishing to marry.[14] He also supported the appointment of Father Martínez to the position of "vicar and ecclesiastical judge" in New Mexico.[15] This latter position gave Father Martínez the power in his own parish or district to "adjudicate in Church matters" that related to civil law.[16]

The Mexican officials in Santa Fe prior to the American occupation shared Bishop Zubiría's respect and admiration for Father Martínez. Martínez was chosen by these officials as advisor to the Americans,[17] and in 1846 Martínez was licensed by the Mexican government as a civil attorney.[18] He was commended by all for his exemplary deportment and character, viewed as a "pillar" in the Taos community, and was a "living legend" in the nineteenth century.[19] Even his birthday was celebrated as a community holiday in Taos.

Although Bishop Lamy was sensitive to the antagonistic feelings Father Martínez had toward him, Lamy attempted to win him over. One of the ways he did so was "to seek the legal counsel of Martínez," whose expertise in both civil and canon law he wished to utilize.[20] He asked Father Martínez to prepare legal briefs on a number of different issues, and conferred with him regarding many matters pertaining to the Church in New Mexico.[21] Bishop Lamy, however, was not completely successful in drawing Father Martínez into his fold. The potential for confrontation remained throughout their association, with Father Martínez never totally accepting Bishop Lamy's authority as his ecclesiastical, intellectual or cultural superior.

The ongoing difficulties between Bishop Lamy and Father Antonio

José Martínez were fueled by conflict over two major issues, the matter of tithes for the support of the Church in New Mexico, and the demands by Martínez and others that Lamy's friend and vicar general, Machebeuf, face an ecclesiastical court trial for allegedly revealing confessional secrets and for abusing ecclesiastical authority in countless ways.[22]

Bishop Lamy had first written to Bishop Zubiría in 1851 requesting he clarify for the priests in New Mexico, the change in religious responsibility. When Bishop Lamy received no reply, he, accompanied by former vicar Juan Ortiz, traveled to Durango for a meeting with Bishop Zubiría and for a further clarification of their respective jurisdictions. Bishop Zubiría faced with the papal document asserting Bishop Lamy's appointment, conceded, promising to inform his priests in New Mexico that they were now responsible to Bishop Lamy. Lamy then returned to Santa Fe. Although Bishop Zubiría could transfer authority, however, he could not transfer allegiance, a fact to which future events would attest. Bishop Lamy went home to continuing difficulties with his recalcitrant New Mexican priests.

During the winter of 1852, Bishop Lamy issued his Christmas pastoral. In this document, the laity were told that they would suffer serious penalties if they did "not contribute generously" to "the upkeep of the Church."[23] Failure to heed the call for tithes, the people were told, would result in the Church's considering them as non-communicants and withholding the sacraments from them.[24] The priests were told that if they failed to enforce the tithing laws they would lose their privilege of saying Mass and administering the sacraments.[25]

The fight between Bishop Lamy and Father Martínez over the tithing regulations and over Lamy's failure to censure Vicar General Machebeuf raged for four years during which time Father Martínez made a terrible nuisance of himself. Finally, however, Father Martínez, who had been unable to make Bishop Lamy concede to any of his demands, offered to step down. Citing old age and ill health, Father Martínez said he would retire on the condition that Bishop Lamy assign a native priest to the Taos parish and that the new priest serve with Father Martínez for a period of time before assuming total responsibility. Bishop Lamy quickly accepted the offer of resignation, but appointed the Spaniard, Father Damaso Taladrid, in Martínez' place.[26]

Father Martínez, who had requested a young priest whom he could train, instead got a haughty, sophisticated Spaniard. Each began undermining the other.[27] Their hostility notwithstanding, Father Martínez continued to say Mass at the Taos church with Father Taladrid's approval.[28] Father Martínez, however, felt that Father Taladrid made it very uncomfortable for him to do so,[29] and, feeling maligned, misunderstood, and mistreated, he built an *oratorio* (a family chapel) in his own home.[30] There, without authorization, he became an independent pastor with his own following. Nor could Father Martínez, let matters rest there. He began publishing open letters in the *Gaceta de Santa Fe* (Santa Fe Gazette) accusing, advising, instructing, and lecturing his superior, Bishop Lamy, as to the proper conduct of his office.[31]

A short time later, Father Martínez requested permission to perform the wedding of his niece, Refugio Martínez, to Pedro Sánchez. Father Taladrid, perhaps as a means of punishing Father Martínez for all the difficulty he had given Bishop Lamy, refused permission. Father Martínez, however, performed the ceremony anyway.[32] This incident first led to Martínez' suspension, and finally to his excommunication during June of 1857.[33] Excommunicated along with Father Martínez was his former student, fellow priest and associate, Father Mariano de Jesus Lucero, pastor at Arroyo Hondo, who assisted Father Martínez in his work.[34]

To add insult to this very grievous injury, Bishop Lamy sent Vicar General Joseph Machebeuf to Taos to tell the parishioners in this village that Antonio José Martínez was no longer of the Church and was to be shunned. The next Sunday, Machebeuf went to Arroyo Hondo where he made the same pronouncements regarding Father Lucero. However, neither the Taosenos nor the Church had heard the last of these apostate priests. Now in total rebellion, the 63-year-old former cleric Antonio José Martínez continued to use the chapel he had built in his home to say Mass and administer the sacraments. Martínez and Lucero, whom Judge Charles Beaubien, Ceran St. Vrain, and Kit Carson, labeled the "Martínez gang," [35] continued to minister to their schismatic parish and to attract a considerable following. The Church would later require that 76 marriages performed by Father Martínez as an excommunicant be revalidated.[36] Although not given as reasons for excommunication, both Fathers Martínez and Lucero may have had common law wives and may have fathered children. Father Martínez' "housekeeper" was Teodora Santisteban y Romero, the daughter of José Romero and María de la Luz Trujillo. The five "Romero" children, with birth dates ranging from 1831 to 1850, are listed on page 443 of Buxton's Early Records.

As Horgan so correctly details, the schism between Father Martínez and Bishop Lamy was an American tragedy, the result of an educated New Mexican native's complete "resistance to foreign authority." Martínez and many of his fellow priests felt that everything Mexican was perceived as wanting, both by Territorial Governor David Meriwether, and by the French prelate, Bishop Jean Baptiste Lamy. Father Martínez, who saw himself as an enlightened man and who was proud of both his Spanish and Mexican heritage, experienced the slights he received as egregious insults and was grievously offended. Martínez could not contain his sense of injustice.[37] He viewed Bishop Lamy as an Anglo, the son of a French peasant, and refused to submit to him. In this sense, it was a clash of cultures. But it was also a clash of temperaments. Martínez, had been and wanted to continue being a master in his own house; he was unable to submit as a servant.[38]

Father Antonio José Martínez, full of outrage to the end, died on July 27, 1867, at the age of 74.[39] He was buried in his own chapel by Father Lucero,[40] who, along with Father Martínez, never accepted Bishop Lamy, the foreigner "who had come to dominate them."[41]

(Jean Baptiste Lamy, made an archbishop in 1875, died on February 13, 1888. Joseph Projectus Machebeuf, made vicar apostolic of Colorado and Utah in 1868, died in 1889.)

16
TWO FAMILIES IN THE THICK OF THINGS

THE BACAS OF SAN MIGUEL, ANTON CHICO, PUERTO DE LUNA AND SANTA ROSA

As previously noted, three of the original *San Miguel del Bado* grantees of 1794 were Diego Baca, **Diego Pedro Manuel Baca** and **Ramón Baca**. They would establish at least three lines of descent for the Bacas at San Miguel and its splinter communities.

José Rafael Albino Baca, born in 1806, was the son of **Diego Pedro Manuel Baca** and Diego's second wife, **María Dolores Leyba**. Albino was a young lad of 15 when the Mexican soldiers escorted William Becknell and his men into San Miguel from the plains. Born a Spaniard, he was to live as a Mexican and die a citizen of the United States, never having lived at any place other than San Miguel. Albino's first marriage on August 28, 1831, was to Teresa Trujillo. He was 25, his wife 19. Two years later, he was a young widower marrying a young widow of 22. She was **María Rosa Altagracia Sena** (the widow of Juan de Dios Sandoval) for whom a community would one day be named. Albino and María Rosa were to have at least three children, Petra, María Gertrudis, and **José Cascelso**, two of whom would marry siblings in a second Baca family, thus doubly cementing their families as *cunados*.

The interrelationships between these various families, Lucero as well as Baca, once the families settled at *San Miguel del Bado*, are truly mind-boggling. (See Charts VI, IX and X.) The intermarriages by the Bacas, for example, constitute a phenomenon repeated in every old New Mexico family. As noted by Chávez in researching his own lineage, certain families tended to form separate groups or clans due to social and regional influences. Both of these latter factors were present in the formation of the Baca clan.

There were, in the 1820s, fewer than 1,000 citizens living in San Miguel and the plazas within the original *San Miguel del Bado* grant. The regional influences for saturation were profound. The social factors influencing these intermarriages were perhaps equally important. These families were of the same social class, and, as one writer put it, "land tended to marry land." One of the *cunados*, noted above, was José Cascelso who was born in 1836 at San Miguel. (The name also appears as Excelso in at least one instance. Celso, the name by which he became known, will be used throughout this discussion.) Celso was a child of 10 when General Stephen Watts Kearny marched through San Miguel on his way to Santa Fe. During this period (1846-1850), Celso was a stockman working with his father. They raised sheep and cattle on the communal grazing lands at the southern reaches of the *San Miguel del Bado* grant where it bordered the decade-old community of *Sangre de Cristo de Antón Chico*.

On December 9, 1851, at the age of 15, Celso married María Sinforiana Baca (I) at San Miguel. Celso and María Sinforiana (I) had at least five children: Rosa, María Ana Celestina, Magdalena, Crescenciano, and **José Placido** who was born on October 5, 1860. The Celso Baca family, like the families of Celso's father and grandfather, lived and ranched at San Miguel where they dealt with the rigors of frontier life on a daily basis. The only outside hostility they had to contend with was an occasional skirmish with the Plains Indians who sought to steal their stock.

CHART IX - Parents of the Third Century, Baca Family

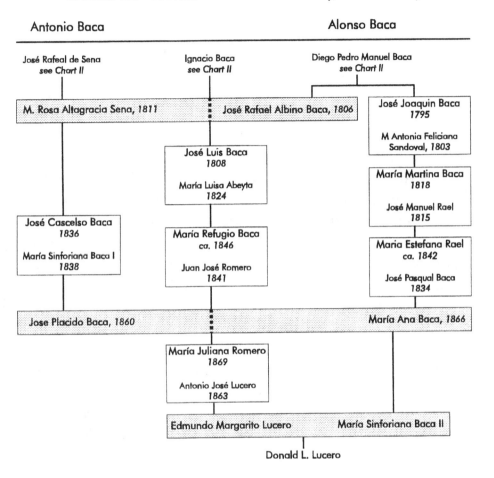

Antonio Baca

Alonso Baca

José Rafeal de Sena
see Chart II

Ignacio Baca
see Chart II

Diego Pedro Manuel Baca
see Chart II

M. Rosa Altagracia Sena, 1811

José Rafael Albino Baca, 1806

José Joaquin Baca
1795

M Antonia Feliciana
Sandoval, 1803

José Luis Baca
1808

María Luisa Abeyta
1824

María Martina Baca
1818

José Manuel Rael
1815

José Cascelso Baca
1836

María Sinforiana Baca I
1838

María Refugio Baca
ca. 1846

Juan José Romero
1841

Maria Estefana Rael
ca. 1842

José Pasqual Baca
1834

Jose Placido Baca, 1860

María Ana Baca, 1866

María Juliana Romero
1869

Antonio José Lucero
1863

Edmundo Margarito Lucero

María Sinforiana Baca II

Donald L. Lucero

At the initiation of the Navajo Wars (1853-1858), the 19-year-old Celso Baca served as a private in the United States army.[1] From 1858 through 1862 he was engaged in freighting merchandise from Independence, Missouri, to New Mexico along the 800-mile route of the Santa Fe Trail.[2] When the American Civil War broke out in 1861, Celso Baca organized a company of soldiers and was commissioned its captain. He served as an officer in Colonel Kit Carson's First Regiment of the New Mexico Volunteers and saw battle at Valverde.[3]

With the Apaches and Navajos precariously established on their reservation in 1864, and the end of the American Civil War reached the next year, Celso Baca, along with others, recognized the potential for financial profit. He wished to obtain government contracts to feed the Apache and Navajo Indians at the *Bosque Redondo* who were as yet unable to feed themselves. He chose for his ranching enterprise an area known as the *Agua Negra* on the Pecos River north of Fort Sumner.

Lying in the cup of a valley at 4,620 feet above sea level, the area of the *Agua Negra* presents interesting surroundings. Circled by purple hills in a semi-desert terrain, the land teems with wildlife: deer, antelope, coyote, fox, badger, and game birds in abundance. The immediate vicinity has many spring-fed lakes, one of which is known as the Blue Hole. A subterranean river feeds this large, seemingly bottomless pool from which more that 3,000 gallons of water flow per minute year-around. It was this grant of approximately 17,000 acres that was given to Antonio Sandoval in 1824. Although Sandoval had been given four times as much land as he had requested, the boundaries of the *Agua Negra* were recognized and firmly established. The *Agua Negra* Land Grant appears to have been on the southwest side of the Pecos near the confluence of this river with El Rito Creek.

The area chosen for settlement by Celso Baca appears to have been on the east side of the Pecos across from the *Agua Negra*. Here, on February 26, 1865, with Marcelino Moya and Lorenzo Bailles, Celso Baca staked a claim to a large portion of the land north and south of present-day Santa Rosa. For his part, Moya selected land which would later become central Santa Rosa, while Bailles took land northwest of the future city.[4] The land taken by all three of these individuals (perhaps under homestead legislation of 1862) appears to have been on the east side of the river in unoccupied territory. The basis on which they laid claim to the land, however, has not been determined. In July of 1854, the United States Congress passed the Homestead Act that allowed any person over 21 years of age to obtain title to 160 acres of public land. The homesteader had to live on the land for four years and improve it.

The Baca, Bailles, and Moya parcels, if obtained under the Homestead Act, would have given the three men a combined area of only 480 acres, hardly enough for a ranch of any note, unless the trio (illegally?) purchased additional homesteads or used the *Agua Negra* for additional pasturage. Encroachment by the trio upon the *Agua Negra*, as subsequent events suggest, may have led to difficulties between the Baca and the Sandoval heirs.

The initial confusion of ownership became more convoluted and chaotic as time went on. At some point, Celso Baca made a claim, and apparently also held title to the *Agua Negra*. One writer has asserted that some years afterwards, in 1884, Baca engaged a José de la Cruz Sandoval (perhaps an heir to the grant) in a fight and beat him to death.[5] Baca is also said to have later lost the deed to the *Agua Negra* in a poker game.[6]

Such assertions regarding Baca and others of his prominence in the old west, however, are fairly common and have become part of their legend. Like Governor Armijo who is alleged to have sold stolen sheep in his climb out of obscurity, Baca is alleged to have been a cattle rustler and a young gun.[7] He was probably neither, possibly both. Most certainly, however, he was an opportunist and an entrepreneur, cagey, crafty and canny.

On June 21, 1860, the United States Congress confirmed Antonio Sandoval's title to the grant. During February of 1877, the grant size was validated at 17,361.11 acres. In 1888, however, the Surveyor General of

New Mexico recommended a reduction in the grant size to 4,438.68 acres due to the initial measurement error of 1824. Nevertheless, secretary of the Interior, Hoke Smith, determined in 1894 that despite the measurement error, the grant could not be reduced below its approximately 17,000 confirmed acres. The owners of the grant in 1896 were R. H. Longwill of Santa Fe; Willie Speigelberg, a wealthy merchant and banker, also of Santa Fe; Lorenzo Labadie of Santa Rosa, a farmer, stock-raiser, and former Indian agent at the *Bosque Redondo*; and Celso Baca. The circumstances of transfer of the grant from its original owner, Antonio Sandoval, to others through the 75-year period, 1824-1909, have yet to be unraveled.[8]

In 1865, the year that don Celso Baca came from San Miguel to the area of the *Agua Negra*, he began construction of his home on land east of the Pecos River. The home, still in existence, was of one story, with adobe walls sixteen inches thick. The home is made up of four enormous rooms, each connecting off a central foyer with a hallway running from the front of the house to the back. So enormous were the rooms, notes an early traveler, that one room was large enough to accommodate a double bed placed in each of its four corners and still have room to spare. On the front and north side of the house was a porch; in the back, accessible from the rear door of the central hallway, was a stone corral. Eave troughs carried water from the corrugated tin roof to a cistern in the corral immediately behind the kitchen. Outside the corral, stood a large beehive adobe oven that the family used for baking. With enormous *vigas* (logs used as joists) supporting the roof, and with its wide-planked floors, it was not a stately mansion by Eastern standards. It was, however, one of the more impressive homes on the western frontier.[9] His home the center of his wide sphere of business influence, don Celso Baca became a man to reckon with.

During the period of its existence, the area of the Baca ranch became known as Eden. What made it Eden, at least to the Bacas, were its beauty and their lives as centered around the home of Celso Baca. The Baca home was the stagecoach stop for the firm of Eugenio Romero Freight and Transfer of Las Vegas as the stage traveled from Las Vegas to *Las Placitas del Río Bonito* (the Little Plazas of the Beautiful River), later known as Lincoln).[10] It was, perhaps, in the "flat-bottomed rig with a fringed canopy top and three seats," that Olive Smith Wiley, author of *A Santa Rosa Story*, made her 1901 trip from Las Vegas to Santa Rosa. She and her grandmother, like many other early travelers of the era, spent their first night in Santa Rosa in the home of Celso Baca.[11] The Baca home was also used as the first church in the area and was rented out for all sorts of public and private events. Celebrations for each of life's passages were staged here: baptisms, confirmations, first communions, weddings, and even some wakes,[12] hosted by the Bacas with the assistance of their *criadas* (servants), doña Rosario and *La Chica*. Anyone of note who visited the area stayed in the Baca home and it was most certainly the centerpoint of life in that area of the country.[13]

With the assistance of a *mayordomo*, the several *caporales* (overseers), and numerous *empleados* (employees), required to operate such an extensive ranch, don Celso Baca ran large herds of both cattle and sheep.[14] Moreover, he constantly searched for ways to widen his sphere of influence. Around 1900, the area of the *Agua Negra* saw an influx of workers who were engaged in laying track for the combined Chicago, Rock Island & Pacific and El Paso and Northeastern Railroads which were approaching the Baca ranch. These workers lived in a tent city and required goods and services. With a town of essentially landless individuals growing in his midst, don Celso opened a butcher shop and placed his younger son, Crescenciano, in charge. For his older son, Placido, however, he had grander designs. He put Placido in charge of the Baca mercantile store and also made him the postmaster and notary public. In 1898, the family started the area's first newspaper, *La Voz Publica* (The Public Voice),[15] as well, and this, too, don Celso gave to Placido. In addition to all of the enterprises directly run by the family, the Bacas also built a facility beside their home which they leased to a firm that operated as the Meline and Eakins Liquor Wholesale and Tobacco Warehouse.[16] Although only the lessor, don Celso was instrumental in selecting William Metzgar as manager and proceeded to involve himself in all aspects of the business. Thus, the Baca family owned, or had control of, the press, the stagecoach stop, the hotel, the community meetinghouse, the mercantile store, the butcher shop, the post office, the notary, and the liquor and tobacco outlet. Having established this extensive empire, don Celso was the *tata* (literally, grandfather) of the village in every sense of the word. He had his finger on the pulse of the community, led it by its arm, and, some would say, had his hand in its collective pocket.

Taking advantage of the fact that he was in an area surrounded by a great number of spring-fed lakes, Celso Baca had one of these springs diverted to water his extensive orchards. When the water was not needed for irrigation, it was further diverted to an area south and east of its irrigation canal where it created a large shallow lake in front of the Celso Baca home.[17] Celso even owned his own carousel, brought by wagon from Chihuahua. On weekends he, his children, and grandchildren, with his peacocks scattering in their wake, would walk to a spot on the El Rito Creek where springs formed a wonderful bathing spot. Here the family would bathe, lie in the grass, and enjoy the fruits of their labors.[18] These activities and surroundings—although spare and Spartan by modern standards—identified the Bacas' life on the frontier as one of privilege.

Although the Celso Baca home was used as the first church in the area, Baca sought to establish more appropriate quarters for religious services. During 1868, it is believed, he began the construction of a chapel which he built across the street from the front of his home. The name of the chapel, *La Capilla de Santa Rosa de Lima* (The Chapel of St. Rose of Lima), was chosen to honor his mother, María Rosa Altagracia Sena Baca, and Isabella de Flores, known to the world as St. Rose of Lima, first canonized saint in the New World.[19] In the dedication of the chapel, don Celso placed on the altar an old statue of St. Rose of Lima which had been brought over the Chihuahua Trail to his home on the Pecos.[20] The chapel became the center of all religious services in the area and, as the center of these activities, lent its name to the community which was beginning to grow around the Baca ranch. The use of the Baca chapel as the communal church continued until 1907 when it could no longer accommodate the growing community.[21]

In 1891, don Celso, a prominent Republican, led the effort to carve Guadalupe County out of the southern reaches of San Miguel County. This effort led to legislative approval and executive confirmation by 1893.[22] In 1896, don Celso was a delegate to the national convention which nominated William McKinley for the presidency.[23] In addition to pursing his many business interests, don Celso also served his new county as territorial senator and representative for several separate terms.[24]

Between 1901 and 1905, don Celso, who held an interest in the First National Bank of Santa Rosa,[25] purchased all of the Marcelino Moya land holdings. He began to divide these, along with those portions of his own ranch that bordered on the village, into homesites for consumptives seeking a healthful environment and to accommodate the remaining railroad workers who were in the community to build operational facilities for the railroad.[26] Although these facilities were originally to be constructed in Eden, now known as Santa Rosa, the railroad quickly moved its roundhouse and turntable to Tucumcari due to the high brine content of the water in Santa Rosa. Despite the move of the railroad facilities, however, Santa Rosa, which came to be known as the city of natural lakes, developed into one of southeastern New Mexico's major trade centers through the efforts of don Celso Baca. Perhaps to a greater degree than most New Mexicans, don Celso Baca was rightfully considered "a patriarch among his people . . . " When he died on May 20, 1909, he was buried beneath the floor of the family chapel.[27]

Although both Placido and his brother Crescenciano Baca were greatly overshadowed by the rotund figure of their father, don Celso, they too were to lead full and interesting lives on the frontier. They grew up in the big house near the confluence of the El Rito Creek and the Pecos River. They attended a private Catholic boys' secondary school and college in Las Vegas conducted by the Jesuits[28] and like each of their forebears, at least initially, lived the lives of stockmen.

Placido was 18 when the rancher John Tunstall was killed and the Lincoln County War began. It is likely that he and all the residents of Santa Rosa knew Billy (the Kid) Bonney, one of the principals in the cattle war.

Bonney, who according to family tradition once ate at the Celso Baca home, would have been just one of many cattle buyers, ranchers, and politicians who sat in don Celso's *sala* to conduct business. Of much more importance than Bonney, however, was former U.S. Vice-president, Levi P. Morton (vice president for Benjamin Harrison, 1889-1893) who represented the railroad in its negotiations with don Celso and his brother-in-law, Benigno Jaramillo, for the purchase of their lands.[29] Placido Baca, Celso's oldest son, must have experienced mixed feelings regarding the sale of the ranch. Along with its surrounding area, the ranch constituted his only home of memory. He had come to the area of Eden from San Miguel or Antón Chico when he was five. It is likely that he believed that some portion of the ranch would someday be his. Now, however, with the sale of the ranch, he diverted his interests to other pursuits.

On November 27, 1882, just a year after Sheriff Pat Garrett killed Billy the Kid in a house near Ft Sumner some 49 miles south of the Celso Baca home, **Placido** married **María Ana Baca** of Antón Chico. María Ana was the daughter of **José Pascual Baca** and **María Estephana Rael**. When the marriage investigation was conducted prior to the publication of the banns, it was determined that Placido and María Ana were fourth cousins, and the couple had to obtain a dispensation to marry. After their marriage, Placido and María Ana initially made their home in the community of Puerto de Luna on the Pecos, just south of the Baca ranch and 11 miles southeast of Santa Rosa. The Puerto de Luna townsite, which appears to have been owned by Melquiades Ramírez and settled about 1862[30] was the Placido Baca home through at least 1897. Two of the Baca children, both named María Guadalupe, were born there in 1895 and 1897. (Neither of these children lived to adulthood.) It was here, too, that don Placido Baca and don Crescenciano Gonzáles founded Placido's second newspaper, the Puerto de Luna News.[31]

Eventually, however, the Placido Baca family, with their *criada*, Rafelita, moved to Santa Rosa where they had at least seven more children: Antonio, Pelagia, Pablo, Rosa, Anita, María Eugenia, and **María Sinforiana Baca** (II) born in 1902.[32]

Although still a gentleman of some privilege, Placido established his own reputation as a prominent and contributing member of each of the communities in which he lived. He was one of the county commissioners appointed by the governor upon the organization of Guadalupe County in 1893. [33] He then served as sheriff in Guadalupe County from 1897 through 1900. During his second term in 1898, he assisted in the capture of a gang of outlaws who had killed a townsman.[34] He also held several other political positions while living in Santa Rosa. He first served a four-year term as deputy county treasurer. Next, he served two years as deputy county clerk followed by two years as county school superintendent. He subsequently held the office of deputy county assessor.[35] Placido, his father, and brother, Crescenciano, continued through 1909 to involve themselves in their community and in the Territory's halting march toward statehood.

THE LUCEROS OF SAN MIGUEL, PUERTOCITO, LAGUNITA/ CHUPADEROS, AND LAS VEGAS

When the aged **Miguel Antonio Lucero** married Guadalupe Martín in 1827, Miguel Antonio's son, **Lorenzo Manuel** was 43, Lorenzo's wife, **María Teresa García**, a young 25. The latter couple had been married by Father Francisco Bragado at the Santa Clara Mission on October 29, 1812, and had apparently come to *San Miguel del Bado* sometime after 1818. Lorenzo and Teresa had at least 10 children, two of whom were **José Pablo** and María Juana Lucero. María Juana, born in 1826, was to be part of the first Lucero-Baca union since those that occurred between the two families in the *Río Abajo* during the previous century. María Juana, widow of José María Herrera, married José Francisco Baca on December 20, 1841, at *San Miguel del Bado*. José Francisco was the son of **José Ramón Baca** and **María Alfonsa Martínez**. José Francisco's brother, **Juan de Jesus**, was in the main line of the Lucero-Bacas that is being followed in this history. (Juan de Jesus and a third brother, José Crescenciano Baca, also married Luceros. These brothers married **María Ramona** and María Buenaventura Lucero, the daughters of **José Miguel Lucero** and **María**

Ramona Angela Gonzáles. The family line involving the second Miguel Lucero at San Miguel is not being followed in this study.)

Born in 1834, **José Pablo Lucero**, the second of the two Lucero siblings noted above, was seven when scattered groups of Texans were housed at San Miguel in the aftermath of the ill-fated Texas-Santa Fe Expedition. If he were not involved in teasing the prisoners or bringing them things to eat, José Pablo was probably at home helping to work the family ranch. For the most part, children knew their place and required little direction. José Pablo would have helped in cutting and gathering wood, drawing water, and tending stock, for such was the life of the *ganadero* (cattleman), and he had been born to it. Along with his five brothers, he must have worked with his father within the Pecos valley and beyond, herding cattle and sheep and trying to keep them and himself out of harm's way.

In 1855, **José Pablo** then 21, married the 13-year-old **María Manuela Salazar** in the church at *San Miguel del Bado*. When he married, José Pablo, like his father and grandfather, lived at Puertocito. María Manuela was the daughter of **Rafael Salazar** and **María Antonia Ribera y Sena**, who, like Miguel Antonio and Lorenzo Manuel Lucero, had come to San Miguel from Chama where the Luceros and Salazars undoubtedly had known each other.

When José Pablo and María Manuela were married in San Miguel, Juan Sena and Marcelino Moya witnessed their marriage. Don Marcelino, who later joined don Celso Baca in establishing a ranching enterprise at Santa Rosa, was apparently also closely associated with the Luceros at Puertocito. In 1838 Moya had also witnessed the marriage of the aforementioned María Juana Lucero to José María Herrera at San Miguel del Bado. Although Moya does not appear to have been a blood relative of either the Baca or Lucero families, he may also have been involved in business pursuits with the Luceros as he was with the Bacas.

CHART X - Parents of the Third and Fourth Centuries, Lucero

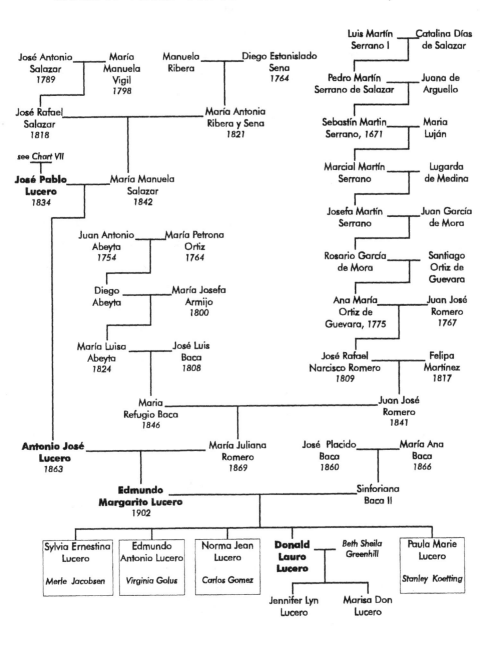

At the time of their marriage, José Pablo and María Manuela lived at Puertocito. Constantly in search of new grazing land, however, the family moved to, and, in fact, may have founded, the splinter community of Lagunita in a river valley adjacent to that of the Pecos. At Lagunita, the José Pablo Luceros built their home on the south bank of the *Cañada de los Tres Hermanos*, a stream only slightly smaller than the Pecos, named for Cipriano Aguilar, Gregorio Zamora and Pantelon Sandoval. Here they established a ranch sited a hundred or so feet above the riverbank.

The area occupied by the José Pablo Lucero ranch became known as Chupaderos,[36] named for the springs from which the ranch drew its water. Here José Pablo and María Manuela, with the assistance of their Indian maid, Andrea, raised a family of four boys and two girls: **Antonio José**, Bonifacio, Lorenzo, Eloy, Francisquita and Florida. We know a little about what life was like for the children of this family from a vignette written by Antonio José sometime after the turn of the century. Antonio, born in 1863, received his elementary education in a one-room schoolhouse either in Lagunita or in a sister community to which the children of the family had to ride on horseback. In the winter, their ride was encumbered somewhat by the requirement that each child bring a log to burn in the school's stove so the building would be heated. Cleofas Jaramillo, author of *Shadows of the Past*, noted the same requirement for her grandfather, Jesus María Lucero, a contemporary of José Pablo Lucero. Obviously, the times required the children's involvement in many of the mundane aspects of providing for their education from bringing in fresh drinking water, to carting one's own chair to school to perhaps even killing rattlesnakes in the school yard.[37]

* * *

The descent of Cleofas Martín Jaramillo from Pedro Lucero de Godoy, demonstrates quite clearly the regional saturation by old New Mexico families. Each of Cleofas' parents (and one of her husband's parents) descends from three Lucero siblings: Jesus María, María Salome and María Manuela Lucero. Their grandparents were the children of Diego Antonio Lucero and Guadalupe Valdes y Trujillo. Diego and Guadalupe had a large and prominent family. In an article that appeared in the *Santa Fe New Mexican* on January 12, 1910, the family is described as "remarkable" by virtue of their wealth. In speaking of four of its daughters, María Manuela, María Cleofas, María Salome, and María Magdalena, the author states, ". . . It has often been said that the four daughters of don Diego Lucero made the wealthiest marriages of their generation in New Mexico."[38] Don Gaspar Street in Santa Fe is named for María Magdalena's husband, don Gaspar Ortiz.[39]

* * *

Despite the difficulties involved in receiving an education in these isolated communities, Antonio José's basic education was apparently a good one. Antonio appears to have been a quick and bright child intent on preparing himself for bigger and better things.

In 1874, or shortly thereafter, Antonio, now 11, began attending a private Catholic boys' school conducted by a group of Italian Jesuits in Las Vegas. Two private citizens of Las Vegas who offered them the use of two houses as a school had lured the men of this order away from Bernalillo. The Jesuit school opened in 1874 in the *Casa Redonda* (Round House; actually, in this case, a *plazuela*) owned by Manuel Romero. The Bacas, Placido and Cescenciano appear to have received room and board in a private home while attending school here. Antonio and his siblings made a change of residence. They moved to Las Vegas with their mother to attend school. She took in sewing to supplement their income while her husband maintained the ranch.[40]

The curriculum, which focused on languages, was demanding, and the Jesuits were tough taskmasters. Elementary and advanced classes were offered in reading, writing, geography, arithmetic, bookkeeping, music, English, Spanish, French, Italian, and Latin. In 1877 the Jesuits began offering studies at the college level and Antonio entered the Jesuit College in a new adobe building on *La Calle de la Acequia* (Ditch Street, later called Gonzáles Street for don Jesus Gonzáles) constructed expressly for its use. He graduated from this institution in 1885 at age 22.

L as Vegas homes in 1862 were simple and sparse by our standards. Ovando Hollister described one in this way:

> Very neat and cozy, the walls nicely whitewashed; the fireplaces small and handy, shaped like the half of an old fashioned bee-hive with a small flue leading out for the chimney. Mattresses rolled up in day into a settee around the walls. A table, stools, skillet, coffee pot comprises the furniture. The ornaments, even among the best class, consist wholly of ordinary prints of sacred subjects mounted in tin frames, and images of saints roughly carved in wood.[41]

The Las Vegas, in which the 11-year-old Antonio lived in 1874, had become quite a community. Founded in 1835 and pushed into prominence by the Santa Fe Trail, it became a community of importance with the opening in 1851 of Fort Union, the departmental headquarters and principal supply depot for the United States Army in the Southwest. Fort Union's presence at *Los Posos* (water holes)[42] on the territory's eastern frontier, twenty-six miles north of Las Vegas, enabled many Las Vegas merchants to make handsome profits by supplying the fort with beef, mutton, timber and wheat.

The fort was also in place to help solve the "Indian problem" and its presence brought a measure of peace to the communities in its midst. The army, using the fort as a staging area, carried the war against the Indians to the Apaches, Utes, Kiowas, and Comanches, in the campaigns of 1854, 1855, 1860, and 1861. Although none of these campaigns achieved great success, they tended to push the Plains Indians away from centralized villages like Las Vegas, assuring the villagers some measure of safety from Indian attack. One of the fort's functions in the area was to prevent attacks such as the following two that occurred in 1850. During that year, while the General Assembly was arguing whether or not to seat Diego Archuleta, a group of Indians attacked a party of travelers on the Santa Fe Trail at

Santa Clara, or Wagon Mound, northeast of Las Vegas. Killed in this attack were eleven persons, seven of whom were members of the Brown party who had previously lost all their mules in a snowstorm.[43] During the same year, the first coach of the mail and stage line from Independence, Missouri, to Santa Fe was attacked in the same area. In this attack the Indians burned the coach and killed the driver and guards.[44]

Besides the seemingly endless caravans that arrived in Las Vegas every year from Independence and St. Louis, farmers and ranchers from the outlying areas used the community as a place of central storage and supply, and the community prospered as a result.

If Antonio Lucero was in Las Vegas on July 4, 1879, he witnessed the event that was to transform the small village into even greater prominence. On this date, the Atchison, Topeka and Santa Fe Railroad entered the town. The scene in Las Vegas upon the entry of the first locomotive was a sight never to be witnessed again in New Mexico. Previously, as the Santa Fe Trail wagons had entered the plaza in Las Vegas, the townspeople had met them with cheers of, "*Los Americanos! Los carros! La entrada de la caravana!*" (The Americans! The carts! The entrance of the caravan!) The wagoneers, for their part, vied with one another in making the most noise by cracking their whips. The sound of these cracking whips was now replaced by the puffing and belching of *El Diablo* (The Devil), the name the villagers of Las Vegas gave to the first locomotive. The tumult provided by the citizenry, however, was no less deafening than it had been at the entry of the wagons. Spectators had come from as far as 200 miles away to see the first train come into town.[45] These people and their wagons covered the hills all around, each vying with one another for an unobstructed view, although many were afraid to approach too closely. Perhaps the 16-year-old Antonio Lucero, along with his parents and the rest of his family, was among those sitting on a hillside waving their hats and cheering as *El Diablo* began its long descent into town from the northern plains.

From a population of approximately 1,000 in 1860, Las Vegas grew into a community of 4,000 by 1880 and 6,000 by 1882. Las Vegas, like Albuquerque, its sister city to the southwest, also had the railroad by

1881 and both communities were growing by leaps and bounds. Not all the growth was positive, however.

During August of 1879, the tubercular ex-dentist and gambler, John Henry "Doc" Holliday arrived from Dodge City and bought a saloon on Center Street in Las Vegas. Unable to leave his Dodge City past behind, however, Holliday was soon confronted by an old antagonist whom he killed. Holliday then successfully evaded the law in Las Vegas and fled back to Dodge City.[46]

During July of the same year, both Billy the Kid and Jesse James came to Las Vegas to enjoy the baths at the Montezuma Hot Springs Hotel north of the village. Although on these occasions both outlaws were quiet, it was not always to be so.[47] Just a year later, Sheriff Pat Garrett of Lincoln County headed a posse that trapped several outlaws at Stinking Springs in present de Baca County, engaging them in a day-long gun battle there. Garrett killed Charley Bowdre and captured Billy Wilson, Dave Rudabaugh, Tom Pickett, and Billy the Kid. These captured men were jailed briefly in Las Vegas before Billy the Kid was transferred to Santa Fe.[48] Worse than Holliday, James, and Billy the Kid, however, was Vicente Silva.

Vicente Silva arrived in Las Vegas in 1875. Silva, like Doc Holliday, first entered Las Vegas as a legitimate businessman. He was the owner of the Imperial Bar off the plaza in Las Vegas. Soon, however, he became the head of a group of robbers and cattle rustlers. The Silva gang claimed to be a member of a second group named the People's Party. When Patricio Maés attempted to resign from the party, the Silva gang held a mock trial in which Maés was accused of planning to betray its illegal activities to the authorities. Maés was first arraigned and then executed by hanging.

The gang next killed Gabriel Sandoval, brother-in-law of Vicente Silva, who was also suspected of having betrayed them. Sandoval's body was dumped into the pit of an outdoor privy where it remained until it was discovered several months later. After this murder, Silva and his men went into hiding in the little village of Los Alamos, 13 miles northeast of Las Vegas.

Having killed his wife's brother, Gabriel Sandoval, Silva now feared that his wife, Telesfora, would betray him. Silva had the couple's adopted daughter, Emma, kidnapped to induce his wife to confer with him at his lair in Los Alamos. Successful in luring his wife to his hideout, Silva killed her and then proceeded to bury her body in an *arroyo* (dry water bed).

With all these retributions and reprisals, each of the men in Silva's gang must have wondered which of them was next. Seeing no end in sight, the men decided to kill Silva and bury him along with his wife.[49] With Silva's death and the incarceration of some of its key gang members, this violent chapter in the history of Las Vegas was ended.[50]

At least four gang members were Luceros, perhaps residents of Las Vegas or of a second community named Los Luceros, located seven miles northeast of Mora. One of these Lucero bandits was Cecilio who was lynched by a mob in Las Vegas during 1893 for the atrocious murders of his cousin, Benigno Martínez, and a second individual named Juan Gallegos. Lucero shot and killed these individuals, smashed their heads with a rock, then tied them to a team of burros and dragged them across the plains. The motivation for these brutal murders is unclear, but may have been related to Lucero's foiled attempt to steal sheep from his cousin.[51] Cecilio's descent from Pedro has not been determined.

While the men of the Silva gang were clearly outlaws who engaged in all kinds of illegal activities, there were other men during this period who could not be so definitely categorized. These men considered themselves upstanding citizens, but became outlaws through their attempts to seek redress for nagging grievances. These men were the *Gorras Blancas*, the white-hooded nightriders in Las Vegas who destroyed the fences of homesteaders and squatters who, they felt, were bent on stealing their land. Their grievances, which began about 1846, dragged on for over 50 years. Their struggle, which was the struggle for Las Vegas, was to provide Las Vegans with their most difficult conflicts through 1912.

If the land grants on the Pecos (claimed by Celso Baca in 1865) were a picture of confusion, the land grants of 1823 and 1835 in Las Vegas were a panorama of chaos. The Las Vegas land grants deserve their own study and are beyond the scope of this book. They present, however, a picture in microcosm of what was happening with land grants throughout the New Mexico Territory in the period from 1846 to 1912. Perrigo, who presents an excellent synopsis of the confusion and terror that gripped Las Vegas in the protracted struggle for the Las Vegas grants, suggests that difficulties centered on several key issues.

The initial grant at Las Vegas embodied 496,446.96 acres with rather clear boundaries: the Sapello River on the north, the *San Miguel del Bado* Grant on the south, the Pecos Mountains in the west, and the less distinct grant of Antonio Ortiz and the "watering place of the mare" on the east.[52] This initial grant was made to Luis C. de Baca in 1823. The next year, perhaps inappropriately, 65,000 acres of the C. de Baca grant contiguous to San Miguel's northern boundary, were given to Salvador Montoya and others as the Tecolote Land Grant.[53] At some point between 1823 and 1835, Luis C. de Baca departed from the area and his land (without the Tecolote piece) was re-awarded to a secondary group of 29 grantees from the community of *San Miguel del Bado*. Very soon thereafter, an additional 118 settlers were added to the original group for a total of 155 families.[54] By 1846, close to 6,000 acres of the Las Vegas grant had been distributed as homesteads, and the population of Las Vegas and its splinter *placitas* numbered approximately 1550.[55] (By 1890 there were at least 30 splinter communities three of which existed in the six miles between west Las Vegas and the hot springs. These were *Plaza de Arriba* [Upper Town], *Plaza Vigil* and *Plaza Llano*. Untold others were in existence by 1912.) The undistributed portion of the enormous grant was held in common by these 155 settlers and was used for grazing sheep and cattle. Then the heirs of Luis C. de Baca appeared on the scene asking for their land.

In 1858, the surveyor-general of the United States, after reviewing Mexican documents regarding the C. de Baca and Las Vegas grants of 1823 and 1835, concluded that both grants were valid. Rather than dispossess the 1,500 people residing on the grant, however, the United States Congress decided to award five tracts, each of 100,000 acres, to the heirs of Luis C. de Baca. These tracts were in locations in the New Mexico Territory where the land was as yet undistributed.[56] Although this took care of the C. de Baca claim it created a new problem. In confirming the claim to the Las Vegas grant, the United States Congress named the Town of Las Vegas trustee for the Las Vegas Grant of 1835. There was, however, no legal entity known as the "Town of Las Vegas." The village of Las Vegas had by 1888 become two communities: the old village surrounding the plaza on the west side of the Gallinas River and the new village which had grown up on the east side of the Gallinas since the advent of the railroad in 1879. This latter village, or new town, had in 1888 been incorporated as the City of Las Vegas and could not, therefore, assert its claim as trustee. (The "City" was re-incorporated in 1895.)

The United States Congress in 1860 secured approval for the Las Vegas grant of 1835.[57] Incredibly, through the subsequent 43 years there was no legal entity to act as trustee for the Las Vegas grant although group after group stepped forward to assert this claim. During this 43-year period, chaos reigned supreme. In the 1880's, for example, a group of 80 Las Vegans, acting on behalf of approximately 800 original grantees and their heirs, determined that the 400,000 or so acres of the grant should be divided among the 800, giving each settler 500 acres a piece. Once the group made this determination, its members began to stake their claims and even to sell the imaginary parcels. In a four-year period alone, at least forty shares of the common land were sold, intensifying the chaos.[58]

On April 26, 1889, desperate villagers rose in rebellion. These villagers, as noted previously, who were to become known as the *Gorras Blancas*, (White Caps) decided they would use every means at their disposal to sabotage the efforts by both legitimate homesteaders and squatters to carve up the land held in common by the Las Vegas grantees.[59] These white-hooded riders cut barbed wire fences, broke fence posts, burned hay stacks and illegally cut railroad ties in their campaign of intimidation. When a grand jury was assembled to bring indictments against the perpetrators, 63 of the *Gorras Blancas* rode around the court house and past the home of the prosecuting attorney.[60] They broke windows at the new court house, congregated in enormous numbers (as many as 300 on one occasion), and rode through the streets firing pistols in the air and intimidating everyone.

The owner and editors of the influential newspaper, *La Voz del Pueblo* (The People's Voice), supported the intent if not the activities of the White Caps. The illegal activities of this group continued unabated until condemned in 1891 by the respected Jesuit newspaper, the *Revista Catolica* (the Catholic Journal). Although the White Caps did succeed in slowing the partition of the common lands, the disposition of the Las Vegas Grant remained unresolved.

Finally, in 1902, District Judge William J. Mills appointed a commission called the "Board of Trustees of the Town of Las Vegas." This Land Grant Board was reconfirmed by an act of the Territorial Legislature on March 22, 1903,[61] and set upon the business of determining land ownership. First, it had the grant surveyed and fought off an attempt by West Las Vegas to incorporate as a town to obtain the grant. The board appears to have set three goals for itself, two of which were in opposition to one another. The first objective was to secure title to family plots for the original grantees and their heirs. The board also wanted to retain common grazing land, but at the same time it wished to keep the land open for further colonization. These last two contradictory goals led to extreme difficulties for the grantees.

Although, many landholders were to lose out in the determinations made by the land grant board, it does not seem that the board's initial decisions, or the parameters it set for its judgments, could have been more equitable.

When the grant was awarded in 1835, the original grantees had each received a certificate (called a *hijuela*) acknowledging their share in it. Recognizing that few of the original settlers or their heirs would be able to produce this document, however, the board provided an alternative way for them to prove their land ownership. It was declared that if the "homesteader" could produce a surveyor's description of his land and an affidavit that he had occupied it for 10 or more years, he would be granted title. No homesteader, however, would be given title to more than 160 acres, a limit apparently suggested by the Homestead Act of 1862. The homesteader, though, if he were able, would be allowed to buy an additional 160 acres. In addition, all the unoccupied grazing land would be held in common for use by the homesteaders whose claims were validated in 1903. No one person could graze more than 4,000 sheep and 400 cattle, and the common watering places were to be kept open.[62]

Although, equitable, these approaches caused some bitterness among those who claimed larger tracts of land. The size of the tracts (up to 320 acres) was small. The grantees had wanted 500 acres and probably needed 5,000 for the ranching enterprises they sought. However, as long as there was common grazing land and an adequate water supply they would be able to make do.

Up until 1906, the board refused to consider offers by individuals or corporations to purchase tracts larger than 160 acres. Nevertheless, it had allowed some claimants to pay for disputed land which in actuality legitimized some awards of several thousands of acres.[63] The board had, however, by the manner in which it conducted its business, respected the allocation of land to individuals and to the community at large. Now, it sought to uphold the third principle of the Spanish and Mexican land grants, that land should be available for further colonization.

Unfortunately, the board's adherence to this principle would eventually lead to the grant's inability to support its settlers. While many recognized that the decisions of the board would lead to this conclusion (as future events would demonstrate) they appeared unable to stop it.

THE WATERING PLACE OF THE MARE

On April 6, 1906, a speculator named A. W. Thompson requested 50,000 acres of land for "colonization."[64] He made a contract with the board to pay $1.25 an acre with a down payment of $10,000. His intention was to sell the land to others for small farms. Less than four months after the initial sale, Thompson transferred his contract to Ira G. Hazzard who told the board that he would pay $1.75 an acre. Hazzard immediately sold 2,000 acres to individuals outside the grant at $6.00 an acre. By November of 1906, Hazzard had sold 19,000 acres. He then transferred his interests to Fred W. Browne who offered to buy more land from the board. The board sold him an additional 100,000 acres at $1.50 an acre with a down payment of only $2,000. Browne's contract stipulated that he settle 75 families on the land. As soon as he did so, he took option on more land.[65]

In the meantime, the Hispanic settlers seemed helpless to stop the board's speculation with their land, speculation that was particularly galling since they derived no benefit from it. The settlers tried unsuccessfully to stop the sales. They also tried and failed to have the board abolished. A monster had been created and, seemingly, it could not be killed.

Speculators sold small farms to families who settled on the eastern plains (known as the "*mesa*"). Initially, these farms were very productive, but because they were "dry" farms (without irrigation), the production soon dropped off. The land on the *mesa* was appropriate for ranching, not for farming, and yet the sales went on and on until 1920 when they began to decline significantly.

During the period 1903-1920, the board settled the claims of 800 settlers and awarded them a total of 17,000 acres. Initially, the board had no money with which to pay its legal fees. Therefore, while it was granting 17,000 acres to 800 families, it paid 26,800 acres to five individuals for services to the board.[66] By 1931 the board had distributed 402,962.9 acres of the original grant for which it had received about $600,000. Approximately half of the proceeds from land sales, grazing leases, and royalties for permits to cut timber had been used for salaries, attorney's fees, taxes, fire-fighting costs and the personal expenses of the board members. The land was gone and, unfortunately, so was most of the money. (The board used some of its proceeds to fund an irrigation project on the northern reaches of the grant. This project, conceived about 1900, ultimately produced a dam to contain the floodwaters from the Sanguiluela Creek, the Sapello and Gallinas Rivers, and the Pecos Arroyo. This irrigation project, which benefited few, if any, of the 1903 residents, was completed in 1921.)[67]

Although it has been alleged that "the board" was Anglo in makeup and bent on giving away the land, the first part of this perception at least is not accurate. Membership on the board was fairly stable, with several prominent Hispanics a party to each of its deliberations. The members met often, worked hard, wrestled with the extremely difficult issues of land ownership and were themselves, except for its secretary who received 2,560 acres in 1905, paid very little.[68] None appears to have profited materially from the sale of the land. The benefit to them, if there was one, may have been in creating a larger community with a more highly charged economic atmosphere. Whatever its motive, however, by its adherence to the principle that the grant remain open to further colonization, the board contributed greatly to the rapid decline of the villages on the Las Vegas grant. In retrospect, while also supporting colonization, the board should have secured an adequate watershed and pasturage for each of its villages. It is likely, however, that no matter what it did, it could not have prevented the eventual decline of the ability of these villages to support themselves. A determination was eventually made that the primary use of water from the Gallinas River was for domestic and public consumption. Water for agricultural use thus became secondary and in some cases ended altogether. But in the final analysis, the over-grazing, the excessive cutting of timber, and the division of land among its many heirs spelled the villages' doom. These shortsighted behaviors would have depleted resources and resulted in the loss of productivity and the eventual demise of some of these villages no matter what decisions the land grant board made along the way. Las Vegas itself, the economic hub of the splinter communities, would survive, but many of the lovely mountain villages sank unwillingly and sadly into extinction.

The protracted struggle for the Las Vegas land grants continued through the period of 1860 to 1903 and beyond, during which time Las Vegas was a very difficult community in which to live. Through the waning years of this conflict (1874-1885), Antonio Lucero attended the Jesuit school, finishing his collegiate studies in 1885. Amid the chaos created by the likes of Billy the Kid, Vicente Silva, and the *Gorras Blancas*, **Antonio Lucero** met and married **María Juliana Romero**, daughter of **Juan Romero** and **Refugio Baca** of lower Las Vegas (a community now known as Romeroville). After their marriage on April 8, 1893, the couple remained in Las Vegas where Antonio embarked on an interesting and distinguished career. By training, a printer, he became associate editor and secretary of a newspaper that began operation in Las Vegas about 1890.[69] The newspaper, *La Voz del Pueblo*, appears to have moved from Santa Fe to Las Vegas during June of 1890. First titled *El Abogado del Estado de Nuevo Mexico* (The Solicitor of the State of New Mexico), the newspaper, which had the largest circulation of any paper in the Territory,[70] was a strong advocate of democratic reform and served as a literary forum for its editors. In his work with this newspaper, don Antonio Lucero became closely associated with its publisher, don Felix Martínez, and his associate editor and former schoolmate at the Jesuit College, don Ezequiel C. de Baca. Each of the three was to play a prominent role in local, territorial and state government.[71]

In 1894-95, Antonio Lucero was a captain in the territorial militia. The *Gorras Blancas* had ceased their activities, but the Las Vegas land question remained unresolved. Antonio's interests were often urbane and academic, sometimes political. He, along with don Ezequiel C. de Baca and others, belonged to a *tertulia*, an educational circle, which met for the purpose of literary discourse and debate. He also participated in a second organization whose purpose was to make it financially possible for gifted but poor students to pursue appropriate education.[72]

During the 1896 presidential campaign, don Antonio, a gifted linguist, served as an interpreter for the famed orator and presidential hopeful William Jennings Bryan in his tour of New Mexico.[73] During this same year, the construction of a university was initiated in Las Vegas. Antonio Lucero, then an instructor of Spanish at East Las Vegas High School, later became a professor of Spanish at the educational facility, first called the New Mexico Normal and later Highlands University. He also worked as an interpreter for the courts, was elected to the territorial legislature, and was one of Las Vegas' leading citizens.

17
STATEHOOD, 1912

THE LONG MARCH TOWARDS STATEHOOD

I n its march toward statehood, New Mexico had walked like a man trying to stride confidently through life with his shoelaces tied together. The Treaty of Guadalupe Hidalgo of 1848 had provided for admission of the Territory to the Union "at the proper time." The question was—when was the proper time? Between 1848 and 1903, New Mexico made 15 bids for statehood, each of which was denied, while newer territories continued to be admitted at every juncture.[1] Statehood appeared out of reach for New Mexico.

When all other approaches failed, the people of New Mexico and Arizona attempted joint statehood during November of 1906. In this referendum, New Mexico voted for the proposal and Arizona against it.[2] With this vote, the stride of the marcher was hobbled even further.

In 1910, however, with Congress no longer able to make excuses, an enabling act was passed which allowed New Mexico to frame yet another constitution prepatory to its admission as a state. The citizens of New Mexico adopted this constitution in 1911. With the adoption of a conservative constitution, the Territory was ready to select candidates for the various state offices. The Democratic Convention was held in Santa Fe on October 5, and William C. McDonald of Lincoln County, chairman of the Democratic Central Committee, was nominated as its candidate for governor. For the offices of lieutenant governor and secretary of state, the convention selected the two former associates of *La Voz del Pueblo*, don Ezequiel C. de Baca and don Antonio José Lucero.[3] This Democratic slate was to prevail in the elections the following year. And, finally, on January 5, 1912, President William H. Taft admitted New Mexico as the 47th state of the Union, and the march was over.[4]

The Republican Convention was held in Las Vegas on September 28, where the colorful Elfego Baca of Socorro was selected as one of its two candidates for the national House of Representatives. Baca was a folk hero and was (next to Billy the Kid) the most legendary figure of the day. The incident that propelled Baca into public life is related by Beck:

> While campaigning for the Spanish candidate for sheriff, Elfego Baca pinned a badge upon his coat, and thus equipped, along with two six-shooters, went off to win votes. While he was electioneering in a small village known as Frisco, a Texas cowboy named McCarthy was busy shooting up the town and intimidating the natives. When the local Justice of the Peace refused to act out of fear, Baca saw an opportunity to distinguish himself as a champion of his people and thereby enhance his own political fortunes. Acting on his own authority, he arrested the Texan and announced that he was going to take him to Socorro for trial.

> The cowboy's fellow Texans were immediately alarmed at this gross insult and doubtless magnified the affair into an uprising of New Mexicans against them. Gathering in force, they ordered Baca to surrender his prisoner. An exchange of shots occurred when Baca refused, and one cowboy was killed. This prompted the Texans to prepare for battle, accompanied by a local deputy sheriff.

> McCarthy was tried in the local Justice of the Peace Court for disturbing the peace and fined five dollars, but the affair was not over. The mob that had gathered was spoiling for a fight, and when Elfego Baca fled to a small shed called a *jacal*, they decided to arrest him for the murder of the cowboy. In the subsequent "battle" Baca defended himself against eighty Texans, killing four of them and wounding eight without receiving so much as a scratch himself in the thirty-six hour battle. [5]

In the subsequent trial, Baca went scot-free. He was nominated as a representative, but despite his notoriety, the Republicans failed to carry the election.[6]

ESTABLISHING A NEW GOVERNMENT

At the time of its admission, New Mexico had a population of 330,000, with most people living on small farms and great ranches. Many hamlets, but only a few cities, dotted its mammoth territory.[7] With an area of 121,666 square miles, it was the nation's fifth largest state. Its Camino Real, which ran from Santa Fe to Chihuahua, was the oldest road in the United States, its capital, Santa Fe, the oldest seat of government. It was to Santa Fe that Antonio Lucero Sr. brought his family in 1912.

Traveling by train, the Lucero family went the 60 miles from Las Vegas to Santa Fe via the Lamy junction. Antonio had bought a home in Santa Fe to which he brought his growing family. In addition to his wife, Juliana, these were Aurora (who stayed behind initially to finish her work at Highlands University), Antonio Lucero Jr., Delia, Julia, Leonor, and **Edmundo**, born in 1902. A seventh child, Arturo, was born that fall, soon after the family arrived in Santa Fe.

Antonio Lucero Sr. served with New Mexico's first state governor, William C. McDonald (1912-1916), and his old friend and editorial associate, Lieutenant Governor Ezequiel C. de Baca.[6] Although their administration got off to an auspicious start, establishing a new government was not easy. In an interesting system devised by New Mexico, the Legislature met for 60 calendar days in odd-numbered years and for 30 calendar days in even years. The Senate was presided over by Lieutenant Governor Ezequiel C. de Baca and a president pro-tem selected by its members. The first task for Antonio Lucero Sr. as secretary of state was to preside over the election of a speaker for the House of Representatives.[8] With this democratic government in place, New Mexico joined her sister states as an equal.

The Luceros, newly established in Santa Fe, suffered an almost immediate tragedy. In 1915, only three years after the birth of her youngest child, Juliana Romero Lucero died leaving seven children ranging in ages from three to twenty-one.

Wednesday, May 19, 1915, dawned cold and with a brisk wind. The chill breeze whipped at the clothing of the hundreds of mourners who entered Santa Fe's cathedral of St. Francis of Assisi. Under the pretty but sad gaze of *La Conquistadora*, the Queen of the Kingdom of New Mexico and its *Villa* of Santa Fe, the casket bearing the remains of Juliana Lucero was placed in the north transept of the cathedral, a remnant of the old adobe church of St. Francis around which the stone cathedral had been built. The surroundings seemed fitting. In contrast to the soaring height of the nave, crossing, choir, and apse, the old *Conquistadora* Chapel, with its venerable adobe walls, seemed small and protective. Amid flickering wax tapers which cast a soft glowing light on the proceedings, Monsignor Antonio Fourchegu, vicar general of the Archdiocese of Santa Fe, prayed a low Mass of Requiem for Juliana. Then, the ceremony over, the casket, borne by Chief Justice C. J. Roberts, Attorney General Frank W. Clancy, former territorial governor, Miguel A. Otero, and Antonio Lucero's esteemed friend, Francisco Delgado, among others left the west front of the cathedral into the cold city which awaited them.[9] A long procession in which many of Santa Fe's most prominent citizens participated, then wound its way through the narrow streets of the capital to the Rosario Cemetery. There, among their many friends who waited beneath leaden skies, the Lucero family stood to say goodbye, each member knowing that a major portion of his or her life was over. Although the children's maternal grandmother (affectionately referred to as "Jujo," the children's rendition of Refugio) stepped in to assist in the care of the children, the family was fractured. The younger Lucero children found it increasingly difficult as time went on to provide direction for themselves. Nevertheless, the elder Antonio had his responsibilities at the statehouse and the adult children at least had their own activities in the new state capital.

Aurora, the oldest at 21, assisted her father and grandmother with the family and, also, worked in her father's office in the statehouse where she became closely acquainted with her father's associates. Governor

McDonald, knowing her academic and cultural background, appointed her to the board of the Panama-Pacific Exposition of 1915.[10] This was an international fair during which the new state hoped to promote itself on the national and international stage. One of Aurora's tasks was to assist in the installation of the New Mexico exhibit, a reproduction of the Franciscan Mission at Ácoma.

In 1916, Antonio Lucero Sr., although still serving as secretary of state for New Mexico, was appointed by the U.S. State Department to serve as interpreter general at the Pan-American Congress in Washington, D.C.[11] Again, New Mexico in its continuing effort to make itself and its citizens known in both political and economic arenas, released Antonio from his duties to serve in this capacity. Aurora accompanied her father. When Antonio was taken ill and had to be hospitalized in Chicago enroute to the conference, Aurora, also a noted linguist, substituted for him. She was appointed as an aide to one of two "ladies' delegations," acted as a hostess and guide, and as an interpreter for speeches delivered in both Spanish and English.[12]

Meanwhile, back in New Mexico, it became obvious that Mexico, and some of its people, were not finished with New Mexico or the United States. During the same year that Antonio Lucero Sr. and his daughter Aurora went to Washington, the Mexican bandit and General of Brigade of the Mexican revolution, named Francisco "Pancho" Villa (real name Doroteo Arango),[13] raided the little town of Columbus in southern New Mexico.[14] This raid at Columbus appears to have been an act of reprisal for President Wilson's support of Villa's rival, Venustiano Carranza, in Mexico's latest revolution. This revolution had as its aegis the dictatorship of Porfirio Díaz who ruled Mexico for over 30 years. During his oppressive regime of political tyranny and economic oligarchy, large landowners, businessmen, and foreign investors prospered while its landless peasants sank deeper into poverty.

In 1911, the 80-year-old Díaz was finally forced from office. He was followed by president-elect Francisco Madero and then General Victoriano Huerta who usurped power. Venustiano Carranza, with the support of the

United States, then led a successful counter-revolution against Huerta. However, after his success, he and some of the other revolutionary leaders began fighting for power.[15] It was during this revolutionary struggle for agrarian and other reforms that Pancho Villa, and the peasant leader, Emiliano Zapata, arose to prominence. In this struggle the United States continued to support Carranza and placed an embargo on the export of guns to those who opposed him. The raid at Columbus did indeed appear to have been an act of reprisal.

The raid may also have been prompted by the failure of Sam Ravel, one of Columbus' merchants, to deliver as promised, a shipment of ammunition to Villa.[16] There is the additional possibility that Villa was after the horses, arms, and ammunition of the Thirteenth United States Cavalry stationed at Camp Furlong, a few miles north of Columbus. If not for these reasons, the attack on Columbus is hard to fathom. An anonymous town in the midst of a dry plain, three miles north of the Mexican border, Columbus' main road was merely a wagon rut leading to Deming, 32 miles to the north. As Rouverol so aptly notes, ". . . it hardly seemed a target worth attacking."[17] Nevertheless, shortly after 4:00 a.m. in the pitch black of March 9, 1916, as many as 500 Villistas attacked the little village. Although Colonel Slocum, in charge of the cavalry at Camp Furlong, had been forewarned of the attack, he did absolutely nothing to protect the village. Once the fighting started, however, the cavalry made a good showing.[18]

Shooting, shouting, setting fires, and breaking down doors, the Villistas appeared to be looking for Ravel. Failing to find him, they burned his store. When they retreated under a hail of machine gun fire, the Villistas left a considerable number of their comrades lying in the dusty street of Columbus. The Americans lost nine civilians and eight soldiers. This invasion was to be the last land attack by a foreign army on the continental United States. It was also to be the last major cavalry operation in American history.[19]

Following the attack at Columbus, Carranza insisted that Mexico be allowed to take care of Villa without interference from the outside.

However, President Woodrow Wilson of the United States ordered a punitive expedition led by General John J. Pershing to enter Mexico, a sovereign nation, in pursuit of Villa. With bitter indignation, Carranza ordered an attack on Pershing by government troops and threatened the United States with war. Wilson, however, although recognizing the threat as a toothless gesture, nevertheless ordered Pershing to withdraw, leaving behind such a degree of hostility and distrust that reconciliation between the United States and Mexico would be a long time coming.[20]

Although New Mexico and the United States may have felt they were through with Mexico, each would soon be confronted with yet another situation in which Mexico played a role, albeit a minor one. Just a year after the United States Cavalry repelled the invasion by a Mexican revolutionary force at Columbus, the United States was again at war. What eventually burgeoned into the First World War began in Sarajevo, the capital of the Austrian province of Bosnia, a place then known to few in the United States. Although this war started with three pistol shots and the death of Archduke Francis Ferdinand and his wife Sophie, it really had as its roots the growth of nationalism, a system of military alliances that creates a balance of power and fosters competition for territory.

The war started in 1914, and at first the United States was successful in maintaining its neutrality. During January of 1917, however, the British intercepted a German message to Mexico that helped persuade the United States to enter the war. The message indicated that Germany had requested an alliance with Mexico in case the United States entered the war against the Central Powers. As payment for this alliance, Germany promised to assist Mexico in recovering some of the land it had lost to the United States after the Mexican War.[21]

Eventually the United States, like 23 other nations, got pulled into the war in an attempt to "make the world safe for democracy." The United States entered the war on April 6, 1917, and Antonio Lucero Jr. was one of those who elected to serve.[22] The United States, one of the Allied powers, was in the war for about a year-and-a-half, during which time the younger Antonio served in the navy. Happily, he returned safely to his own career in New Mexico. When the war was over, he became the assistant adjutant general under Adjutant General Yeager.[23] He began this appointment just at the time his father completed his tenure as secretary of state.

Antonio Lucero Sr. served as New Mexico's first secretary of state from 1912 until 1918, the year his oldest son returned from the European theater. At the conclusion of his two terms of office, Antonio and his younger children returned to Las Vegas where the family bought a large, pretty, year-old home on Hot Springs Boulevard. This house was to be the home of the next three generations of this branch of the Lucero family.

With the death in 1916 of Felix Martínez, the former owner of *La Voz del Pueblo*, Antonio Lucero Sr., became president of the *La Voz* Publishing Company.[24] He also returned to academic life. He was a member of the board of regents at Highlands University, maintained his interest in politics, and continued with the publishing business.

In 1917, Congress approved the 18th Amendment to the Constitution that prohibited the export, import, manufacture, sale, and transportation of alcoholic beverages in the United States. Antonio Lucero Sr. neither smoked nor drank, and during the war in Europe, may have been one of those who had argued that using grain to make liquor was unpatriotic. By 1919-20, when Prohibition came into effect in the United States, he became the first federal Prohibition director for New Mexico. It was from his home on Hot Springs Boulevard that Antonio Lucero Sr. carried out his work against the illegal manufacture and sale of liquor that was being conducted in northern New Mexico.[25]

With all these activities, the elder Antonio didn't have much time for his children, and the younger ones especially suffered. In 1920, when he ran for Congress in his final bid for public office, the ages of his children were: Aurora twenty-six, Antonio Jr. twenty-four, Delia twenty-two, Julia twenty, **Edmundo** eighteen, Leonor sixteen, and Arturo eight, with the three youngest children living at home.

Don Antonio José Lucero died during June of 1921. Following his death the Lucero children tried to maintain their home in Las Vegas but eventually found this impossible. With both parents gone, they were a leaderless group. Ultimately, with the 22-year-old Delia accepting responsibility for her youngest brother, the remaining members of the family rented out the Lucero home and scattered to the four winds.

After his father's death in 1921, Edmundo was completely at loose ends. When his mother died in 1915, he was only 13 and attending school in Santa Fe while his father worked at the state capitol. He completed his elementary education and entered St. Michael's High School but only attended sporadically. No one seemed to notice. At his father's death, he was 19, not a child, yet not an adult either, and, unlike his older siblings, he was seemingly without direction or purpose. One of the "pick-up" jobs offered him was to ferry a racecar from Las Vegas to Raton, a small community on the New Mexico-Colorado border. This was a great lark for a 19-year-old, and he seized the opportunity. He successfully drove the car as far as Springer, about mid-way between Las Vegas and Raton, where he had car trouble and had to request assistance from a second driver in Las Vegas. While waiting for this driver, Edmundo slept in the loft of a garage in Maxwell, a small community north of Springer. He was offered a job in the garage and since nothing was waiting for him on his return to Las Vegas, he stayed in Maxwell. He did subsequently return to Las Vegas, however, and in 1922, at the age of 20, Edmundo used his new-found mechanical skills to take a job as a car-inspector/mechanic with the Atchison, Topeka and Santa Fe Railroad. He was to hold this job for 45 years.

While **Edmundo** had been growing up in Santa Fe and Las Vegas, **Sinforiana Baca** (II) (or "Sinnie," as she was called), had been growing up in Santa Rosa only 60 miles away. Since the Lucero and Baca families had been associated with the newspapers, La Voz del Pueblo and La Voz Publica (with the latter being published on the La Voz del Pueblo Press), it is certain that their fathers, Antonio Lucero, Sr. and Placido Baca, knew each other. As children, though, Edmundo and Sinnie did not meet. Since statehood, Sinnie's father, Placido, had served as United States Commissioner in Guadalupe County,[26] while the Baca family continued to assert influence in Santa Rosa.

Upon completing high school, Sinnie, a lovely, auburn-haired, brown-eyed 18-year-old with diploma in hand, began teaching at various rural schools in the Santa Rosa area. She taught at *Puerto* (near Puerto de Luna), at Giddings (in a one-room school house), and then at Antón Chico. During the school year while at Puerto and Giddings, Sinnie boarded with local families whose children were among her pupils. When she taught in Antón Chico, She boarded with the Abercrombies, a prominent family who lived in this village.[27]

Each summer Sinnie attended college at Highlands University in Las Vegas where she worked toward teacher certification. One fall, while attending a teacher's convention in Las Vegas, she met the very handsome Edmundo Lucero. Sinnie Baca's recollection of this encounter is delightful. She had attended a dance with a friend named Cecilia Gonzáles and had caught the eye of a tall, hazel-eyed, handsome Galician standing among the crowd. They may have spoken to each other at the dance, although she doesn't remember, but in any case, toward the end of the evening, the dashing Edmundo offered the young women a ride home. Edmundo was driving an open "touring" car. The back seat was uncovered and full of snow. Although the snow was brushed off, someone still had to sit on the cold, wet seat. After much debate as to who the victim would be, Sinnie drew the seat next to Edmundo. They were married in 1923.[28]

CHANGES

The twentieth century brought change to New Mexico but it was neither sweeping nor rapid.[29] There were, most certainly, pockets of development here and there, fueled especially by the railroad. These pockets were relatively insignificant, however, in terms of major changes through the mid-1950s. To be sure, the state's clean air, wonderful climate, and remarkable light attracted artists to Santa Fe and to Taos, but for the most part, New Mexico continued separate and apart from its sister states through the middle of the century. Ironically, it was this very isolation (as well as World War II), which placed it at the forefront of events that would change the world.

On December 7, 1941, the Japanese attacked Pearl Harbor in the South Pacific, and the United States was forced for a second time to become part of a world at war. During 1942, the United States determined to push the new science of atomic energy toward the development of an atomic bomb. One of the key figures in the development of this bomb was J. Robert Oppenheimer who as an adolescent had attended a boys' school in isolated northern New Mexico. A corps of engineers had been organized to develop this bomb, and when it was searching for a site for its secret laboratories, Oppenheimer suggested the Los Alamos Ranch School for Boys.[30] This school was located on the Pajarito Plateau 25 miles northeast of Santa Fe.

Called the "Manhattan Project," the work was funded in 1942. By July 16, 1945, the corps of engineers had a bomb ready for testing. Again, the need for isolation resulted in the selection of the test site on the White Sands Missile Range between Socorro and Alamogordo, along the Dead Man's Route of Bernard Gruber. The bomb developed at Los Alamos was tested at the Trinity Site of the White Sands Missile Range.

The scientific research, which had led to the development of the atomic bomb, was to result in the location of some of the world's most important research laboratories in New Mexico. With the Los Alamos Scientific Laboratory as its parent, the village of Los Alamos eventually grew into a scientific community of 15,000. The associated Sandía Base and Laboratories at Albuquerque caused that city's population to soar from 35,000 in 1940 to 96,000 in 1950 and to a remarkable 201,000 in 1960 with fully a third of New Mexico's citizens living there.[31] After World War II, the peacetime use of nuclear energy continued to be explored in Los Alamos and Albuquerque with research being conducted in chemistry, medicine, metallurgy and physics.

18
EPILOGUE, SIMPLE GIFTS: 1923–1958

THE GIFTS: LUCERO/BACA

'Tis the gift to be simple, 'tis the gift to be free
'Tis the gift to come down where we ought to be,
And when we find ourselves in the place just right
'Twill be in the valley of love and delight

—A Shaker Hymn, Elder Joseph Brackett, c 1848

My parents, Ed and Sinnie Lucero, had five children, born in three clusters which made, at least for the children, three separate families. The first of these clusters was composed of my sister Sylvia and brother Edmundo Antonio (Buddy), born in 1925 and 1926 respectively. There was then an unusual gap of seven years before my sister Norma Jean was born in 1933. I followed in 1935. Again, a magical seven years elapsed before my sister Paula was born in 1942. If Sylvia, Buddy, and my parents comprised the first cluster in our family, and Norma Jean, my parents, and I the second, then Paula and my parents constituted the third. The lines of distinction among these three groupings are most apparent when one looks at the year 1946. By that year, Sylvia and Buddy had graduated from high school and were off starting lives of their own. Neither was living at home. On the other hand, Norma Jean and I, at thirteen and eleven, were beginning the journey of adolescence. Although Paula was a delightful four-year-old, she entered little into our thinking or our play.

Born in 1935 in the middle of the Great Depression (1929-1941), a second event of major consequence to our area ended in the year of my birth. This was a drought during which no rain fell from the fall of 1932 until May of 1935. I was only six when the United States entered the

Second World War. As neither my 15-year-old brother nor my 39-year-old father was required to serve in this war, the more benign issues of rationing and civil defense brought its reality home. How one could believe that the Japanese might attack New Mexico is now beyond my comprehension. We had, however, our blackout drills in which we were required either to cover the windows of our homes with opaque material or extinguish our lights. I recall standing with other members of my family in the front yard of our home in a darkened and silent town. As we peered into the starlit night, I actually thought that we might see Japanese aircraft approaching Santa Fe or Albuquerque. These air raid drills were, for this six year old, not rehearsals, but very real events, fraught with danger and menace.

If the Japanese aircraft were illusionary, however, rationing was not. One had, in 1945, to present coupons for the purchase of meat at the grocery store. Moreover, Norma Jean and I devoted every Saturday to foraging expeditions for toilet paper and soap for the laundry and bath. We may have had a closet-full of these items upstairs in our home, but no matter—you could never have enough of either of these commodities.

My parents were at once frugal, sensible, hard working and patriotic. My mother may have hoarded soap, but she did so out of the conviction that one could never be too clean. My mother baked bread once a week, pastry almost daily, and canned food in season. We had our own kitchen garden, raised rabbits for the table and contributed to the war effort.

My father's patriotic efforts were in a different vein. Under his direction, I collected metal and rubber items from among our neighbors. My father and I then took these materials all the way to "New Town" where an enormous wire enclosure was placed in the middle of the intersection at Sixth Street and Douglas Avenue. One might have thought this would have created an obstruction, but with very few cars on the streets, the enclosure, full of tin cans and the soles of old shoes, presented no obstacle.

During the war years, I can only remember two mechanical devices that were used in our home. The first of these worked very well, the second hardly at all. The first was a *maquina* or *maquinita* (little machine), a small, hand-cranked meat grinder with three cutters. My mother apparently ground meat for everything, empanaditas, enchiladas, beef patties, and so on. The first two of these were delicacies and not daily fare. There were, however, a myriad of other dishes, which called for the use of the *maquinita*, and it was in almost daily use in our home.

The second mechanical device was our washing machine. This washing machine was, by my reckoning, at least 350 years old and may well have been in use at San Gabriel. I looked forward to washday with dread! On that day I would come home from school to find this ponderous machine in the middle of the kitchen. This murderous device, which rattled, bounced, crunched, and leaked oil all over the floor, was flanked on one side by a large, empty washtub sitting on a green wooden chair, and on the other by my Madonna of a mother. My mother, with damp forehead and matted hair, tried valiantly to keep the washing machine and tub in one unit.

My job was even more heroic. My mother would start washing at mid-day, timing the first load to finish at my arrival from school. My task was to hold the gears of the washer's wringer in place with a large stick that my father had fashioned for just this purpose. During the previous centuries, the task I was performing had been accomplished by a small lever on the cover of an enclosed gearbox that had served to switch the rotation of the wringers and to lock them in place. Now, with all else lost, the gear "shifter" and "place-holder" were a long stick and an 11-year-old child. I hated washday!

There were, in addition to washing clothes, a few other tasks that caused almost as much aggravation. We had beautiful hardwood floors throughout our home and the task of keeping them beautiful fell to my sister Norma Jean and me. Our job was to spread paste wax on the floors and, on our hands and knees, to polish them until we could see the reflections of our faces and our chandeliered ceilings. To be sure, when my mother was busy elsewhere, we stood on the towels and polished with our feet and, on occasion, attempted to slide from one side of the room to the other. For the most part, however, we were closely supervised and when not pulling our wagon through the community looking for soap, we spent Saturday polishing floors. There was, in our family, a continuing question as to the order of precedence relative to the virtues of cleanliness and godliness. The question was never resolved to anyone's satisfaction. Other chores were seasonal, the two most onerous of which occurred in the spring. The first of these chores was pulling weeds in our big backyard. The assignment was to weed the area between the back porch and what had been a carriage barn where my paternal grandfather had kept his "revenuing" equipment. The second was sweeping the enormous porch that fronted our entire house. Both of these latter tasks fell to me. I was supervised in the weeding by my mother who would first pull two weeds to show me how it was done. My oldest sister, Sylvia, supervised the sweeping, having been assigned the task of ensuring that the porch was immaculate. Our weeds were, without question, larger, thicker, and denser than were those in any yard in New Mexico.

But if pulling weeds required a Herculean effort, sweeping the porch was a trial by fire. Our closest neighbors, the Elmer Pettines, had three enormous cottonwood trees which tried their very best to seed a forest of cottonwood on our front porch. My job was to stop this assault. It was like trying to bail the ocean! I would begin at one end of the porch and very quietly stroke at the cotton piling at my feet. The task was to sweep with soft light strokes so as to move the cotton, but without causing any movement of air. It was impossible! No matter how light the stroke, how deft the movement, some of the cotton moved forward, while much of it moved back. It went on and on. Stroke. Move back. Stroke. Move back. The cotton swirling about the broomhead and upon invisible currents of air blew around my head and moved insidiously back to where it had originally lain. Through all of this, my sister Sylvia would stand peering at me, first through the enormous picture window in our living room and then through its companion window in my parents' bedroom. It was a never-ending struggle. I hated those trees, I disliked the porch, and I couldn't wait for Sylvia to go away to school!

My parents, it seemed, were often away from home. Extremely

outgoing and gregarious, they had many friends and were always visiting, playing cards or going dancing. When my parents were away from home for the evening, we were left in the care of our "working girls," Claudita and Trini. It didn't occur to me until many years later that Claudita and Trini were a team composed of a mother and daughter. They worked for my parents doing spring-cleaning, preparing for large family gatherings, and baby-sitting. Our working girls did not live in and did not perform such murderous tasks as pulling weeds, washing clothes, polishing floors, or sweeping porches, but what they did do was scare us to death.

Claudita and Trini had a wonderful way with children. During the summer we were allowed to play outside until it grew dark and I recall very clearly our being left with them on many of those summer evenings. Whichever one was in charge of us would be busy in the house finishing some chore or sitting on the porch swing, with cotton swirling about her head, watching our play. "Hide-and-go-seek" and "Statues" were our favorite games. Come dark, however, it was the responsibility of the women to get us into bed and settled down for the night. How they accomplished this was by telling us stories about ghosts, or the bogey-man, or, more often, about the *llorona*, a woman who was grieving over the loss of her children whom she had killed (probably because they wouldn't go to bed, I thought at the time). Although we were fascinated by these stories and loved to hear them, we were also extremely frightened by them. If they were meant to scare us into submission, getting us into bed and keeping us there, they succeeded. Many a warm summers evening I lay suffocating beneath my blankets, afraid to take my head out from underneath the covers. We learned to be rather compliant children.

We had a car, but like everyone else's, it was up on blocks in the backyard. The Second World War had ended during July of 1945, but rationing and shortages were still the order of the day, with neither tires nor gasoline available. Thus, our world consisted of those places to which we could walk or ride our bikes. I think that it is important to note that while the absence of transportation must have been a hardship for my father who had to walk over a mile to work in every weather, it was no problem whatsoever to Norma Jean or me. That was just the way things were, and we never thought twice about it.

We grew up in Las Vegas which was composed of two incorporated communities, East Las Vegas and West Las Vegas, each with approximately 6,000 people. In an extremely wasteful system, we had two of everything: two police stations, two fire departments, two school systems, and two town governments. Although we grew up in West Las Vegas, we operated in both communities. The elementary schools, which Norma Jean and I attended, were Our Lady of Sorrows in West Las Vegas and Normal Elementary in East Las Vegas. Our Lady of Sorrows was a parochial school located off the plaza, the scene of so much history during the past 100 years. It was here that the Santa Fe Trail wagons had rested before their final leg to Santa Fe. It was here that General Kearny had taken New Mexico for the United States. The ring of buildings just behind those that front the plaza have also seen much history. Vicente Silva's Imperial Saloon used to be in the second tier of buildings at the southwest corner of the plaza, while the jail that had housed Billy the Kid once occupied the building behind the one on the northwest corner.

Although Our Lady of Sorrows School was an impressive structure built in the Spanish design of an open *plazuela*, its most important feature to me was the 106-year-old *acequia* that bisected the property. This irrigation canal, one of the original two dug for the village, teemed with water bugs and crayfish that we delighted in catching. Apart from having to read aloud with tremendous pride a vignette in our elementary school textbook that had been written by my paternal grandfather, I best remember the *acequia*.

As noted previously, our world during the period from 1941 to 1951 was defined by where we could walk, hike, or ride our bikes. We went pretty far afield. Most often our hikes took us to and beyond the *creston*, the mountainous escarpment immediately behind our home. Here we played among the rocks that had hidden the women and children of Las Vegas during the American invasion of 1846. We rode our bikes north to the hot springs, to the gypsy encampment on the Gallinas River below our home, and northeast about seven miles to York's Lake. In beautiful surroundings backdropped by the 10,263 foot two granite massifs of Hermit's Peak, we were completely unfettered and free.

Eventually, however, rationing and shortages became things of the past and my parents again had a car on the road. In my recollection, there were only a few paved streets in West Las Vegas, the four main arteries leaving the plaza: Bridge Street, South Pacific, West National, and Hot Springs Boulevard. Later, New Mexico Avenue was added to this list, but in 1950, travel by car was still an adventure. The trip from Las Vegas to Santa Fe, which now takes less than an hour, could, in the early 1950s, take several hours. Although we were interested in the destination, getting there was half the fun. Sometimes we would go to Santa Fe in the beat-up station wagon belonging to my uncle Ed Sena, but more often, we would go in my parents' car.

It was on one of these trips in early spring that we stopped in San Ysidro, a village on the Pecos River, to visit with some of our relatives. On our approach to the village, I recall seeing a group of the townsmen walking through their fields carrying a throne on their shoulders. They were carrying a statue of San Ysidro, patron saint of the village, through the fields, invoking a blessing on their lands, ditches and ditch gates. Although they seemed quite different from me in terms of their connection to the land, I was aware that they were enacting a ritual with centuries of precedence, and I felt a oneness with them. Whether hiking, biking, or going on motor excursions with my family, I experienced these days of my childhood as among my happiest.

Of all the excursions, and there were many during the years I lived at home, I remember best two which seem particularly representative of New Mexico and of my family. The first of these involved an attempt by my family (guided by my uncle Arthur Lucero) to drive to the Lucero ranch that was located but 17 miles into the mountains west of Las Vegas. The Luceros had a 640-acre ranch, perhaps one of those validated in 1903, located in an area known as *Los Valles de San Gerónimo* (the Valleys of St. Jerome) or Mineral Hill. This ranch was, along with our home on

Hot Springs Boulevard, a portion of the inheritance from my paternal grandfather. My father had parlayed his seventh share of both of these parcels into sole ownership of the house. His siblings, who retained ownership in the ranch, leased it to my uncle Carlos Baca for cattle raising. One could, across tortuous mountain terrain, reach the ranch by horseback or by horse-drawn wagon. As we were to find out, however, the high centers in the dirt road, and the boulders, which jutted through the rutted surface, made passage by car an impossibility. Although the ranch was only 17 miles away, I never saw it.

The second excursion, one to Storrie Lake, tells a great deal about my father. Most of our picnics took us up into the Gallinas Canyon or to Storrie Lake where my father could fish. Each of these picnic sites was readily accessible: Gallinas Canyon by the Elk Mountain Road and Storrie Lake by the Seventh Street Extension. The former, however, gave my father little opportunity for pathfinding as the scenic Elk Mountain Road was the only way one could reach the village of Gallinas and the north fork of the Gallinas River. Storrie Lake, on the other hand, gave full reign to his creativity.

Storrie Lake was only five miles north of Las Vegas. No matter, my father, who was always looking for a "shortcut," decided to reach the lake by way of Upper Las Vegas or Upper Town. This beautiful drive took us north toward the hot springs, across the Gallinas River, by the mansion of don José Albino Baca (I), and then south along the east bank of the stream.[1] When my father felt the time was ripe, we headed off on one of the rutted intersecting roads, traveling northeast to approach the lake now about three miles away. We ended up eating our picnic lunch in a lovely field amid a herd of cattle, within sight of the lake but barred from access by line after line of barbed wire fences. We never got to the lake on this occasion, but we did get to see a lot of New Mexico this way.

My appreciation of New Mexico's history and my family's place in it came from many sources. Perhaps the most important of these sources was my Aunt Aurora, the oldest of my father's many siblings, whom we often visited in Santa Fe. Even in a community of quaint houses and odd surrounds, my Aunt Aurora's home in an old dance hall of the 1880s was conspicuously eccentric. For example, her bathroom door was a louvered contraption from the old saloon which neither met the threshold at the bottom nor the doorjamb on top. Filled with family heirlooms, the house had among its furnishings my paternal grandmother's wedding chest and large wooden jewel case. Aunt Aurora also had my grandmother's *olla* (cooking pot), a treasured heirloom that had been passed down for generations. My Aunt Aurora was, in many respects, the repository of all that we were as a family. She had co-authored a study that sought to preserve the oral traditions and folk dances that in the 1940s were still extant in New Mexico. In 1948, she published her *Literary Folklore of the Hispanic Southwest*, an anthropological subject on which she was considered an authority. It was through my Aunt Aurora that I developed an appreciation for folk cultures in general and for the folk society of New Mexico in particular. She made me feel a connectedness, a sense of pride, and in a way I cannot explain, a sense of ownership and responsibility. I did not merely reside in the adobe kingdom, I was one of its custodians. There were many wide gaps in my knowledge of New Mexico and of my forebears, but I began the voyage of discovery around 1950 that has resulted in this book.

AMONGST FAIR FLOWERS

In 1957 I received my undergraduate degree in history from New Mexico Highlands University where a number of my family had received degrees, some even serving as members of its faculty. After college, I taught in Santa Rosa where I spent countless hours walking around and sitting within the Baca chapel where my maternal grandfather, Placido, granduncle Crescenciano, and great-grandfather, Celso, had been buried. I would drive to Puerto de Luna and to Antón Chico to explore and re-explore these villages. I knew, as Marcel Proust had instructed me, that in the voyage of discovery it was not new landscapes that I sought, but new eyes with which to see them. On quiet afternoons I roamed beneath sterling skies through cornfields and orchards. With my eyes cast downward, I scanned the surfaces of newly plowed furrows looking for remnants of the past:

And the children in the apple tree
Not known because not looked for
But heard, half heard in the stillness . . . [2]

I loved these excursions and, although I returned from them with little new knowledge, I gained on each occasion a greater appreciation for the land and its people.

After completing the school year in Santa Rosa in June of 1958, I left New Mexico for a required two-year stint in the military, returning later to attend graduate school and, once I had moved to another state, to visit my parents as often as possible. When I left New Mexico in those beginning days of the summer of 1958, it was with an expanding perspective and a greater understanding regarding my family. There was, however, much exploring yet to be done. My sister, Norma Jean, and her husband, Carlos Gomez, whose genealogical work assisted me to complete the present study, later joined me in this exploration. In attempting to define our present status in this research I am reminded of something T. S. Eliot wrote in Four Quarters:

We shall not cease from exploration
And the end of all our exploring
Will be to arrive where we started
And know the place for the first time.[3]

AFTERWORD

I f isolation placed New Mexico at the forefront of an industry that required solitude and secrecy, it also resulted in the preservation of historic and architectural treasures that could probably have been destroyed by modernization in more populated areas. A sense of New Mexico's Spanish colonial past is still much in evidence in the villages of Arroyo Hondo, Chimayo, Ranchos de Taos, Santa Cruz, Trampas, and Truchas. These places have changed little in 300 years.

A taste of life in the eighteenth century may be experienced at *El Rancho de las Golondrinas* at La Ciénega where life in a Spanish colonial village is depicted at this living museum. The "Ranch of the Swallows," the former home of **Miguel de la Vega y Coca** (c1710), and then his son-in-law, **Diego Manuel Baca**, once served as the last station on the Camino Real from Mexico City to Santa Fe. This restored village which features the Coca and Baca homes in a beautiful setting at any season, is open to the public through the Summer and early Fall. Here the visitor is encouraged to participate in village life by engaging in candle making, grinding, threshing, carding and weaving.

A sense of life in the nineteenth century can still be savored in Los Luceros. It was here, at a military outpost above San Gabriel, that Oñate's men built a small fort during the period between 1598 and 1610. This was also the site upon which Sebastián Martín Serrano built his 24-room *plazuela* after the Spanish colonists returned from exile in 1693. It is believed that the Sebastián Martín home of the very early 1700s remains as a portion of the great house at Los Luceros, one of the best-preserved nineteenth century haciendas in New Mexico.[1]

On the eastern fringe of the state, New Mexico's colonial past of the early 1800s is preserved in the Pecos River villages of San Ysidro, San José, San Miguel, Villanueva, El Cerrito, and Antón Chico. All of these villages, but especially San José and El Cerrito, carry nineteenth century

New Mexico well into the twenty-first century.[2]

The most intact remnant of the nineteenth century, however, is Las Vegas. Although a few homes from the mid-1800s still survive in Las Vegas, many of the homes and buildings are remnants of the period from 1880 to 1899, the era when Las Vegas was among New Mexico's most important trade centers. These homes and buildings are representative of territorial, Italianate, Victorian, and Queen Anne architecture and design, and fully 900 of these historic and architectural treasures survive and are listed in the National Register of Historic Places.

The lovely homes in Las Vegas grew up around Lincoln and Carnegie Parks and along the grid of streets emanating from these two residential centers in East Las Vegas. In West Las Vegas, structures of the nineteenth century and early twentieth century circle the West Las Vegas Plaza and line the west side of the formerly stately drive which leads north out of town toward the hot springs. Here among the last group of homes on this drive, three or four blocks from the plaza, is the house bought by Antonio Lucero Sr. He lived in it until his death in 1921. Shortly after 1923, it became the home of his son, Ed, and Ed's bride, Sinnie.

This is the home in which I was born and where I was raised. Here, among my grandfather's books, I developed a love for history and anthropology—studies that I hoped would be my life's pursuit. Although I never abandoned my search for potsherds and worked stone, the real artifacts of my collecting expeditions became the tales related by voices half heard in the stillness, and the knowledge I gained regarding my ancestors; a lively pastoral people, tenacious, self-sufficient, inordinately proud and individualistic, and isolated in the extreme. They established one of the oldest of the transplanted cultures to be found in the New World and, older than most, one that has had time to take root and flower.

As I became imbued with the spirit of the past, my grandparents' struggles became mine. I walked and herded with them for 800 miles, froze in the snow, and shared their grief as they buried loved ones in nameless graves throughout the Spanish borderlands. As time went on, I came to know, love and respect them and their story became the more endearing to me. Somehow in sharing their struggles, I felt responsible for them. I couldn't rest until I had them safely tucked behind adobe walls. And once this was accomplished, my responsibility to them was to provide them with a memorial, and to place them correctly in New Mexico's history. This study will never be completed. Others, I am sure, will continue in the exploration. However, with the publication of this treatise I hope that I have given them voice, and that their names and deeds will live forever in the Adobe Kingdom.

APPENDIX I

A SELECTED LIST OF SURVIVORS OF THE PUEBLO INDIAN REVOLT, 1684

The destitute condition of the colonists after the Pueblo Indian Revolt of 1680 cannot be better illustrated than by the descriptions provided as a result of the visitations conducted at the various settlements at *Guadalupe del Paso* four years later. This census, made by Attorney General Juan Severino Rodríguez from 11 to 14 September 1684, demonstrates clearly that the condition of the refugees had been little improved in the intervening period—this, the season of the fourth harvest. The following is an abridged version containing some of *The Adobe Kingdom* principals. In this version changes have been made in the spelling and listing of proper names to coincide with their listing in the Genealogical and Subject Index.

REAL DE SAN LORENZO

Continuing, I came to this *Real de San Lorenzo* (after the visitation at *Corpus Christi de la Ysleta*) which is today one league from El Paso and in the same conformity, made the inspection as follows:

The family of Pedro de Leyva consists of eight persons. They have no provisions because a cornfield which he planted has been eaten piecemeal ear by ear of corn. Clothing, in the same manner as the rest. He has six horses, a saddle, firearm and sword.

The family of the Captain Francisco de Anaya Almazán (II) consists of four persons. He has a small cornfield, but does not know how much will be harvested because they have been eating it ear by ear of corn. Clothing, somewhat decent. He has five horses, a saddle, firearm and sword.

The family of **Antonio Lucero de Godoy** (I) consists of six persons. They have no provisions nor cornfield because they had nothing to plant. Clothing, like all the rest. He has two horses, a saddle and a firearm.

The family of the *Sargento Mayor* Ignacio Baca consists of twenty-two persons. He has a small cornfield which in the same manner as those above, they are eating from. He has twenty goats which they milk for their sustenance. Clothing, with some decency he and his wife, the others badly worn-out, others completely naked. He has six horses, a saddle, firearm, sword, dagger and a leather jacket.

The family of Francisco Lucero de Godoy consists of 11 persons. They have no provisions nor cornfield because he did not have time to plant. Clothing, he quite well dressed, his wife somewhat decent, and the rest almost naked.

The family of **Juan Pacheco** consists of seven persons. They have no provisions or cornfield. He has fourteen goats with whose milk they sustain themselves. Clothing, like all the rest. He has three horses, a saddle, firearm and sword.

The family of the widow of **Pedro Varela Jaramillo** consists of 15 persons. They are extremely poor.

The family of Juan Griego consists of seven persons. They are extremely poor. He has a horse and a saddle.

The family of Captain José de Leyva Nevares consists of eight persons. They have no provisions. Clothing, like all the rest, he, his wife and a small child and all others naked. He has three horses, a saddle, sword and leather jacket.

The family of Captain **Cristóbal Baca** (II) without provisions. Clothing, the same as the others. He has six horses, a saddle, firearm, sword, dagger and leather jacket.

The family of *Sargento Mayor Lorenzo de Madrid, Alcalde Ordinario* consists of six persons. They have no provisions. Clothing, that which he and his wife wear is somewhat decent, the others are almost naked. He has two horses, a saddle, firearm, sword and dagger.

The family of Lazaro de Mizquia consists of eight persons. They have no provisions. Clothing, his wife dresses somewhat decent, his is indecent, and all others are naked. He has two horses, a firearm, saddle, and sword.

The family of Pedro Hidalgo consists of three persons. He planted a cornfield, but eaten ear by ear of corn along with the loss of some of it due to lack of water, it appears that it will harvest two or three *fanegas* of corn. Clothing, he and his wife somewhat decent, the others very badly dressed. He has three horses, a saddle, firearm, and sword and leather jacket.

The family of Captain don **Fernando Durán y Cháves** (II) consists of nine persons. He has twenty *fanegas* of corn for provisions. Clothing, he and his wife somewhat decent and the rest naked. He has seven horses, a saddle, firearm and sword.

The family of doña **Bernardina de Salas y Trujillo**, widow, consists of nine persons. She has four *fanegas* of corn that she finished harvesting. Clothing, very indecent.

The family of **Manuel Baca** consists of four persons. They are the same as above (extremely, extremely, poor, without anything).

The family of Domingo de Herrera consists of six persons. They have for provisions a *fanega* of corn which he recently harvested from his cornfield in addition to what they had eaten piecemeal. Clothing, the same as the above, poor. He has a saddle and a firearm.

The family of Nicolás Lucero de Godoy consists of five persons. They have no provisions. Clothing, indecent and the children completely naked.

The family of Captain Felipe Romero consists of ten persons. He has a small cornfield which as it appears will harvest from three to four *fanegas* of corn. Clothing, some very indecent, others naked. He has five horses, saddle, firearm, sword and leather jacket.

The family of *Sargento Mayor* **Juan Lucero de Godoy** consists of fifteen persons. He has a small cornfield which as it appears will harvest from six to eight *fanegas* of corn. Clothing, he indecent, his sons and servants almost naked. He has a horse, saddle, firearm and sword.

The family of **Antonio de Montoya** consists of six persons. He has a cornfield which as it appears will harvest from six to eight *fanegas* of corn. Clothing, he and his wife very indecent, the others naked.

The family of *Maestre de campo* **Francisco Gómez Robledo** consists of thirty-one persons. He has a small cornfield which should harvest from ten to twelve *fanegas* of corn. Clothing, some indecent, others badly worn out. He has two horses, a saddle, firearm, sword and dagger.

The family of the *Maestre de campo* Juan Domínguez de Mendoza consists of 16 persons. He should harvest from what he has planted from 35 to 40 *fanegas* of provisions. Clothing, somewhat decent and his servants ragged. He has 30 horses and mules, all the arms, and a son with all the arms.

The family of *Sargento Mayor* Diego Lucero de Godoy (I) consists of ten persons. He has his provisions together with the *Maestre de campo*, his father-in-law [Juan Dominguez de Mendoza]. Clothing, some decency in dress. He has six horses, saddle and all the arms.

The family of *Alferes* (Ensign) **Alonso García de Noriega**, the younger, consists of ten persons. He has two and one-half *fanegas* of wheat and a small cornfield which will harvest three or four *fanegas* of corn. More was lost due to the shortage of water. Clothing, he indecent, his wife decent and the others almost naked. He has three horses, saddle and all arms.

The family of **Juan Antonio Montaño de Sotomayor** consists of seven persons. He has a cornfield which will harvest four *fanegas* of corn. Clothing, very indecent, and the children naked. He has a horse, saddle and firearm.

The family of Luis Martín Serrano, the younger, consists of seven persons. They are exceedingly poor.

The family of **Juan García de Noriega** consists of eight persons. Provisions, he has ten *fanegas* [of corn]. Clothing, his wife somewhat decent, he and the others with worn-out [clothes]. He has three horses, saddle, firearm, sword and dagger.

The family of *Maestre de campo* **Alonso García**, Lieutenant Governor and Captain General, consists of 23 persons. They have 20 *fanegas* (of corn) for provisions. Clothing, he and his wife with some decency, the others with very worn-out clothes. He has 40 horses and mules, saddle and all arms.

This visitation was made by me, said Attorney General with due legality accompanied by the *Sargento Mayor* Luis Granillo and Francisco Romero, Secretary of the *Cabildo*, who acting in true faith signed it with me at this Pueblo of *Nuestra Señora de Guadalupe del Paso* on the 14th day of the month of September of 1684.

Juan Severino Rodríguez de Zuballe (rubric)
Luis Granillo (rubric)
Francisco Romero de Pedraza (rubric)

(There are) 109 families at Ysleta, *Real de San Lorenzo*, and *Venerencia de Guadalupe* which is called Paso.

List of soldiers of the *Presidio* of San José in the Province of New Mexico.

(Roque de Madrid with ten horses; José Domínguez de Mendoza with four horses; **Juan de Pérea** with three horses.

Diego de Montoya with four horses; José de Madrid with five horses; Antonio Gómez Robledo with five horses; Francisco Márquez with six horses

All of which the said soldiers are actually serving their terms with arms ___?___, firearms, swords and lances. The others have defensive arms. And so that it is made known to the King, the Viceroy, and the knowledge of New Spain, I the present __?__ __?__ before the Governor and Captain General, on the 30th day of the month of May of this present year of 84 accounted for __?__ and I signed it.

don Pedro Ladrón de Guebara Secretary of Government and War

Published by special permission of The New Mexico Genealogical Society. The complete census will appear in its forthcoming publication, *New Mexico Exiles Residing in the El Paso Area, 1684*, (J. Richard Salazar, Transcriber; J. Richard Salazar and Eloise Arellanes, Translators; Della Montoya, Editor and Compiler).

APPENDIX II

The following, an abridged version of the census conducted by Governor Diego de Vargas from December 22, 1692 to January 2, 1693, taken at *Pueblo de Paso* and *Real de San Lorenzo*, contains some of the principals of *The Adobe Kingdom*. This census was conducted for the purpose of ascertaining the number of settlers to be taken from the El Paso settlements to recolonize New Mexico. In this version changes have been made in the spelling and listing of proper names to coincide with their listing in the Name Index.

I have named as witnesses to accompany me on the visit (to be made in order to take the census), Sergeant Major Francisco de Anaya Almazán (II), ordinary *alcalde* of first vote, and Captain **Juan García de Noriega**, *alguacil mayor* of the *cabildo*. Don Diego de Vargas Zapata Luján Ponce de León. Before me, Alonso Real de Aguilar, secretary of government and war.

Pueblo de Paso

First I visited the house of Captain **Antonio de Montoya**, ordinary *alcalde* of second vote, married to **María Hurtado**, with eight children, three males and five females: Juan, eighteen years of age, Andrés, fourteen years old, and Antonio, a babe in arms, **Juana**, thirteen years old, **María**, eleven years old, Antonia, seven, Nicolása, five, and Thomása, three years of age.

Captain **Juan García de Noriega**, *alguacil mayor* of the *cabildo*, married to **Francisca Sánchez de Ynigo**, with three sons and a daughter: Juan Antonio, eleven years old, Francisco, seven years old, José, five years old, María, two years old. Also found in the said house were the following servants: Juana, eighteen years of age, Luisa, twenty years old, Gertrudis, seven years old, Bernardino, four, María, five years old, Mónica, five years old, Alonso three years old, Matheo, one year old, Antonio nine years old.

Adjutant **Antonio Lucero de Godoy** (I), councilman (*regidor*), married to **Antonia Varela de Losada** [or **de Pérea**], with three sons and two daughters: **Antonio** (II), five years old, Juan, three years old, Diego, one year old, Martína, fifteen years old, Bernardina, seven years old. Also two sisters, one a widow named Gerónima, without children, and the other María, eighteen years old, and an orphan girl, eleven years old.

Diego de Montoya, councilman, married to María Josefa de Hinojos, with six children: Salvador, three years old, Juan Esteban, five years old, Antonio, three years old, María de la Rosa, eight years old, Luisa, four years old, Juana, two years old. Also, in the same house, two married servants named Antonio and Ana Durán, his wife. He says that as a loyal vassal of his Majesty he is very willing to enter (New Mexico) and settle there with his wife and children when I, said governor and captain general enter.

Sergeant Major **Juan Lucero de Godoy**, married to doña Isabel de Salazar. He declares as his children Mathias, thirty years old, Cayetano Lucero, forty years old, and Barbara, one year old. He states that he has four servants: María, Juana, Josefa, and Juan. And he says that as a loyal vassal of his Majesty, he is very willing to enter (New Mexico) with his family whenever I, said governor and captain general, enter to colonize the said kingdom.

Sergeant Major Bartolomé Gómez Robledo, bachelor. He declares as his family the following persons: doña Juana Ortiz, his widowed sister, doña Ana María Robledo, doña María Ortiz, Francisca, Lucía, María Rosa, doña Ana Gómez, Gregoria, and Francisca. Also four female and two male servants named Magdalena, Petrona, María, Ana, Luis, and Sebastián. And he says that he will enter [New Mexico] with me, said governor and captain general, only to construct his house and irrigation ditch, and after this is done he will return and enter with all of the above persons.

Captain Lazaro de Misquia, married to doña María Lucero de Godoy, with five children, three males and two females, named Alonso, thirteen years old, Domingo, eleven years old, and Francisca, seven years old. Also José, twelve years old, who is their nephew. And he says that he will enter (New Mexico) with the said governor alone, and that later he will return for his family.

Juan Antonio Montaño de Sotomayor, married to **Isabel Jorge de Vera**, with seven children, four of whom are males, named Antonio, eight years old, José, seven years old, Lucas, six years old, Manuel, three years old. **Polonia**, eleven years old, María, five years old, and Leonor, two years old. Also two servants, Juan and the Indian José; a married woman, whose husband is absent, named Isabel Lucero de Godoy, with a daughter named Micaela, seven years old; also an Apache girl. He says that as a loyal vassal of his Majesty he is very willing to enter

(New Mexico) whenever ordered to do so, but that for the present he will enter only to rebuild a house, and will return for his family later.

Hernán Martín Serrano (II), married to María Montaño, with a daughter named Pasquala, fourteen years old. He says that he is very willing to enter and settle [in New Mexico] when I, said governor and captain general, enter.

Domingo de Herrera, married to María Martín, with six children, four of whom are males, named Marcos, seven years old, Francisco, nine years old, Juan, four years old, Mathias, two years old, Antonia, ten years old, and Josefa, eleven years old. And he says that he is willing to enter with his entire family to settle in New Mexico when I, said governor and captain general, enter.

Sebastián Martín Serrano, married to **María Luján**, with a son named Martín, one year old. He says that he is willing to enter [New Mexico] with his family when I, said governor and captain general, enter.

Cristóbal Durán y Cháves (II), bachelor, with his sister and her three children named Lorenzo, seven years old, Alejo, five years old, and Ana María, nine years old. He says that if he had sufficient provisions to enter [New Mexico] he would do so. He also has two brothers named Sebastián, thirteen years old, and Miguel, nine years old, and a sister named María, twelve years old.

Maestre de campo **Alonso García**, married to doña **Teresa Varela**. He states that he has twelve servants: Juana, twenty years old, Bernardino and his wife named Josefa, Cristóbal, Francisca, Magdalena, Catalina, María, another María, another María, Juan, Antonio, and Catalina. He says that as a loyal vassal of his Majesty he is willing to enter and settle in the said kingdom of New Mexico, but that he finds himself without the means to take his family either on foot or on horse, although he is very willing to do so. I told him that I, said governor and captain general, would assist him in every way possible in the said matter.

Doña **Bernardina de Salas y Trujillo**, widow of Captain **Andrés Hurtado**, with a daughter named doña Mariana Salas Orozco, eighteen years old and a stepdaughter named Juana, with two daughters and a son, named María, fourteen years old, Bernardina, eight years old, and José, four years old.

Captain don **Fernando Durán y Cháves** (II), married to doña **Lucía Hurtado de Salas y Trujillo**, with nine children named Bernardino, sixteen years old, Pedro, fifteen, Antonio, fourteen, Isabel, thirteen, Francisco, eleven, Luis, nine,

Nicolás, six, María, four, and Catalina, one. Also a servant named Francisca, twenty-eight years old, and a child named Ventura, five years old.

Real de San Lorenzo

Sergeant Major Francisco de Anaya Almazán (II), ordinary *alcalde* of first vote of the *cabildo*, married to doña Felipa Cedillo Rico de Rojas, with three children, two males and one female: Salvador, ten years old, Antonio, eight years old, María, four years old. Also, an orphan named María, fifteen years old, a widowed sister of his named doña Ynes de Anaya, her son named José, twenty-one years old, her servant girl, and an Indian named Antonia. He says that he has been serving his Majesty for over forty years at his own expense, and that he never had an *encomienda*; that at the time of the general uprising in New Mexico he was on one of the frontiers as the leader of six men under his charge, and that upon hearing of the said uprising he was unwilling to abandon the said frontier; and that on the said occasion he lost his wife and children. He said that without help he cannot move his family because he is extremely destitute, to which I, said governor and captain general, answered that which is stated above with regard to the order and command of his Excellency the viceroy, Conde de Galve, to which I refer.

Sergeant Major *Lorenzo de Madrid*, married to doña *Ana María de Anaya Almazán*, without children. He states that he has five servants named Luisa, thirty years old, Paula, nine years old, Eugenia eight years old, Juan Francisco, eight years old, Cristóbal, fourteen years old, and Pedro, a babe in arms. He says that he has been serving his Majesty in New Mexico and these parts for forty-one years, having been an *encomendero* in the said kingdom, and that as a loyal vassal of his Majesty he is willing to enter and settle in the said kingdom if his Majesty gives him the necessary aid; that he will enter to build a house and will take his family later.

Captain **Pedro Cedillo Rico de Rojas**, widower, with two sons named **Juan Cedillo Rico de Rojas**, twenty-three years old, and Joaquin Cedillo Rico de Rojas, sixteen years old, the former being absent, having gone to *tierra firme*, and an Indian woman. He says that he needs much help before he can move to the said kingdom of New Mexico.

Captain Pedro de Leyva (II), married to María de Nava, with two sons and three daughters named Diego, six years old, Juan, three years old, María fifteen years old, Antonia, ten years old, and María Magdalena, one year old. Also a servant named María who has three children named Luis, eight years old, Juan Antonio, five years old, Caietano, one year old, and another servant named Antonio, ten years old. Also found in the said house were an unmarried niece thirty years old named Juana, with two children, José nine years old, and Juana, eight years old. He says that he is willing to enter and settle in the said kingdom if his Majesty provides him with all of the necessary assistance because he is poor and on foot, and that he has been in his service for twenty-five years without ever having received any favors.

Pedro Hidalgo, married to Ana Martín Griego Montoya, with two daughters and four sons named Nicolás, sixteen years old, Alonso, twelve years old, Cristóbal, eleven years old, Francisco, eight years old, María, seven years old, Marta, four years old, and an orphan named Bernardina, five years old. Also six servants named María, forty years old, with two children, Antonio, fourteen years old, Josefa, twelve years old, Gertrudis, nine years old, Bernardino, four years old, Salvador, nine years old, Isabel, thirty years old. He is willing to enter and settle in the said kingdom, and to serve his Majesty as ordered, if he is provided with the assistance. He says that he has served him (his Majesty) in the said kingdom and has participated in the *entradas* which have been made, at his own expense; that he will go in order to build his house and that his family will enter later if given assistance.

Manuel Baca, married to **María de Salazar**, with three sons and three daughters named Antonio, nine years old, **Diego Manuel**, one year old, Gregorio Baca, three years old, María, thirteen years old, Josefa, seven years old, Bernardina, five years old. He says that he is willing and ready to fulfill his Majesty's orders if given the necessary assistance with which to enter and settle in the kingdom of New Mexico.

Audencia de Guadalajara, legajo no. 139, *Archivo General de Indias, Seville*
Espinosa, J. Manuel, "Population of the El Paso District in 1692," in
MIDAMERICA Vol. XXIII (January, 1941), 61-84.

NOTES

INTRODUCTION

1. Ralph Emerson Twitchell, *The Leading Facts of New Mexico History*, (Albuquerque: Horn and Wallace, 1963), 8-9.
2. *The American Heritage Book of Indians*, Alvin M. Josephy, Jr., Ed. (New York: American Heritage Publishing Company, Inc., Simon and Shuster, 1961), 10, 12.
3. Ibid., 9, 15.
4. Rev. James T. Burke, *This Miserable Kingdom*, (Las Vegas: Our Lady of Sorrows Church, 1973), 114.
5. Edward H. Spicer, *Cycles of Conquest*, (Tucson, The University of Arizona Press, 1989), 444-448, 449-451; John Kessell, *Kiva, Cross & Crown*, (Albuquerque, University of New Mexico Press, 1990), 66; Josephy, *Indians*, 118.
6. Marc Simmons, "*Colonial Cornucopia*," *New Mexico Magazine* (January, 1992), 68.
7. Simmons, *Cornucopia*, 68; Antonia Fraser, *Mary Queen of Scots* (New York, Dell Publishing Company, 1971), 163.
8. Kessell, *Kiva*, 90.
9. Margaret Yeo, *The Greatest of the Borgias* (Milwaukee, The Bruce Publishing Company, 1952), 29.
10. Henry Bamford Parkes, *A History of Mexico*, (Boston: Houghton Mifflin Company, 1988), 39-41.
11. Ibid., 52-53.
12. Burke, *Miserable*, 57-59.
13. Paul Horgan, *The Great River*, (Hanover: University Press of New England, 1984), 981.
14. Álvar Nuñez Cabeza de Vaca, *The Journey of Álvar Nuñez Cabeza de Vaca* (Chicago: The Rio Grande Press, 1964), 38.
15. Burke, *Miserable*, 62.
16. Horgan, *River*, 99.
17. Burke, *Miserable*, 64.
18. Horgan, *River*, 105.
19. Burke, *Miserable*, 65.
20. Ibid., 68.
21. Horgan, *River*, 106.
22. Ibid., 106-107.
23. Burke, *Miserable*, 68-69.

24. David Weber, *The Spanish Frontier in North America* (New Haven: Yale University Press, 1992), 46.
25. Burke, *Miserable*, 72.
26. Burke, *Miserable*, 73; Weber, *Frontier*, 47.
27. Burke, *Miserable*, 74; Weber, *Frontier*, 48.
28. Horgan, *River*, 112-119.
29. Burke, *Miserable*, 74-75.
30. Josephy, *Indians*, 118.
31. Horgan, *River*, 121-123; Burke, *Miserable*, 71.
32. Horgan, *River*, 130-136.
33. Horgan, *River*, 136-137; Burke, *Miserable*, 76-77.
34. Horgan, *River*, 140-141.
35. Ibid., 144-145.
36. Paul Horgan, *The Centuries of Santa Fe* (New York, E. Dutton and Co., Inc., 1956), 31; Burke, *Miserable*, 78.
37. Burke, *Miserable*, 81; Paul Horgan, *Conquistadors in North American History* (New York, Farrar, Straus and Giroux, 1966), 186; Horgan, *Centuries*, 31.
38. Burke, *Miserable*, 81.
39. Burke, *Miserable*, 81; Daniel J. Boorstin, *The Discoverers* (New York, Random House, 1983), 632.
40. Boorstin, *Discoverers*, 632; Burke, *Miserable*, 82.
41. Marc Simmons, *The Last Conquistador, Juan De Oñate and the Settling of the Far Southwest*, (Norman, The University of Oklahoma Press, 1991), 50.
42. Ibid., 51-52.
43. Ibid., 54.
44. Horgan, *River*, 155-157; Burke, *Miserable*, 85.
45. This was the same year in which a special child was born in Peru. Isabella de Flores y de Oliva was born on April 20, 1586. She captured the imagination of the world in 1671 as St. Rose of Lima when she became one of Catholicism's most popular saints. In 1868, a small adobe chapel in New Mexico was dedicated to her and to a Baca parent of the saint's name.
46. Horgan, *River*, 157-160. Castaño de Sosa's motives have never been satisfactorily explained. His superior, Governor Luis de Carvajal, had been jailed for the crime of having failed to denounce his sisters who were accused of Judaistic practices. Carvajal was prosecuted, deprived of his office, and died in prison. One historian has speculated that Castaño de Sosa, perhaps himself a Judaizer, may have been attempting to escape beyond the long arm of the Inquisition. Private conversation with Stanley M. Hordes, Ph.D., Visiting Scholar, Latin American Institute, *Hacienda de Los Luceros*, September 15, 1991; Cecil Roth, *A History of the Marranos* (New York, Meridian Books, Inc., 1959), 276.
47. Simmons, *Oñate*, 123-124; Burke, *Miserable*, 87-88.

1
COLONIZATION

1. Simmons, *Oñate*, 13-58.
2. Burke, *Miserable*, 89.
3. Simmons, *Oñate*, 87.
4. Fray Angélico Chávez, *Origins of New Mexico Families* (Santa Fe, Museum of New Mexico Press, 1954), 110.
5. Ibid.
6. Ibid., 6.
7. Ibid., 48.
8. Ibid., 87.
9. Simmons, *Oñate*, 93-96.
10. Simmons, *Oñate*, 100-101; Herbert E. Bolton, ed., *Spanish Exploration in the Southwest*: 1542-1706, (New York: Barnes and Noble, Inc., 1963), 202.
11. Josephy, *Indians*, 106.
12. Burke, *Miserable*, 38.
13. Simmons, *Oñate*, 96-97; Burke, *Miserable*, 94.
14. Burke, *Miserable*, 104.
15. Simmons, *Oñate*, 109-111; Bolton, *Explorations*, 203.
16. Burke, *Miserable*, 99.
17. Kessell, *Kiva*, 78.
18. Chávez, *Origins*, 71-72.
19. Sixty years old when he began the trek, he was the first colonist to die in New Mexico. He was buried along the trail on May 21, 1598 near a great bluff still called Robledo.
20. Kessell, *Kiva*, 18.
21. Bolton, *Explorations*, 203; Simmons, *Oñate*, 109-114.
22. Simmons, *Oñate*, 116; Horgan, *Conquistadores*, 230.
23. Simmons, *Oñate*, 117-118; Aurora Lucero-White Lea, *Literary Folklore of the Hispanic Southwest* (San Antonio, 1953), 21.
24. Simmons, *Oñate*, 118; Kessell, *Kiva*, 80.
25. Kessell, *Kiva*, 81.
26. Kessell, *Kiva*, Ibid.
27. Adolph F. A. Bandelier, *The Gilded Man* (New York, The Rio Grande Press, 1893), 232; Simmons, *Oñate*, 148-149.
28. Simmons, *Oñate*, 135-136.
29. Kessell, *Kiva*, 85.
30. The Jews when attacked by the Romans at Masada
31. Simmons, *Oñate*, 139-145; Kessell, *Kiva*, 86.
32. Bolton, *Spanish Explorations*, 212, 222; Kessell, *Kiva*, 87; Simmons, *Oñate*, 146-148.
33. Chavez, *Origins*, 11.

34. Chavez, *Origins*, 77.
35. Conjecture, based on the results of an archaeological dig conducted at Yunge Oweenge during 1959—1961 by a team from the University of New Mexico. *When Cultures Meet: Remembering San Gabriel del Yunge Oweenge*. (Santa Fe: Sunstone Press, 1987), 10-38.
36. Simmons, *Cornucopia*, 67.
37. Kessell, *Kiva*, 89; Simmons, *Oñate*, 160-161.
38. Chávez, *Origins*, 9.
39. Simmons, *Oñate*, 169-170.
40. Chávez, *Origins*,9.
41. Bolton, *Spanish Explorations*, 268, 280; Simmons, *Oñate*,172-173.
42. Simmons, *Oñate*, 183; Kessell, *Kiva*, 92-93; Burke, *Miserable*, 110.
43. Simmons, *Oñate*, 184; Burke, *Miserable*, 110-111.
44 Simmons, *Oñate*, 185.
45 Simmons, *Oñate*, 185-194.

2
A NEW CAPTAIN AND CAPITAL

1. Frances Levine, *Down Under an Ancient City*, in *Santa Fe: History of an Ancient City*, David Grant Noble, ed. (Santa Fe, School of American Research Press, 1989), 9-10.
2. Ibid., 14, 17; Robert Mayer, "*Lost Pueblo Found in Agua Fria*," in *Santa Fe Reporter*, January 25, 1989.
3. Levine, *Down Under*, 11.
4. Bandelier, *Gilded Man*, 284.
5. Levine, *Down Under*, 12.
6. Fray Angélico Chávez, *Chávez a Distinctive American Clan of New Mexico*, (Santa Fe, William Gannon, 1989), 4.
7. Joseph P. Sánchez, "*The Peralta-Ordonez Affair and the Founding of Santa Fe*," in *Santa Fe: History of an Ancient City*, David Grant Noble, ed. (Santa Fe, School of American Research Press, 1989), 27.
8. Ibid., 28.
9. Ibid.
10. Ibid.
11. Bandelier, *Gilded Man*, 287. One of the buildings of this *barrio*, which became known as *Analco* meaning over the water...of the *Río de Santa Fé*, is now known as "the oldest house," ca 1694.
12. Sánchez, *Peralta-Ordonez*, 27.
13. Bandelier, *Gilded Man*, 243.
14. Kessell, *Kiva*, 95.
15. Kessell, *Kiva*, 94.
16. Sánchez, *Peralta-Ordonez*, 31.

17. Sánchez, *Peralta-Ordonez*, 32; Kcsscll, Kiva, 96.
18. Sánchez, *Peralta-Ordonez*, 33.
19. Ibid.
20. Ibid.; Kessell, *Kiva*, 97.
21. Kessell, *Kiva*, Ibid.,
22. Sánchez, *Peralta-Ordonez*, 34.
23. Ibid.
24. Kessell, *Kiva*, 97.
25. Sánchez, *Peralta-Ordonez*, 35.
26. Ibid.; Kessell, *Kiva*, 97.
27. Kessell, *Kiva*, 97.
28. Sánchez, *Peralta-Ordonez*, 36.
29. Ibid., 38.
30. Chávez, *Origins*, 59.
31. Burke, *Miserable*, 121.
32. Kessell, *Kiva*, 99. (Although, Juan Martínez de Montoya, appears to have been one.)
33. Sánchez, *Peralta-Ordonez*, 30.
34. Brebner, *The Explorers*, 26.
35. Kessell, *Kiva*, 187.
36. Kessell, *Kiva*, 98.
37. Ibid., 99; Simmons, *New Mexico: A Bicentenial History*, (New York, W. W. Norton and Company, Inc., 1977), 55.
38. Kessell, *Kiva*, 187.
39. Ibid., 99.
40. Burke, *Miserable*, 119.
41. Sánchez, *Peralta-Ordonez*, 30.
42. Marc Simmons, *A Bicentenial History*, 55-56; Ramon A. Gutiérrez, *When Jesus Came the Corn Mothers Went Away*, (Stanford, Stanford University Press, 1991), 159-160.
43. Chávez, *Origins*, 4.
44. Ibid., 59.
45 The Gómezes were also closely associated with the Bacas. The sponsors at the baptism of Francisco Gómez Robledo were Governor Felipe Sotelo Osorio and doña Isabel de Bohórquez. She was the wife of don Pedro Durán y Cháves (I) and sister of Antonio and Alonso Baca.
46. Kessell, *Kiva*, 186.
47. Ibid., 19.
48. Ibid., 20

1. Kessell, *Kiva*,109.
2. Kessell, *Kiva*,107.
3. Kessell, *Kiva*, 138; Alfred B. Thomas, *After Coronado: Spanish Exploration Northeast of New Mexico, 1696-1727* (Norman, University of Oklahoma Press, 1969), 11; Herbert Howe Bancroft, *History of the North Mexican States and Texas, Volume I-1531-1800* (San Francisco, A. L. Bancroft and Company Publishers, 1884), 384, 390.
4. Kessell, *Kiva*, 155-156
5. Ibid., 158.
6. Ibid., 159.
7. Ibid.
8. Ibid., 160.
9. Ibid., 161.
10. Ibid.
11. Simmons, *Bicentenial History*, 64.
12. Kessell, *Kiva*, 162-163.
13. Ibid., 164.
14. Ibid.
15. Chávez, *Origins*, 83. For a different and expanded version of this tragedy see *The Rosas Affair* by this author.
16. Kessell, *Kiva*, 115-116, 165; John A. Crow, *Spain: The Root and the Flower* (New York, Harper and Row Publishers, 1963), 198-199; Gutiérrez, *Corn Mothers*, 231-232.
17. Kessell, *Kiva*, 161.
18. Chávez, *Origins*, 15, 12, 89.
19 Kessell, *Kiva*, 174.
20. Tim MacCurdy, "The Embattled Life of an Eccentric Governor," in *New Mexico Magazine* (March, 1990), 50-55.
21. Kessell, *Kiva*, 175.
22. Ibid., 176.
23. Ibid.
24. Ibid., 178; re: inability to speak the Pueblo language; Ibid., 337-339.
25 This may have been the *Hacienda de San Antonio de Sevilleta* owned by Felipe Romero and Jacinta de Guadalajara y Quiros. The Piro pueblo in the vicinity was named Sevilleta by Oñate in 1598 because of the resemblance of the location to that of Seville, Spain.
26. France V. Scholes, *Troublous Times in New Mexico* (Albuquerque, The University of New Mexico Press, 1942), 95.
27. Ibid., 93, 95.
28. Kessell, *Kiva*, 184.

29. Ibid., 216.
30. Ibid., 187.
31. Ibid., 188.
32. Ibid., 192.
33. Ibid., 193; Chávez, *Origins*, 1.
34. Kessell, *Kiva*, 193; Chávez, *Origins* 4.
35. Chávez, *Origins*. 87.
36. Kessell, *Kiva*, 196.
37. Ibid., 198.
38. Chávez, *Origins*, 21.
39. Kessell, *Kiva*, 199.
40. Kessell, *Kiva*, 200.
41. Ibid., 205.
42. Ibid., 207.
43. Ibid.

4
EXPULSION

1. *Albuquerque Journal*, November 18, 1988.
2. Burke, *Miserable*, 132.
3. Joseph P. Sánchez, *Twelve Days in Santa Fe: History of An Ancient City*, David Grant Noble, ed., (Santa Fe, School of American Research Press, 1989), 41.
4. Kessell, *Kiva*, 226.
5. Simmons, *Bicentennial History*, 66.
6. Sánchez, *Twelve Days*, 42.
7. Chávez, *Origins*, 70, Robert Silverberg, *The Pueblo, Revolt*, (Lincoln, University of Nebraska Press, 1994), 114.
8. Kessell, *Kiva*, 241, Silverberg, *Revolt*, Ibid.
9. Nancy Hunter Warren, *Villages of Hispanic New Mexico* (Santa Fe, School of American Research Press, 1987), 46. A description of one these homes was provided Fabiola C. de Baca by her grandmother. Built around a square called a *placita*, the *plazuela* had living quarters on one side. A second side was given to storerooms, granaries and workshops. A third side accommodated the corrals or wagons while the fourth, "which completed the square, was a high wall with one entrance—a massive gate of hand-hewn timbers."
10. Fabiola Cabeza de Baca, *We Fed Them Cactus* (Albuquerque, The University of New Mexico Press, 1954), 4.
11. Charles Winick, *Dictionary of Anthropology* (Totowa, New Jersey, 1968), 447, Silverberg, *Revolt*, 115.
12. Sánchez, *Twelve Days*, 43.
13. Ibid., 39; Silverberg, *Revolt*, 116-117.
14. Sánchez, *Twelve Days*, 45.

15. Ibid.
16. Ibid., 44.
17. Fray Angélico Chávez, *La Conquistadora* (Santa Fe, Sunstone Press, 1975), 8-11.
18. Ibid., 44-45.
19 Chávez, *Origins*, 4
20. Kessell, *Kiva*, 235.
21. Ibid., 237.
22. The route takes its name from Bernard Gruber, a Sonora-based German peddler who was killed in 1670 while escaping from confinement in the Sandía *alcaldia*. Gruber had been imprisoned by the Inquisition for selling little slips of paper which he claimed would assure the owner of 24-hours of protection. The site where he was apparently murdered by his Apache companion, was once known as *El Aleman* (the German); Ibid., 211-215; Chávez, Clan, 46.

5
EXILE: 1680–1693

1. Chávez, *Origins*, 25.
2. Horgan, *River*, 292; Silverberg, *Revolt*, 128; Sánchez, *Twelve Days*, 51.
3. Chávez, *Origins*,2.
4. Ibid., 10.
5. Ibid.
6. Horgan, *River*, 295; Silverberg, *Revolt*, 137
7. Silverberg, *Revolt*, 138-139.
8. Kessell, *Kiva*, 241.
9. Horgan, *River*, 297; Silverberg, *Revolt*, 141.
10. Kessell, *Kiva*, 240-241.
11. Chávez, *Clan*, 47, 51; Later settlements in this vicinity were *San Elizario* and *San Marcial*. Interestingly, although *Guadalupe del Paso* was settled by 1661, *Corpus Christi de Ysleta*, which was founded in 1681, is considered by many residents in Texas to be her oldest community.
12. Chávez, *Origins*, 60.
13. Ibid.
14. John L. Kessell, "*By Force of Arms*," in *Santa Fe: History of an Ancient City*, David Grant Noble, ed. (Santa Fe: School of American Research Press, 1989), 53.
15. Kessell, *Kiva*, 243.
16. Kessell, "*Arms*," 54.
17. Chávez, *La Conquistadora*, 49-50.
18. Kessell, "*Arms*," 54.
19. Ibid., 55, Chávez, *Origins*, 209-210.
20. Kessell, *Kiva*, 248. Chávez, *Origins*, 4. This young man drowned two years later while crossing the Rio Grande.
21. Ibid., 69-70.

22. Ibid., 49.
23. Ibid., 27.
24. Ibid., 53-54.
25. Ibid., 68.
26. Ibid., 81.
27. Kessell, *Arms*, 54-56.
28. Ibid., 56; Kessell, *Kiva*, 254.
29. Kessell, *Kiva*, 255; Kessell, "*Arms*," 56.
30. Chávez, *La Conquistadora*, 48.
31. Ibid., 67; Chávez, *Origins*, 286.
32. Chávez, *Origins*, 10.
33. Ibid., 10-11.
34. Gutiérrez, *Corn Mothers*,144; Horgan, *River*, 317; John Francis Bannon, *The Spanish Borderlands Frontier* (Albuquerque, University of New Mexico Press 1970), 88; Weber, *Frontier*, 139.
35. Ibid; Kessell, "*Arms*," 57; Kessell, *Kiva*, 256.
36. Chávez, *La Conquistadora*, 57-58.
37. Ibid., 57.
38 Kessell, "*Arms*," 57; Horgan, *River*, 317.
39. Kessell, *Kiva*, 256-257.
40. Chávez, *Origins*, 279.
41. Kessell, *Kiva*, 260.
42. Kessell, "*Arms*," 58; Kessell, *Kiva*, 262; Chávez, *La Conquistadora*, 60.
43. Kessell, *Kiva*, 262; Kessell, "*Arms*," 58.

6
RAPPROCHEMENT: 1693–1706

1. Kessell, *Kiva*, 266-270.
2. Ibid., 267.
3. Kessell, "*Arms*," 60.
4. Burke, *Miserable*, 152; Chávez, *Origins*, 284.
5. Chávez, *Origins*, 129, 193.
6. Kessell, *Kiva*, 267.
7. *New Mexico Place Names*, T. M. Pearce, ed. (Albuquerque, The University of New Mexico Press, 1965), 148; Kessell, "*Arms*," 60.
8. The Durán y Cháves family lived on land known as *El Tunque*. During November of 1705, Bernardo Durán y Cháves was killed while playing a prank on his cousin who mistook him for an Indian. Following this accident, Bernardo's grief-stricken father, don Fernando Durán y Cháves (II), moved south to Atrisco where other family members lived. Don Fernando later sold his *estancia* to Manuel Baca who lived on land inherited from Manuel's father, Cristóbal (II). The contiguous estates of Baca and Durán y Cháves, along with the estates of

Baca's relatives, the Gallegos and the Montoyas, became the present Bernalillo. Chávez, *Clan*, 61-62.

9. Kessell, *"Arms,"* 60.
10. Kessell, *Kiva*, 284-285.
11. Ibid., 287-289; Kessell, *"Arms,"* 61.
12. Burke, *Miserable*, 154; Chávez, *Origins*,141.
13. Chávez, *Origins*, 141.
14. Kessell, *Kiva*, 293.
15. Ibid.
16. Ibid.
17. Chávez, *La Conquistadora*, 50; Kessell, *"Arms,"* 59.
18. Kessell, *"Arms,"* 59.
19. Ibid., 61.
20. Ibid., 62.
21. Chávez, *Origins*, 209; Chávez, *Clan*, 56.
22. Chávez, *Origins*, 141.
23. Ibid., 144.
24. Ibid., 141.
25. Chávez, *Origins*, 141; *Place Names*, 24. We now know that Juana (*La Vieja*) was Manuel's sister rather than his daughter, and that he had two additional children: Gregorio, born c 1689 [and thus too young to bear arms in 1693], and Bernardina, born c 1690. They were omitted from the original list of settlers who returned to New Mexico.
26. Chávez, *Origins*, 144; Chávez, *Clan*, 88-89.
27. Kessell, *Kiva*, 367-368.
28. Chávez, *Origins*, 144.
29. Virginia L. Olmstead, *"Spanish Enlistment Papers of New Mexico 1732-1820,"* in *National Genealogical Quarterly* (Washington, September, 1979), 236.
30. Kessell, *"Arms,"* 63; Chávez, *Clan*, 59-60.
31. Kessell, *Kiva*, 303.
32. Chávez, *Clan*, 60.
33. Chávez, *Origins*, 209
34. *Place Names*, 5.

7

LAND GRANTS AND SETTLEMENTS: 1706–1794

1. *New Mexico Past and Present: A Historical Reader*, Richard N. Ellis, ed. (Albuquerque, The University of New Mexico press, 1971), 51.
2. Chávez, *Origins*, 60.
3. Kessell, *Kiva*, 314.
4. Ralph E. Twitchell, *The Leading Facts of New Mexican History* (Albuquerque, The Torch Press, 1917), Vol. I, entry 698.

5. *Place Names*, 152.

6. *Albuquerque Journal*, November 18, 1988.

7. Although Fray Angélico Chávez initially identified these women as the children of don Fernando Durán y Cháves and Elena Ruiz Cáceres, he later states that the women were in fact the daughters of Miguel Luján and the aforementioned Cáceres. He suggests that Durán y Cháves may have been María Luján's biological father, as stated in her will, but was not married to Elena Cáceres, her biological mother. Miguel Luján and Elena Cáceres did escape the 1680 massacre with two daughters. The Luján women may have been these children and thus perhaps were half-sisters. Chávez, *Origins*, 22; Chávez, *Clan*, 36-37, 289.

8. Chávez, *Origins*,104, 289.

9. *National Register of Historic Places, Item 9, 2.*

10. Chávez, *Origins*, 222.

11. Margaret L. Buxton, *The Family of Lucero de Godoi: Early Records* (Albuquerque, The New Mexico Genealogical Society, 1981), 36.

12. Ibid., 24.

13. David Muench, *New Mexico* (Portland, Charles H. Balding, Publisher, 1974), 34.

14. *Place Names*, 24. Chavez, *Origins*, 141. Manuel Baca was one of those accused of cruelty to the Indians. A leader among the soldier-colonists of the *Río Abajo*, he once gathered 40 Queres Indians along with the Albuquerque contingent for a campaign against the Hopi. He headed other Indian campaigns as well, with Nicolás Lucero de Godoy likely serving under his command. However, the Indians of the three pueblos of Cochiti, Santo Domingo, and San Felipe complained about their treatment at the hands of Manuel and his sons, and for this, the *alcaldia* of Cochiti was taken from him in 1718. As additional punishment, he was required to go on the next two campaigns against those Indians still railing against Spanish rule. Bowed, but unbroken, Manuel and his wife, María de Salazar, lived out their lives on their *estancia* in Bernalillo.

15. Adrian H. Bustamante, "*Espanoles, Castas y Labradores,*" in *Santa Fe: History of an Ancient City*, David Grant Noble, ed. (Santa Fe, School of American Research Press, 1989), 68.

16. Warren A. Beck, *New Mexico: A History of Four Centuries* (Norman, Oklahoma, University of Oklahoma Press, 1969), 89.

17. Buxton, *Lucero*, 35.

18. In 1750, the Lunas were living at the *Rancho de San Clemente*, a former settlement near present-day Los Lunas. The San Clemente Land Grant, west of Los Lunas from the Río Puerco to the Rio Grande, was given to Felix Candelaria in 1716, and subsequently was sold to the Luna family. The grant was approved by the United States Congress and awarded to the Luna heirs in 1899. *Place Names*, 142.

19. Ibid., 121.

20. Buxton, *Lucero*, 25.

21. Ibid., 300.
22. Fray Angelico Chávez, "*The Authentic New Mexican—A Question of Identity*." An address presented at the inaugural symposium and inauguration of Gerald W. Thomas as the sixteenth president of New Mexico State University.
23. M. Morgan Estergreen, *Kit Carson: A Portrait in Courage* (Norman, University of Oklahoma Press, 1962), 32.
24. Arthur L. Campa, *Hispanic Culture in the Southwest* (Norman, University of Oklahoma Press, 1979), 254.
25. Kessell, *Kiva*, 186.
26. Campa, *Hispanic Culture*, 252.

8
THE PUEBLO LEAGUE, THE PLAINS INDIANS AND THE
GENIZARO

1. Kessell, *Kiva*, 312-319.
2. Ibid., 301.
3. Ibid., 439-441.
4. *Place Names*,126.
5. Ibid., 76.
6. *Indians*, 377.
7. Kessell, *Kiva*, 357, 380.
8. Ibid., 372-383.
9. *New Mexico Past and Present*, 83.
10. Bancroft, *Volume I*, 648-649.
11. Kessell, *Kiva*, 398.
12. Ibid., 400.
13. Ibid., 401.
14. Ibid.
15. Ibid., 403.
16. Ibid., 366-368.
17. Ibid, 366.
18. Ibid.
19. According to Fray Angélico Chávez, the term as used in Spain means "born of a stranger." In New Spain, however, the term had a different meaning, a faulty derivation of the Turkish word janizary (janissary in English) which referred to former slaves of captive nations who had been formed into special military units. In New Mexico, on the other hand, the term referred to Christianized, hispanicized and detribalized Indians who became part of the Hispanic community. Chávez, *Clan*, 127-128.
20. Kessell, *Kiva*, 545.

9
TO THE CENTRAL PLAINS: 1794–1810

1. Francis Louis Crocchiola, *The San Miguel del Bado New Mexico Story* (Pep, Texas, Pampa Print Shop, 1964), 3.
2. Ibid.
3. David Weber, *Foreigners in their Native Land*, (Albuquerque, University of New Mexico Press, 1973), 30-32.
4. Kessell, *Kiva*, 355, 415-416.
5. Crocchiola, *San Miguel*, 7; Kessell, Kiva, 442.
6. Kessell, *Kiva*, 416-417.
7. Ibid., 348, 353.
8. Ibid., 416.
9. Weber, *Foreigners*, 30-32.
10. Kessell, *Kiva*, 340.
11. Ibid., 417.
12. Ibid.
13. Ibid., 418; Marc Simmons, *Spanish Government in New Mexico* (Albuquerque, The University of New Mexico Press, 1990), 79. A *vara* was a measurement equal to a "rod" of thirty-three and one-half inches. This measurement was sometimes made using the skin of a sheep or other animal. A more precise measurement of land was gained by using a pre-measured cord, usually one of a 100 "rods" in length.
14. Kessell, *Kiva*, 418.
15. Crocchiola, *San Miguel*, 6.
16. Kessell, *Kiva*, 442.
17. Kessell, *Kiva*, 434.
18. Richard Nostrand, *The Hispano Homeland*, (Oklahoma, University of Oklahoma Press, 1992), 77.
19. Kessell, *Kiva*, 439, 441.
20. Cromie, *Restored Towns*, 308.
21. Chávez, *Origins*, 286.
22. Ibid., p. 134; *Albuquerque Journal*, 1981.
23 Chávez, *Origins*, 9, 59, 108, 286.
24. Chávez, *La Conquistadora*, 72.
25. Chávez, *Origins*, 287.
26. Kessell, *Kiva*, 505.
27. Ibid., 385.
28. Josiah Gregg, *Commerce of the Praires* (Copyright, University of Oklahoma Press, 1954), 63.

10
ENCROACHMENT AND INDEPENDENCE: 1739–1821

1. Kessell, *Kiva*, 387.
2. Ibid., 387-391.
3. Leroy R. Hafen and Carl Coke Rister, *Western America* (New York, Prentice Hall Inc., 1950), 184; Bannon, *Borderlands*, 205, 216-217.
4. Ibid., *Western America*, 184-186.
5. Kessell, *Kiva*, 424-425.
6. E. A. Mares, "*The Many Faces of Padre Antonio José Martínez: A Historiographic Essay*," in *Padre Martínez: New Perspectives from Taos* (Millicent Rogers Museum, Taos, 1988), 23, Bannon, *Borderlands*, 211, Parks, *History of Mexico*, 146-165.
7. Chávez, "*Authentic New Mexican.*"
8. Ibid.
9. Simmons, *Bicentennial History*, 109.
10. Janet Lecompte, "*When Santa Fe Was a Mexican Town*" in *Santa Fe: History of an Ancient City*, David Grant Noble, ed. (Santa Fe, School of American Research Press, 1989), 83.
11. Simmons, *Bicentennial History*, 109.
12. Lecompte, "*Mexican Town*," 83.
13. Simmons, *Bicentennial History*, 109-110.
14. Hafen, *Western American*,110, Lecompte, 83.
15. Kessell, *Kiva*, 448-449; Rosemary Nusbaum, *The City Different and the Palace* (Santa Fe, The Sunstone Press, 1978), 17-18.
16. Beck, *Four Centuries*,110.
17. Ibid., 112.
18. Findley, "*Santa Fe Trail*," 107.
19. Gregg, *Commerce*, 76-77.
20. Ibid., 77.
21. Ibid.
22. Lynn I. Perrigo, *Gateway to Glorieta* (Boulder, Pruett Publishing Company, 1982), 8.
23. Rowe Findley, "*Along the Santa Fe Trail*," in *National Geographic*, March, 1991, 98-122.

11
PERMANENT SETTLEMENTS: 1821–1835

1. *Place Names*, 9.
2. Ibid., 163-164.
3. David A. Delgado, *Early New Mexico Governors Had Active Interest in Santa Rosa*, (Santa Rosa, undated), 2-3.
4. Andrés S. Hernández, *Chronology of Events Related to the Agua Negra Grant in New*

Mexico (Santa Rosa, 1985), Unpublished Manuscript.

5. *New Mexico Blue Book*, (Santa Fe, 1977-1978), 10.
6. Kessell, *Kiva*, 448.
7. Ibid., 452-453.
8. Ibid., 454. Father Caballero and most of the remaining Franciscans left New Mexico for the last time in 1828. The order was expelled by the Mexican National Congress amid rumors that Spain planned to "invade and reconquer" Mexico.
9. Campa, *Hispanic Culture*,194.
10. Lucero-White Lea, *Literary Folklore*, 215; Cleofas M. Jaramillo, *Shadows of the Past* (Santa Fe, Second Printing), 31-34.
11. Lucero-White Lea, *Literary Folklore*, 214-216.
12. *Place Names*, 85.
13. Perrigo, *Gateway*, 8.

12
CULTURAL CONFLICT: 1835–1845

1. Warren, *Villages*, 45.
2. *Place Names*, 162.
3. Chávez, *Origins*, 21-22; *Place Names*,162.
4. Beck, *Four Centuries*, 105.
5. Harvey Lewis Carter, *Dear Old Kit: The Historical Kit Carson* (Norman, University of Oklahoma Press, 1968), 38.
6. M. Morgan Estergreen, *Kit Carson: A Portraait in Courage* (Norman: University of Oklahoma Press), 86.
7. Buxton, *Lucero*, 87.
8. Simmons, *New Mexico*,138.
9. Mares, *Faces*, 10.
10. Ray John de Aragón, *"Padre Antonio José Martínez: The Man and the Myth,"* in *Padre Martínez: New Perspectives From Taos* (Millicent Rogers Museum, Pan American Publishing Company, Taos, 1988), 127.
11. Mares, *Faces*, 24.
12. De Aragón, *Padre Martínez*, 127.
13. Ibid.
14. Mares, *Faces*, 37.
15. Ibid.
16. Ibid., 36.
17. Ibid.
18. De Aragón, *Padre Martínez*, 125.
19. Mares, *Faces*, 38.
20. Lecompte, *Mexican Town*, 87.
21. *New Mexico Blue Book*, 10.

22. Horgan, *River*, 572-573.

23. Chávez, *Origins*, 137.

24. Lecompte, *Mexican Town*, 87.

25. Gregg, *Commerce*, 79.

26. Beck, *Four Centuries*,122.

27. De Aragón, *Padre Martínez*, 136.

28. Beck, *Four Centuries*, 22.

29. There is no consensus as to the origin of this colorful name. Some have suggested that it derives from *estacada* or stockade, a reference to a geological barrier which defines one of its boundaries. A second explanation suggests that the name derives from the need by people of the Arkansas-Chihuahua caravans to mark their trail with stakes on the otherwise featureless plain. *Place Names*, 89.

30. Horgan, *River*, 571-580.

31. Susan Magoffin, Stella M. Drumm, Ed., *Down the Santa Fe Trail and into Mexico: The Diary of Susan Shelby Magoffin* (New Haven, Yale University Press, 1926), 119-120. A more favorable fictional account of the life of Gertrudis Barceló is provided by Ruth Laughlin in *The Wind Leaves No Shadow*.

32. *Place Names*, 167.

33. Buxton, *Lucero*, 336c.

34. April Koop, "*La Tules: Gambling Lady Had Stake in Santa Fe's Colorful History*," in *New Mexico Magazine*, October, 1991, 92.

35. *Nuestras Mujeres*, Tey Diana Rebolledo, ed. (Albuquerque, El Norte Publications, Academia, 1992), 20.

36. Horgan, *Santa Fe*, 175; Ruth Laughlin Barker, *Caballeros: The Romance of Santa Fe and the Southwest* (New York, D. Appleton and Company, 1931), 59, 178.

37. Lecompte, *Mexican Town*, 91.

38. Lecompte, *Mexican Town*, 89.

39. Chávez, *Origins*, 141.

13

OCCUPATION AND REBELLION: 1845–1847

1. Rodolfo Acuña, *Occupied America*, (New York, Harper Collins Publishers, 1988), 13.

2. John P. Wilson, "*The American Occupation of Santa Fe*" in *Santa Fe: History of an Ancient City*, David Grant Noble, ed. (Santa Fe, School of American Research Press, 1989), 98.

3. Wilson, *American Occupation*, 97-99.

4. Chris Emmett, *Fort Union and the Winning of the Southwest* (Oklahoma, University of Oklahoma Press, 1965), 24.

5. Wilson, *American Occupation*, 100.

6. Emmett, *Fort Union*, 32, Horgan, *River*, 722.

7. Wilson, *American Occupation*, 103; Horgan, *River*, 722.
8. Emmett, *Fort Union*, 30; Horgan, *River*, 723-724. James Magoffin, accompanied by Senator Thomas H. Benton, had met with the Secretary of War and the President of the United States before leaving with Kearny. He appears to have been an emissary sent by President Polk to negotiate with Governor Armijo.
9. Perrigo, *Gateway*, 12.
10. Emmett, *Fort Union*, 34.
11. Proclamation at Las Vegas Museum.
12. Phillip St. George Cooke, *The Conquest of New Mexico and California* (New York, 1878), 305.
13. Emmett, *Fort Union*, 36.
14. Lecompte, *Mexican Town*, 87.
15. Ibid., 93.
16. Ibid., 87.
17 Lecompte, *Mexican Town*, 89. The lance, although seemingly a primitive weapon, could, in the hands of the right man, inflict a serious blow to the man equipped with a firearm. Kit Carson, with Fremont in California, noted that the Mexican troops killed and wounded many of the American troops by the use of the lance, Carter, *Dear Old Kit*, 114.
18 Two of these *presidial* soldiers were **Juan de Jesus Baca**, father of **Pascual Baca**, and **Antonio Baca**, father of **María Sinforiana Baca** (I)
19. Ibid.
20. Ibid., 89-90.
21. Ibid., 90.
22. Wilson, *American Occupation*, 102.
23, Lecompte, *Mexican Town*, 95.
24. Wilson, *American Occupation*, 108.
25. Lecompte, *Mexican Town*, 82.
26. It's possible that Kearny could not have made a worse choice. Bent's contempt for the people he was to lead was pathetic. In Bent's letter to a friend before the American occupation, he punctuated his description of the New Mexicans with this statement: "The Mexican character is made up of Stypidity (sic), Obstanacy, (sic) Ignorance—duplicity and vanity." Emmett, *Fort Union*, 26.
27. Wilson, *American Occupation*, 108.
28. Lecompte, *Mexican Town*, 84.
29. Wilson, *American Occupation*,111; Emmett, *Fort Union*, 51, for other principals.
30. Wilson, *American Occupation*, 111-112; Emmett, *Fort Union*, 51-52.
31. Wilson, *American Occupation*, 112; Emmett, *Fort Union*, 54.
32. Emmett, *Fort Union*, 56-57.
33. Ibid., 57; Estergreen, *Kit Carson*, 172-176.
34. Wilson, *American Occupation*, 113.
35. Emmett, *Fort Union*, 62-67; Mares, *Faces*, 27-29.

14
THE TERRITORIAL PERIOD: 1846–1912

1. Rodolfo Acuna, *Occupied America*, 18-20;
2. Ibid., 11.
3. J. M. Roberts, *The Pelican History of the World*, (London, Penguin Books, 1976), 712-715.
4. Robert W. Larson, *New Mexico's Quest for Statehood 1846-1912* (Albuquerque, The University of New Mexico Press, 1968), 18; Emmett, *Fort Union*, 87.
5. Perrigo, *Gateway*, 16; *Legacy of Honor, The Life of Rafael Chacón, A Nineteenth Century New Mexican*, ed. Jacqueline Dorgan Meketa, (Albuquerque, University of New Mexico Press, 1986), 125-126.
6. Larson, *Quest*, 84;
7. Meketa, *Legacy of Honor*, 165-167.
8. For a more complete discussion of the events leading to the confinement to a reservation of the Navajos, the reader is referred to *The Long Walk*, perhaps the definitive study in this regard. L. R. Bailey, *The Long Walk* (Los Angeles, Westernlore Press, 1964), 164, Horgan, 831-832.
9. The word Apache is from a Zuñi word meaning "enemy." The Zuñi used the term to describe a new group of Indian invaders who took over lands at the abandoned Tewa pueblo of Navahu. The Zuni called them Apache de Navahu, or "enemies at the pueblo of Navahu." This group became the Navajo. The name Apache was then applied by extension to other blood-related people all over the Southwest. Indians, 375; Spicer, Cycles, 218-220, 241-243.
10. This personality profile,which describes their strengths and weaknesses of the New Mexicans as paradoxically often one and the same, was suggested by Crow's discussion of the polarization of Spanish psychology and culture: *Spain: The Root and the Flower*, pages 1-22.)
11. Larson, *Quest*, 106.
12. Ibid., 119.
13. Ibid., 124-125.
14. Ibid., 123.
15. Ibid., 140.
16. Ibid., 79; The same sentiment had been expressed as early as 1853. See Emmett, *Fort Union*, n 19, 169; Horgan, *River*, 861.

15
TERRITORIAL VIOLENCE, CORRUPTION AND SCHISM

1. Anselmo F. Arellano, *Through Thick and Thin: Evolutionary Transitions of Las Vegas Grandes and Its Pobladores*, December 1990, Ph.D, Dissertation, (Albuquerque, University of New Mexico, 1990), 107-109.
2. Larson, *Quest*, 66; Emmett, Ibid., 102-103.

3. Ibid., 94.

4. Frederick W. Nolan, *The Life and Death of John Henry Tunstall* (Albuquerque, The University of New Mexico Press, 1965), 267-370; Ralph Looney, *Haunted Highways: The Ghost Towns of New Mexico* (New York, Hastings House Publishers, 1968), 49.

5. Robert M. Utley, *"Billy the Kid Country,"* in *American Heritage Magazine*, April 1991, 66; Looney, *Ghost Towns*, 52.

6. *Place Names*, 98.

7. Larson, *Quest*, 143; Frances León Swadesh, *Los Primeros Pobladores: Hispanic Americans of the Ute Frontier* (Notre Dame, University of Notre Dame Press, 1974), 68-73, 84-88.

8. Paul Horgan, *Lamy of Santa Fe* (New York, Farrar, Straus and Giroux, 1976), 18, 22.

9. Ibid., 73.

10. Ibid., 70.

11. Ibid., 108.

12. Ibid., 113.

13. Ibid., 114.

14. De Aragón, *Padre Martínez*, 137.

15. Ibid.

16. Ibid.

17. Ibid., 136.

18. Ibid., 138.

19. Ibid., 125, 129.

20. Ibid., 140.

21. Ibid., 142.

22. Ibid., 141.

23. Ibid.

24. Ibid., 128, 141; Horgan, *Lamy*, 249.

25. De Aragón, *Padre Martínez*, 141.

26. Mares, *Faces*, 31.

27. De Aragón, *Padre Martínez*, 143.

28. Thomas J. Steele, S. J., *"The View From the Rectory,"* in *Padre Martínez: New Perspectives from Taos* (Millicent Rogers Museum, Taos, 1988), 89.

29. De Aragón, *Padre Martínez*, 142.

30. Steele, *The View*, 77, 81.

31. Horgan, *Lamy*, 242, 250.

32. Steele, *The View*, 74.

33. Horgan, *Lamy*, 242.

34. Steele, *The View*, 81. Father Lucero's descent from Pedro Lucero de Godoy appears to be as follows: Gregorio 6, Salvador Manuel 5, Diego (II) 4, Antonio I 3, Juan 2, Pedro 1.

35. Ibid., 93.

36. Ibid., 73, 75-76, 78.
37. Horgan, *Lamy*, 250.
38. Ibid., 251; Steele, *The View*, 89-90.
39. Mares, *Faces*, 10.
40. Steele, *The View*, 82; Horgan, *Lamy*, 353.
41. Horgan, *Lamy*, 243.

16

TWO FAMILIES IN THE THICK OF THINGS

1. He was one of the first native New Mexicans to do so. Although the New Mexicans had been commended for their loyalty and zeal while serving in volunteer regiments, they were not allowed to join the regular army until 1855. *History New Mexico Illustrated, Volume II* (1907), 817; Emmett, *Fort Union*, 194-195.
2. Ibid.
3. Ibid.
4. David A. Delgado, *"Founder of Santa Rosa: don Celso Baca's Family Tree,"* in *Santa Rosa News*, June 28, 1990, 6.
5. Ibid.
6. Ibid.
7. Delgado, *Don Celso*, 6.
8. Hernández, *Agua Negra Grant*. The Labadies and Bacas were closely tied. Lorenzo and Reyes Labadie became the sponsors in 1870 for María Ana Celestina Baca, daughter of Celso and Sinforiana Baca (I).
9. Olive Smith-Wiley, *A Santa Rosa Story*, 1973, 9-10. The home was, perhaps, a cut above the frontier standard for the times. President Andrew Jackson [1829-1837] had running water piped into the White House for the first time, and President James Polk [1845-1849], added the first ice box and gas lights. The first telephone was installed in the executive mansion in 1879, and the first typewriter in 1880. In 1889, the White House had only one bathroom.
10. Delgado, *Don Celso*, 6.
11. Wiley, *Santa Rosa*, 9-10.
12. David A. Delgado, *La Capilla de Santa Rosa Remains Endearing to the New Mexico Travelers*, (Undated) 4.
13. During the Spanish period, 1598-1821, the term don, perhaps an acronym for *de origin noble* (of noble origin), was reserved for the governor. Only very rarely was it used for any other person. The term doña, however, did not have the same lofty connotation. It was used as a term of respect for many women. By 1821, the term don was used for owners of land, property, or individuals of influence. By 1846, the terms don and doña were used for those in the village whose mature years gave them status.
14. David A. Delgado, *"Rustic Sojourns in Guadalupe County. Who Owned Guadalupe*

County?" in *Santa Rosa News*, August 11, 1988.

15. *History Illustrated*, 818.
16. David A. Delgado, *Santa Rosa Cattle Kings Dealt One Last Hand for Hacienda de Agua Negra Land Grant Title*, (Undated).
17. Wiley, *Santa Rosa*, 24.
18. Delgado, *La Capilla*, 3.
19. *Place Names*, 149-150.
20. Delgado, *Cattle Kings*, 3.
21. A record, found by Carlos Gómez among the Antón Chico baptisms of 1895, calls the 1868 date into question. This record, which is an account of a visit during July of 1895 by Archbishop Placid Louis Chapelle [1894-1897] to the *paroquia* of Antón Chico, contains this statement: "don Celso Baca *esta edificando una capilla* ..." Should this read, "*edificante*," edifying? meaning to "improve spiritually" rather than "build?" The statement, as is, suggests that the chapel was being built in 1895, 27 years after the date given by Fabiola Cabeza de Baca. Cabeza de Baca, *Cactus*, 75.
22. *History Illustrated*, 816.
23. Ibid., 817.
24. Ibid.
25. Ibid.
26. David A. Delgado, *Santa Rosa de Lima Church*, (Undated), 1-2.
27. Late in life, several years after the death of María Sinforiana Baca (I), don Celso married Vivianita Villanueva. Celso Baca Obituary in *Santa Fe New Mexican*, May 21, 1909.
28. *History Illustrated*, 817.
29. Delgado, *Don Celso*, 6.
30. *Place Names*, 127.
31. Francis Louis Crocchiola, *The Puerto de Luna New Mexico Story*, (Nazareth, Texas, 1969), 12.
32. At least one of these children attended school in Saint Louis. María Sinforiana (II) relates that she, her father, and grandfather escorted her sister Pelagia by train to school in St Louis. This trip, in 1907, first required a two-day ride by stagecoach from Santa Rosa to the railhead at Las Vegas, a distance of only 60 miles.
33. *History Illustrated*, 818.
34. Ibid.
35. Placido Baca Obituary. Undated.
36. Aurora Lucero-White Lea, "*Our Treasury of Spanish Folklore*," in *New Mexico Folklore Record Volumn IX 1954-1955*, 15.
37. Jaramillo, *Shadows*, 29; Cabeza de Baca, *Cactus*, 156.
38 Buxton, *Lucero*, 456-457.
39. Jaramillo, *Shadows*, 93.
40. Oliver LaFarge, *Behind the Mountains* (Boston, 1956), 165-166.

41. Perrigo, *Gateway*, 6-7.
42. Emmett, *Fort Union*, 3-20. In its 40-year history (1851/05-15-1891), a number of principals in this narrative were to command this post: Lt. Col. Phillip St. George Cooke, 11-04-1853/03-11-1854, 05-07-1854/09-17-1854; Col. Christopher Carson, 12-23-1865/04-21-1866; Col. Nathan Dudley, 11-18-1876/ 08-23-1877 (arrested and court martialed) 01-14-1880/June, 1880
43. Larson, *Quest*, 34.
44. Perrigo, *Gateway*, 15-16.
45. Ibid., 19.
46. Ibid., 74.
47. Ibid., 22.
48. Ibid., 74-75; *Place Names*, 160; Utley, *"Billy the Kid,"* 76-78.
49. Perrigo, *Gateway*, 75. Following the murders of her adoptive parents, friends sent Emma to a Presbyterian school near Taos where a teacher from Kansas adopted her.
50. Perrigo, *Gateway*, Ibid., 82-84; Cabeza de Baca, *Cactus*, 93-120; Looney, *Ghost Towns*, 6672.
51. Looney, *Ghost Towns*, 66-72; Cabeza de Baca, *Cactus*, 93-95.
52. Perrigo, *Gateway*, 101.
53. Ibid., 101-102.
54. Ibid., 103.
55. Ibid.
56. *Place Names*, 12-13.
57. Perrigo, *Gateway*, 104-105.
58. Ibid., 106.
59. Nancie L. Gonzalez, *The Spanish-Americans of New Mexico* (Albuquerque, The University of New Mexico Press, 1969), 90.
60. Perrigo, *Gateway*, 110.
61. Ibid., 117.
62. Ibid., 118-120.
63. Ibid., 120-121.
64. Ibid., 121.
65. Ibid.
66. Ibid., 119.
67 Ibid., 124-126.
68. Ibid., 123.
69. Ibid., 90; Cabeza de Baca, *Cactus*, 96.
70. Anselmo F. Arellano, *"Governor Don Ezequiel C. de Baca,"* in *Las Vegas Grandes* (Las Vegas, 1985), 23.
71. *La Voz del Pueblo* had a subsidiary in Santa Rosa. This was *La Voz Publica* published by Placido Baca. The latter publication was printed on the presses at *La Voz del Pueblo* in Las Vegas. Placido Baca and Felix Martínez, owner of *La Voz del Pueblo*, were cousins. Delgado, *Don Celso*, 6.

72. Arellano, *Don Ezequiel*, 22-23.
73. "*Aurora Lucero-White Lea, Teacher Folklorist,*" in *The Santa Fe Scene* (Santa Fe, January 9, 1960), 4.

17

STATEHOOD, 1912

1. *New Mexico Blue Book*, 64.
2. Larson, *Quest*, 250.
3. Perrigo, *Gateway*, 90-92.
4. Larson, *Quest*, 304.
5. Beck, *Four Centuries*, 172-173. Elfego's descent from Cristóbal Baca (I) is as follows: Francisco Baca (9), José Miguel Baca (8), Juan Dionisio Baca (7), Juan Felipe Baca (6), Juan Antonio Baca (5), Manuel Baca (4), Cristóbal Baca (II) (3), Alonso Baca (2), Cristóbal Baca (I). For a more complete discussion regarding this genealogy see *Herencia*, January 1995.
6. C. de Baca was himself to become governor in 1916. De Baca County is named for him. His descent from Cristóbal (I) is as follows: Tomas Dolores C. de Baca (10), Juan Antonio C. de Baca (9), Luis María C. de Baca [this branch of the family reverting to the use of the full ancestral name at this point] (8), Juan Antonio Baca (7), Antonio Baca (6), the unmarried Josefa Baca (5), Manuel Baca (4), Cristóbal Baca (II) (3), Alonso Baca (2), and Cristóbal Baca (I). The descent of author Fabiola C. de Baca from Cristóbal (I), has but one more rung: Graciano C. de Baca (11). Fabiola C. de Baca wrote *We Fed Them Cactus*.
7. Muench, *New Mexico*, 39.
8. On February 18, 1917, Governor Ezequiel C. de Baca (1917 –), who had succeeded McDonald as governor, died while still in office. His lieutenant governor, Washington E. Lindsey (1917-1918) succeeded him. During February of 1918, Governor Lindsey was out of state attending a conference in Chicago and visiting Camp Kearney in California. During the waning weeks of the winter of 1918, Antonio Jose Lucero Sr. served as governor of New Mexico. "*El Secretario de Estado Antonio Lucero Gobernador Interino,*" in *La Voz del Pueblo*, undated.
9. The remaining active pallbearers were Carlos Abreau, Judge Lorin C. Collins, Judge N. B. Laughlin, Dr. Frank Marron y Alonso, Nathan Salmon, and Superintendent of Instruction Alvin N. White. Juliana Lucero Obituary in *Santa Fe New Mexican*, May 18, 1915; *Santa Fe New Mexican*, May 19, 1915; *La Voz del Pueblo*, undated.
10. *Santa Fe Scene*, 4
11. Ibid.
12. Ibid., 4-5.
13. Horgan, *River*, 911.
14. Ibid., 925.

15. Ibid. 911-912.
16. Jean Rouverol, *Pancho Villa: A Biography*, (Garden City, New York, Doubleday and Company, Inc.1972), 13.
17. Ibid.
18. *"Witnesses Claim Columbus People Had Warning Three Days Before Villa Raid,"* in *Las Vegas Daily Optic*, February 7, 1920; Looney, *Ghost Towns*, 193.
19. Looney, Ibid., 199; *New Mexico Magazine*, (March, 1991), 7.
20. Horgan, *River*, 928-926
21. Ibid., 937-939.
22. *Santa Fe Scene*, 6.
23. Ibid.
24. Perrigo, *Gateway*, 151.
25. Interview with Arthur Lucero, Albuquerque, 1990; Named Prohibition Director, in *Las Vegas Daily Optic*, January 3, 1920; *"What We Aim to Do"* in *Las Vegas Daily Optic*, January 24, 1920.
26. Interview with Sinforiana Baca (II), Las Vegas, 1990, Placido Baca Obituary. Undated.
27. Ibid.
28. Ibid.
29. Muench, New Mexico, 39.
30. Ibid.
31. Ibid.

18

EPILOGUE, SIMPLE GIFTS: 1923–1958

1. José Albino Baca (I) was one of eleven children of Vicente Baca and Francisquita Montoya. Their son, José Albino Baca (II), was married to Marguerite Pendaries. One of the six children of the latter couple was Consuelo Baca. She was married to Oliver LaFarge whose delightful account of this family is memorialized in his book, *Behind the Mountains*.
2. T. S. Elliot, *Four Quartets: Little Giddings*, in the *Complete Poems and Plays, 1909-1950*, (New York: Harcourt, Brace, World, Inc., 1971) 145.
3. Ibid.

AFTERWORD

1. *National Register, Item 9, 3-4.*
2. Elmo Baca, *"Pecos Valley Villages Stand Proud,"* in *New Mexico Magazine* (October, 1990), 87-98.

BIBLIOGRAPHY

ALL SOURCE MATERIALS, WHETHER PUBLISHED OR
UNPUBLISHED, ARE HERE GROUPED IN A SINGLE ALPHABET.

Acuña, Rodolfo. *Occupied America*. New York, Harper Collins Publishers, 1988.

Anonymous. *An Illustrated History of New Mexico. Its Sources and People* (Los Angeles, Chicago, New York), 1907.

Antonio José Lucero Obituaries. Antonio Lucero, Former Secretary of State, Dead; For Years Leader of Democrats. Prominent Citizen Passes Away at Las Vegas Suddenly: About to Resume Editor's Chair. *Santa Fe New Mexican*, June 27, 1921; Antonio Lucero Dies Suddenly at Home on the Boulevard Today. *Las Vegas Daily Optic*, June 27, 1921.

Arellano, Anselmo F. *"Through Thick and Thin: Evolutionary Transitions of Las Vegas Grandes and Its Pobladores,"* Ph.D. Dissertation, University of New Mexico, 1990.

Arellano, Anselmo F. and Julian Josue Vigil. *"Las Vegas Grandes on the Gallinas 1835-1985"* Las Vegas: *Editorial Teleraña*, 1985.

Baca, Elmo. *Pecos Valley Villages Stand Proud*, in *New Mexico Magazine*. October, 1990.

Bailey, L. R. *The Long Walk*. Los Angles: Westernlore Press, 1964.

Bancroft, Hubert Howe. *History of the North Mexican States and Texas, Volume I, 1531-1800*. San Francisco: A. L. Bancroft and Company Publishers, 1884.

Bandelier, Adolf F. A. *The Gilded Man*. Chicago: The Rio Grande Press, 1962.

Bannon, John Francis. *The Spanish Borderlands Frontier*. Albuquerque, University of New Mexico Press, 1970.

Beck, Warren A. *New Mexico: A History of Four Centuries*. Norman: University of Oklahoma Press, 1969.

Beerman, Eric. *"The Ancestors of Álvar Nuñez Cabeza de Vaca,"* in the *Louisiana Genealogical Register, Vol. XXXV, Number 2, June 1988*.

Bolton, Herbert Eugene. *Spanish Exploration in the Southwest 1542-1706*. New York: Barnes and Noble, Inc., 1963.

Boorstin, Daniel J. *The Discoverers*. New York: Random House, 1983.

Brebner, John Bartlet. *The Explorers of North America 1492-1806*. Garden City, New York: Doubleday and Company, Inc., 1955.

Burke, James T. *This Miserable Kingdom*. Las Vegas: Our Lady of Sorrows Church, 1973.

Bustamante, Adrian H. "*Españoles, Castas y Labradores*," in *Santa Fe: History of an Ancient City*. David Grant Noble, ed. Santa Fe: School of American Research Press, 1989.

Buxton, Margaret L., ed. *The Family of Lucero de Godoi: Early Records*. Albuquerque: The New Mexico Genealogical Society, 1981.

Cabeza de Vaca, Álvar Nuñez. *The Journey of Álvar Nuñez Cabeza de Vaca*. Translated by Fanny Bandelier. Chicago: The Rio Grande Press, 1964.

Cabeza de Baca, Fabiola. *We Fed Them Cactus*. Albuquerque: The University of New Mexico Press, 1954.

Cabeza de Vaca, James Hugo." *Captain Don Bartolomé Baca Governor of New Mexico, 1823 Thru 1825*," in *Herencia*, Volume I, October, 1993.

Campa, Arthur L. *Hispanic Culture in the Southwest*. Norman: University of Oklahoma Press, 1979.

Carter, Harvey Lewis. *Dear Old Kit: The Historical Kit Carson*. Norman: University of Oklahoma Press, 1968.

Celso Baca Obituary. Celso Baca Who Died Last Night at Santa Rosa. Patriarch Among His People and Political Leader. He Answers the Last Summons. *Santa Fe New Mexican*. May 21, 1909.

Chávez, Fray Angélico. "*But Time and Chance: The Story of Padre Martínez of Taos, 1793 1867*. Santa Fe: The Sunstone Press, 1981.

———. *A Distinctive American Clan of New Mexico*. Santa Fe: William Gannon, 1989.

———. *La Conquistadora: The Autobiography of an Ancient Statue*. Santa Fe: Sunstone Press, 1983.

——. *Origins of New Mexico Families: In the Spanish Colonial Period*. Albuquerque: The University of Albuquerque, 1973.

——.*Origins of New Mexico Families: In the Spanish Colonial Period*. Santa Fe: The Museum of New Mexico Press, *Revised edition, 1992*.

——. *"The Authentic New Mexican: A Question of Identity."* An address presented at the Inaugural Symposium and inauguration of Gerald W. Thomas as the sixteenth president of New Mexico State University. Undated.

Cooke, Phillip St. George. *The Conquest of New Mexico and California, an Historical and Personal Narrative*. New York: G. P. Putnam's Sons, 1878.

Crocchiola, Francis Louis. *The San Miguel del Bado New Mexico Story*. Pep, Texas, 1964.

Cromie, Alice. *Restored Towns and Historic Districts of America*. New York: E. P. Dutton, 1979.

Cronon, William. *Changes in the Land: Indians, Colonists, and the Ecology of New England*. New York. Hill and Wang, 1983.

Crow, John A. *Spain: The Root and the Flower*. New York: Harper and Row Publishers, 1963.

Delgado, David A. *Don Celso Baca's Family Tree*, in the *Santa Rosa News*, June 28, 1990.

——. *Early New Mexico Governors Had Active Interest in Santa Rosa*. Undated.

——. *La Capilla de Santa Rosa Remains Endearing to New Mexico's Tourists*. Undated.

——. *Rustic Sojourns in Guadalupe County. Who Owned Guadalupe County?* in *Santa Rosa News*, August 11, 1988.

——. *Santa Rosa Cattle Kings Dealt One Last Hand for Hacienda de Agua Negra Land Grant Title*. Undated.

——. *Santa Rosa de Lima Church Celebrates 80th Feast Day of Patroness of the Americas*. August 23. Undated.

Dunham, Harold H. *"Spanish and Mexican Land Policies and Grants in the Taos Pueblo Region, New Mexico."* *Pueblo de Taos* v United States. Docket No. 357, Indian Claims Commission, December, 1959.

Eliot, Thomas Stearns. *"Four Quartets: Little Giddings"* in *The Complete Poems and Plays 1909-1950*. New York: Harcourt, Brace, World, Inc., 1971.

Ellis, Richard N., ed. *New Mexico Past and Present: A Historical Reader*. Albuquerque: The University of New Mexico Press, 1971.

Emmett, Chris. *Fort Union and the Winning of the Southwest*. Copyright, University of Oklahoma Press, 1965.

Esquibel, José Antonio. *"Esquibel Families in Eighteenth Century New Mexico,"* in *New Mexico Genealogist, Volumes XXXI, Nos. 1 and 2, March and June, 1992*.

Estergreen, M. Morgan. *Kit Carson: A Portrait in Courage*. Norman: University of Oklahoma Press, 1962.

Findley, Rowe. *"Along the Santa Fe Trail,"* in *National Geographic*, March, 1991.

Fraser, Antonia. *Mary Queen of Scots*. New York: Dell Publishing Co., Inc., 1971.

Gonzáles, David and Jonathan A. Ortega. *"Onofre Baca-Socorro Lynching Victim and His Brother Elfego Baca—An American Legend,"* in *Herencia*, Volume 3, Issue 1, January 1995.

González, Nancie L. *The Spanish-Americans of New Mexico: A Heritage of Pride*. Albuquerque: The University of New Mexico Press, 1967.

Gregg, Josiah. *Commerce of the Prairies*. University of Oklahoma Press, 1954.

Gutiérrez, Ramón A. *When Jesus Came the Corn Mothers Went Away. Marriage, Sexuality, and Power in New Mexico, 1500-1846*. Stanford: Stanford University Press, 1991.

Hafen, Leroy R. and Carl Coke Rister. *Western America: The Exploration, Settlement, and Development of the Region Beyond the Mississippi*. New York: Prentice Hall, Inc., 1950.

Hernández, Andrés S. *Chronology of Events Related to the Agua Negra Grant in New Mexico*. Santa Rosa, 1985.

Hollister, Ovando J. *Boldly, They Rode: A History of the First Colorado Regiment of Volunteers*. Lakewood, Colorado: Golden Press, 1949.

Horgan, Paul. *Conquistadors: In North American History*. New York: Farrar, Straus and Giroux, 1966.

——. *The Great River*. Hanover: University Press of New England, 1984.

——. *Lamy of Santa Fe: His Life and Times*. New York: Farrar, Straus and Giroux, 1976.

——. *The Centuries of Santa Fe*. New York: E. P. Dutton and Co., Inc., 1956.

Jaramillo, Cleofas M. *Shadows of the Past*. Santa Fe: Ancient City Press, Undated.

Jeffries, Olen C. "*Holiday in Santa Rosa*," in *New Mexico Magazine*, October, 1965.

Josephy, Alvin M., Jr. *The American Heritage Book of Indians*. American Heritage Publishing Company, Inc. Simón and Schuster, 1961.

Juliana Romero Lucero Obituaries. Mrs. Antonio Lucero Wife of Secretary of State, Dies at Her Home Here: City Shocked By News of Passing of Highly Esteemed Wife of State Officer. *Santa Fe New Mexican*, May 18, 1915; Impressive Scenes at Funeral Services of Late Mrs. Lucero. Hundreds of Friends Gather to Pay Tribute to Memory of Late Wife of Secretary of State. *Santa Fe New Mexican*, May 19, 1915; *La Voz del Pueblo*, May 22, 1915.

Kendall, George Wilkins. *Narrative of the Texan Santa Fe Expedition*. 2 Volumes. Austin: The Stick Company, 1935.

Kessell, John L., "*By Force of Arms*," in *Santa Fe: History of an Ancient City*. David Grant Noble, ed. Santa Fe: School of American Research Press, 1989.

——. *Kiva, Cross and Crown: The Pecos Indians and New Mexico 1540-1840*. Albuquerque: The University of New Mexico Press, 1987.

Koop, April. "*La Tules: Gambling Lady Had Stake in Santa Fe's Colorful History*," in *New Mexico Magazine*, October, 1991.

La Farge, Oliver. *Behind the Mountains*. Boston: Houghton Mifflin Co., 1956.

Larson, Robert W. *New Mexico's Quest for Statehood*. Albuquerque: The University of New Mexico Press, 1968.

Laughlin Barker, Ruth. *Caballeros*. New York: D. Appleton & Company, 1931.

Lecompte, Janet. "*When Santa Fe Was a Mexican Town*," in *Santa Fe: History of an Ancient City*. David Grant Nobel, ed. Santa Fe: School of American Research Press, 1989.

Levine, Frances, *"Down Under an Ancient City,"* in *Santa Fe: History of an Ancient City*. David Grant Nobel, ed. Santa Fe: School of American Research Press, 1989.

Looney, Ralph. *Haunted Highways: The Ghost Towns of New Mexico*. New York: Hastings House, Publishers, 1968.

Lucero-White Lea, Aurora. *Literary Folklore of the Hispanic Southwest*. San Antonio: The Naylor Company, 1953.

Lucero-White Lea, Aurora. *"Our Treasury of Spanish Folklore,"* in *New Mexico Folklore Record*. Volume IX 1954-55. Undated.

Magoffin, Susan Shelby. *Down the Santa Fe Trail and into Mexico: The Diary of Susan Shelby Magoffin*, Ed. by Stella M. Drumm. New Haven: Yale University Press, 1926.

Mayer, Robert. *"Lost Pueblo Found in Agua Fr*ia," *Santa Fe Register*, January 25, 1989.

MacCurdy, Tim. *"The Embattled Life of an Eccentric Governor,"* in *New Mexico Magazine*, March 1990.

McClure, Judy. *"Pancho Villa Commemoration."* *New Mexico Magazine*, October, 1990.

Mikele, Jacqueline Dorges, ed. *Legacy of Honor, The Life of Rafael Chacón. A Nineteenth Century New Mexican*, Albuquerque, University of New Mexico Press, 1986.

Miller, Michael. *"Land Dispute Sparks Gun Duel: Sprawling Bartolomé Baca grant raises a fury,"* in New Mexico Magazine, January 1989.

Muench, David and Tony Hillerman. *New Mexico*. Portland: Charles H. Balding, Publisher, 1974.

National Genealogical Society Quarterly. Washington: National Genealogical Society, September, 1979.

National Register of Historic Places Inventory-Nomination Form. Los Luceros Hacienda. Item No. 7. Undated.

New Mexico Blue Book: 1977 through 1992.

Noble, David Grant, ed. Santa Fe: History of an Ancient City. Santa Fe: School of American Research Press, 1989.

Nolan, Frederick W. The Life and Death of John Henry Tunstall. Albuquerque: The University of New Mexico Press, 1965.

Nostrand, Richard. *The Hispano Homeland*. Norman, University of Oklahoma Press, 1992.

Nusbaum, Rosemary. *The City Different and the Palace*. Santa Fe: The Sunstone Press, 1978.

Ortega, Jonathan A. *"Vacaville, California Founded by New Mexico's Baca Family,"* in *Herencia*, Volume 1, October, 1993.

Padre Martínez. New Perspectives from Taos. Taos: Millicent Rogers Museum, 1988.

Parkes, Henry Bamford. *A History of Mexico*. Boston, Houghton Mifflin Company, 1988.

Pearce, T. M., ed. *New Mexico Place Names: A Geographical Dictionary*. Albuquerque: The University of New Mexico Press, 1965.

Perrigo, Lynn. *Gateway to Glorieta: A History of Las Vegas, New Mexico*. Boulder: Pruett Publishing Company, 1982.

Placido Baca Obituaries. Prominent Guadalupe Man Dies; *Sentida Defunción*; Funeral Services Here Monday for Placido Baca. undated.

Roberts, M. *The Pelican History of the World*. London, Penguin Books, 1987.

Rebolledo, Tey Diana , ed. *Nuestras Mujeres*. Albuquerque, El Norte Publications, Academia, 1992.

Roth, Cecil. *A History of the Marranos*. New York: Meridian Books, Inc., 1959.

Rouverol, Jean. *Pancho Villa: A Biography*. New York: Doubleday and Company, Inc., 1972.

Santa Fe Scene. Santa Fe: January, 1960.

Sánchez, Joseph. *"The Peralta Ordonez Affair and the Founding of Santa Fe,"* in *Santa Fe: History of an Ancient City*. David Grant Noble, ed. Santa Fe: School of American Research Press, 1989.

———. *"Twelve Days in August,"* in Santa Fe: History of an Ancient City. David Grant Noble, ed. Santa Fe: School of American Research Press, 1989.

Scholes, France V. *Troublous Times in New Mexico. 1659-1670.* Albuquerque: The University of New Mexico Press, 1942.

Silverberg, Robert. *The Pueblo Revolt.* Lincoln: University of Nebraska Press, 1994.

Simmons, Marc. *"Colonial Cornucopia,"* in *New Mexico Magazine*, January, 1992. New Mexico:

———. *A Bicentennial History.* New York: W. W. Norton and Company, Inc., 1977.

———. *Spanish Government in New Mexico.* Albuquerque: The University of New Mexico Press. 1990.

———. *The Last Conquistador: Juan de Oñate and the Settling of the Far Southwest.* University of Oklahoma Press, 1991.

Spicer, Edward H. *Cycles of Conquest.* Tucson, the University of Arizona Press, 1989.

Stratton, Eugene Aubrey. *Plymouth Colony: Its History and People, 1620-1691.* Salt Lake: Ancestry Publishing, 1986.

Swadesh, Frances León. *Los Primeros Pobladores: Hispanic Americans of the Ute Frontier.*Notre Dame: University of Nortre Dame Press, 1974.

Thomas, Alfred Barnaby. *After Coronado: Spanish Exploration Northeast of New Mexico, 1696—1727.* Norman: University of Oklahoma Press, 1969.

Tobias, Henry J. *A History of the Jews in New Mexico.* Albuquerque: University of New Mexico Press, 1990.

Twitchell, Ralph E. *The Leading Facts of New Mexico History.* 5 Volumes, Cedar Rapids, Iowa: The Torch Press, 1911-17. New Edition, Sunstone Press, 2008.

———. *The Leading Facts of New Mexico History.* Albuquerque: Horn and Wallace, 1963.

Utley, Robert M. *"Billy the Kid Country,"* in *American Heritage Magazine*, April, 1991.

Warren, Nancy Hunter. Villages in Hispanic New Mexico. Santa Fe: School of American Research Press, 1987.

Weber, David. *Foreigners in their Native Land*. Albuquerque, University of New Mexico Press, 1973.

———. *The Spanish Frontier in North America*. New Haven, Yale University Press, 1992.

Westphall, Victor. *The Public Domain in New Mexico: 1854-1891*. Albuquerque: The University of New Mexico Press, 1965.

What We Aim To Do. Statement of Antonio Lucero, Prohibition Director. Las Vegas: *Optic and Live Stock Grower*. January, 24, 1920.

When Cultures Meet: *Remembering San Gabriel del Yunge Oweenge* . Santa Fe: Sunstone Press, 1987.

Wiley, Olive Smith. *A Santa Rosa Story*, 1973.

Wilson, John P. "*The American Occupation of Santa Fe*," in *Santa Fe: History of an Ancient City*. David Grant Noble, ed. Santa Fe: School of American Research Press, 1989.

Winick, Charles. Dictionary of Anthropology. Totowa, New Jersey, 1966.

Witnesses Claim Columbus People Had Warning Three Days Before Villa's Raid, in *Las Vegas Daily Optic*, February 7, 1920.

Yeo, Margaret. *The Greatest of the Borgias*. Milwaukee: The Bruce Publishing Company, 1952.

Zamora, William. "*New Mexico's Zamora Family*," in *Herencia*, Volume 2, January, 1994.

GENEALOGICAL NAME INDEX

The genealogical determinations made in this study result from research conducted over a number of years using hundreds of historical and genealogical sources. The following methodology was used to establish these relationships:

- Definite proof linking parent and child in the form of a birth, baptismal, marriage or death record; marital investigation; legal proceeding; military enlistment paper; Spanish, Mexican, Territorial or State Census; and/or a will.
- Newspaper accounts, obituaries, and interviews, and
- Especially in the murky seventeenth century where definite proof is often lacking, reasonable assumptions stated as such. The source for each entry is listed.

A legend for abbreviations and sources follows. Names emboldened in this index represent possible, probable, and confirmed lines of descent to the author. Italicized names represent hypothesized relationships. Names in regular script represent members of the extended Baca or Lucero de Godoy families or as designated in the entry. Some of the people listed in this index are not in the text.

ABBREVIATIONS FOR NAME INDEX:

B: Date of Birth
Bap: Date of Baptism
Bur: Buried
D: Date of Death
M: Date of Marriage
SL: Still Living
( ): Locations of births, deaths or marriages
(1) First spouse, (2) second spouse, etc.
Dates are month, day, year.
(copy): Copy of document
Obit: Found in obituary

LEGEND FOR SOURCES:

Those sources with an asterisk are also listed in the Bibliography with more specific information.

AASF: Archives of the Archdiocese of Santa Fe
AK: *The Adobe Kingdom*
*Buxton: *The Family of Lucero de Godoi: Early Records* by Margaret Buxton
Census: Spanish or Mexican census of New Mexico: 1750, 1790, 1823, 1830, 1845, New Mexico Genealogical Society
*Cab: *Caballeros* by Ruth Laughlin Barker
*Chance: *But Time and Chance: The Story of Padre Martínez of Taos*, (1793-1867) by Fray Angélico Chávez
Chávez: A Distinctive American Clan of New Mexico by Fray Angélico Chávez
*Conq: *La Conquistadora* by Fray Angélico Chávez
*Corn Mothers: *When Jesus Came, the Corn Mothers Went Away* by Ramón Gutiérrez
*Delgado: David Delgado. See Bibliography
Doña Ana: New Mexico's southern most county on the Rio Grande
Fed. Census: U. S. Census Records for the Territory of New Mexico taken every ten years from 1850. U. S. Census Records for the State of New Mexico 1920
Film: Microfilm number
Gómez: The genealogical research of Carlos Gómez (unpublished) using, primarily, the following sources: Special Collections Branch of the Albuquerque Public Library; Church of Jesus Christ of Latter Day Saints Genealogical Branch Library (Family History Center); State of New Mexico Records Center and Archives, Santa Fe
IGN: International Genealogy Index. May be found in the Genealogical Branch Library of the Church of Jesus Christ of Latter Day Saints, and in the Special Collections Branch of the Albuquerque Public Library.
*Kiva: *Kiva, Cross and Crown: The Pecos Indians and New Mexico, 1540–1840* by John Kessell
*NMPN: *New Mexico Place Names*, T. M. Pierce, Editor.
*Oñate: *The Last Conquistador: Juan de Oñate and the Settling of the Far Southwest* by Marc Simmons
*Origins: *Origins of New Mexico Families: In the Spanish Colonial Period* by Fray Angélico Chávez, 1973 edition and revised edition, 1992.
SEP: "Spanish Enlistment Papers of New Mexico." National Genealogist Quarterly, Vol. 67, 1979
SMDB: *San Miguel del Bado Records*, New Mexico's community of third importance in 1821. *San Miguel del Bado Census of 1841*, transcribed by Julian Josue Vigil

Anaya Almázan, Juana de: (D 1696) (San Ildefonso) Wife of Ignacio Baca (Origins 10-11), AK 140

Anaya, Ynes de: (Salamanca, Spain) Wife of **Pedro de Almázan** (Origins 3), AK Chart II

Apodaca, Juana Teresa: Wife of **Juan Esteban Velásquez** (M 12-20-1772) (Santa Fe), (Origins 310), AK Chart VII

Archibeque, María Guadalupe: Wife of **Salbador Gonzáles** (Gómez)

Arechuleta, Asencio de: (B 1572) (Eibar, Guipúzcoa) (D by 1626) Son of **Juan de Arechuleta**; husband of **Ana Pérez de Bustillo**, One of Oñate's men, he was described as having a medium build, black beard, and a slight wound on the forehead. (Origins 6, 87) (NMPN 10), AK 43, 52, Charts IV and VIII

Arechuleta, Juan de: (D 07-21-1643) Son of Ascencio de Arechuleta; one of the men beheaded in Governor Rosas affair (Origins p. 6-7, 63, 131), AK 93, Chart IV

Arechuleta, María de: Daughter of **Ascencio de Arechuleta**; wife of Juan Márquez (Origins 6), AK Chart IV

Baca/Vaca , see also C. de Baca

Baca, Alonso: (B 1601) (San Gabriel) Son of **Cristóbal Baca** (I). His wife's name is unknown (Origins 11) (Clan 20, 62) (Kiva 138, 154, 194, (526 n 57), AK 60, 86, 93, 106, 122, 132, Charts I, IV, VI, and IX

Baca (II), Alonso: (D 1696) (San Ildefonso) Son of Ignacio Baca (Origins 11, 141), AK 140

Baca, Ana: (D 1680) (Taos) (Lived at her *Estancia del Alamo*, Santa Fe) Daughter of **Antonio Baca**; wife of Francisco López de Aragón (Origins 10, 54-55) (Clan 36), AK Chart IV

Baca, Andrés: (D 1696) Son of Ignacio Baca (Origins 11), AK 140

Baca, Anita: (B 1900 ?) Daughter of **José Placido Baca**; wife of Adolfo Sena. AK 256

Baca, Antonio: (B 1708) (Appears to have been one of the grantees in 1762 of the *Nuestra Senora de la Luz de Las Lagunitas* between the Río Puerco and Cebolleta Mountains. Inherited the Pajarito Grant.) Antonio was the son of Josefa Baca; husband of Mónica de Cháves (M 06-16-1726) (Albuquerque) (Origins 144, 161) (Clan 85, 88-89) (NMPN 3, 110, 116) (Corn Mothers 326)

Baca, Antonio: (B 1596) (Mexico City) (D 07-21-1643) (Santa Fe) Son of **Cristóbal Baca** (I), husband of **Yumar Pérez de Bustillo**; one of the men beheaded in the Governor Rosas affair (Origins 10, 87) (Clan 16, 19-20) (Kiva 165, 531 n 34), AK 60, 78, 92-94, 106, 122, 133, 143, 149, Charts I, IV, VI and IX

Baca, Antonio: (B 1680 ?) (D 12-04-1761) Son of **Manuel Baca**; husband of María de Aragón (B 1685) (Mexico City) (M 06-12-1706) (D 09-01-1751) (Origins 128, 141) (Clan 110-111) (Corn Mothers 255-56), AK 133, 142

Baca, Antonio: (B 1811) Son of **Manuel Baca** and **Pascuala Cisneros**; husband of **María Josefa Gonzáles** (M 08-20-1826) (SMDB) (census 1790 SF) (census 1841 SMDB) (Film 016775) (Gómez)

Baca, Antonio Emilio Ramón: (B 04-10-1901) (Santa Rosa) Son of **José Placido Baca** (Gómez), AK 256

Baca, Baltazar: Son of Bernabé Baca, husband of (1) Manuela Rael de Aguilar (M 07-17-1738) (D 1758), (2) Rafaela Baca (M 05 or 09-11-1762) (Origins 145) (Clan 139) (NMPN 13, 120, 136) (Corn Mothers 210)

Baca, Bartolomé: (B Belen) (D 04-30-1834) (Tome) Served: 1823-1825. Son of Diego Domingo Baca, husband of María de la Luz Cháves (B 05-02-1790) (Albuquerque) (D 11-03-1844) (Tome) (Origins 144)

Baca, Bernabé: (Possibly Bernabé Jorge) (B 1692) (D 1762) (Possible grantee of the *Pueblo Viejo* at La Ciénega in 1701) Bernabé was the husband of Margarita Baca (Mata) (B 10-05-1705) (M 05-28-1718) (Origins 145) (Clan 76, 140, 142)

Baca, Carlos: (B 10-19-1901) Husband of Delia Lucero

Baca, Celso: (Alternately José Cascelso or Excelso) (Bap. 04-07-1836) (SMDB) (D 05-20-1909) (Santa Rosa) (Consolidated the holdings at Santa Rosa) (The community takes its name from the family chapel dedicated to St. Rose of Lima and Celso's mother Maria Rosa Sena.) Son of **José Rafael Albino Baca**; husband of (1) **María Sinforiana Baca** (I) (B 1838) (M 12-09-1851)(SMDB) (Copy), (2) Vivianita Villanueva (Fed. Cs. 1870) (Bap. in film 017001, SMDB Baptisms) (Film 016875, Ribera Baptisms) (M of CB to SB in Film 016878, Ribera Marriages) (NMPN 149-150) (Gómez), AK 143, 247, 248, 250-257, 265. 292, Chart IX

Baca, Consuelo: Daughter of José Albino Baca (II), wife of Oliver LaFarge (NMPN 119), AK FN Chapter 18

Baca, Crescenciano: (Bap. 04-09?-1866) (SMDB) Son of **Celso Baca**, husband of Manuela Serrano (M 10-09-1885) (Antón Chico) (Film 0016875, Ribera Baptisms), AK 248, 250-257, 261, 292

Baca (I), Cristóbal: (B 1567-70) (Mexico City) Son of Juan de Vaca, husband of **Ana Ortiz Pacheco** (Mexico City). One of Oñate's reinforcements, this parent was described in 1600 as having a good stature, dark complexioned, and well featured. (Origins 9-10) (Clan. 3, 16) (NMPN 12), AK 55, 57, 59, 62, 66, 76-77, 132, 175

Baca (II), Cristóbal: (D by 1687 ?) (Lived in Santa Fe) Son of **Alonso Baca**, husband of **Ana Moreno de Lara (Trujillo)** (Origins 10) (Clan 62, 68), AK 122, 127, 133, 139, 142, Chart I

Baca (III), Cristóbal: (D 1739) Son of **Manuel Baca**, husband of (1) Apolonia de la Vega y Coca (B 1701)(D 03-07-1734), (2) Manuela Márquez (M 11-09-1734) (Origins 141, 144, 82, 89), AK 133, 142

Baca, Diego: A San Miguel del Bado grantee (Kiva 433 ?), AK 170, 247

Baca, Diego Manuel: (B 1691-1703) (D 03-29-1727) (Lived at *La Cañada de Guicú*-La Ciénega). Diego Manuel was the son of **Manuel Baca**; husband of **María de la Vega y Coca** (Origins 141-144) (Kiva 368), AK 133, 142-143, 294, Chart VI

Baca, Diego Pedro Manuel: (Bap. 06-05-1748) (Santa Fe) (D before 01-02-1831) Son of **Nicolás Baca**; husband of (1) **Ana María Esquibel** (M 03-05-1770) (Castrense), (2) **María Dolores Leyba** (M 04-11-1798) (Copy) On July 1, 1779 this parent was described as a farmer, 5' 3" in height, 27-years-of-age (he was actually 31), with black hair and eyebrows, dark eyes, dark skin, thin beard, and moles at the end of the left side of his nose and on his right leg. (Bap. in Film 0016903) (Both M's listed in Film 016905) (Film 0016903, Santa Fe Baptisms) (Copy) (census 1790, *Presidio* of Santa Fe) (Film 016906, Santa Fe Burials 77) (SEP 231) (Gómez), AK 143, 170, 247, Charts VI and IX

Baca, Elfego: (B 1865)(D 1945) Son of Francisco Baca, husband of Frances Pohmer (NMPN 60-61, 132), AK 274

Baca, Gertrudis: Daughter of **Antonio Baca**; wife of **Antonio Jorge de Vera** (Origins 10, 51) (Clan 108-109), AK 122, Chart I

Baca, Gregoria: Daughter of **Antonio Baca**; wife of Antonio de Albizu (Origins 2, 10), AK 122

Baca, Ignacio: (B 1657) (D by 1689) Son of **Cristóbal Baca** (II); husband of Juana de Anaya Almázan. One of the refugees of 1680, this 24-year-old was described in 1681 as tall and slim, with an aquiline face, fair complexion, wavy red hair, with no beard. (Origins 10) (Clan 50), AK 123, 133, 140

Baca, Ignacio: (B 1762?) Son of **Juan Esteban Baca**; husband of **María Vitalia Tafoya** (M 05-29-1797) (Origins 144), AK Charts VI and IX

Baca, Isabel de Bohórquez: (B 1586-87) (Mexico City) (Lived at *Arroyo del Tunque*, San Felipe). Isabel was the daughter of **Cristóbal Baca** (I); wife of **Pedro Durán y Cháves** (I) (Origins 10, 19) (Clan 7-8, 16-17, 62, 71), AK 60, 78, Charts I, IV and VI

Baca, José: (B 1664) (D 07-03-1687) Son of **Cristóbal Baca** (II); husband of **Josefa Pacheco**. In 1681, the 17-year-old José was described as of medium, thick-set stature, with a beardless face, large eyes and chestnut hair (Origins 10, 84, 141), AK 133

Baca (I), José Albino: (B 03-01-1828) (D 01-09-1905) Son of Vicente Baca; husband of Dolores Gallegos (B 11-01-1827) (Abiquiu) (D 01-09-1904), AK 291

Baca (II), José Albino: (B 06-23-1876) Son of José Albino Baca (I); husband of Marguerite Pendaries (M 1897), AK FN Chapter 18

Baca, José Crescenciano (or Crescencio): (B 1809-16) Son of **José Ramón Baca**; husband of María Buenaventura Lucero (M 05-27-1834) (SMDB) (Delig. #7 05-21-1834) (Gómez), AK 157

Baca, José Francisco: (B 1819) Son of **José Ramón Baca**; husband of María Juana (or Juana María) Lucero (M 12-20-1841) (Copy) (census 1841) (Gómez), AK 257

Baca, José Joaquin: (B 1795) Son of **Diego Pedro Manuel Baca**; husband of **María Antonia Feliciana Sandoval** (M 07-29-1812) (SMDB) (census 1841) (Gómez), AK Charts VI and IX

Baca, José Luis: (Bap. 06-23-1808) Son of **Ignacio Baca**; husband of **María Luisa Abeyta** (Gómez) Charts IX and X

Baca, José Pascual: (Bap. 05-22-1834) (SMDB) Son of **Juan de Jesus Baca**; husband of (1) María de Jesus Bustamante (B 1838) (SMDB) (M 04-11-1852) (SMDB), (2) **María Estefana Rael** (M 07-22-1861) (Bap. Film 017001, SMDB Baptisms) (Fed. Cs. 1880) (M of JPB to MJB in Film 0016878) (M JPB to MER, Film 0016627, Antón Chico Marriages) (Film 016875, Ribera Baptisms) (Gómez), AK 256, Chart IX.

Baca, José Placido: (B 10-05-1860) (SMDB) (D 11-16-1937) (Santa Rosa) Son of **Celso Baca**; husband of **María Ana Baca** (M 11-27-1882) (Copy) (Bap. in Film 0016875) (M in Film 016627) (Film 0169875, Ribera Baptisms, 339) (Copy) (Gómez), AK 248, 250-257, 261, 292, Charts IX

Baca, José Rafael Albino: (B 1806) Son of **Diego Pedro Manuel Baca**; husband of (1) Teresa Trujillo (M 08-28-1831) (SMDB) (Copy), (2) **María Rosa Altagracia Sena** (M 01-23-1833) (SMDB) (Copy), (3) Dolores Marques (M 02-21-1852) (SMDB) (Copy) (JRAB to TT Film 017002) (JRAB to DM Film 016878) (JRAB to MRAS Film 0017002) (DM to TT 0828-1831) (DM to MRAS 01-23-1833)) (census 1823) (Gómez), AK 247, Charts VI and IX

Baca, José Ramón: (B 1782 ?) (D by 05-21-1834) Husband of **María Alfonsa Martín(ez)**, AK 170, 247, 257

Josefa Baca: (B 1685-86) (*Guadalupe del Paso*) (D 1746 ?) (Lived at *El Sitio de San Ysidro de Parjarito*) Daughter of **Manuel Baca** (Origins 144) (Clan 63, 88-89, 111) (NMPN 116), AK 142, 205-206

Baca, Juan Antonio: Son of **Manuel Baca**; husband of (1) María Gallegos (M 08-02-1716) (Bernalillo), (2) Petronila García Jurado (Origins 141) (NMPN 24), AK 133, 142, 153

Baca, Juan Antonio: (B 1722) Son of Antonio Baca; husband of María Romero (B 1728) (M 09-17-1753) (Origins 144, 152) (Clan 89) (NMPN 12)

Baca, Juan de Jesus: (B 1806) (D before 03-13-1853) Son of **José Ramón Baca**; husband of **María Ramona Lucero**; (M 04-28-1826) (SMDB) (Film 017878, Ribera Baptisms, 42)

(Film 016875, Ribera Baptisms) (Census 1841) (M in Film 0016675) (Gómez), AK 257

Baca, Juan Esteban: Son of **Diego Manuel Baca**; husband of **Teodora Terrus** (Origins 144), AK 143, Chart VI

Baca, Juan Manuel: (Founder of Vacaville, California) Son of José Miguel Baca; husband of (1) María Dolores Bernal (M 06-15-1815) (Santa Fe), (2) Estephana Martínez.

Baca, Juana,: Daughter of **José Baca**; wife of **Nicolás Ortiz Nino Ladron de Guevara** (II) (Origins 41), AK 133

Baca, Juana (Maria ?): Daughter of **Cristobal Baca** (II). On February 20, 1703 she was given a grant of land on the Rio Grande between the Santo Domingo and Cochiti Pueblos. (Origins 141, 144) (Clan 63, 109), AK 205

Baca, Juana de Zamora: Daughter of **Cristóbal Baca** (I); wife of Simón Pérez de Bustillo (Origins 9, 88) (Clan 13, 16), AK 78, 93, Charts I and IV

Baca, Leonor: (D 1696) Daughter of Ignacio Baca; wife of Pedro Sánchez de Inigno (B 1673?) (Origins 11, 141), AK 140

Baca (Vaca), Luis: (Toledo) (Origins 11), AK 55

Baca, Magdalena: Daughter of **Celso Baca** (Gómez), AK 248

Baca, Manuel Antonio: Justice at San Miguel (Kiva 424), AK 180, 187, 228

Baca, Manuel: (B 1656-59)(D by 1727) Son of **Cristóbal Baca** (II); husband of **María de Salazar**. In 1681, this parent, at approximately 25 years of age, was described as having a good thick-set build, a ruddy face, thick beard, and wavy hair. (Origins 10, 141) (Clan 61, 63, 71, 83, 87), AK 127, 133, 142-143, 206, Charts I and VI

Baca, Manuel: Son of **Diego Manuel Baca**; husband of (1) Leonarda Fernández, (2) Margarita Tafoya (1750), (3) Juana Silva (M 1768) (Origins 144)

Baca, Margarita: Daughter of Ignacio Baca, wife of Diego Lucero de Godoy (II) (Origins p. 11, 141)

Baca, María Ana: (Bap. 07-09-1866) (Antón Chico) (D 1942) (Santa Fe) Daughter of **José Pascual Baca**; wife of **José Placido Baca** (M 11-27-1882) (Antón Chico) (IGI) (Gómez), AK 256, Charts IX and X

Baca, María Ana Celestina: (Bap. 04-17-1870) (Copy) Daughter of **Celso Baca** (Gómez), AK 248

Baca, María Eugenia: (B 1910) (D 1985) (Albuquerque) Daughter of **José Placido Baca**; wife of Anthony Dominic García (D) (Albuquerque), AK 256

Baca, María Gertrudis: (B 1837) Daughter of **José Rafael Albino Baca**; wife of José Pablo Baca (Bap. 03-16-1834) (SMDB) (M 12-09-1851) (SMDB) (M in Film 0169875, Ribera Baptisms, 311) (Copy) (Gómez), AK 247

Baca, María Guadalupe (I): (B 12-12-1895) Daughter of **José Placido Baca** (Gómez), AK 256

Baca, María Guadalupe (II): (B 10-16-1897) Daughter of **José Placido Baca** (Gómez) AK 256

Baca, María Magdalena: (Lived in Santa Fe) Daughter of **Manuel Baca**; wife of José Vásquez de Lara (San Juan, Mexico) (M 02-03-1694) (Origins 141, 306), AK 142

Baca, María Magdalena: (B 06-05-1702) (D 1740) (Murdered by Márquez) Daughter of **Manuel Baca**, wife of (1) Diego Antonio Montoya, (2) Juan Márquez (M 1735) (Origins 141) (Clan 63), AK 142

Baca, María de Villanueva (or **Villarubia) Ortiz**: (B 1582) (Mexico City) Daughter of **Cristóbal Baca (I)**; wife of **Simón de Abendaño** (Origins 1, 9-10) (Clan 16), AK Charts I and VI

Baca, María Martina: (Bap. 02-01-1818) Daughter of **José Joaquin Baca**; wife of **José Manuel Rael** (Gómez), AK Chart IX.

Baca, María Refugio: (B 1846-51) Daughter of **José Luis Baca**; wife of **Juan José Romero (II)** (M 01-03-1862) (Fed. Cs. 1870, 1880) (Gómez), AK 271, 276, Charts IX and X

Baca (I), María Sinforiana: (B 1838) Daughter of **Antonio Baca**; wife of **Celso Baca** (M 12-09-1851) (SMDB) (Delig.) (census 1841, SMDB, listed as "Serafina") (Gómez), AK 248, Chart IX

Baca (II), María Sinforiana: (B 1902) (Santa Rosa) (D 1999) (Albuquerque) Daughter of **José Placido Baca**; wife of **Edmundo Margarito Lucero** (M 09-19-1923), AK 256, 281-296, Charts IX and X

Baca, Nicolás: Son of **Diego Manuel Baca**; husband of **Teodora Fernández de la Pedrera** (M 1747) (Santa Fe) (D 1794) (Origins 144), AK 143, Chart VI

Baca, Pablo: Son of **José Placido Baca**; husband of (1) Guadalupe Márquez, (2) Rebecca Salazar (Gómez), AK 256

Baca, Pelagia: (B 1891) (D 1974) Daughter of **José Placido Baca**; wife of Sunción Coronado Gonzáles (D 1960) (M Copy), AK 256

Baca, Petra: Daughter of **José Rafael Albino Baca**; wife of Benigno Jaramillo (M 01-25-1860) (Copy) (Gómez), AK 247

Baca, Rosa: (D 1696) Daughter of Ignacio Baca (Origins 11), AK 140

Baca, Rosa: (D 1755) Daughter of Joseta Baca, wife of (Manuel) Miguel Lucero de Godoy (II) (Origins 144)

Baca, Rosa: (Bap 07-12-1871) (Antón Chico) Daughter of **Celso Baca** (IGI 451) (Gómez), AK 248

Baca, Rosa: (B 08-28-1904) (Santa Rosa) Daughter of **José Placido Baca**; wife of Eleuterio Padilla (B1905) (Fed. Cs. 1910) (Gómez), AK 256

Baca, Vicente: (B 1784) (Bur. 11-05-1846) Son of Miguel Baca and María de los Reyes Padilla (B 1760) grandson of Baltasar Baca; husband of María Francisquita Montoya (B 1796).

C. de Baca, Ezequiel: (B 1864) (D 02-18-1917) Served: 1917, Son of Tomás Dolores C. de Baca; husband of Margarita C. de Baca (Clan 90) (NMPN 46), AK 272-273, 275

C. de Baca, Fabiola: Daughter of Graciano C. de Baca; wife of Carlos Gilbert, AK FN 6, Chapter 17

C. de Baca, Graciano: Son of Tomás Dolores C. de Baca, AK FN 6, Chapter 17

C. de Baca, Juan Antonio: (B 12-01-1783) (D 02-1835) (Lived at *Rancho de Peña Blanca*) Juan Antonio was the son of Luis María C. de Baca; husband of Josefa Gallegos y Cháves (Origins 153), AK FN 6, Chapter 17

C. de Baca, Luis María: (B 10-26-1754) (Santa Fe) (D 1827) (Peña Blanca) (Grantee of the *Ojo de Espiritu Santo* west of the Jémez Pueblo, 05-24-1815. Grantee of the Vegas Grandes, 1823) Luis María was the son of Juan Antonio Baca; husband of (1) María Josefa López (M 11-24-1777) (D 04-02-1797), (2) Ana María Sánchez (M 04-11-1798), (3) María Incarnación Lucero (B 03-28-1791) (M 1810) Luis María *Baca* was described on March 12, 1776 as a farmer, 5' 3" in height, 23 years of age, with black hair and eyebrows, beardless, fair skin and a scar above his right eyebrow. (Origins 152-153) (SEP, 232) (Clan 89-90) (NMPN 12-13, 67, 82, 85-86, 131, 136, 150, 167, 174) (Buxton 426b, 487), AK 173, 184, 193, 266-267

C. de Baca, Tomás Dolores: (B 1830) Son of Juan Antonio C. de Baca; husband of Estefanita Delgado, AK FN 6, Chapter 17

Cabrera, Josefa de: (B 1663) Wife of **Alonso de Medina.** This parent was described as having an aquiline face, large eyes, and a small nose (Origins 307)

Carvajal, Agustin de: (B 1620-30) (D 1680) (Angostura) Son of **Juan de Vitoria Carvajal**; husband of (1) María Márquez, (2) Estefania Enríquez (B 1641), (3) Damiana Domínguez de Mendoza (B1630) (D 1680) (Angostura) (Origins 15, 25) (Clan 20, 22, 43), AK 93, Chart IV

Carvajal, Gerónimo de: (B 1630) (D by 1680) (Lived at his *estancia, Nuestra Senora de los Remedios de los Cerrillos*) Gerónimo was the son of **Juan de Vitoria Carvajal**, husband of Margarita Márquez (B 1643) (Origins 15) (Kiva 182, 189, 206), AK 98, 107

Carvajal, Juan de Vitoria: (B 1561-62) (Ayotepel, NS) Son of **Juan de Carvajal**; husband of **Isabel Holguín**. One of Oñate's original settlers, this parent was described in 1598, and later in 1600, as having a medium stature and a chestnut beard, well-featured and having a mark on the right side of the face above the left eye. (Origins 14) (Clan 22-23) (Kiva 77) (Juan Holguín 258), AK 42, 47, 55, 175, Chart II

Carvajal, Juana de: (B 1624 ?) (D 1683) (San Lorenzo) Probably the daughter of **Juan de Vitoria Carvajal**; Juana was the first wife of **Juan Lucero de Godoy** (Origins 16, 60), AK 126, Chart II

Carvajal, (María) (Holguin): Daughter of **Juan de Vitoria Carvajal**; wife of **Fernando Durán y Cháves (I)** (Origins 15, 20) (Clan 22), AK Chart I

Catiti, Alonso: Son of **Diego Márquez** (Clan 36) (Kiva 240-241, 535 n 13), AK 111, 124-125

Sedillo/Cedillo

Cedillo Rico de Rojas, Casilda de: Daughter of **Pedro de Cedillo Rico de Rojas**; wife of **Cristóbal Varela Jaramillo** (Origins 198, 285), AK 152, Chart II

Cedillo Rico de Rojas, Pedro de: (B 1611 ?) (Queretaro, NS) (D by 1698) (Sedillo, 23 miles east of Albuquerque, is named for him.) Pedro was the husband of **Isabel López de Gracia** (Origins 103, 285) (NMPN 152) AK Chart II

Cháves/Chavez (Durán y Cháves)

Durán y Cháves Bernardo: (B 1675) (Buried 11-19-1705) (*El Tunque*) Son of **Fernando Durán y Cháves (II)**; husband of Francisca de Misquia (M 01-02-1699) (Santa Fe) (D 1714 ?) (Origins 161) (Clan 41, 59, 61, 63, 80-82), AK 139

Durán y Cháves (II), Cristóbal: (B 1664-65) (Lived at present Ranchos de Taos.) Son of **Fernando Durán y Cháves**. One of the exiles of 1680, this 16 year-old was described as tall and swarthy, with a mole on the right cheek. (Origins 21, 22) (Clan 36)

Durán y Cháves (I), Fernando: (B 1609-1617) (D before 1669) Son of **Pedro (Gómez ?) Durán y Cháves (I)**; husband of **(María) Carvajal (Holguín)** (Origins 14-15, 19-20), AK Chart I.

Durán y Cháves, Fernando (or **Fernández**): (B 1647) (Lived at present Ranchos de Taos). Probable son of **Agustin de Cháves**. In 1681, this 34 year old parent was described as tall and thin, of good features, and having a thick, black beard. (Origins 21, 22) (Clan 35, 37, 45, 49) (NMPN 56, 81, 134, 162), AK 195

Durán y Cháves (II), Fernando: (B 1641-51) (D by 1716) (Atrisco) (Lived at *El Tunque*, Bernalillo). Son of **Fernando Durán y Cháves (I)**; husband of **Lucía Hurtado de Salas y Trujillo**. At 40-years of age, this parent was described as having a good stature with a fair and ruddy complexion (1681). (Origins 20, 49, 160) (Clan 19, 35, 37-38, 41-42, 44-48, 50-

54, 56-67) (Conq. 57) (NMPN 12, 16, 32, 91, 134, 162), AK 134, 139, 143, Chart I

Durán y Cháves, Nicolás: (B 1690) (Atrisco) (D 1768 ?) Son of **Fernando Durán y Cháves** (II), husband of **Juana Moñtano** (M 07-20-1714) (Origins 163), AK Charts I and VI

Durán y Cháves (I), Pedro (Gómez ?): (B 1550-56) (Valverde de Llerena) (D 1626 ?)(Atrisco) (Lived at *El Tunque*, Bernalillo) Son of **Hernán Sánchez Rico** (or **Fernando Gómez Rico**); husband of **Isabel de Bohórquez (Baca)**. One of the reinforcement citizen-soldiers who arrived in 1600. This parent was described briefly as a well-built man of good features. (Origins 19) (Clan 3-4, 6-9, 11-13, 15-18, 72) (Conq. 27) (NMPN 32, 167, 171), AK 78-79, Charts I and IV

Durán y Cháves (II), Pedro: (B 1610-27) (Santa Fe) (Lived near Isleta) Son of **Pedro Durán y Cháves (I)**; husband of Elena Domínguez de Mendoza (Origins 21) (Clan 21, 24, 27-28, 3537, 42, 45-47, 51, 53, 71), AK 93-94, 106, 121

Durán y Cháves, Rosa Gertrudis: (B 1714) (D 04-17-1763) (Albuquerque), Daughter of **Nicolás Durán y Cháves**; wife of **Francisco de Silva** (M 09-12-1729) (D 04-17-1763) (Origins 163, 289) (Clan 131), AK Chart VI

Concepción, Juana de la: Wife of **Andrés de Santisteban** (Origins 284), AK Chart VII

Cruz, María de la: (Mexico City) Wife of **Juan Pérez de Bustillo** (Origins 87), AK 43, Chart II

Durán y Cháves (See Cháves/Chavez)

Esquibel, Ana María: (B 1760) Daughter of **Gerónimo Esquibel**; first wife of **Diego Pedro Manuel Baca** (M 03-05-1770) (Castrense), AK Chart VI

Esquibel, Gerónimo: (B 1710) Possibly the son of **Juan Antonio Esquibel**; husband of (1) **Francisca Tenorio de Alba**; (M 02-30-1746) (Santa Fe), (2) Josefa Felipa Ramírez (B 1743) (Origins 293?)

Esquibel, María Antonia de la Luz: (B 1734) Wife of **Pablo Antonio de Sena** (M 07-07-1772) (Origins 287) (Gómez), AK Chart VI

Esquibel, María Josefa: Wife of **Juan Andrés Gonzáles** (M 07-08-1805) (SMDB) (Gómez)

Fernández de la Pedrera, Juan: (B 1665-69) (Moñdonedo, Galicia) (D 07-28-1745) (Albuquerque). Son of **Santiago Fernández de la Pedrera**; husband of (1) María Jurado de Gracia (M 04-24-1695), (2) **María Peláez** (M 1710) (Albuquerque) (Origins 174), AK Chart III

Fernández de la Pedrera, Santiago: (Madrid, Spain) Husband of **Francisca de los Ríos** (Origins 174), AK Chart III

Fernández de la Pedrera, Teodora: (D 01-26-1794) Probably the daughter of **Juan**

Fernández de la Pedrera. Teodora was the wife of (1) **Nicolás Baca** (M 1747), (2) Miguel Tenorio de Alba y Corona (M 1758) (Origins 144, 174-175, 293), AK 143, Charts III and VI

Fernandez Valerio (See Valerio)

García, Alonso: (B 1627-37) (Zacatecas) (Lived at his *estancia* of San Antonio south of Sandía) Alonso was the husband of **Teresa Varela**. This parent was described in 1681 as having a good physique, partly gray hair, protruding eyes, and an aquiline face. (Origins 33, 34) (Clan 29, 44-46, 91) (Kiva 237), AK 115, 118-120, Chart VIII

García, Francisco: (B 09-25-1745) (Santa Cruz) Son of **Juan Esteban García de Noriega**; husband of **Manuela Martín** (Origins 182) (Gómez), AK Chart VIII

García, María Teresa: (Bap. 02-07-1802) Daughter of **Santiago García**; NOTE: **Santiago**, married to **María Encarnacion Velásques**, was the son of **Francisco García** and **Manuela Martín**. Encarnación appears to have been the daughter of **Juan Esteban Velásquez** and **Juana Teresa Apodaca** (or **Velarde**) (M 12-20-1772). Santiago and Encarnación were married 10-08-1799. Three of their daughters, Clara de la Ascención, María Manuela, and **María Teresa** married three sons of **Miguel Antonio Lucero de Godoy**. **María Teresa** was the wife of **Lorenzo Manuel Lucero de Godoy** (M 10-29-1812) (Bap. for SG, Film 016971, Santa Cruz) (Santa Clara census 1818, 180) (Gómez), AK 182, 257, Charts VII and VIII

García, Santiago: (Bap. 07-26-1773) (Santa Cruz) Son of **Francisco García**; husband of **María Encarnación Velásquez** (M 10-08-1799) (Santa Clara) (Book of Baptisms B-35 Frame 365) (Gómez), AK Charts VII and VIII

García de la Mora, Juan: (B La Villa de Pozuelo de Almagro, Toledo, Spain) Son of **Juan García de la Mora** and **Manuela Gonzalez**: husband of (1) María de Hornero (M Porzuelo de Calatrava), and (2) **Josefa Martín Serrano** (M 08-03-1735) (Origins 184) (Buxton has him as "José," 38b, 38c, 356), AK Chart X

García de la Mora, María del Rosario: Probably the daughter of **Juan García de la Mora**, María was the wife of **Santiago Ortiz Nino Ladrón de Guevara** (M 04-23-1759) (Origins 184, 249), AK Chart X

García de Noriega (II), Alonso: (B 1651) (D 1696 ?) (Sevilleta) Son of **Alonso García**; husband of (1) **Ana Jorge de Vera**, (2) María Luisa Godines. This parent was described in 1681 as swarthy and pock-marked with a large nose and long, straight hair (Origins 34), AK Charts I and VIII

García de Noriega, Juan: (B 1658) Son of **Alonso García**; husband of (1) Margarita Márquez, (D before 1680), (2) **Francisca Sánchez de Ynigo**. In 1681 this parent was described as of medium build with a long face and chestnut hair. (Origins 34, 181), AK Chart VIII

García de Noriega, Juan Esteban: (B 1696) (lived at Santa Cruz) Son of **Juan García de**

Noriega; husband of **Luisa Gómez Luján del Castillo** (M 06-23-1721) (San Ildefonso) (Origins 182), AK Chart VIII

García de Noriega, María Luisa: (B 08-12-1708) (Albuquerque) (D 07-03-1767) (Santa Fe) Daughter of **Tomás García de Noriega**; wife of **Tomás Antonio de Sena** (M 04-22-1723) (Santa Fe) (Origins 182, 286, 287) (Delig.) (Alonso, Clan 29), AK Charts VI and VIII

García de Noriega, Tomás: (B 1685) (Albuquerque) Son of **Alonso García de Noriega** (II); husband of **Juana Hurtado** (M 01-07-1705) (Origins 181-182), AK Charts I and VI

Gómez, Carlos: (B)(Las Vegas) (D)(Albuquerque) Son of José de Jesus Leodoro Gómez, husband of Norma Jean Lucero, AK 293

Gómez, Francisco: (B 1576-87) (Coina, Portugal) (D 1656-57) (Santa Fe) (Had an *estancia* at *Los Barrancas* near Sevilleta, Socorro) Served: 1641-1642; Son of **Manuel Gómez**, husband of **Ana Robledo** (Origins 35-36, 94) (Clan 13, 131-132) (Conq. 12, 20-26, 28-30, 33, 36, 38); (Kiva 109, 111, 114, 139, 159, 161, 165, 185-186, 522-23 n 41, 524 n 14), AK 73, 77-78, 85-86, 89, 95, Chart III

Gómez Luján del Castillo, Luisa: Possibly the daughter of **Antonio** or **Bartolomé Gómez Robledo**. Luisa was the daughter of **Juana Luján** and wife of **Juan Esteban García de Noriega** (M 06-23-1721) (Origins 182, 187, 188) AK Chart VIII

Gómez Robledo, Andrés: (B 1639-43) (Native of Santa Fe) (D 1680) (Santa Fe) Son of **Francisco Gómez**; husband of **Juana Ortiz** (**Baca**) (Origins 37, 187) (Clan 14) (Conq. 28, 39, 44, 56), AK 117, Chart III

Gómez Robledo, Francisca: (D 1680) Daughter of **Francisco Gómez**; second wife of **Pedro Lucero de Godoy**, (Origins 36, 59, 60) (Conq. 39), AK 77, 117, Charts II and V

Gómez Robledo, Francisco: (B 1628) (Santa Fe) (D by 1693) (Lived in the Pojoaque area) Son of **Francisco Gómez**. One of the refugees of 1680, the 53-year-old Francisco was described as having a good stature and features, with red hair and mustache, and partly gray (Origins 36) (Clan 13, 132) (Conq. 26, 28, 36, 38-42, 44, 48, 56, 87) (Kiva 175, 181, 184, 192, 224, 228, 232, 260, 522-23 n 41, 530 n 20), AK 77, 101-102, 105, 108, 113-114, 158-159, Chart V

Gómez Robledo, Margarita: Daughter of **Andrés Gómez Robledo**; wife of **Jacinto Peláez** (M 1691) (*Guadalupe del Paso*) (Origins 37, 256), AK Chart III

Gonzáles, Josefa de la Ascención: Wife of **Hernán Martín Serrano** (II) (Origins 72), AK 152, Chart VIII

Gonzáles, Juan Andrés: (B 12-01-1781) Son of **Salbador Gonzáles**; husband of **María Josefa Esquibel** (M 07-08-1805) (SMDB) (Gómez)

Gonzáles, María Josefa: (Bap. 02-22-1810) (SMDB) Daughter of **Juan Andrés Gonzáles**, wife of **Antonio Baca** (M 08-20-1826)(SMDB) (Gómez)

Gonzáles, María Ramona Angela: (B 1783?) (Buried 08-01-1833) (La Questa) Daughter of **Pablo Gonzáles**, wife of **José Miguel Lucero** (M 11-01-1807) (Taos) (Gómez) (Buxton 94), AK 258

Gonzáles, Pablo: Husband of **María Medina** (Gómez)

Gonzáles, Salbador: Husband of **María Guadalupe Archibeque** (Gómez)

Herrera, Josefa de: Possibly the daughter of **Juan de Herrera**; Josefa was the wife of **Domingo Martín Serrano** (Origins 45-46, 73), AK Chart VII

Herrera, Juan de: (B 1580) (Mexico City) (D before 1680) (Lived at Santa Cruz) Son of **Francisco de Herrera**, husband of **Juana (Ana) López del Castillo** (D before 1680) One of the reinforcements of 1600, this 20-year-old parent was described as of medium height, round-faced, with a beard starting to grow. (Origins 45, 196), AK 56, Chart VIII

Hinojos/Ynojos

Hinojos, Hernando Ruiz de: (B 1562) (Cartaya, Condado de Niebla) (D by 1632) Son of **Juan Ruiz**; husband of **Beatriz Pérez de Bustillo**. One of Oñate's original colonists, the 36-year-old Hernando was described in 1598 as having a good stature and a chestnut beard. (Origins 48, 87), AK 43, 52, Chart IV

Hinojos, Juan Ruiz de: Son of **Hernando Ruiz de Hinojos**; one of the men beheaded in Governor Rosas affair. (Origins 48), AK 93, Chart IV

Hinojos, María Josefa de: Daughter of **Aparicio de Hinojos**, adopted daughter of **Andrés Hurtado**; wife of **Diego de Montoya** (II) (Origins 236)

Hinojos, Sebastián Rodríguez de: (D 1598) (Âcoma) Son of **Juan Ruiz** (Origins 48), AK 52-53

Holguín, Isabel: Daughter of **Juan López Holguín**; wife of **Juan de Vitoria Carvajal** (Origins 14, 81), AK Chart II

Hurtado, Andrés: (B 1628) (Zacatecas) (D by 1680) Husband of **Bernardina de Salas y Trujillo** (or **Orozco/Osorio**) (Origins 49, 108) (Clan 67-68, 71), AK 127, 144, Chart VI

Hurtado, Diego: Son of **Andres Hurtado**; husband of **Josefa de la Fuente** (Origins 49-50)

Hurtado, Juana: Daughter of **Andrés Hurtado**, (Origins 49) (Clan 83), AK 119, 130

Hurtado, Juana: Daughter of **Diego Hurtado**; wife of **Tomás García de Noriega** (Origins 49, 50), AK Chart I

Hurtado de Salas y Trujillo, Lucía or **Luisa** (**Lucía de Salazar**): (D 02-03-1729) Adopted daughter of **Andrés Hurtado**; wife of **Fernando Durán y Cháves** (II) (Origins 20-21, 49, 160-61) (Clan 87-88), AK Chart I

Hurtado, María: (D 03-22-1726) (Buried in the Conquistadora Chapel, Santa Fe) Daughter of **Andrés Hurtado**; wife of **Antonio de Montoya** (M 1679) (Origins 78, 235-236), AK Chart VI

Hurtado, Martín: (B 1659-72) (D 10-17-1734) Son of **Andrés Hurtado**: husband of Catalina Varela

Jorge de Vera, Ana: Daughter of **Antonio Jorge de Vera**; wife of **Alonso García de Noriega** (II) (Origins 34, 51), AK Chart I

Jorge de Vera, Antonio: (D before 1680) Probably the son of **Manuel Jorge**. Antonio was the husband of **Gertrudis Baca**. (Origins 51), AK Chart I

Jorge de Vera, Isabel: (B 1660) (D 11-25-1736) Daughter of **Antonio Jorge de Vera**; wife of **Juan Antonio Moñtano de Sotomayor** (Origins 76, 233-234), AK Chart VII

Jorge, Juan: (B 1565) (Los Lagos, Spain ?) Son of **Juan Jorge Griego**; Described briefly in 1600 as tall and dark (Origins 51), AK Chart III

Jorge, Manuel: Probably the son of **Juan Jorge**. Manuel was the first husband of **María Ortiz Baca de Vera** (Origins 51), AK Charts I and III

Leyba, María Dolores: (B 1781 ?) Second wife of **Diego Pedro Manuel Baca** (M 04-11-1798) (Gómez), AK 247, Chart VI

Lobrera, María Barbara: (B 1781 ?) Probably the daughter of **Francisco Lobrera**. **María Barbara** was the wife of **Alonso Rael** (Gómez)

López, Catalina: (Toledo, Spain) Wife of **Pedro Robledo** (Origins 93), AK 47, Chart III

López de Gracia, Andrés: (First lived at *San Antonio de Isleta*, later first *alcalde mayor* at *Guadalupe del Paso*). Possibly the son of **Esteban López** (Origins 55-56)

López de Gracia, Isabel: (D by 1692) Daughter of **Andrés López de Gracia**; wife of **Pedro de Cedillo Rico de Rojas** (Origins 103, 285), AK Chart II

López del Castillo, Juana (Ana): (D before 1680) Daughter of **Matías López del Castillo**; wife of **Juan de Herrera** (Origins 55, 279-280), AK Chart VIII

López del Castillo, Matías: Husband of (an **Arechuleta**, daughter of **Asencio**) (Origins 55), AK Chart VIII

López Holguín, Juan: (B 1560-62) (Fuente Ovejuna, Spain) Son of **Juan López Villasana**, husband of **Catalina de Villanueva**. One of the reinforcements of 1600, this parent was of good stature, black bearded, with a mark on the left eye and 40 years old (Origins 81), AK 56, Chart II

López Robledo, Lucía or **Luisa**: Daughter of **Pedro Robledo**; wife of **Bartolomé Romero** (Origins 93, 95), AK Chart III

López Sambrano, Andrés: (B 1618-21) (San Miguel, NS) First husband of *Ana María de Anaya Almázan* (Origins 4, 58, 60), AK Chart II

López Sambrano de Grijalva, Josefa: Daughter of Andrés López Sambrano, wife of Francisco Lucero de Godoy (Origins 58, 60) (Conq. 44-45), AK Chart II

López Villafuerte, Juana: (B 1603) Daughter of **Francisco López** (Jerez, Spain); wife of **Francisco de Anaya Almázan** (Origins 3-4), AK Chart II

Lucero/Lucero de Godoy

Lucero, Jr., Antonio José: (B 1896) Son of **Antonio José Lucero, Sr.**; husband of Blanche Hyett, AK 275, 279-280

Lucero, Sr., Antonio José: (Bap. 10-07-1863) (Puertocito) (D 06-27-1921) (Las Vegas) Son of **José Pablo Lucero**; husband of **María Juliana Romero** (M 04-08-1893) (Las Vegas) (Obit) (M Film 0016511) (copy) (Bap. Film 016875) (Ribera Baptisms) (NMPN 23?, 73, 102) (Gómez), AK 260-261, 271-273, 275-277, 280, 295, Chart X

Lucero, Arturo Francis Paul: (B Santa Fe) (D) (Albuquerque) Son of **Antonio José Lucero, Sr**, husband of Dortha Louraine Regensberg (B 12-30-1915) (Guadalupita ?) (M 05-30-1937) (D 10-07-1993) (Albuquerque), AK 275, 280, 290

Lucero, Aurora: (B 02-08-1894) (Las Vegas) Daughter of **Antonio José Lucero, Sr**, wife of (1) Garner D. White, (2) King Lee. (Film 016875, Ribera Baptisms) (Gómez), AK 275-277, 280, 291-292

Lucero, Bonifacio: (Bap. 09-29-1866) (SMDB) (D 1918-19) Son of **José Pablo Lucero**; husband of Raquel Ellsworth (B 1876) (M 10-17-1892) (Las Vegas) (FC 1910) (Bap. MF 0016875) (Gómez), AK 260

Lucero, Diego Antonio: (B 11-13-1787) (San Juan) Son of Antonio José Lucero; husband of Guadalupe Valdés (Alvares?) y Trujillo (B 1803) (M 05-13-1816) (Buxton 381-385), AK 260

Lucero, Donald Lauro: (SL) (B)(Las Vegas) Son of **Edmundo Margarito Lucero**; husband of Beth Sheila Greenhill (nee Greenberg) (SL) (B)(Bayonne, NJ) (M 10-23-1969), AK 284-296, Charts IX and X

Lucero, Edmundo Antonio: (B 10-28-1926) (Las Vegas) (D 08-14-1985) (St. Thomas, Virgin Islands) Son of **Edmundo Margarito Lucero**; husband of Virginia Golus (SL) (B Loup City, Nebraska) (M 07-28-1957) (Reno, Nevada), AK 284-293, Chart X

Lucero, Edmundo Margarito: (B 12-16-1902) (Las Vegas) (D 08-12-1969) (Las Vegas) Son of **Antonio José Lucero, Sr.**; husband of **María Sinforiana Baca** (II) (M 09-19-1923), AK 275, 280-293, 295-296, Charts IX and X

Lucero, Eloy: Son of **José Pablo Lucero**; husband of Isabelita Gonzáles, AK 260

Lucero, Florida: Daughter of **José Pablo Lucero**. AK 260

Lucero, Francisca Alfonsa: Niece of Juan Lucero de Godoy (II); wife of Salvador Durán de Armijo, AK 199

Lucero, Francisquita: Daughter of **José Pablo Lucero**; wife of Jacobo Valerio, AK 260

Lucero, Jesus María: (B 1833-34) Son of Diego Antonio Lucero; husband of Cleofas Anaya (B 1840-42) (Buxton 467), AK 260

Lucero, José Antonio: A *San Miguel del Bado* grantee, AK 170

Lucero, José Miguel: (B 1782 ?) Possibly the son of **Julian Lucero**; husband of **María Ramona Angela Gonzáles** (M 11-01-1807) (Taos) (Film 016559, Pecos) (Copy) (Buxton 94) (Gómez), AK 257

Lucero, José Pablo: (Bap. 01-14-1834) (SMDB) Son of **Lorenzo Manuel Lucero**; husband of **María Manuela Salazar** (M 08-04-1855) (SMDB) (Delig. #58, 1008) (Fed. Census. 1860-70-80) (NMPN 81) (Bap. Film 0017001) (Gómez), AK 257-260, Chart X

Lucero, Julian: Husband of **Ana María Vallejos** (Gómez).

Lucero, Juliette (Julia): (B 09-27-1900) (Santa Fe) (D 01-18-1984) Daughter of **Antonio José Lucero, Sr.**, wife of Edmundo Sena. AK 275, 280, 290

Lucero, Julian Antonio: (B 11-28-1767) (San Juan) Son of Salvador Manuel Lucero; husband of María Barbara Antonia Cisneros (Bap. 03-15-1780) (San Juan) (Buxton 200-202) AK 196

Lucero, Leonore: (B 1904) Daughter of **Antonio José Lucero, Sr.**; wife of (1) Alfonso Wright, (2) Fred Lucero, AK 275, 280

Lucero, Lorenzo: (Buried 01-20-1882) (Las Vegas) Son of **José Pablo Lucero** (Gómez). AK 260

Lucero, Manuel Salvador: (B 12-13-1797) (Bosque, San Juan) (Consolidated the holdings at Los Luceros) Manuel Salvador was the son of Julian Antonio Lucero; husband of (1) Soledad Quintana, (2) María Josefa Mestas (M 11-19-1820) (Buxton 203, 355-56)(NMPN 123). AK 196-197, 228

Lucero, María Buenaventura: (B 1809-19) Daughter of **José Miguel Lucero**; wife of José Crescenciano Baca (M 05-27-1834) (SMDB) (Census 1841). AK 257

Lucero, María de la Luz: (B 05-12-1812) (Taos) Daughter of Pablo Antonio Lucero; wife of Santiago Martín(ez) (Bap. 07-29-1804) (Taos) (Buxton 333, 334), AK 197

Lucero, María Cleofas Gabriela: (B 03-18-?) Daughter of Diego Antonio Lucero; wife of Vicente García (Buxton 466), AK 261

Lucero, María Delia: (B 01-12-1898) (D 11-?-1980) (Santa Fe) Daughter of **Antonio José Lucero, Sr**.; wife of Carlos Baca (B 10-19-1901), AK 275-281, 291

Lucero, María Juana: Daughter of **Lorenzo Manuel Lucero**; wife of (1) José María Herrera (M 12-02-1830) (SMDB), (2) José Francisco Baca (M 12-20-1841) (SMDB) (M MJL with JMH in Film 0017002, M MJL with JFB copy), AK 257

Lucero, María Magdalena: (B 01-28-1827) (San Juan) (D 01-10-1910) Daughter of Diego Antonio Lucero; wife of Gaspar Ortiz y Alarid (B 1824-25) (M 07-26-1848) (San Juan) (Buxton 464) AK 261

Lucero, María Manuela: (B 1822 ?) (Buried 02-08-1907) (El Rito) Daughter of Diego Antonio Lucero; wife of José Pablo Gallegos (B 01-25-1817) (M 08-09-1837) (D 08-14-1896) (Buxton 455-458) AK 260-261

Lucero, María Ramona: (B 1809-11) Daughter of **José Miguel Lucero**; wife of (1) **Juan de Jesus Baca** (M 04-28-1826), (2) Juan Andrés Estrada (B 1799) (M 03-13-1853) (SMDB) (M with JAE copy, Film 16878) (census 1841) (Film 0016559) Bap. of twins establishes relationship. (Gómez), AK 157

Lucero, María Rita Juliana: (B 01-14-1776) Daughter of Salvador Manuel Lucero; wife of Alonso Hermenigildo Sisneros (D 10-04-1809) (Taos) (Buxton 191), AK 204

Lucero, María Salome: (Bap. 10-22-1818) (San Juan) Daughter of Diego Antonio Lucero; wife of José Vicente Martín(ez) (B 1800) (M 05-01-1839) (Buxton 441-442, 454), AK 197, 260

Lucero, Mariano de Jesus: (B 04-03-1813) (Embudo) (Cleric) Possible son of Gregorio Lucero de Godoy (Buxton 354)

Lucero, Norma Jean: (SL) (B)(Las Vegas) Daughter of **Edmundo Margarito Lucero**; wife of Carlos Gómez (D) (Albuquerque), AK 284-293, Chart X

Lucero, Paula Marie: (SL) (B)(Las Vegas) Daughter of **Edmundo Margarito Lucero**; wife of Stanley Koetting (SL) (M 08-18-1962) (Las Vegas), AK 284-293, Chart X

Lucero, Salvador: May be Manuel Salvador Lucero (Buxton 203, 355-356), AK 196

Lucero, Sylvia Ernestina: (B)(Las Vegas) (D)(Albuquerque) Daughter of **Edmundo Margarito Lucero**; wife of Merle E. Jacobsen (B 1923) (Montrose, Colorado) (D 1968) (Dallas, Texas) AK 284-293, Chart X

Lucero de Godoy, Antonia Gregoria: (D 12-06-1736) Daughter of Francisco Lucero de Godoy; wife of Andrés de Montoya (M 01-24-1698) (Origins 236) (Buxton 16a), AK Chart V

Lucero de Godoy (I), Antonio: (B 1650-55) (D by 1712) Son of **Juan Lucero de Godoy**; husband of (1) a blood niece of Juan Domingo de Mendoza (D 1680), (2) **Antonia Varela de Losada** (or **de Perea**) (M by 1685) (Origins 61, 209, 257) (Buxton 11) (Cab.103) (Corn Mothers 219, 228, 232-33, 237), AK 117, 128, 132, 141-142, 144, 148, 152, Charts II and V

Lucero de Godoy (II), Antonio: (B 1687-91) (D before 1750) Son of **Antonio Lucero de Godoy** (I); husband of **Francisca Varela Jaramillo** (M 09-27-1712) (Albuquerque) (Origins 209) (Buxton 19) (NMPN 24), AK 128, 141-142, 152-154, 199, Charts II and V

Lucero de Godoy (I), Diego: (B 1643) (Grantee of the Lucero de Godoy, Taos) Probably the son of **Pedro Lucero de Godoy**. Diego was the husband of (1) ? (D 1680) (Taos), (2) María Domínguez de Mendoza (M 02-16-1681). One of the exiles of 1681, Diego was described as tall and slender, with a fair, ruddy complexion and long, red hair (Origins 60) (Buxton 26, 397-399) (Clan 25) (Kiva 199-202) (NMPN 93, 97, 134), AK 107, 109, 112, 120, 122-123, 148-150, 195

Lucero de Godoy (II), Diego: (B 1687) (Buried 04-02-1752) Son of **Antonio Lucero de Godoy** (I); husband of (1) Margarita Baca (M 07-05-1716), (2) Ana María Martín (M 02-03-1726) (Origins 209) (Buxton 22), AK 197

Lucero de Godoy, Francisco: (B 1645) Son of **Pedro Lucero de Godoy** and his second wife Francisca Gómez Robledo; husband of (1) Josefa López Sambrano de Grijalva, (2) Catalina de Espinola (M 1695). One of the exiles of 1680, this 35 year old was described as tall and erect, with a thick beard, a wound-scar on his mustache, and another on the right side of his nose (Origins 172, 209-210) (Buxton 7) (Conq. 45, 48, 73) (Kiva 248, 257, 260 262, 272), AK 109, 115, 129, 132, 135, Charts II and V

Lucero de Godoy, Gregorio: (B 1793) Son of **Miguel Antonio Lucero de Godoy**; husband of María Clara de la Asencion García (Bap. 08-15-1800) (M 10-29-1812) (M in Film 016993, Santa Clara) (Film 16859 and 016975) (census 1841) (Gómez), AK 171

Lucero de Godoy, José Antonio: (Grantee of one *fanega* of planting land on the Santa Fe River, 09-20-1732.) Possibly the son of Antonio Lucero de Godoy (II), José was the husband of María Antonia Fernándes (Buxton 49) (NMPN 77), AK 148

Lucero de Godoy, José de Jesus: (B 1800) Son of **Miguel Antonio Lucero de Godoy**; husband of (1) María Manuela García (Bap. 10-21-1805) (M 09-17-1820) (SMDB) (Copy), (2) Juana Nepomucena Martín (B 1801)(M 02-23-1827) (SMDB) (MF 16775, Galisteo) (Santa Clara Census 1818) (M to MMG in MF 0016075) (M to JNM in MF 0016775) (Gómez), AK 171, 182-183, 189-191, 258

Lucero de Godoy, José Manuel (Gregorio ?): (Bap. 10-18-1839) Son of **Miguel Antonio Lucero de Godoy**, husband of María Dolores Ocaña (B 1839) (M 01-25-1855) (SMDB) (DM) (Census 1841 #216) (M in MF 0016878) (Gómez), AK 193

Lucero de Godoy, Josefa: (B 1730) (Buried 07-11-1763) Daughter of (Manuel) Miguel Lucero de Godoy ; wife of Domingo de Luna (M 12-21-1745) (Origin 60, 209) (Buxton 5) (Clan 56, 71, 87), AK 156

Lucero de Godoy, Juan: (B 1622-24) (Lived at Pueblo Quemado, Agua Fria) Son of **Pedro Lucero de Godoy**; husband of (1) Luisa Romero, (2) **Juana de Vitoria Carvajal**, (3) Isabel de Salazar (M 01-14-1689) (San Lorenzo). One of the exiles of 1680, this 57 year old parent was described as having a good stature with a large, pock-marked aquiline face and a crooked nose. (Origins 60, 209) (Buxton 5) (Clan 56, 71, 87), AK 77, 101-102, 108-109, 126-128,132-133, 141-142, Charts II and V

Lucero de Godoy, Juan Cristóbal: (Bap. 11-29-1830). Son of **Miguel Antonio Lucero de Godoy,** husband of Margarita Sais (M 01-08-1854) (Las Vegas) (M in Film 0016878) (Gómez), AK 193

Lucero de Godoy, Juan de Dios: (B 1656) (D 03-04-1703) Son of **Juan Lucero de Godoy**; husband of María Varela (M 1681). At age 25, he was described as robust, of medium height, and having good features, a thick, black beard, and wavy hair (1681). (Origins 61, 209) (Buxton 10), AK 109, 132, 151

Lucero de Godoy, Juan Ignacio: (B 1720 ?) Son of **Antonio Lucero de Godoy (**II); husband of **María Rosa Santisteban** (Buxton 19-20, 79), AK 153-155, Charts V and VII

Lucero de Godoy, Lorenzo Manuel: (B 1784) Son of **Miguel Antonio Lucero de Godoy**; husband of **María Teresa García** (M 10-29-1812) (M Santa Clara Mission, copy, Film 016993) (Census 1841 SMDB) (Roll 30 NMSRA) (Gómez), AK 171, 182-183, 257-258, Charts, VII and VIII

Lucero de Godoy, Luisa: Probably the daughter of **Pedro Lucero de Godoy**. Luisa was the wife of Pedro Montoya de Esparza (Origins 60, 77), AK 96

Lucero de Godoy, María: Daughter of **Pedro Lucero de Godoy**; wife of Lazaro de Misquia (Origins 60, 74-75) (Clan 80), AK 96

Lucero de Godoy, María Dolores: (B 1798) Daughter of **Miguel Antonio Lucero de Godoy**; wife of Juan Esteban Velasquez (B 1783) (Gómez), AK 171

Lucero de Godoy, Miguel Antonio: (Bap. 06-13-1755) (Cochiti) Son of **Juan Ignacio Lucero de Godoy**; husband of (1) **María Rosa Valdés** (M 08-26-1783) (Santa Clara) (D 1811), (2) Guadalupe Martín (M 02-22-1827) (SMDB) (Buxton 79, 152) (Santa Clara Marriages, Roll 30 NMSRA, copy of M with MRV and GM) (Cochiti Mission Records, 532?) (census 1818, Santa Clara) (Kiva 454) (Bap. Film 0016757) (M with GM in MF 0016075) (Gómez), AK 154, 157, 171, 176, 189, 257, 191, Charts V and VII

Lucero de Godoy (II) (Manuel) Miguel: (B 01-06-1710) (D 01-25-1766) (Fuenclara) Son of Miguel Lucero de Godoy (I) (D 06-15-1709). Manuel (known as Miguel (II)) was born six months and twenty-one days after the death of his father.) Miguel (II) was the husband of (1) Rosa Baca (M 1729) (D 06-29-1755) (Tome), (2) Antonia Cháves (Origins 211, 327) (Buxton 53) (Clan 96, 120, (Miguel I, 32), AK 156

Lucero de Godoy, Nicolás: Son of **Juan** or Francisco **Lucero de Godoy** (Origins 61), AK 113-114, 144

Lucero de Godoy, Nicolás: (B 1646) (Santa Fe) (D 04-27-1727) Probably the son of **Juan Lucero de Godoy**. Nicolás was the husband of María Montoya (D 01-12-1740) (Origins 209) (Buxton 12), AK 132, 144

Lucero de Godoy, Pedro: (El Viejo) (B 1588) (Origins 59), AK 73

Lucero de Godoy, Pedro: (El Mozo) (B 1600) (Mexico City) (D before 1680) Husband of (1) **Petronila de Zamora**, (2) Francisca Gómez Robledo (Origins 59-60) (Buxton 3) (Clan 70, 80) (Kiva 185-186, 188-190, 192, 216) (NMPN 93), AK 73, 76, 95, 102, 128, 175, Charts II and V

Lucero de Godoy (II), Pedro: Son of **Pedro Lucero de Godoy** (El Mozo) (Origins 59-60), AK 77, 109

Lucero de Godoy (III), Pedro: (B 1662) Son of **Juan** or Nicolás **Lucero de Godoy**, described in 1681 at 19 years of age as having a medium, thickset stature, with a beardless face, black hair, and large eyes (Origins 61, 209), AK 132, 144

Lucero de Godoy, Ynez: Probably the daughter of **Pedro Lucero de Godoy**. Ynez was the wife of Juan de la Escallada (Origins 29, 60(Buxton 7), AK 96

Luján, Josefa: Daughter of Miguel Luján; wife of Felipe Antonio de Sisneros. (Origins 21-22, 64, 213), AK 151

Luján, Juana: Daughter of Matías Luján and Francisca Romero; wife of Francisco Martín; armourette of Antonio or Bartolomé Gómez Robledo (Origins 36, 187), AK Chart VIII

Luján, María: (D 1765?) Probably the daughter of Fernando Durán y Cháves; wife of Sebastián Martín Serrano (Origins 21-22, 213) (Clan 36), AK 151, 195, Chart X

Luján, Miguel: (D 1694) Husband of Elena Ruiz Cáceres (Origins 64, 213) (Clan 36), AK FN 7, Chapter 7

Luna, Antonio de: (D 08-09-1729) Probably the son of Diego de Luna (B 1635), (described in 1681 as tall with a long face and having long, straight hair.) Antonio was the husband of Jacinta Peláez (M 05-29-1718) (Origins, 65, 214) (Clan 75-76) (NMPN 91, 94), AK 156

Luna, Domingo de: Probably the son of Antonio de Luna; husband of (1) Josefa Lucero de Godoy (M 02-21-1745) (D 07-11-1763), (2) María Baca (Origins 214) (Buxton 267-268) (Clan 76, 138), AK 156

Luna, Margarita de: Daughter of **Miguel de San Juan** (*Guadalupe del Paso*), wife of (1) **Pedro Martín Serrano**, (2) Esteban Durán (M 02-02-1727) (Origins 283) (Clan 81-82), AK 156, Chart VII

Madrid, Lorenzo de: (B 1633) Son of *Francisco de Madrid (II)*; husband of (1) Antonia Ortiz (Baca ?) (2) *Ana María de Anaya Alnazan*, (3) Juana Domínguez. Described in 1680 as tall and swarthy with black hair and beard and with a lame arm. Adoptive father of **Lucía de Madrid**. Origins 66, 216), AK 131, Chart II

Madrid, Lucía de: Adopted daughter of *Lorenzo de Madrid* and *Ana María de Anaya Almázan*. Lucia was the wife of **Pedro Varela Jaramillo**. (Origins 66, 68), AK 131, Chart II

Márquez, Diego: (B 1623?) (D 07-21-1643) Son of **Gerónimo Márquez**; husband of **Bernardina Vásquez** (Origins 69) (Kiva 535 n 13), AK 93, 115, Chart IV

Márquez, Gerónimo: (B 1560) San Lucar de Barrameda) (San Lucar la Mayor) Son of **Hernán Muñoz Zamorano** (Or **Hernán Martín Sambrano**). Briefly described in 1600 as swarthy and black bearded. (Origins 69) (Oñate 119123, 128, 135-136, 138, 140, 167, 171-173, 184, 188), AK 52-53, 58

Márquez, Margarita: (1643) Daughter of **Diego Márquez**; wife of Gerónimo de Carvajal (Kiva 182, 206), AK 98, 107

Martín/Martín(es)z

Martín, Ana: Wife of Diego Lucero de Godoy (II), AK 197

Martín, Guadalupe: Daughter of Tomás Martín; second wife of **Miguel Antonio Lucero de Godoy**, AK 190, 257

Martín, Josefa: Daughter of **Marcial Martín Serrano**; wife of **Juan García de la Mora** (Origins 184) (Buxton 38b, 38c, 356), AK Chart X

Martín, Juan Miguel: Husband of **María de la Luz Ortiz** (Gómez)

Martín, Juana Nepomucena: Daughter of Tomás Martín; wife of José de Jesus Lucero de Godoy, AK 19-192

Martín, Manuela:Wife of **Francisco García**, AK Chart VIII

Martín, María Dolores: (B 1798) (Santa Fe) Daughter of **Juan Miguel Martín**; wife of **José Manuel Rafael de Sena**, AK Chart VI

Martín, María Gertrudis: Daughter of **Pedro Martín Serrano**; wife of **Francisco Valdés**, AK 156, Chart VII

Martín, María Paula: Wife of **Juan José Sandoval** (Gómez)

Martín, Tomás: Husband of Petra Romero (Gómez), AK 190-191

Martín Gonzáles, Tomasa: (B 1690) (Buried 02-20-1727) (Conquistadora Chapel, Santa Fe) Daughter of **Hernán Martín Serrano (**II), wife of **Bernardino de Sena**, AK 152, 175, Chart VIII

Martínez, María Alfonsa: (B 1787) Wife of **José Ramón Baca** (M 02-20-1802) (SMDB), AK 257

Martín Serrano de Salazar, Pedro: Son of **Luis Martín Serrano** (I); Husband of **Juana de Argüello** (B 1648), AK 149, 152, 155-156, Chart X

Martín Serrano, Antonio: (B 1673) Son of **Pedro Martín Serrano y Salazar**, husband of (1) Ana María Gómez (M 1700), (2) Felipa de Villavicencio, (3) Magdalena Sedillo (M 1734) (Origins 223), AK 150

Martín Serrano, Blas: Son of **Domingo Martín Serrano**; husband of **Rosa de Vargas Machuca** (M 02-01-1705) (Origins 222) (Buxton 29-30) (Clan 143), AK 155, Chart VII

Martín Serrano, Domingo: (B 1646-49) (Santa Fe) (D 02-27-1735) Possibly the son of **Luis Martín Serrano** (I); husband of Josefa de Herrera. One of the refugees of 1680, this parent was described as having a good stature, with a long face, thick beard, and long, black hair. (Origins 73, 222) (Buxton 40), AK 152, 155-156, Chart X

Martín Serrano (I), Hernán: (B 1556-58) (Zacatecas, NS) Son of **Hernán Martín Serrano**; husband of **Juana Rodríguez**. One of Oñate's original colonists, this parent was described in 1598 as tall of stature, sparse-bearded and pockmarked (Origins 71-72) (NMPN 97), AK 47, 149, Chart X

Martín Serrano (II), Hernán: (B 1599-1608) (San Gabriel) (Lived at Santa Cruz) Son of **Hernán Martín Serrano** (I); husband of (1) María Montaño, (2) Catalina Griego, (3) **Josefa de la Asencion Gonzáles**. One of the refugees of 1681, this parent was described as of good stature, robust, with a gray beard, partly gray hair, and a film on his left eye (Origins 72), AK 152, Chart VIII

Martín Serrano (I), Luis: Son of **Hernán Martín Serrano** (I); husband of **Catalina Días de Salazar**, (Origins 72), AK 94, 98, 149, Chart X

Martín Serrano (II), Luis: (B 1631-33) Son of **Luis Martín Serrano** (I); husband of Antonia de Miranda. Described in 1681 as having a good slender physique, dark complexion, black hair and beard and a mole on his left cheek. (Origins 72-73, 222), AK 152

Martín Serrano, Marcial: (Lived at La Soledad) Son of **Sebastián Martín Serrano**; husband of **Lugarda de Medina** (Buxton 17, 38b, 41, 43), AK Chart X

Martín Serrano, Pedro: (Buried 05-12-1768) (Grantee of the *Piedra Lumbre*, 02-12-1766). Son of **Blas Martín Serrano,** husband of **Margarita de Luna** (Buxton 29-30), AK 149, 155-156, Chart VII

Martín Serrano, Sebastián: (B 1671-74) (Consolidated the holdings at *La Soledad* above San Juan) Son of **Pedro Martín Serrano de Salazar**; husband of **María Luján** (M *Guadalupe del Paso*) (1692) (Origins 223) (Buxton 37-38 38b, 38c, 40) (Clan 36) (NMPN 24, 85, 152), AK 148-152, 155-156, 166, 294, Chart X

Medina, Alonso de: Husband of **Josefa de Cabrera** (Origins 307)

Medina, María: Wife of **Pablo Gonzáles** (Gómez)

Medina de Cabrera, María: (B 1673) (Mexico City) Daughter of **Alonso de Medina**; wife of **José Luis Valdés**. Her sister, María de Medina, was the first wife of **Miguel de la Vega y Coca**. (Origins 301), AK Chart VII

Mendez, Elvira: wife of **Gonzalo Pelaez** (Origins 256)

Moñtano, Juana: (Buried in Santa Fe) Daughter of **Juan Antonio Montaño de Sotomayor**; wife of **Nicolás Durán y Cháves** (Origins 163, 233-234), AK Chart I

Moñtano, Polonia: (B 1681-82) (*Guadalupe del Paso*) Daughter of **Juan Antonio Montaño de Sotomayor**; wife of **Salvador de Santisteban** (Origins 233-234), AK Chart VII

Montaño de Sotomayor, Juan Antonio: (B 1651) (Mexico City) (D by 1696) Husband of **Isabel Jorge de Vera** (Origins 76, 233-234), AK Chart VII

Montoya, Andrés de: (D 08-03-1741) Son of **Antonio de Montoya**; husband of (1) Antonia Gregoria Lucero de Godoy, (M 01-24-1698) (2) María Sisneros (M 07-1734) (Kiva 322) (NMPN 8) (Buxton 16a), AK Chart V

Montoya, Antonio de: (B 1638-49) (D before 1725) Husband of **María Hurtado** (M 1679) (Origins 78, 235-236), AK Chart VI

Montoya, Antonio de: (B 1696) (D 1745) Son of Diego Montoya; husband of (1) Bernarda Baca, (2) Jacinta Peláez (M 1737) (Origins 214), AK 156

Montoya, Bartolomé de: (B 1572) (Cantillana, Spain) Son of **Francisco de Montoya** (Cantillana), husband of **María de Zamora**. One of the reinforcements of 1600, this parent was described briefly as short of stature, and black bearded. (Origins 77) (Clan 69, 86) (NMPN 103), AK 55, 77, Chart II

Montoya, Diego de: (B 1658) Possibly the Diego de Montoya described in 1681 as the husband of María Josefa de Hinojos (Ynojos) With broad shoulders, good features, a thick beard, and long straight hair (Origins 78, 236), AK 205

Montoya, Diego de: (Texcoco, NS) (D by 1661) Son of **Bartolomé de Montoya**; husband of (1) Ana Martin, (2) **María Ortiz de Vera** (Origins 77, 112), AK Charts I and III

Montoya, Isabel de: Daughter of **Diego de Montoya**; wife of **Miguel de San Juan**. (M 1710) (Origins 236, 283), AK Chart VII

Montoya, Josefa de: Daughter of Andrés de Montoya; wife of (1) Manuel Silva (M 1717) (D 1720), (2) José de Santisteban (M 12-25-1720) (Origins 236, 284) (Buxton xvi)

Montoya, Juana de: Daughter of **Antonio de Montoya**; wife of **Francisco Palomino Rendón** (Origins 236, 284)

Montoya, Luisa (or **Lucía**) **de**: Daughter of **Diego de Montoya**; wife of **Francisco de Trujillo** (Origins 77, 108) (Clan 46, 60, 71), AK 144, 206, Charts I and VI

Montoya, María de: (B 1681-82) (D 08-22-1750) (Santa Fe) Daughter of **Antonio de Montoya**; second wife of **Miguel de la Vega y Coca** (M 1699) (Santa Cruz) (Origins 307-308), AK Chart VI

Moreno de Lara (Trujillo), Ana: (B Bernalillo) Daughter of **Diego de Trujillo**; wife of **Cristóbal Baca** (II) (Origins 10, 107-108), AK 122, Chart I

Olguín, Ana: Wife of **Juan de Vargas Machuca** (Origins. 306), AK Chart VII

Ontiveras, Josefa de: (Lived at Santa Cruz) Amourette of **José Valdés**, (1) wife of a Bustos or Bustillos (Origins 301) (Buxton ix), AK Chart VII

Ortiz Baca, Juana: Possibly the daughter of **Manuel Jorge** and **Maria Ortiz de Vera**, or **Baca. Juana** was the wife of **Andrés Gómez Robledo** (Origins 37, 51, 77), AK Chart III

Ortiz de Vera, María: (B 1623 ?) (Santa Fe) Daughter of **Diego de Vera**; wife of (1) **Manuel Jorge**, (2) **Diego de Montoya** (Origins 51, 77, 112), AK Charts I and III

Ortiz, María de la Luz: (B 1765) Wife of **Juan Miguel Martín** (Census 1790) (Gómez)

Ortiz Pacheco, Ana: (Mexico City) Daughter of **Francisco Pacheco**; wife of **Cristóbal Baca** (I). (Origins 9) AK 56, 59, Chart I

Ortiz, Nicolás: (B 1618) Husband of María Pérez de Bustillo (Origins 83, 88) (Clan 19), AK 92-94, 106, 149, Chart IV

Ortiz Nino Ladrón de Guevara, Ana María: (B 1775 ?) Daughter of **Santiago Ortiz Nino Ladrón de Guevara**; wife of **Juan José Romero** (I) (M 04-07-1790) (Santa Fe) (Census 1790) Gómez), AK Chart X

Ortiz Nino Ladrón de Guevara, Francisco: (D 03-11-1749) (Santa Fe) Son of **Nicolás Ortiz Nino Ladrón de Guevara** (II); husband of **Francisca Montoya** (M 1730 ?) (D 04-08-1750) (Santa Fe) (Origins 249)

Ortiz Nino Ladrón de Guevara (I), **Nicolás**: (B 1653) (Mexico City) Son of **Nicolá de Ortiz**; husband of **María Ana** (**Mariana**) **de Vargas Barba Coronado**. In 1693 this parent was described as of medium height, with a sharp nose, large eyes, and a bald head. (Origins 247)

Ortiz Nino Ladrón de Guevara (II), **Nicolás**: (B 1681-83) (Mexico City) (D 1742 ?) (Santa Fe) Son of **Nicolás Ortiz Nino Ladrón de Guevara** (I); husband of **Juana Ortiz** or **Baca**. (M 11-12-1702) (Bernalillo) (D 06-27-1729). In 1693 this parent, then 10 or 12

years old, was described as having a freckled aquiline face, a high forehead, and a broad nose. (Origins 51, 247-49)

Ortiz Nino Ladrón de Guevara, Santiago: Son of **Francisco Ortiz Nino Ladrón de Guevara**; husband of **María del Rosario García de La Mora** (Origins 184, 249), AK Chart X

Peláez, Gonzalo: Husband of **Elvira Mendez** (Origins 256)

Peláez, Jacinta: (D 01-27-1766) (Tome) Daughter of **Jacinto Peláez**; wife of (1) Antonio de Luna (M 05-29-1718), (2) Antonio de Montoya (M 1736 or 1737). (Origins 214, 228, 236, 256) (Clan 75-76), AK 156

Peláez, Jacinto: (B 1670) (Villanueva de las Montanas, Asturias, Spain) (Grantee of La Majada at Jacona near San Ildelfonso, February 10, 1695). Son of **Gonzalo Peláez**; husband of (1) **Margarita Gómez Robledo** (M 1691) (*Guadalupe del Paso*), (2) Isabel Durán y Cháves (Origins 37, 256) (NMPN 83), AK Chart III

Peláez, María: Daughter of **Jacinto Peláez**; wife of **Juan Fernández de la Pedrera** (M 1710) (Albuquerque) (Origins 174, 256), AK Chart III

Pendaries, Marguerite: (B 1876) Gascon in New Mexico was named by her grandfather, Jean Pendaries, (B 1832) for his native Villebrumien in Gascony, France. Marguerite was the wife of José Albino Baca (II) (NMPN 63, 119)

Perea, Juan de: (B 1663-69) (*Guadalupe del Paso*) (D by 1701) Husband of **Aldonsa Varela**. Described briefly in 1681 this parent was slender and swarthy with thick straight hair. (Origins 86-87, 257), AK Chart II

Pérez de Bustillo, Ana: (B 1581) Daughter of **Juan Pérez de Bustillo**; wife of **Asencio de Arechuleta** (Origins 87), AK Chart IV

Pérez de Bustillo, Beatriz: (B 1593) Daughter of **Juan Pérez de Bustillo**; wife of **Hernando Ruiz de Hinojos** (Origins 87), AK Chart IV

Pérez de Bustillo, Catalina: (B 1612) Daughter of **Juan Pérez de Bustillo**; wife of **Alonso Varela Jaramillo** (Origins 87, 110), AK Charts II and IV

Pérez de Bustillo, Juan: (B 1558) (Mexico City) Son of **Simón Pérez** (B 1525) (Mexico City); husband of **María de la Cruz**. One of the original colonists of 1598, this 40-year-old parent was described as small of stature, gray-bearded, and having a wart on the left side of the face. (Origins 87) (Oñate 97), AK 43, Chart II

Pérez de Bustillo, María: Daughter of **Simón Pérez de Bustillo**; wife of Nicolás Ortiz (Origins 88) (*The Rosas Affair*), AK 90-95, Chart IV

Pérez de Bustillo, Nicolás: (D 07-21-1643) Adopted son of Simón Pérez de Bustillo (Origins 88), AK 93, Chart IV

Pérez de Bustillo, Simón: (B 1576) (Mexico City or Zacatecas) Son of **Juan Pérez de Bustillo**; husband of Juana de Zamora (Baca). Also, one of the original colonists of 1598, this 22-year-old was described as of medium height, dark and freckled, with a sparse beard (Origins 87-88) (Clan 16), AK 43, 78, 93, Charts I and IV

Pérez de Bustillo, Yumar: (B 1591) Daughter of **Juan Pérez de Bustillo**; wife of **Antonio Baca** (Origins 87) (Kiva 154), AK 43, 78, 93, Charts I and IV

Pettine, Emidio (Elmer): Son of Michael Pettine, husband of Dolores Baca. Dolores was the daughter of Miguel Baca (B 05-07-1860) and Margarita Frank, granddaughter of José Albino Baca (I) (Lucero), AK 287

Rael, Alonso (B 1780 ?): Husband of **María Barbara Lobrera** (Gómez)

Rael, José Manuel: (B 1815) Son of **Alonso Rael**; husband of (1) María Antonia Velasquez, (2) **María Martina Baca** (M 04-28-1840) (SMDB) (Copy) (Census 1841) (Gómez), AK Chart IX

Rael, María Estephana: (B 1842-47) (Antón Chico ?) Daughter of **José Manuel Rael**; wife of **José Pascual Baca** (M 07-22-1861) (Antón Chico) (Copy) (M of JMR, Film 017002) (MER to JPB, Film 016627) (Census 1841) (Fed Cs. 1910) (Gómez), AK 256, Chart IX

Ribera, Manuela: Possibly the wife of **Diego Estanislado Sena** (Gómez), AK Chart X

Ribera y Sena, María Antonia: (B 1821) Probably the daughter of **Diego Estanislado Sena, María Antonia** was the daughter of **Manuela Ribera**; wife of **José Rafael Salazar** (Gómez), AK 258, Chart X

Robledo, Ana: (B 1604) (San Gabriel) Daughter of **Bartolomé Romero**; wife of **Francisco Gómez**. The village and county of Doña Ana in southern New Mexico are reputed to commemorate her. (Origins 36, 94) (NMPN 48), AK Chart III

Robledo, Francisco: (B 1580) (Valladolid or Zamora, NS) Son of **Pedro Robledo** (Origins 93), AK 47

Robledo, Pedro: (B 1538) (*El Carnero*, a native of Maqueda, Spain) (Buried 05-21-1598) (*Cruz* or *Paraje de Robledo*/Robledo Campsite). Son of **Alejo Robledo**; husband of **Catalina López**. This 60-year-old parent, the first colonist to die in New Mexico, was described briefly in 1598 as of good stature and completely gray. He was buried near the present village of Robledo (which takes its name from him or from his granddaughter, Ana Robledo) on the west bank of the Rio Grande between Doña Ana and Radium Springs. Mount Robledo, 10 miles south of Radium Springs, is named for him. He left four red-headed sons to carry on the colonizing effort. Origins 93) (Conq. 23, 50) (NMPN 48, 137) (Oñate 96, 103), (*A Nation of Shepherds*) AK Chart III

Robledo (II), Pedro: (B 1578) (Temazcaltepeque, NS) (D 12-1598) (Ácoma) Son of **Pedro Robledo**. Twenty-years-old in 1598, Pedro was described as having a good stature and a scanty beard. (Origins 93) (Oñate 136), AK 53

Rodríguez, Juana: Wife of **Hernán Martín Serrano** (I) (Origins. 71-72), AK 47, Chart VII

Rodríguez de Salazar, Sebastián: (B 1582) Husband of **Luisa Días** (Origin 72, 95)

Romero, Bartolomé: (B 1563) (Corral de Almaguer, Spain). Son of **Bartolomé Romero** and **Maria de Adeva**; husband of **Lucía López Robledo**. This parent was described in 1598 as being of good stature, dark, and black-bearded. (Origins 95) (KCC 89, 118) (NMPN 137), AK Chart III

Romero, Domingo: (B 1738 ?) Probably the son of **Antonio Romero de Pedraza**; **Domingo** was the husband of **Lugarda Montoya** (B 1745 ?) (M 07-08-1759) (Origins 271) (Census 1790) (Gómez)

Romero Juan José (I): (Bap. 03-18-1767) Son of **Domingo Romero**; husband of **Ana María Ortiz Nino Ladrón de Guevara** (M 04-07-1790) (Santa Fe) (Census 1790) (Gómez), AK Chart X

Romero, Juan José (II): (B 03-05-1841) (Santa Fe) (D 1879 ?) Lived at La Ciénega) Son of **José Rafael Narciso Romero**; husband of **María Refugio Baca** (M 01-03-1862) (Santa Fe) (Fed Census 70) (Gómez), AK 271, Chart X

Romero, María Juliana: (B 01-27-1869) (Las Vegas) (D 05-17-1915) (Santa Fe). Daughter of **Juan José Romero** (II), wife of **Antonio José Lucero, Sr**. (Birth record copy, Film 016811, 198, Book 2 Las Vegas) (Fed. Cs. 1880) (Obit) AK 271, 276, Chart X

Romero, José Rafael Narciso: (B 07-30-1809) Son of **Juan José Romero** (II) (Bap. 1767); husband of **Felipa Martínez** (B 1817-19) (Gómez), AK Chart X

Romero de Pedraza, Antonio: (D 11-19-1736) (Lived at La Cienegilla) Possibly the son of **Francisco Romero de Pedraza** and **Francisca Ramírez de Salazar**. **Antonio** was the husband of **Nicolasa del Castillo** (M 04-30-1726) (D 01-08-1783) (Origins 171)

Ruiz Cáceres, Elena: Wife of Miguel Luján (Origin 22, 64) (Clan 6), AK

Salas, Antonio de: (B 1617) (Mexico City) Probably the stepson of Pedro Lucero de Godoy (El Viejo ?); second husband of **María de Abendaño** (Origins 60, 97, 100, 112) (Clan. 70-71) (Kiva 182), AK 94, Charts I and III

Salas y Trujillo, Bernardina de: Daughter of **Francisco de Trujillo**; wife of **Andrés Hurtado** (Origins 49, 108) (Clan 56, 68, 71, 88), AK 127, 132, 144, 152, Chart VI

Salazar, Catalina Días de: Daughter of **Sebastián Rodríguez de Salazar**; wife of **Luis Martín Serrano** (I) (Origins 72, 95, 222), AK Chart X

Salazar, Isabel de: Possibly the daughter of Bartolomé de Salazar. Isabel was the adopted daughter of **Andrés Hurtado**, and **Bernardina de Salas y Trujillo**. Isabel was the third wife of **Juan Lucero de Godoy** (Origins 49, 60, 101) (Clan 56, 87), AK 127, 132, Chart II

Salazar, José Antonio: (B 1789) (Lived at Santa Clara) Husband of **María Manuela Vigil** (Census 1818) (Gómez), AK Chart X

Salazar, José Rafael: (B 1818) Son of **José Antonio Salazar**; husband of **María Antonia Ribera y Sena** (Census 1845) (Gómez), AK 258, Chart X

Salazar, María de: Possibly the daughter of Bartolomé de Salazar. **María** was the adopted daughter of **Andrés Hurtado** and wife of **Manuel Baca** (Origins 10, 101) (Clan 87), AK 127, Chart I

Salazar, María Manuela: (Bap. 02-22-1842) (San Juan) (Copy) Daughter of **José Rafael Salazar**; wife of **José Pablo Lucero** (M 08-04-1855) (Delig. 1008) (Fed. Cs. 1860-1870-1880) (Bap. in Film 0016981) (Gómez), AK 258, Chart X

Sánchez de Inigo, Francisca: Probably the daughter of **Juana (Ana) López del Castillo** and **Juan de Herrera**; **Francisca** was the wife of **Juan García de Noriega** (M 05-04-1681) (Origins 4, 280), AK Chart VIII

Sánchez de Inigo, Pedro (or Pedro López de Yniquez): (B 1673-74) (D by 1720) Son of **Juana (Ana) López del Castillo**; husband of (1) Leonor Baca (M 01-07-1692) (*San Lorenzo delPaso*) (D 1696) (Taos), (2) María Luján (M 1698) (Bernalillo) (Origins 11, 141, 279-280)

Sandoval, Juan de Dios: (Buried 11-10-1831). First husband of **María Rosa Altagracia Sena** (Gómez), AK 247

Sandoval, Juan José: Husband of **María Paula Martín** (Gómez)

Sandoval, María Antonia Feliciana: (B 1803) Daughter of **Juan José Sandoval**; wife of **José Joaquin Baca** (Census 1841) (Gómez), AK Chart X

San Juan, Miguel de: (*Guadalupe del Paso*) (Will of 05-12-1768) Husband of **Isabel de Montoya** (M 1710) (Origins 236, 283), AK Chart VII

Santa Cruz (Pérez de Bustillo), Diego: (B 1591) (Zacatecas) (D by 1661) Foster son of **Juan Pérez de Bustillo**; husband of Gregoria de Arechuleta (Origins 87-88, 102)

Santiestaban/Santisteban/Santistevan

Santisteban, Andrés de: (Mexico City) Husband of **Juana de la Concepción** (Origins 284), AK Chart VII

Santisteban, José de: (B 1698) Son of **Salvador de Santisteban**; husband of Josefa Montoya (M 12-25-1720) José, then 22, was one of the few survivors of the ill-fated Villasur expedition of 1720. One of his fellow men-at-arms, Manuel Silva, was killed in this battle. José then married Manuel's young widow, Josefa. (Origins 284) (Buxton xvi)

Santisteban, María del Carmen: (B *Cañada de Cochiti* ?) (Bur. 04-25-1829) (Taos) Daughter of

Juan Santisteban and María Francisca Trujillo; wife of Antonio Severino Martín (M 03-25-1787) (Abiquiu) (Chance 13, 15, 19-30)

Santisteban, María Rosa: Daughter of **Antonio de Santisteban Coronel**; wife of **Juan Ignacio Lucero de Godoy** (Origins 392, revised edition) (Gómez), AK 154, Charts V and VII

Santisteban, Salvador de: (B 1679-80) Son of **Andrés de Santisteban**; husband of **Polonia Moñtano** (M 12-20-1695) (Santa Fe) (Origins 284), AK 138, Charts V and VII

Santisteban Coronel, Antonio de (B 1708): Son of **Salvador de Santisteban**; husband of **Francisca Fernández Valerio**, (M 09-11-1728) (Santa Cruz) (Origins 392) (Buxton 54b, 73, 79, 81, 85), AK Charts V and VII

Sedillo See Cedillo

Sena, Agustin de: Husband of **María Ynez de Amparano** (Origin 286), AK 132, Chart VIII

Sena, Diego Estanislado: (B 1764) Possibly the husband of **Manuela Ribera** (Gómez), AK Chart X

Sena, Pablo Antonio de: (B 1732) Probably the son of **Tomás Antonio de Sena**; probable husband of (1) Antonia Gertrudis de la Peña (M 11-11-1753) (Santa Fe). Pablo Antonio was the husband of (2) **María Antonia de la Luz Esquibel** (M 07-07-1772) (Santa Fe) (Origins 287) (Census 1790, Santa Fe) (M of PAS to AGP and MAE, Film 0016905) (Copy of latter) (Gómez), AK 176, Charts VI and VIII

Sena, Tomás Antonio de: (B 1706 ?) (D 02-11-1781) (One of three grantees of the Cayamungue). Son of **Bernardino de Sena**; husband of **María Luisa García de Noriega** (M 04-22-1723) (Santa Fe) (Origins 286-287) (Delig.) (Census 1750) (Conq. 67) (Kiva 385, 391, 395, 547 n 29) (NMPN 44) (Gómez), AK 175-176, 218, Charts I, VI and VIII

Sena y Valle, Bernardino de: (B 1684-87) (Tezcuco, Valley of Mexico) (D 11-11-1765) (Santa Fe) (Buried at San Miguel Church) Son of **Agustin de Sena**; husband of (1) **Tomasa Martín Gonzáles** (M 02-08-1705) (Santa Fe), (2) Manuela de Roybal (B 05-13-1727) (D 05-1778). With his foster parents in 1693, this parent, at approximately nine-years-of-age, was described as having a round dark face, large eyes, and a thick nose (Origins 286) (Conq. 67-68, 72) (NMPN 153), AK 132, 152, 174-175, Chart VIII

Sena, María Rosa Altagracia: (Bap. 09-02-1811) (Santa Fe) Daughter of **José Manuel Rafael de Sena**; wife of (1) Juan de Dios Sandoval (M 09-30-1825) (Copy), (2) **José Rafael Albino Baca** (M 01-23-1833) (SMDB) (IGI) (Film 016903) (Gómez), AK 176, 247, Chart IX

Sena, José Manuel Rafael de: (Bap. 06-10-1776) (Santa Fe). Son of **Pablo Antonio de Sena**; husband of (1) ? , (2) **María Dolores Martín** (Film 016903) (Census 1823) (Gómez), AK 176, Chart VI

Silva, Antonio de: (B 1670) (Queretaro, NS.) (Lived at Santa Cruz, Bernalillo, Albuquerque) (D 05-25-1732) (Albuquerque). One of the colonists of 1693, this parent, son of **Salvador**, was described as having a round dark face, large eyes, and a sharp nose. His wife **Gregoria Ruiz**, daughter of **Juan**, and born in Mexico City in 1671, was described as having a broad and pockmarked face. (Origins 288)

Silva, Francisco de: Son of **Antonio de Silva**; husband of **Rosa Gertrudis Durán y Cháves** (Origins 163, 288), AK Chart VI

Silva, María Augustina de: (B 09-09-1739) Daughter of **Francisco de Silva**; wife of **Pedro Tafoya** (Origins 289), AK Chart VI

Sisneros, Felipe Antonio de: (B 1660) (Buried 08-09-1706) (Zuni). Probably the son of Vicente Cisneros, Felipe Antonio was the husband of Josefa Luján (Origins 104, 289), AK 150-151, 155, 166

Tafoya, María Vitalia: (B 1785) Daughter of **Pedro Tafoya**; wife of **Ignacio Baca** (M 04-29-1797 ?) (Belen) (c 1821, *La Partido de La Cienega*) (*Herencia*, July, 1994, p. 37) (Gómez), AK Chart VI

Tafoya, Pedro: (B 1750 ?) Husband of **María Agustina de Silva** (Gómez), AK Chart VI

Terrus, José Francisco: (Vigue, Cataluña, Spain) (D 05-25-1745). Husband of **Antonia Páez Hurtado** (M 03-21-1734) (Santa Fe) (D 09-19-1760) (Origins 294) (AASF Reel 3, Frame 21)

Terrus, Teodora: Daughter of **José Francisco Terrus**; wife of **Juan Esteban Baca**. (Origins 144, 294), AK 143, Chart VI

Trujillo, Diego de: (B 1611-13) (Mexico City) (D 1682) (Casas Grandes) (Lived at his *estancia, Paraje de las Huertas*, four leagues from the Sandía Pueblo) Husband of **Catalina Vásquez**, (Origins107-108), AK 175.

Trujillo, Francisco de: Son of **Diego de Trujillo**; husband of **Luisa (or Lucía) de Montoya** (Origins 77, 108) (Clan 68-69, 71, 87) (NMPN 170), AK 144, Chart I

Trujillo, Teresa: (B 1812) Wife of **José Rafael Albino Baca** (M 08-26-1831) (SMDB) (Gómez), AK 247

Vaca, Diego de See Baca, Diego de

Valdés(z)

Valdés y Bustos, Francisco: (B 1731 ?) Son of **José Valdéz**; husband of (1) Lugarda Martín, (2) **María Gertrudis Martín** (3) Diega Tafoya (Buxton ix) (Gómez), AK 156, Chart VII

Valdés, José: Son of **José Luis Valdés**; amour of **Josefa de Ontiveras** (Origins 301), AK Chart VII

Valdés, José Luis: (B 1664) (Oviedo, Spain). One of the "gentlemen soldiers" brought from Spain by Diego de Vargas in 1693 (D 03-04-1703) (Zuñi). Husband of **María Medina de Cabrera** (Origins 301), AK Chart VII

Valdés, María Rosa: (B 1768 ?) (D 1811) Daughter of **Francisco Valdés y Bustos**; wife of **Miguel Antonio Lucero de Godoy** (M 08-26-1783) (Santa Clara) (Buxton 79, 152), AK 156-157, 171, Chart VII

Valerio

Fernández Valerio, Francisca: Daughter of **Martín Fernández Valerio**; wife of **Antonio de Santisteban Coronel** (Origins 398) (Buxton, 79, 81, 85), AK Charts V and VII

Fernández Valerio, Martín: (Sombrerete, NS) (B 1682) (D 05-13-1752). Perhaps the son of *Jose Valerio Martinez*, **Martin** was the husband of **María Montoya** (Origins 302), AK Chart VII

Vallejos, Ana María: Wife of **Julian Lucero** (Gómez)

Varela, Aldonsa (Alfonsa): (D by 1701) Wife of **Juan de Perea**; sister of **Teresa Varela** who was married to **Alonso Garcia** (Origins 257, 399 revised edition), AK Chart II

Varela (Jaramillo or **Losada), Teresa**: Wife of **Alonso García**; sister of **Aldonsa Varela** (Origins 33-34, 399 revised edition), AK Chart VIII

Varela de Losada (or de Perea), Antonia: Possibly the daughter of **Juan de Perea**, **Antonia** was the wife of **Antonio Lucero de Godoy** (I) (Origins 61, 209, 257), AK 128, Chart II

Varela de Losada (I), Pedro: (B 1574) (Santiago de Compostela, Spain) Son of **Pedro Varela**. One of Oñate's original colonists, this 24 year old was described in 1598 as having a good stature and a red beard. (Origins 110)

Varela Jaramillo, Alonso: (B 1566-68) (Santiago de Compostela, Spain) (D 1633) (La Ciénega) (Lived at La Ciénega). Son of **Pedro Varela**; husband of **Catalina Pérez de Bustillo**. One of Oñate's original colonists, this parent was described as of good stature, with a chestnut beard, and 30-years-old. (Origins 87), AK 43, Charts II and IV

Varela Jaramillo (II), Alonso: (B ? 1600 ?) Son of **Alonso Varela Jaramillo** (Origins 110), AK Chart II

Varela Jaramillo, Cristóbal: (B 1665) Son of **Pedro Varela Jaramillo**; husband of (1) **Casilda de Cedillo Rico y Rojas**, (2) Leonor Luján Domínguez. A refugee of 1680, this parent was described as of medium build, with a ruddy, plump, and beardless face (Origins 110), AK 144, 152, Chart II

Varela Jaramillo, Francisca Antonia: Daughter of **Cristóbal Varela Jaramillo**; wife of **Antonio Lucero de Godoy** (II) (M 09-27-1712) (Albuquerque) (Origins 209), AK 152-153, Charts II and V

Varela Jaramillo, Pedro: (B 1620) (Santa Fe) (D by 1692). Probably the son of **Alonso Varela Jaramillo** (II); husband of **Lucía de Madrid** (Origins 110)

Vargas Machuca, Juan de: (B 1663) Husband of **Ana Olguín** (Origins 306), AK Chart VII

Vargas Machuca, Rosa de: (B 1690) Daughter of **Juan de Vargas Machuca**; wife of **Blas Martín Serrano** (M 02-01-1705) (Origins 73, 222, 306), AK Chart VII

Vásquez, Bernardina: (Lived at Los Cerrillos) Probably the daughter of **Francisco Vásquez**, Bernardina was the wife of **Diego Márquez** (Origins 15, 112)

Vásquez, Catalina: (B 1621) (Santa Fe). Possibly the daughter of **Diego Márquez.** Catalina was the daughter of **Bernardina Vásquez** and wife of **Diego de Trujillo.** Catalina Vásquez and **Diego de Trujillo** were the parents of **Ana Moreno de Lara**, wife of **Cristóbal Baca** (II), and of **Francisco de Trujillo**, husband of **Luisa de Montoya** (see AK Chart I). (Origins 69, 107-108, 112)

Vásquez, Francisco: (B 1570) (Cartaya, Spain) Son of **Alonso Alfran** (Cartaya). One of the original colonists of 1598, this parent was described briefly as of good stature and having a red beard (Origins 112), AK 42

Vega y Coca, María de la: Daughter of **Miguel de la Vega y Coca**; wife of **Diego Manuel Baca** (Origins 307-308), AK 142, Chart VI

Vega y Coca, Miguel de la: (B 1677) (Mexico City) (Lived at La Ciénega). Son of **Cristóbal de la Vega**; husband of (1) Manuela de Medina, (2) **María Montoya** (M 1699) (D 08-22-1750) With the colonists of 1693, this parent was described as fair-complexioned, with an aquiline face and small eyes. (Origins 307-308), AK 294, Chart VI

Velasco (Velásquez), Lorenzo Inocencio: Probably the son of **Diego de Velasco** (B 1668). Lorenzo was the husband of **María Mestas** (M 06-19-1735) (Nambe) (Origins 309-310)

Velásquez, Juan Esteban: (B 1739) (D 10-08-1819) (*La Cucilla*, Santa Clara) (Lived at *La Cuchilla de Ortega*) Son of **Lorenzo Inocencio Velasco** (**Velásquez**); husband of **Juana Teresa Apodaca** (M 12-20-1772) (Santa Fe) (Origins 310), AK Chart VII

Velásquez, María Encarnación: (B 1782) (D 09-30-1838) (SMDB). Probably the daughter of **Juan Esteban Velásquez**, María Encarnación was the wife of **Santiago García** (M 10-08-1799) (Santa Clara) (Gómez), AK Charts VII and VIII

Vera, Diego de: (B 1593) (Canary Islands). Son of **Pedro de Vera Perdomo** and **María Betancur** (La Laguna, Tenerife). Paternal grandparents: **Hernán Martín Baena** (Jerez de los Caballeros) and **Catalina García** (La Laguna, Tenerife). Maternal grandparents:

Antonio Pérez (La Graciosa, Canary Islands) and **Catalina Aponte** (Garachico, Tenerife) **Diego** was the husband of (1) A wife in Tenerife in the Canaries from whom he was not divorced, and (2) **María de Abendaño** (M 1622). Diego was required by the Inquisition to return to his wife in Tenerife and his marriage to María was annulled (Origins 1, 100, 112), AK Chart I and III

Vera Ortiz, María de: See **Ortiz de Vera, María**

Vitoria Carvajal, Juan de: See **Carvajal, Juan de Vitoria**

Vigil, María Manuela: (B 1796) Wife of **Juan Antonio Salazar** (Gómez), AK Chart X

Villafuerte, María de: Wife of **Francisco López** (Origins 3), AK Chart II

Villanueva, Catalina de (Fuente Ovejuna): Wife of **Juan López Holguín** (Origins 81), AK Chart II

Villanueva, Vivianita: Second wife of **Celso Baca** (MF 016989, Santa Rosa Baptisms) (Gómez), AK FN 27, Chapter 16

Zamora, Catalina de: Daughter of **Pedro Lucero de Godoy**, wife of Diego Pérez Romero, AK 77, 102, 105, Chart V

Zamora, María de: (Mexico City at San Sebastián) Daughter of **Pedro de Zamora**, wife of **Bartolomé de Montoya** (Origins 77) (Clan 86), AK 55, 77, Chart II

Zamora, Petronila de: (B 1600 ?) Daughter of **Bartolomé de Montoya**; first wife of **Pedro Lucero de Godoy** (Origins 77), AK 55, 77, Charts II and V

INDEX

CPSIA information can be obtained
at www.ICGtesting.com
Printed in the USA
LVHW012248081020
668387LV00001B/59